Applying Perform

Live Art, Socially Engaged
Affective Practice

Nicola Shaughnessy
University of Kent, UK

First published 2012
Published in paperback 2015 by
PALGRAVE MACMILLAN

Palgrave Macmillan in the UK is an imprint of Macmillan Publishers Limited, registered in England, company number 785998, of Houndmills, Basingstoke, Hampshire RG21 6XS.

Palgrave Macmillan in the US is a division of St Martin's Press LLC, 175 Fifth Avenue, New York, NY 10010.

Palgrave Macmillan is the global academic imprint of the above companies and has companies and representatives throughout the world.

Palgrave® and Macmillan® are registered trademarks in the United States, the United Kingdom, Europe and other countries.

ISBN 978–0–230–24133–6 hardback
ISBN 978–1–137–52585–7 paperback

This book is printed on paper suitable for recycling and made from fully managed and sustained forest sources. Logging, pulping and manufacturing processes are expected to conform to the environmental regulations of the country of origin.

A catalogue record for this book is available from the British Library.

A catalog record for this book is available from the Library of Congress.

Typeset by MPS Limited, Chennai, India.

For Gabriel and in memory of Virginia Sharp (1963–2008)

Contents

List of Illustrations

Acknowledgements

The author and publishers wish to thank the following for permission to reproduce copyright materials:

Canterbury Museum for permission to use Jack Waller's story.

The photographers and artists who kindly gave me permission to reproduce their images: Reckless Sleepers, Bruce Damonte, Patrick Baldwin, Steve Hickey, Magic Me and the Moving Lives Group, Wendy Ewald, Graeme Rose, Peter Fry, Paul Sutton and Max Allsup, Tim Mitchell, and Kevin Kennefick.

An earlier version of 'Digital Transportations' has been published in: 'Truths and Lies: Exploring the Ethics of Performance Applications', *Research in Drama Education* 10.2 (2005): 201–12. I am grateful to the Taylor & Francis Group for their permission to use this work.

I also wish to acknowledge the London International Festival of Theatre Living Archive and to thank staff at Goldsmiths Special Collections for their help and support with my research and permissions to use material.

I am extremely grateful to Paula Kennedy, Commissioning Editor of Literature and Performance at Palgrave Macmillan for publishing the book and for steadfast support during the period of writing. Thanks are also due to Benjamin Doyle, Assistant Editor at Palgrave for his rigour and efficiency in keeping the book on track. I am deeply indebted to the book's copy editor, Penny Simmons, for her care, engagement, efficiency and support during the production period and to the staff at Palgrave for help and advice on the manuscript. It has been a pleasure to work with the whole publication team.

I wish to extend my gratitude to the University of Kent for two periods of study leave at the beginning and end of the research process. Material from the book has been presented to the Applied and Social Theatre Group at the UK's annual conferences of the Theatre and Performance Research Association, as well as the American Society for Theatre Research working group: Cognitive Science in Theatre, Dance and Performance. I would like to thank colleagues in both working groups, as these discussions have informed the development of the research. In particular, I wish to thank Amy Cook, John Lutterbie and Bruce McConachie for encouraging me to bring a cognitive perspective to my work in applied theatre and performance.

To the practitioners who have contributed so generously and taught me so much, a huge thank you, especially to Margaret Ames, Martha Bowers,

Helena Bryant, Sue Mayo and Magic Me, Vayu Naidu, Pablo Pakula and Daisy Orton at Accidental Collective, Paul Sutton and C&T, Jonathan Petherbridge and the London Bubble, Arti Prashar and Spare Tyre, Melanie Wilson, James Yarker and Kerrie Reading at Stan's cafe, Jacqui Russell and Chicago Children's Theatre, and Mole Wetherell.

I am grateful for conversations with Hans Thies Lehmann and Richard Schechner during their tenure as Leverhulme Research Professors at the University of Kent. My discussion of post-dramatic theatre and rasaesthetics benefited from this dialogue.

I am indebted to colleagues and students in the School of Arts (past and present) at the University of Kent, who have been extremely supportive. Particular thanks are due to Jill Davies for critical acumen, as well as reminders of the need for balance and short emails in the early stages of writing; Paul Allain for being an excellent research mentor and for resolving headaches, and to members of the research centre for Cognition, Kinesthetics and Performance, especially Fran Barbe and Helen Brooks (a excellent digital native). Thanks also to Sian Stevenson and Jayne Thompson for inspirational practice and for Sian's room with a view. Special thanks are due to those who have worked closely with me during the book's production: Jonathan Friday for all his support and conviction, and Melissa Trimingham who always believed in this project and for ongoing dialogue about embodiment, cognition and autism. I am particularly indebted to Robert Shaughnessy for childcare, cooking and conversations all of which have kept this project live.

Finally, a thank you to my children for keeping this in perspective and for helping when it was needed; thanks to Caitlin for being in tune, Nat for brothering and Erina for being herself. Special thanks are due to Gabriel for helping me to perceive differently and for enabling me to fully understand the importance and value of applying performance.

Preface: Defining the Terms

At the beginning of writing, there is a loss. What cannot be said.

(de Certeau, 1984: 195)

As its title suggests, this book explores applications of performance practices in educational, social and community contexts. The writing is situated in the spaces between making and performance, exploring the processes of creating work variously defined as collaborative, participatory and socially engaged.

The difficulties of writing about the ephemeral medium of performance continue to be a source of critical discussion (Phelan, 1993; Schneider, 2011). 'Loss', in the context of writing about performance, is associated with the death of the 'live' event. De Certeau's reference to 'what cannot be said' invokes the difficulties of writing about a medium as elusive as performance and of negotiating the absence and presence of events which have happened but which remain as memory and cannot be recovered.

At the end of writing there is also loss (not least in the material edited out and the practices not featured, as well as deceased performance events) as a process comes to its end, but this closure is also a beginning as a book, like performance, enters production and reaches its audience. At the beginnings and ends of writing about performance, moreover, there is something to be gained through remembering and recreating. The decomposing corpse of performance is, after all, transforming into something else, a different kind of performance matter. And we write about performance because it matters.

Applying is derived from the Latin *applicare*, its etymological sense being 'to bring things in contact with one another' to 'join' to 'connect' and, figuratively to 'devote (oneself) to', 'give attention'.[1] Implicit in this terminology is the concept of 'care': practitioners of applied theatre and performance care about and/or care for the communities they are working with; the work is often politically or pedagogically motivated; it has conscience, integrity and commitment. The process of applying performance is a bringing together of elements to create change, to make something new. Thus, in writing about these processes, there is gain (as well as loss). Writing about performance is itself a/gain as the work is recovered in a different form and shared with an audience of readers who may not have experienced the original. As Helen Nicholson has written:

> Whilst the performative moment may be lost or (rather more accurately) embodied only in the collective memories of the participants, the written word remains open for re-interpretation and invites critical questioning.

Analysis of, and reflection on, performative events keeps them alive by breaking down the polarity between process and product, between past and present, theory and practice. Furthermore, a written text enables a wider audience to participate in the event by inviting them to take an imaginative journey into the performance space. In this conceptualization, writing for publication is an act of generosity.

(2006: 1)

Writing about the terminology of 'applied' drama/theatre in the same editorial, Nicholson draws attention to a change of wording in *Research in Drama Education's* (*RIDE*) published aims as being for those interested in '*applying performance practices* to cultural engagement, educational innovation and social change' (Nicholson, 2006: 2; my emphasis). The term 'performance' is used by Nicholson to acknowledge 'the distinctive place of community, educational and applied theatre within contemporary theatre making'.

The broad spectrum of practices featured within this study draw upon the forms, vocabularies, technologies and methodologies broadly associated with contemporary theatre and performance: 'devising', 'performance art', 'durational', 'site/place responsive', 'intermedial' are all terms associated with the work discussed here. Like Mike Pearson, 'I prefer "performance": to embrace the fullest range of practices originating in theatre and visual art and to demonstrate affiliations with the academic field of performance studies' (Pearson, 2010: 1). Much of the work featured can also be defined in the context of 'live art', a term used by a number of practitioners to refer to their own work and to the practices I discuss:

The term Live Art is not a description of a singular form or discipline, but a cultural strategy to include processes and practices that might otherwise be excluded from more established curatorial, cultural and critical discourses. A strategy to acknowledge ways of working that do not sit easily within received structures and strictures and to privilege artists who choose to operate across, in between and at the edges of more conventional artistic forms to make art that invests in ideas of process, presence and experience as much as the production of objects or things; art that is immediate and real; and art that wants to test the limits of the possible and the permissible.

(Keidan, 2004: 9)

This positioning of working across and between disciplines and forms, is particularly pertinent to artists engaged in *applying* performance; hybrid practices which, like performance itself, evade definition, refusing to be constrained by categorical frameworks. Thus to conceive of this work as a strategy is a useful means of conceptualizing the practices discussed. The commitment of live artists to finding 'new languages for the representation of ideas, new ways of activating audiences and new strategies for intervening in public life' (ibid.: 9) is shared by many applied theatre practitioners who similarly seek to find new ways of engaging audiences as participants, developing, where appropriate, interventionist strategies to challenge or to transform existing systems of representation, hierarchies and ideologies. Whilst contemporary forms of performance are often considered to be modes of 'art theatre' and non-utilitarian (art for art's sake), the work featured in this book demonstrates that some live art has a social intention and function and is increasingly seeking to challenge the dualisms of the aesthetic and non-aesthetic (or what might be considered as pure versus applied theatre, as discussed in Part I). The twenty-first-century tendency to involve children in both the making and performance of contemporary theatre for adults, for example, can be seen as an indication of live artists moving beyond elitist perceptions of theatre for and by grown-ups as they explore the relations between children and adults, their influences upon each other, identity formation and the liminal, transitory space of adolescence. Examples include the CAMPO trilogy of theatre works with children, made for an adult audience (Josse De Pauw's *üBUNG*, Tim Etchells's *That Night Follows Day* and Gob Squad's *Before Your Very Eyes*), Fevered Sleep's *On Ageing* as well as Mark Storer's *Fat Girl Gets a Haircut and Other Stories* (discussed in Part II in the context of autobiographical performance). This work occupies the space between applied theatre and live art, between modes of 'doing' and 'not doing', learning and playing, the space between autonomous art and engaged art which Rancière conceptualizes in *The Politics of Aesthetics* as the 'becoming life of art' (2006).[2] Challenging the relations between modernism and postmodernism, autonomous art and the avant-garde, Rancière reconfigures and recontextualizes aesthetics as a 'regime of identification of art' (differentiated from what he defines as 'ethical' and 'representational' regimes) in which the aesthetics of art as art (the 'resistant' form) and art as life coexist in a simultaneous and complementary relationship. Rancière's theories, in conjunction with Bourriaud's 'relational aesthetics' (2002), offer a conceptual middle way for considering the social value and efficacy of contemporary art practices.[3] The role and experience of both the spectator and the community in which the art is produced is central to the re-evaluation of efficacy in these relational and participatory practices and encounters. Efficacy, moreover, is also defined in terms of the participant's experience as affect theory brings together aesthetic and socially engaged perspectives. Throughout this study, then, different genealogies are engaged in dialogue as contemporary relational art is linked to post-dramatic theatre. Thus post-dramatic theatre, live art and applied performance converse, conjoined by shared interests in audience engagement, innovation, affect and a commitment to the social value of the arts.

My analysis of the processes involved in 'encounters' between performers, participants and spectators draws on recent studies of cognition and performance to theorize these relationships. In his preface to *Performance and Cognition*, Bruce McConachie invites scholars to 'incorporate many of the insights of cognitive science into their work and to begin considering all of their research projects from the perspective of cognitive studies' (McConachie and Hart, 2006: x). This is the first full-length study to consider applied theatre from the perspective of cognitive studies and in so doing engages in dialogue with a range of other disciplines – philosophy, anthropology and education. A cognitive approach is 'applied' to explore how learning is embodied, to discuss concepts of 'transformation' through performance, to analyse the experience of the participant/spectator and the processes involved in the production of meaning.

As I am not a trained scientist, much of the discussion involves what Tim Etchells refers to in his practice as creative borrowing (Etchells, 1999). By appropriating perspectives and insights from cognitive science, postmodern performance theory and applied theatre practice, this study brings into dialogue disciplines that have previously engaged in debate. Rhonda Blair confronted similar challenges in bringing together science, acting and postmodern theory. As she has explained, 'some of the difficulties of working in an integrated way with acting, performance theory and science grow out of common and mistaken artificial binaries such as science vs. art, thinking vs. feeling and reason vs. emotion. However, my task has been made easier by the plasticity and openness of Acting as a discipline to embrace interdisciplinarity' (Blair, 2008: 5). In applied theatre and performance, interdisciplinarity is also a feature of the field, with work informed by, for example, educational theory, cultural and human geography, psychology, gender theory and, more recently, affect theory. Thus the field is open to a range of theoretical perspectives; a cognitive approach offers a means of conceptualizing perception, memory, embodiment and transformation, exploring how practitioners and participants 'engage with and become engaged by [applied] performance' (McConachie, 2008: 8).

Mind the gap

For Rhonda Blair, although 'there is something true in many "practice-centered" and "theory-centered" perspectives ... there is also something missing, and this missing thing is located in a more thorough investigation of the integration of these perspectives' (2008: xi). Her book explores actor training from this perspective and John Lutterbie has developed this further (2011). These studies of actor training complement McConachie's work on spectatorship as explorations of cognition and performance. Cognitive neuroscience has reconceptualized our understanding of how we learn, the way we think and how we engage with our environment. Perception, memory, identity and subjectivity, agency, relations and interactions with others, emotions, empathy, embodiment, affect are prevalent themes of both applied theatre scholarship and cognitive studies and this book endeavours to bring them into dialogue with each other. Even the divisions between Eastern and Western approaches to performance are interrogated. The subtitle to George Lakoff and Mark Johnson's study is *The Embodied Mind and Its Challenge to Western Thought*. There are some surprising synergies between the teaching and practices of Eastern aesthetics and the cognitive perspectives explored here, particularly in terms of embodiment (see my discussion of Rasa in Parts I and III).

Integrating these concepts involves challenging the dualisms of theory and practice, mind and body, self and other by conceiving of these concepts as dynamic, iterative and integrated. The turn to 'affect' in applied theatre gestures towards this (Thompson, 2009; Nicholson, 2011); performance theorists articulate similar perspectives about emotion/feeling, body and pleasure in a related turn to spectatorship, a recognition that meaning in performance is not dependent on the semiotics of the *mise-en-scène*, but involves the embodied engagement, understanding and experience of the audience (Shepherd, 2006). Anna Fenemore, a scholar practitioner, brings both perspectives together with clarity and insight when she writes 'on being moved by performance' (2003). She coins her own terminology in this article (as discussed in Chapter 3 Performing Lives), but what she is writing about can be conceptualized through the cognitive perspectives on performance articulated by McConachie (2008) and Stephen Di Benedetto (2010). A cognitive approach considers feelings as emotions 'brought into consciousness ... [so that] affective responses become an ongoing part of the feedback loop of spectating' (McConachie and Hart, 2006: 6).

Many of the practices discussed in this book are identified with post-modern paradigms, although some of the theoretical perspectives emerging from postmodernism engage in argument with cognitive neuroscience. As Blair summarizes: 'from these postmodern perspectives, both science and acting lack sufficient cultural contextualization and therefore require rigorous interrogation' (2008: 5). These postmodern perspectives have, however, been challenged as cynical, reductive and inappropriate as theoretical paradigms for twenty-first-century performance:

> Progressive ideals and practices clash with postmodern theory's intransigent and homogenizing world view, that is to say, with its now inherent conservatism (whereas once upon a time – specifically the late 1970s and early 1980s – it was radical), postmodern theory, once nemesis and destroyer of the author, the sign and the metanarrative, has itself become an authorial patriarch of conformist cultural commentary; a burning yet myopic critical sign; an oppressive metanarrative beyond compare within the history of critical theory.
>
> (Dixon, 2007: 7)

Dixon cites Stephen Wilson's suggestion that artists can choose to locate their work within one of three theoretical paradigms: a contemporary version of modernism (privileging the autonomy of the artist and artefact), a new form of deconstructive postmodernism, or practices exploring new technologies (Wilson, 2002: 26). I suggest that a fourth possibility is socially engaged art praxis; evidence of the turn to this paradigm can be seen in Shannon Jackson's study, *Social Works: Performing Art, Supporting Publics* (2011).

Minding the 'gaps' in this study (meaning a careful negotiation of these in-between spaces) also involves being situated in between performance disciplines. Mark Storer (a practitioner discussed in the context of applied theatre and featured in Part II, Chapter 3, 'Performing Lives') describes himself as 'working in the space between live art and theatre'[4] and this book is similarly situated in between live art and what Richard Schechner and James Thompson refer to as 'social theatre' (Schechner and Thompson, 2004). As such, it extends current definitions of applied performance, embracing some of the forms emerging from participatory arts practice: 'public', 'participatory' and 'collaborative' modes of contemporary art.

Methodologies, form, content

The methodology involved an autoethnographic perspective through fieldwork (participating in workshops and performances) and interviews. Autoethnography is defined by Norman Denzin as writing which draws upon ethnography and autobiography (2003). My account brings a personal perspective to the work discussed, as the experiential engages in dialogue with the social, cultural and critical. The case studies are similarly chosen as indicative practices which function (as in phenomenology) as 'examples [which] are the methodological language through which the deep structures of experience are explored' (van Manen, 1979: 5). As applied theatre and performance generally takes place outside of the public space of theatres and galleries and is often 'bespoke', developed for particular communities in a particular context, the work is not readily accessible, is difficult to document (due to the ethics of participant-centred practices) and hence requires 'thick' description as a means of making the material visible.

According to McConachie, ' the two major approaches that theatre scholars have used to understand how we process visual information from the stage – phenomenology and semiotics – cannot, by themselves, reveal our dual modes of processing ... semiotics makes no foundational distinctions between looking at the physical world and watching intentional human action' (2008: 57). In both applied theatre and many contemporary modes of performance, the production of meaning is even more complex, involving multiple (rather than dual) modes of processing through work which involves embodied, sensorial and experiential engagement, where the 'audience' or 'spectator' is positioned as 'partaker' to use Schechner's terms.[5] Applying performance, like live art, 'invests in ideas of process, presence and experience as much as the production of objects or things ... art that seeks to be alert and responsive to its contexts, sites and audiences' (Live Art, 2009).

Cognitive science offers a useful framework, then, for understanding the processes of applying performance: reception, meaning making, identity formation, social interaction, group behaviour, emotional systems, processes of change, and even morality, can all be conceptualized through this developing body of theory. Whilst it is important to emphasize the hypothetical nature of cognitive thinking (it makes no claims to be 'truth'), this body of work has challenged our assumptions about how the mind/brain works as well as calling into question some theories which have historically informed theatre and performance scholarship, particularly psychoanalysis and semiology. For McConachie, however, 'cognitive studies offers a more empirically responsible path to knowledge in cultural history than psychoanalysis' (McConachie and Hart, 2006: 54).

Part I explores this further, establishing the theoretical and historical contexts for the study. In the avant-garde, we can identify the pioneers, politics and principles for applying performance. Cognitive perspectives provide a framework for conceptualizing the interventionist approach to performance, the changed relations between performers and spectators and the emancipation of performance as well as spectators, as performance moved beyond building-based theatre and galleries and into public space. A section on principles suggests a taxonomy for applying performance, identifying seven features which link the range of practices discussed and which emerged from the field work phase of my research.

Part II focuses upon practices and has three chapters: Chapter 3, 'Performing Lives', explores a range of work in which auto/biographies are the source material for applying performance, drawing on traditions of performance art and documentary modes of performance. This chapter uses cognitive theory to explore the construction and performance of identities and lives. In Chapter 4 the focus moves from 'who' to 'where' in a discussion of 'placing performance.' McConachie (2007) and Jeff Malpas (1999) argue that place is central to how we perceive and conceptualize and this is endorsed in a range of research discussing site responsive performance.

Digital technologies are also part of the environment we inhabit in the twenty-first century, contributing to the language we speak and, increasingly, becoming an extension of the object world. Multimedia theatre has developed into a particularly significant strand of contemporary performance practice, as evident in the work of, for example, Blast Theory, The Builders Association, Company in Space, Troika Ranch and Stelarc. Described by Steve Dixon as an 'emergent avant-garde' (2007: 7), the pervasive influence of digital technologies on performance and in everyday life is similarly evident in the processes and practices of applying performance. Chapter 5, 'Digital Transportations', discusses how computer technologies and digital media are being used in conjunction with live art and performance in educational and social contexts. The vocabularies of 'digital natives' (to use Mark Prensky's contested terms) articulate and create new perspectives, new modes of communication and new kinds of interactivity.

Part III explores the participant perspective, engaging with current debates in applied theatre and performance concerning aesthetics, ethics and affect. Questions to be asked here are: 'who' it is for? what is the 'outcome'? and is this 'aesthetic' (with particular reference to Erika Fischer Lichte's analysis) or not? Drawing on Claire Bishop's work (2004, 2006), I question some of the practices emerging from the turn to affect, particularly the 'disneyfication' of some forms of so called 'immersive' performance and the influence of this on applied performance. Participation is, however, a defining feature of applied performance and the final part of the book explores a range of examples examining how and why this is *affective* practice.

Throughout the book I have endeavoured to integrate form and content by producing forms of writing which affect as well as analyse. Academic writing, like all forms of writing, is auto/biographical and this is no exception. Chapter 3, on performing lives, opens with a personal perspective from a live artist on her experience of applying performance, while my discussion of working with dementia also includes an autobiographical element. Chapter 4, on place, takes the reader on a range of journeys and experiences – from the Kent coast to the United States and back again.

The structure of the book is also shaped by the content, particularly the connectionist model of cognition. According to Elizabeth Wilson, a feminist neuroscientist, cognitive processing involves 'the spread of activation across a network of interconnected, neuron-like units .... It is the connections between these units, rather than the units per se, that take on the pivotal role in the functioning of the network' (Wilson, 1998: 6). The chapters of the book are conceived to function like neurological units and it is the connections between them which generate meaning. To some extent the tripartite structure can function autonomously as three independent parts of a whole. Whilst Part I establishes a contextual framework, Part II involves a flexible spatial arrangement and the chapters on the various practices can be read in any order; although Part III is conceived as a finale and conclusion, it is also free standing. The seven principles of applying performance (pedagogy, process, play, presence, participation, performance and pleasure) provide links across and between chapters. The book is not structured according to the settings in which the work is created, but in accordance with various modes of contemporary performance. Each part could be a book-length study and is designed to work as a touchstone to provoke further discussion, to stimulate new ideas for new applications, and to provide working examples of the integration of theory and practice within a cognitive framework. Linking the various elements together is cognitive theory, a context for creating dialogue, encounters, connection and conceptual coherence, keeping it all in play. As McConachie asserts, 'performance matters, and cognitive studies can help to show how and why this is so' (2008: xii).

Part I
Histories and Contexts

1
Setting the Scene: Critical and Theoretical Contexts

> *If we wish to see how contemporary drama and theatre might engage with the 'great liberal motives' underlying most conceptions of democracy, then we should be looking to resistant and transcendent practices which valorise the autonomous subject while reinforcing collective (or community) identities.*
>
> (Kershaw, 1998: 73)

'Resistant' and 'transcendent' are terms readily associated with applied theatre and performance. The performance work featured within this book shares ideological and political objectives that are espoused through practices which have the potential to challenge, innovate and transform, respecting and promoting individual agency as well as embracing collective identities. Kershaw's comment in his millennial volume coincided with a crisis in theory (Eagleton, 2003). New models were needed for new forms and an emergent new world order. Digital revolution, political revolution and upheaval, global economic anxieties and ecological concerns about sustainability and the environment are part of the twenty-first-century climate of change with new temporalities, materialities and ontologies. In terms of temporality, the mediatization of events means they no longer take place in particular times and places, distance no longer matters in the context of Skype, while the past is being returned to the present through new technologies for recovering, preserving and documenting. We seek to possess the past through a commodification of history. Family archives become part of our material identities; theatre archives become 'live'. Performance documentation is a means of keeping the past in a continuous present, a refusal to accept the past as loss.

Linked to this are fundamental concerns about the nature of identity. Theorization of the performative construction of social identities creates a new kind of cultural schizophrenia (Butler, 1993), a reconfiguration of R. D. Laing's notion of the 'divided self', whereby gender and speech

3

are 'acts' and presence signifies absence. Laing's concept of 'ontological insecurity' is a twenty-first-century malaise, contributing to our preoccupation with materiality, as we preserve anything that contributes to a sense of individual or collective identity. Kershaw's comment is also compatible with the theoretical positions engaged in this book, which respond to the variously brave, angry or frightened new worlds of the twenty-first century with new paradigms that challenge the dichotomies of self and other through a discourse of embodiment and affect where thinking and feeling are conjoined.

Remembering Brith Gof

PAX, Aberystwyth railway station, 1991

It's 16 October 1991 and an audience gathers on a platform of Aberystwyth railway station. As the 19.57 departure for Shrewsbury pulls out, horn sounding by arrangement, the performers of Cyrff Yswyth, a local dance company with several disabled members, are revealed across the tracks on the platform opposite. Over the next fifteen minutes, their choreographic routines avoid the large trolleys from which 'ground-workers' vigorously spread soil and spray water and envelop them in smoke – workers who will then drag felled trees through the audience, shepherding them into the glass-roofed station concourse where all will eventually congregate: where a small orchestra, vocalists and narrators perch on the roof of a newspaper kiosk and four performers are suspended on pulley systems from the ironwork rafters.

PAX, the second of Brith Gof's large-scale works, involved a descent of angels: fragile when examined and persecuted by the workers, vengeful in their retribution and eventual ascent. Announced as 'a reflection on the state of the planet in ten movements', its dramaturgy attended two questions: could angels survive in current environmental conditions? Would we know them if we saw them?

(Pearson, 2010: 69)

In his essay on site specificity and Dutch community theatre, Eugene van Erven draws on the work of Mike Pearson and Michael Shanks to make the following comment on Brith Gof's practices:

But although the work of Brith Gof … goes considerably beyond the use of site as backdrop to delve archaeologically into local histories, the people residing in these places only provide anecdotal information and are then invited to watch the structurally, visually, and technologically complex concoctions of 'outsider' artists, who at all times maintain executive control over the creative process.

(Van Erven, 2007: 28)

The issues at stake here are central to the ethics and aesthetics of making performance in social, community and educational contexts: the role of the artist, the relations between performers and participants and between process and performance. Van Erven advocates the aesthetic potential of place ('space made meaningful by human actions') as a stimulus for making performance in conjunction with the stories of community participants, who, he suggests, should play a part in artistic decisions. Implicit (but not explicit) in Van Erven's discussion is the role of *affect* in the practice of place. The conceptualization of place making in terms of theories of affect (Casey, 2001; Clough and Halley, 2007; Soja, 1989; Thrift, 2007) has particular significance for the theory and practice of applied theatre and performance and is resonant in current research within the field.[1] The importance of an affective perspective, recognizing and responding to the experience of place as well as the doing and making activities which produce it is evident in the work of Margaret Ames, a community artist, dance movement therapist and lecturer in Drama and Theatre Studies at Aberystwyth University. For Ames, a Brith Gof performer who worked with a disabled dance company as the choreographer and movement director for *PAX*, the production is remembered somewhat differently:

> Aberystwyth railway station. We waited on the platform. The last train was like a curtain opening the show: we had to work around the train timetable and the logistics of getting the audience from the platform into the other space, onto the concourse. The struggle to pull people off the platform was part of the dramaturgy, needing to get to the concourse for the right point in the score. Some of the audience were concerned about how the disabled performers were being moved by the other performers. They missed the sophistication of the work. We were moving large groups of people into a space through a dramaturgy and choreography. Site was never a backdrop. Things move through you as you move through things. These knowings emerge from spectacle but don't have to be ground in spectacle. The station, this station was important as the place of performance. Coming from Wales, Brith Gof maintained a marginal perception of life and this was at the heart of the work: sensitivity about indigenous culture, heritage, language, lived experience, the everyday, shaping the way you dream.[2]

Ames offers a counter-perspective to Van Erven's conceptualization of Brith Gof's work, emphasizing the centrality of the lived experience, the emotional resonance and *felt* dimension of place as being integral to the aesthetics and ethics of the performances. She recalls the 1984 miners' strikes, throwing coins into buckets as she ran through the streets of Swansea (working as both a nurse and performer during the 1980s) to participate in *Pandaemonium: The True Cost of Coal*. The piece was performed in a functioning Methodist chapel; Ames remembers the banks of choirs, nurses in uniform, ex-miners and the audience, conjoined as a 'congregation'. These were not community choirs, she explains, but choirs of people, nuanced groupings who had come together, creating a huge wall of sound. The volume of sound was 'profoundly emotional' whilst the personal and communal in this context was also profoundly political. In the vast scale of the work, professional performers were largely lost. The boundaries between artist and audience dissolved as the event shifted into something complex, unravelling and deeply communal: a body of people, participating in an event. For its audiences, Brith Gof's work was much more than a spectacle to be observed; it was made to witness, to perceive, to grapple with.

The issues identified in this short example – ethics and aesthetics in participatory modes of practice, the affect of the work on performers and audience, the importance of process and the relations between making and performance are critical considerations to my discussion of *affective* practice.

Affective practice

Kinesthetic knowledge and understanding is at the heart of applied theatre practice where participatory performance is used to 'effect' change (defined variously as 'transformation' or 'transportation') through its 'affect' on participants (Nicholson, 2005; Thompson, 2009). Drama activities in educational, social and community contexts involve practitioners and participants as 'active producers' (rather than consumers) who 'are enabled to move ... through creative activity, towards a valuable goal of applied theatre praxis: social transformation' (Sutton, 2005: 32–3). Thus for the applied theatre practitioner, empathy might be considered to be an important feature of their practical and ethical engagement with the 'client group'. Empathy, however, is a somewhat vexed concept as a term which has been used somewhat pejoratively by contemporary performance scholars and practitioners. This is due largely to the theories and practices of Bertolt Brecht (a seminal influence in the field of applied theatre), whose references to 'crude empathy' and mimesis have a tendency to be misunderstood and simplified in the critique of 'identification' (Brecht, 1964). As Jill Bennett observes in *Empathic Vision: Affect, Trauma and Contemporary Art:* 'What is wrong with [crude empathy] is, of course, that another's experience ... is assimilated to the self in the most simplistic and sentimental way; anything beyond the audience's immediate experience remains beyond comprehension ... we fail to respect the difference between their suffering and our own' (2005:111). Bennett's study rehabilitates empathy through its focus on forms of art which affect through embodied modes of perception that simultaneously provoke 'critical enquiry'. As she explains:

This conjunction of affect and critical awareness may be understood to constitute the basis of an empathy grounded not in affinity (*feeling for* another insofar as we can imagine *being* that other) but on a *feeling for* another that entails an encounter with something irreducible and different, often inaccessible.

(Bennett, 2005: 10)

This notion of an empathetic 'encounter' with something enigmatic and generally regarded as 'inaccessible' promoting kinesthetic and critical empathy provides an apt introduction to the work discussed here under the rubric of applied performance.

The naming of applied performance

In a series of interviews I conducted as part of the research for this book, I was asked the same two questions by the majority of practitioners I spoke to. Firstly, they asked me to explain the terms 'applied theatre' and 'performance' and, secondly, they wanted to explore the implications of having their work discussed in this context. The over-riding concern was how their work would be evaluated and an insistence on the status of their work as 'art'.

In writing about the theories and practices associated with what has become known as 'applied theatre' we need to be clear about the terminology we are using. Applications of theatre involve a diversity of participatory practices in educational, social and community contexts (e.g., schools, prisons, hospitals, museums, care homes) or with particular cultural groups (particularly in terms of the contested term 'theatre for development' or TfD). In discussions of the terminology (Jackson, 2007; Nicholson, 2005; Prendergast and Saxton, 2011; Prentki and Preston, 2008; Schechner and Thomspon, 2004), some common themes emerge which can be broadly summarized in terms of functionality and beneficence. Thus when theatre is applied *to* something, it is in order to achieve a particular objective which is generally defined in terms of change, learning or 'development', although the latter is a contested term due to its association with cultural hegemony and the 'developing world'. The interventionist agenda allied with theatre for development (often abbreviated TfD) and the pursuit of social change raise a series of questions to be addressed later concerning the agent for change, the politics of cultural intervention and the problems of cultural hegemony.

Three core principles can be identified which appear to be fundamental to definitions of applied theatre. First is the importance of context; 'applied' generally refers to theatre which operates outside of 'mainstage' and 'mainstream' traditions (in a range of 'non-traditional' settings). Secondly, there is a sense of it having a utilitarian purpose and, thirdly, it will involve an active engagement with its audience who are generally constituted as participants. Thus for Nicholson, 'the point is that theatre is applied to different contexts, audiences and situations and for specific purposes.'[3] The concept of purpose is fundamental as this underlies the 'application'. That is, the theatre activity or event has an objective beyond the production of an artistic artefact. Whilst a number of commentators have referred to this objective as 'transformation', Nicholson uses Richard Schechner's discussion of the terminology suggesting that 'transportation' is more appropriate and in so doing raises some key questions:

> If applied drama is socially transformative, is it explicit what kind of society is envisioned? If the motive is individual or personal transformation, is this something which is done *to* the participants, *with* them, or *by* them? Whose values and interests does the transformation serve? Seen in this light, the idea of transportation suggests greater scope for creativity and unpredictability than that of transformation.
>
> (Nicholson, 2005: 12)

The publication of three key texts in the early to mid-2000s helped to establish applied theatre as a discreet area of enquiry in Theatre Studies and raised further questions about terminology: Philip Taylor's *Applied Theatre: Transformative Encounters in the Community* (2003), James Thompson's *Applied Theatre: Bewilderment and Beyond* (2003) and Helen Nicholson's *Applied Drama: The Gift of Theatre* (2005). Taylor's introductory study discusses the function and practice of applied theatre as well as addressing some of the issues involved in terms of ethics and evaluation. Interestingly, the practices featured focus on the generation of scripts, improvised scenarios and role-play. This model is the basis of drama therapy as well as many other applications of drama to social, community or educational settings. One could argue that 'applied drama' might be a more appropriate title for this study if 'drama' is understood as an activity or process involving the composition of scenarios, actions and representation (generally associated with acting 'in role' and the production of scripts). Taylor, however, allies 'drama' with classroom-based educational activities, where drama is used as a teaching method and associates the practices in his book with the theatre in education movements of the late twentieth century. As Nicholson observes, drama and theatre are terms that are used 'flexibly and interchangeably' in discussions of the area. Preferring the title *Applied Drama* for her study, she points to the association of theatre with specialist building-based work produced for spectators to see (and cites the origins of the term *theatron*: viewing place) (2005: 4–5). By using the term 'theatre' in her subtitle, Nicholson emphasizes her holistic approach in recognizing 'the importance of all forms of theatre practice and performance as they are applied to specific contexts and different audiences'. Nicholson's book is a constructive development of Taylor: she offers an overview of theoretical concepts with reference to a range of practical examples in educational and community contexts. What Nicholson foregrounds are the ideological commitments underpinning applied drama: '[it] is fortified by a robust understanding of the politics of cultural difference, in which questions of citizenship, pedagogy and praxis are neither individualized nor privatized, but acknowledged as both a positive attribute of contemporary society and as a site of struggle' (2005: 15).

One of the objections to the use of the label 'applied theatre' is that it implies other forms of theatre are therefore 'pure' (Colleron and Spencer, 1998; Nicholson, 2005; Prentki and Preston, 2008). The problem here is a concern that theatre which is 'pure' by virtue of being non-utilitarian will be considered as superior to its applied counterpart and that working with groups of 'non-actors' to create performance in 'non-theatre' spaces might be regarded as a secondary activity to the primary one of making 'pure' art for its own aesthetic merits. Tim Prentki (in his review of Taylor's book) counters this with an eminently quotable rebuff: 'a theatre which lacks application is merely a product of the leisure industry.'[4] Yet as Jeanne Colleran and Jenny Spencer note in writing about the difficulties of defining 'political' theatre, 'the aesthetic-versus-political binary that underwrites such declarations is far easier to recognize than to escape. Theatre performances, like other instances of cultural production are decidedly "impure acts", simultaneously socially implicated and socially critical, an apparatus for the construction of meaning rather than an index to it' (Colleran and Spencer, 1998: 1). In applied theatre, moreover, the spectator's active engagement is fundamental to its construction and ideology; Nicholson emphasizes this in her discussion of the terminology: '[it] relates to work which is orientated towards aspects of social change, personal development and community building through various forms of participation in drama, theatre and other performance practices'(2005: 90).

The terms of the debate were challenged in 2009 by the publication of Thompson's paradigm-shifting *Performance Affects: Applied Theatre and the End of Effect* in which his experience of a drama project at a rehabilitation centre for child soldiers and the subsequent massacre which he fears *may* have been connected, causes him to radically question and problematize the purposes and practices of applied theatre in contexts of social crisis or conflict:

> The argument to be made, in light of this project ... is that applied thea-tre's claims need to be re-examined and a politics of the practice needs to be rearticulated (or perhaps rediscovered) so that it is decoupled from any possible complicity, however tenuous, with incidents of violence.
>
> (Thompson, 2009: 16)

Thompson's book initiated the turn to 'affect' in applied theatre research and debates about ethics and aesthetics became a focus of concern. Nicholson's subsequent *Theatre, Education and Performance* (2011) also asks searching questions about efficacy; situating theatre education in the context of a globalized economy, she explores the impact of theatre on education and vice versa and the dialogues between twentieth- and twenty-first-century pedagogies and performance practices.

In applied theatre and performance, we can argue, the focus for evaluation shifts from performer to partaker as the learner/audience for whom the work is created. Whilst some might consider this to be a vertical approach in terms of power structures ('good' group go to 'bad' group) and in contrast to the horizontal modes of collaboration involved in devising performance, the vertical model is not appropriate or relevant to the practices discussed here. Devising is a collaborative methodology, underpinning the processes involved, while performance provides a liminal space in which participants can play, engaging conceptually, spatially and imaginatively through experiment and experience – a place where theatre and learning meet.

Nicholson draws upon Elizabeth Ellsworth's concept of the 'materiality of learning' which 'recognizes that the physical environment, the place of learning, and the movement of bodies in space are integral to the experience of learning' (Nicholson, 2011: 9). This embodied pedagogy Nicholson argues, challenges the mind/body and reason/emotion dualisms underpinning the individualism of Western educational paradigms. Ellsworth's understanding that 'learning always takes place in relation' (2005: 55) in conjunction with notions of 'situated learning' (Lave and Wenger, 1991) links to cognitive theory, particularly Wilson's connectionist model which conceives of knowledge as being created through interdependent processes conjoining the brain and body. Cognitive science similarly challenges the dualisms associated with child development theory and psychoanalysis, positing a social model of 'cognitive communities' whereby infants learn through the development of empathy and memory, engaged through social interaction; as McConachie has noted in his discussion of spectatorship, 'contrary to Lacan, infants are rapid, proactive learners in their search for sociality; they use their mirror neuron systems with significant others to build numerous capacities for later interactions, including social relations basic to language and the arts' (2008: 82). McConachie also questions Judith Butler's conception of performative constructions of gender, which, he argues, 'denies significant intentionality to infants, who only gain subjectivity after their enculturation ... Lacanian Othering assumes that the self and social others are often natural antagonists. In contrast, the mutual mirroring that occurs all the time between the self and others assumes that there is a natural basis in infancy and social relationships for human cooperation' (82). These cognitive perspectives can be mapped on to Nicholson's reconceptualizing of pedagogical and aesthetic models (with reference to Gregory Bateson's notion of the mind being structured as an ecological system in conjunction with Ellsworth's materiality of learning):

> Rather than seeing the world in terms of different domains of knowledge, in which objective knowledge is privileged over subjective feeling or local know-how, there is an increasing search for ways of thinking and learning that acknowledge their interdependence.
>
> (Nicholson, 2011: 8)

Cognitive perspectives facilitate this goal of joined-up thinking and learning, linking neurological responses to the motor system and emotion. Embodied interaction is conceived as fundamental to learning and agency, while empathy, imagination and social engagement are embraced as central engines of meaning. Nicholson's mapping metaphor is also prevalent in cognitive science (Wilson, 2005) and offers an alternative to the vertical/horizontal paradigms which conceptualize authorities of knowledge.

In contemporary art, the shifting emphasis from artist to spectator (via participatory, collaborative and public modes of art) similarly challenges traditional notions of aesthetics as well as the notion of art as object and commodity. As in applied theatre, the distinctions between creator/performer/perceiver are blurred as performers and participants engage in creative dialogue through action/interaction. This discussion is developed in Part III, where the interplay between ethics and aesthetics in participatory performance is explored.

In terms of cognitive theory, it has been argued that there is 'an evolutionary continuity between action recognition, imitation and language' (Iacoboni 2005: 22) and this can be linked to a complex dynamic between self and other. According to Susan Hurley, one model 'connects a shared information space for perception and action with a shared information space for self and other, while at the same time illustrating how the distinctions between perception and action, self and other, and possible and actual can be overlaid on these shared information spaces' (Hurley, 2005: 1). Questions of the self, the construction of identity, the formation of subjectivity and the concept of the 'other' are, of course, fundamental to postmodernism, a theoretical discourse which, for better or worse, has informed contemporary performance practices. As Kershaw ruefully observes: 'if you write about *contemporary* performance, either you are *with* the post modern or you're not' (Kershaw, 1999: 7). Kershaw identifies the possibilities and problems of the postmodern for performance practice:

> Drama and theatre can significantly contribute to the collective and individual creation of autonomous subjects, especially through an engagement with systems of formalized power in an effort to create radical freedom. Such freedom can be achieved through actions which combine

resistant *and* transcendent ideological dynamics, which oppose dominant ideologies and also at least gesture to possibilities beyond them. Postmodernism is useful to this project because its pluralism opens up a rich range of approaches to the creation of resistance.

(Kershaw, 1998: 76)

The problem, however, as Kershaw acknowledges, is that postmodernism's critique of subjectivity and commitment to relativism is incompatible with the various notions of agency, autonomy and community underpinning socially engaged theatre. Thus although postmodernism might be deemed to be a globally relevant paradigm whose pluralism offers marginalized communities positions of equality, ultimately it can be seen to deny a culture an 'absolute artistic, cultural, spiritual or historical truth' (Chin, 1989: 163). For the purposes of this study, Hans-Thies Lehman's concept of the 'post dramatic' is a useful development of postmodernist performance theory. Lehman's discussion of semiotics, the aesthetics of space, the representation of the body and the use of media illuminate the practices discussed here. Central to Lehman's thesis is the shift from representation as the focus of dramatic enquiry to the relations between actor and audience: 'the turn to performance is ... always a turn towards audience as well ... Performance has the power to question and destabilize the spectator's construction of 'identity' and the 'other' – more so than realist mimetic drama, which remains caught in representation and thus often reproduces prevailing ideologies' (Lehman, 2006: 5). Lehman's thesis can be seen as a development of Denzin's call for a 'turn to a performance-based approach to culture, politics and pedagogy' (Denzin, 2003: 24) which involves a Barthesian death of the traditional audience (albeit within the rubric of postmodernism):

under this postmodern performance aesthetic, the traditional audience disappears. The postmodern audience is both an interactive structure and an interpretive vehicle ... As existential collaborators they are co-constructed by the event ... postmodern audience members are neither voyeurs nor spectators; they are not passive recipients of a performance event. Rather, audience members are participants in a dialogic performance event, an event that is emancipatory and pedagogical.

(Denzin, 2003: 41)

The dialogue between audience and performer in postdramatic theatre has an interesting synergy with mirror neuron theory in terms of the focus on the relation between the perceiver and the perceived. As Vittorio Gallese explains, 'to perceive an action is equivalent to internally simulating it. This enables the observer to use her/his own resources to experientially penetrate the world of the other by means of a direct, automatic and unconscious process of simulation' (Gallese, 2008).

So what are the implications here for the active spectator in 'postdramatic' theatre and the practices in social contexts which are discussed in this book as 'applied performance'? Many of the examples cited by Karen Jürs-Munby in her introduction to the English edition of *Postdramatic Theatre* are practitioners and companies who make performance through the process of devising (The Wooster Group, Station House Opera, Forced Entertainment, Goat Island, etc.), practices in which the emphasis is on experimentation and play in rehearsal oriented towards 'process and improvisation rather than textual analysis and technique' (Govan, Nicholson and Normington, 2007: 32). Devising processes emphasize the importance of play while research on children's play has identified 'dramaturgies resembling those of avant-garde devising groups' (Guss, 2005: n2).

The discovery of mirror neurons has huge significance for our understanding of play in terms of child development theory and, by extension, performance theory. If 'the playful activity of all primates derives from their mimetic observations of life' (Govan, 2007: 32), mirror neurons enable us to understand that in humans, this mimetic activity has evolved into a more complex observation in which the individual mentally embodies the behaviour of the other and that the assimilation of this felt experience and knowledge will inform any representation. This evolutionary movement from imitation to embodiment is analogous to the emergence of devised performance as a methodology and form whose fluidity and flexibility offers a more appropriate means of exploring and representing the complexity of contemporary lives.

Thus the title of this book, *Applying Performance*, reflects its focus on contemporary performance practices within social and educational contexts and the implications of a shift from a theatre dominated paradigm to a performance centred one in the twenty-first century. The book explores the political, social and educative implications of the different forms of contemporary performance discussed. As Helen Nicholson argues, drawing upon Pierre Bourdieu's analysis of the 'politics of purity', practitioners in applied drama have often distanced themselves from 'mainstream' theatre practices and spaces which have been considered the preserve of the middle class (Nicholson, 2005: 7). Against the backdrop of globalization, corporate capitalism and consumerism, applied theatre practitioners are generally working from positions which are both within (inside an institution or working within a particular community setting) and outside institutional structures (as the practitioner will generally come from outside the institution or community), thereby inhabiting a somewhat anomalous position. This can be viewed positively as a creative space where interventions can happen (Kershaw, 1999; Nicholson, 2005). However, the problems of this position have been wittily articulated by John Fox's account of the parachute artist who dipped into a community, 'stirred things up" and went away again.[5] There are lessons to be learned from the fierce debates surrounding Theatre for Development, not the least of which is the need for decisions about cultural production to be negotiated amongst stakeholders and for practitioners to ensure that they engage with the 'experienced' community rather than the 'imagined' one so that, explains Nicholas Rowe (with reference to his dance based work in Palestine) 'the cultural interventionist can consider the impact of the intervention on the various ideals co-existing in the community, not just the one emerging from a dominant or centralized narrative. In doing so, the pluralistic nature of local cultural decisions becomes more apparent' (2007). Thus for the practitioner, applying performance in educational and community settings, there are crucial political and ethical questions which need to be addressed concerning who the work is for and what it is intended to achieve.

2
Pasts, Pioneers, Politics

Avant-garde and radical theatres

The dialogue between the avant-garde (both the historical avant-garde of the early twentieth century and the neo avant-garde of the 1960s and 1970s) and applied modes of performance during the twentieth-century provides the contextual framework for this study, connecting historical and contemporary artists who have a common interest in socialist politics, social activism, audiences, community engagement, marginalized groups and collaborative methodologies. Miwon Kwon has identified Russian Constructivism and the Dessau Bauhaus as 'precedents' for 'art in public interest' (2004: 106). The historical context for this study is the fecundity of work considered as 'radical' and 'interventionist,' associated with the avant-garde, challenging disciplinary boundaries and institutional contexts through practices which emancipated art from galleries and theatres, as performance took to the streets, engaging its publics through social and collaborative modes which repositioned art as 'work' (rather then contemplative leisure), orientated towards political change and, at its most extreme, revolution. Although the historical avant-garde, the neo avant-garde and applied theatre and performance maybe appear to be somewhat uneasy bedfellows the creative tensions between these sets of practices (all of which share a commitment to effecting social change) has produced work which is radical and interventionist in a narrative which can be seen to include Russia's Blue Blouses, the Red Megaphones in Germany, the 1930s Worker's Theatre Movement in Britain and the United States, Futurism, Dada, Expressionism, Constructivism, Situationism, the Federal Theatre, Living Theatre, Group Theatre, Bread and Puppet, San Francisco Mime Troup and El Teatro Campesino.

Emerging from 'oppositional' and 'popular' theatres (Nicholson, 2005), applied forms of theatre are defined in opposition to practices considered to be self-regarding, introspective and narcissistic. There is, however, a danger here of a false dichotomy which celebrates applied theatre as the form with social conscience and integrity in opposition to the bourgeois practices of the 'academy' (Kershaw, 1999; Nicholson, 2005).

In trying to trace a genealogy of applied performance, it is important to be aware that this is not a homogonous phenomenon. Tim Prentki and Shelia Preston trace the history of 'applied theatre' and its 'hybrid practices' through the educational and political reforms of the twentieth century in the United Kingdom and United States: 'the roots of applied theatre grew in the soil of progressive radical peoples movements in various places around the world' (2008: 11, 13). The practices referred to as avant-garde in the annals of twentieth-century theatre history have been variously defined and the terminology does not refer to a definitive set of characteristics. Nevertheless, we can identify features associated with avant-garde aesthetics which have contributed to the performance practices discussed here: the blurring of boundaries between life and art; the use of 'devising' methodologies to create performance; the challenging of the hierarchies of directors and writers; and the changing relations between audience and performers, particularly in terms of participatory or collaborative modes of practice. Precedents are Happenings, Fluxus instructions and 1970s performance art, all of which were driven by a commitment to democracy, emancipation, intervention and a desire to 'activate' the spectator, changing the 'conditions' and power relations of artistic production. Theoretical tracts such as Walter Benjamin's 'The Author as Producer' (1970), Umberto Eco's *The Open Work* (1989) and Roland Barthes's 'The Death of the Author' (1968) were endemic to the shifting practice and its challenge to modernism. As Eco writes:

> The poetics of the 'work in movement' (and partly that of the 'open' work) sets in motion a new cycle of relations between the artist and his audience, a new mechanics of aesthetic perception, a different status for the artistic product in contemporary society. It opens a new page in sociology and in pedagogy, as well as a new chapter in the history of art. It poses new practical problems by organizing new communicative situations. In short, it installs a new relationship between the *contemplation* and the *utilization* of a work of art.
>
> (1989: 22–3)

There are strong parallels here with critical writing about applied theatre and debates about the artefact, aesthetics and art as instrument (Jackson, 2007; Nicholson, 2005, 2011; Thompson, 2009).

Numerous commentaries have endeavoured to create a historiography of avant-garde performance and in so doing, as Kershaw eloquently protests: 'too many aesthetic eggs are being placed in the same historical basket' (Kershaw, 1999: 60). Applied performance is situated in the gap between 'performance' and 'theatre'. It is not art for art's sake or an elitist aesthetic; its practitioners describe themselves as artists and clearly consider this role as one which is socially responsive. The practices featured in this book engage in a dialogue with both the work of their contemporaries in contemporary performance and their antecedents in political theatre and the avant-garde. As Nicholson has noted, 'although theatre and performance have been characterized as separate sites of struggle, there has been, of course, much productive dialogue between these two related modes of cultural practice.' Moreover, as she emphasizes, they are not 'fixed' and stable categories but are 'sites of experimentation', 'continually in play' (2005: 9).

At key points in twentieth-century theatre history, theatre workers have drawn upon radical practices to promote social change: thus 'the history of political, radical and alternative theatres has allied applied drama to cultural activism' (Nicholson, 2005: 8). These pioneering practices can be seen as the context for the contemporary forms of applied performance featured in this study. The war-torn political landscape of the first part of the twentieth century functioned as a seed-bed for the post-war interventionist theatres which followed. Derek Paget offers a succinct summary:

> a good deal of radical theatre practice was expunged from Russian theatre history in a Stalinist period of 'Socialist Realism' in the arts ... practices developed in the USSR of the 1920s were imported into Germany later in the decade, then transferred via immigrant communities to the USA. Information from all three sources percolated into the UK both by the front (European) and back (US) doors.
>
> (1990: 49)

Paget points to the influence of the Blue Blouse groups, who can be considered as a precursor to the applied theatre practices which subsequently emerged. Erwin Piscator, Brecht and Hallie Flanagan visited the Soviet Union, while a Blue Blouse company toured Germany in 1927. Informed by the revolutionary theory and practices of Meyerhold and Eisenstein, the Blue Blouses drew upon popular performance traditions (song, burlesque, vaudeville) to produce documentary theatre in non-theatre spaces (often outdoors) in the form of 'dramatic living newspapers' bringing education, news and politics and propaganda to the workforce. Eschewing naturalism (as bourgeois), the Blue Blouses practised 'social realism' and incorporated their experiences of industrial life into their performance methods. A particularly insightful reading of a 1930s agitational sketch can be found in Simon Shepherd's discussion of how the body makes meaning in performance. Shepherd cites a piece by a 1930s workers' group (*Tempo Tempo*) as an example of how body rhythm in performance mirrored the social environment in which the work was situated:

> [*Tempo Tempo*] was explicitly connected to a sense of temporal flow in society. [It] addressed itself to industrial workers with experience of monotonously regulated time ... The connection between rhythmic delivery and

the supposed experience of industrial production is made explicit. And the precision of the link between the performance and its audience's culture in turn demonstrates the sketch's authority to speak to them – and for them.

(Shepherd, 2006: 89)

This analysis of how body rhythm works on the bodies of its audience can be theorized in terms of mirror neurons being the neurological basis of the kinaesthetic response. The crux of Shepherd's thesis is this: 'a play's rhythm works on an audience. It does so through the agency of the performer's body rhythm which stimulates response in audience bodies. The audience are not, however, without their own rhythm, which is derived from their everyday lives. In watching, the rhythm of their bodies may be confirmed or drawn into a new rhythm by the play' (2006: 85). This kinesthetic and empathic response is central to the transformative potential of theatre and performance as a medium which is experiential and in which knowledge is embodied. It is also the basis for considerations of spectatorship from the perspective of cognitive studies. In Shepherd's example, what is being described can be conceptualized as 'entrainment' in and through performance as bodily rhythms are synchronized like clock rhythms: 'the agitational sketch *Tempo Tempo* used verse rhythms to image the effects of capitalist factory speed-up on the workforce – and then used the same rhythms to celebrate the effects of the new Soviet Five Year Plan' (147). This form of agitational propaganda was hugely influential and cognitive theory helps us to understand why: 'group dynamics, including audience behaviour, always affect individual cognition'(McConachie, 2008: 31). This, as McConachie explains, can motivate political engagement: 'the feeling of communitas that sometimes unites an audience' can provide a context for 'political change' (2008: 97).

The histories, theories and practices of applied theatre and performance are, of course indebted to Brecht's seminal influence and his concept of 'epic' theatre, committed to social change and social justice' (see Willett, 1964). Crucial to Brecht's concept of *Verfremdunkseffekt* is his desire to provoke critical engagement in theatre through an aesthetic which defamiliarized the 'natural', ordinary and familiar by making the dramatic situation 'strange', in order to provoke audiences to look again, to question and to understand the social and historical contexts in which they are situated: 'to hand the world over to [the workers'] minds and hearts for them to change as they think fit' (Willet, 1964: 185).

The Living Newspapers produced by Flanagan's Federal Theatre Project are precursors of applied performance as social projects written, produced and performed by a marginalized social group (unemployed theatre professionals) using methodologies which anticipate contemporary forms of performance. As Paget perceives:

In its use of a wide vocabulary of technical devices, the Living Newspaper has obvious connections with the radical theatrical movements in Europe.

There was the agit-prop attention to information and the non-naturalistic styles of rapid transformation which originated with the peripatetic troupes of the USSR and Germany; there were the cross-cutting techniques of cinema and the montage structures of European cabaret/music hall brought into the theatre by the likes of Meyerhold and Piscator.

(1990: 55)

As radical theatre projects which were also a 'union of popular entertainments with people's theatre' (Malpede Taylor, 1972), the Living Newspapers could be considered in the context of Ilka Saal's critique as an example of America's 'persistent *vernacularisation* of political issues, that is, their translation into a language commensurate with the cultural experience of a broad public steeped in consumer culture' (Saal, 2007: 102). This 'vernacular praxis of political theatre' (to which Saal attributes the failure of Brecht's relations with Theater Union) anticipates the work of theatre companies such as C&T in the United Kingdom who draw upon the conventions of television, video and digital technologies and reappropriate them for theatre.

Saal distinguishes between the 'historical avant-garde' (Burger, 1984) and what she terms the 'vernacular'. The former constitutes a 'moment' in modernism where 'bourgeois art, having completed its differentiation from the social sphere, suddenly became aware of both its own institutional character as well as its utter social inconsequentiality' (Burger 1984: 27; Saal, 2007: 108). This gave rise to the political theatres of Brecht, Piscator and Meyerhold, all of which are indebted to 'the iconoclasm of the historical avantgarde' (Saal, 2007: 108). Many of the characteristics associated with applied performance praxis can be traced back to these forms of political theatre: the commitment to an aesthetics of innovation, social intervention and the challenging of existing paradigms, particularly in terms of relations between performers and audience. Applied performance is also indebted to the 'vernacular' political praxis identified by Saal which deploys 'the language of an established culture industry'. Drawing upon Fredric Jameson's work (1991), Saal defines 'vernacularity in political theatre as the capacity to speak the language of a proven, that is, commercially successful, sign system' (Saal, 2007: 109). The use of techniques drawn from film, television, digital technologies and gaming by applied performance practitioners today (as discussed in Part II, Chapter 5, 'Digital Transportations'), particularly in their work with young people can be seen as a contemporary form of 'vernacular' praxis. Whilst critics might question the political efficacy of forms of theatre which employ forms and methods associated with consumerism, Saal suggests we reconsider our criteria for assessing the political value of performance and raises some critical questions concerning the politics of form and agency:

> shifting the emphasis from the critique of the commodity to the analysis of the various intricate ways in which cultural practices interact with and

within relations of power .... What kind of political agenda motivates their choice of form and public? In what kind of social change are they interested? How radical are their intentions? What exactly is their vision of a new, better society?

(2007: 109)

These are questions arising from Saal's discussion of 1930s political theatre which remain pertinent to many of the practices discussed in this book.

The interplay between avant-garde and radical theatres in the United States during the twentieth century is critical to the development of the practices discussed here as examples of 'applied performance'. A diverse range of companies and practitioners can be identified on the historical map as points of influence and reference: companies such as the Living Theatre, the Open Theatre, characterized by Bigsby as the 'radical right', became increasingly politically engaged in the context of the 1960s civil rights movement, Vietnam and the Free Speech Movement. Conversely, as various commentators have noted, left-wing activist companies such as Bread and Puppet, the San Francisco Mime Troupe and El Teatro Campesino engaged in forms of aesthetic experiment more readily associated with the avant-garde (Bigsby, 1985, Cohen-Cruz, 2005, Govan, Nicholson and Normington, 2007).

One of the most significant legacies of avant-garde and radical theatres is the changing relationship between performer and audience. The Living Theatre, founded in 1947 by Julian Beck and Judith Malina, pioneered the participatory practices which are one of the defining characteristics of applied performance. Judith Malina had studied with Piscator and the company's ideology and methods reflect his influence. Although interested by the experimental and revolutionary aspects of the avant-garde, Beck questioned its solipsistic aspects. Beck, writes Christopher Bigsby, 'came to reject that kind of theatre in which individuals are required to sit isolated from one another in the dark and live by proxy, surrendering their freedom and their imagination to those on the stage who alone can move and act' (Bigsby, 1985: 63). As the company's name indicated, the Living Theatre's core principle was to breakdown the barrier between art and life. To this end the company prioritized the body and physical expression over 'literary' language and involved members of the public in performance events. The oft cited 'body pile' is the most famous example of this, where audiences for *Paradise Now* (1968) were invited to undress and join each other onstage in a physical declaration of sexual liberation prior to being carried by actors on to the streets to the refrain 'The theatre is in the street. The street belongs to the people. Free the theatre. Free the street. Begin', at which point the police usually intervened (Tytell, 1997: 228). This was a theatre of celebration and protest where spectators participated in performance making. The participatory element is one of the defining characteristics of applied performance.

Bread and Puppet Theatre

In discussions of avant-garde aesthetics and the relations between the experiments of the 1920s and 1930s and those of the neo avant-garde (1960s and 1970s), the concept of mimesis becomes central to debates about representation and the relations between art and life. Bürger's analysis has been questioned by several critics, most notably Hal Foster, who argues that mimesis has the capacity to function as social critique, framing and objectifying the everyday through art to provoke critical debate and questioning (Foster, 1996). Practitioners of visual and object theatre (in particular Oskar Schlemmer in the Bauhaus) explored the relationship between art and non-art, using methods which were developed in community performance contexts. One of the most significant pioneers for this work is Peter Schumann. Bread and Puppet Theatre, which Schumann founded in 1963, is an important part of the historical map in terms of their commitment to the concept of community as well as their methods and (perhaps as a consequence) their long history which continues into the twenty-first century. As John Bell observes:

> the longevity of Bread and Puppet Theatre, Living Theatre and San Francisco Mime Troupe does not fit the neat periodicity that theatre critics and historians like to impose on Twentieth-Century theatre. Despite the constant work of these companies over several decades, it makes for a clearer evolutionary narrative to peg them to the 'sixties'. Criticism can then focus on postmodernist theatre and performance art that developed out of and (to a degree) in relation to the expansive and often excessive performance of the 1960s.
>
> (1998: 34–5)

These companies, moreover, defy categorization as a well as periodization. Whilst some readers might contest their inclusion in a book which purports to be about 'applied' performance practices, there are many features of the work produced by these companies which are shared by practitioners of applied theatre and performance. These can be summarized as follows:

The work is interventionist: i.e., committed to making a change.
The work is produced in educational, social or community contexts.
The work is 'experimental', generally using non-naturalistic techniques.
The work is either participatory or promotes some form of active engagement with its audience.

Bread and Puppet can be broadly defined as avant-garde 'political' theatre, committed to producing work in and for local communities; 'puppetry was always political', according to Peter Schuman (Bell, 1998: 33). Throughout its history, Bread and Puppet Theatre has been associated with and committed to intervention. The company's street shows, indoor productions and street processions have been described as 'the theatrical center of anti-Vietnam War activity in the 1960s' (Bell, 1998: 35). Sponsored by various anti-war activists in the United States and Europe, the company's work after the end of the Vietnam War (1975) continued to engage in international politics and policy. Bread and Puppet's critique of global political and post-Cold War international issues was as radical in style as it was in content. Schummann's avant-garde aesthetic has been discussed in relation to 'Happenings', John Cage, Dada, the Wooster group and the visual theatre of Robert Wilson (Kourilsky, 1971). Although the work of these practitioners is distinguishable from the 'paratheatre' of Bread and Puppet, Schumann's aesthetic has many of the characteristics associated with postmodern performance in terms of its hybridity, non-realism, use of new technologies (albeit in a deliberately primitive form), while the relations between performer and audience in puppet theatre have been described as 'a kind of automatic *Verfremdunkseffeckt*' (Bell, 1998: 39). The haptic bodies of multimedia performance can be seen to have evolved from Schumann's puppets: 'This form of puppet theatre involves the constant juxtaposition of objects and other stage elements (music, spoken text, light) in a multilayered theatrical spectacle both grounded in real political issues ... and yet capable of abstract, open-ended meanings' (Bell, 1998: 39). Above all, however, Schumann's commitment to explore the possibilities of community performance determined the company's evolution, and, somewhat ironically, its downfall in terms of the end of the Domestic Resurrection Circus. A victim of its own success, Bread and Puppet, in spite of Schumann's attempts to avoid commercialism, struggled to cope with the increasing popularity and scale of Schumann's annual festival: multiple campgrounds, food and clothing vendors as well as various forms of merchandise accompanied the performances and ultimately threatened its integrity.

What Schumann's theatre has remained committed to throughout its long history (and in its current formation) is a community *performance* aesthetic. Whilst community theatre is generally associated with the production of plays (devised or specially commissioned) about, for, and generally presented by, a specific community (featuring local actors in pieces about local history or issues), community performance is more likely to be disruptive of the social fabric, engaging in provocation or protest through activities and events which draw upon the carnivalesque and spectacle in an aesthetic more readily associated with Artaud than Stanislavski (Kuppers, 2007a).

Bread and Puppet's work can be seen in terms of performance autoethnography as 'a civic, participatory, collaborative project. It is a project centered on an ongoing moral dialogue involving the shared ownership of the performance project itself. Together, members of the community, as cultural workers, create the performance text and the performance event' (McCall, [2000] 2003: 426).

Welfare State International

A commitment to experimental and interventionist forms of community performance also characterizes the work of Welfare State International in the United Kingdom, a company which has some similarities to Bread and Puppet and which also enjoyed longevity.

Founded in 1968 by John Fox and Boris Howarth, Welfare State International (Welfare State) produced unique forms of community performance drawing upon popular performance, puppetry, carnival, sculpture, pyrotechnics, dance, music, and fire and ice technology to create community celebratory events. The company's production of highly visual forms of performance reflects the art school background of its founders, whilst its sense if itself as being radical and interventionist is also attributable to the art school culture of the 1960s. The company situated itself physically and ideologically outside of 'middle-brow/middle-class' theatre, committing itself to the creation of work which was accessible to a wider public audience. One of the distinguishing features of the company was the location of projects in both public and private contexts. As well as large-scale public events, the company also produced 'events' such as naming ceremonies and barn dances. Like Bread and Puppet, Welfare State's participatory events often involve feasting as part of the community celebration. This conjoining of performance with communal eating is part of a tradition which extends into applied performance in the twenty-first century.[1] In documenting the history of Welfare State, Tony Coult cautiously associates the company with the avant-garde: 'Although they operated within the then current utopian avant-gardism, they were also trying to uphold a tradition of popular entertainment against the mind-blown elitist experimentation of the time' (Coult and Kershaw, 1983: 6). Crucially, for Welfare State, 'the objective was not to be judged on the quality of performance per se but to be listened to.' The evolution of the company, as discussed by Kershaw, involved a movement away from artefact and towards participatory community forms of performance: 'an aesthetic adventure searching the hinterlands between populist community carnival and exclusive experimental theatre' (Coult and Kershaw, 1982: 216). The company's splitting in 1976 and the defection of many of its members to form the performance art company IOU is indicative of the tensions between its aesthetic and social orientations. As Kershaw observes, 'it is notable that the company's increasing shift towards a commitment to community, to working *with* people as much as *for* them, has coincided with the onset of the post-punk, post-modernist free markets' (Coult and Kershaw, 1982: 206). Embracing contradiction and flirting with nostalgia in their commitment to integrating the old with the new, Welfare

State's projects explored community identities, histories and futures. Their interests in rites of passage moved between the intimate, private celebrations associated with birth, marriage and death (revisionary forms of Victor Turner's life-crisis ceremonies) to the production of large-scale public events and rituals responsive to the community contexts in which they were created. Welfare State's performances operated in liminal spaces, where identities were in transition and, as such, their work can be seen to anticipate contemporary performance ethnographies in terms of Denzin's analysis (2003). This terminology is fundamental to my definition and discussion of applied performance:

> Performance autoethnography inhabits a postmodern culture ... The performance text-as-event is situated in a complex system of discourse where traditional and avant-garde meanings – of the real, the hyperreal, mimesis and transgression, audiences, performances, performance video and performance art pedagogy – all circulate and inform one another ... These texts-as-performances challenge the meanings of lived experience as simulated performance. ... bringing audiences and performers into a jointly felt and shared field of experience. In this field memory operates. Each participant enters the performance from the standpoint of his or her own past experiences.
>
> (Denzin, 2003: 36–7)

This 'shared field of experience' is a also a 'place of learning' in terms of Nicholson's analysis and Ellsworth's pedagogy, 'a complex moving web of interrelationalities' (Ellsworth, 2005: 55; cited in Nicholson, 2011: 9). Denzin also refers to experiences being 'evoked, not explained' in this physical, visceral space of performance, thereby alluding to the affective potential for partakers of this experience.

By way of example, Kershaw offers an insightful analysis of the interaction between performers and participants in Welfare State's Barn Dances whereby a traditional and conservative social event becomes a vehicle for 'transportation' (Nicholson, 2003; Schechner, 1983) through radical theatre techniques:

> the Barn Dance animated a community-forming process between actors and audience, and ... this process was a result of the dynamic produced by the incorporation into the 'safe' form of the barn dancing of the 'threatening' images and action created by the company, and the incorporation of the audience, through increasingly active participation, into the company's performance. The complexity of that dynamic seemed to make the community-forming process available to a wide range of different types of audience.
>
> (Coult and Kershaw, 1983: 162)

Many of the paradoxes Kershaw identifies in Welfare State's projects are, however, characteristics of the case studies to follow: 'simple and complex, tacky yet beautiful, accessible yet opaque' (Kershaw, 1999: 201). Whilst Welfare State are regarded by Kershaw as 'the sharp edge of a radical knife that aims to cut through the hegemonic bindings of a pathological normality', he anticipated the end of the road with 'the ideological paralysis of post-modernism ... tightening its grip on Western Culture' (201). Welfare State's final performance was in 2006. Its legacy continues in the work of LanternHouse and in the solo work of John Fox as well as being a pioneering influence on many of the practices discussed here.

Performance work created within specific community contexts carries with it a series of ethical responsibilities and raises issues and questions which are explored in relation to each of the case studies featured in this book. Welfare State's legacy is a particularly important one in this respect as they established working practices which demonstrated 'respect for a community's life – inner and outer' (Kershaw and Coult, 1983: 11). Central to this was the use of a reconnaissance team who would be based at the site well in advance of a project (weeks and sometimes months) and would undertake the necessary field work research whilst establishing a relationship with the community and an understanding of the context in which the work was to be situated. This 'allows local people to adjust to an input ... and it allows for images from the landscape and from the stories and experience of local people to filter back to the main architects of the project' (Coult and Kershaw, 1983: 11).

The problems and politics of intervention

We can see from the work of the Living Theatre, Bread and Puppet and Welfare State how performance has functioned in community contexts throughout the twentieth century as pedagogy, politics and art. Performance has been used for the purposes of protest and to promote social change. In the dialogue between the avant-garde and applied theatre and performance, the relations between performer and audience are shifting, identities are questioned and, to use a well-worn phrase, the personal becomes political. Performance has been used in a range of contexts to interrogate identities, to challenge oppression, to question social norms and to move towards change. As Denzin observes in his powerful and provocative manifesto 'The Call to Performance':

> Performance is an act of intervention, a method of resistance, a form of criticism, a way of revealing agency ... Performance becomes public pedagogy when it uses the aesthetic, the performative, to foreground the intersection of politics, institutional sites, and embodied experience ... In this way performance is a form of agency, a way of bringing culture and the person into play.
>
> (2003: 9)

As a discourse associated with 'intervention', 'resistance' and 'criticism', performance is thus a particularly powerful medium. Its uniqueness and importance in pedagogical terms is linked to mirror neuron theory through the concept of kinaesthetic learning and embodiment. Without reference to neurological theory Denzin recognizes the significance of performance in terms of knowledge and understanding: 'a performance authorizes itself not through the citation of scholarly texts, but through its ability to evoke and invoke shared emotional experience and understanding between performer and audience' (13). The dialogue between performer and participant/audience in the practices discussed here involve complex interactions in liminal spaces. Performance is thus associated with 'doing', 'being' and 'becoming'.

The political potential of the performative (as discussed at length by Denzin) and its exploitation in Third World contexts has been a source of some debate and controversy. Boal has championed 'Theatre of the Oppressed' and numerous social groups have used performance as a means to raise consciousness of issues concerning gender, race, discrimination and poverty and to campaign for justice and equality (Boal, 1985, 1995; Etherton, 1988; Garoian, 1999). Hardly surprisingly, applied theatre and performance has its critics and some of the practices associated with it raise ethical and moral concerns, particularly in terms of authority and agency. This brings me to the issues surrounding what has become known as 'theatre for development' (TfD). Pierre Bourdieu refers to a form of symbolic violence associated with the phrase 'cultural development:' (Bourdieu, 1984). Cultural hegemony in various manifestations can be seen to have operated through many of the international 'aid' and 'development' programmes established in the late part of the twentieth century. There is a danger that interventions proposed in the name/service of 'development' perpetuate the ideologies of the funders and this can threaten existing cultural practices. Critics of TfD recognize this tendency and advocate the need for an alternative paradigm – one which recognizes and values 'local' cultural practices and respects the integrity of the existing culture. Following the philosophical approaches of Franz Fanon and Paolo Freire, this 'alternative paradigm', as Rowe has written, considers 'how local practices might be supported, enhanced and diversified in order to ensure their continuity within the local community, and in order to support the local community's cohesion ... [it] promotes a local community's collective right to be equal and active negotiating parties in such interactions' (Rowe, 2007). Denzin explores related issues in his discussion of 'the ethics and practical politics of performance autoethnography'; he calls for a 'moral ethnography that presumes a researcher who builds collaborative, reciprocal, trusting and friendly relations with the person he or she studies' (Denzin, 2003: xii).

The contemporary performance techniques featured in this study facilitate and enable interventions which are dialogic and reciprocal largely through participatory practices. Rowe refers to cultural interventions as 'adaptations' rather than 'developments', which can be allied to Nicholson's use of the term 'transportation' and Kershaw's 'transcendence' in preference to 'transformation'. Thus in terms of the interventionist purposes of applied performance, the practices and philosophies explored here involve a self-referential critique through which all participants explore, question and create performance conditions which are self-aware, which acknowledge paradox and contradiction, and which embrace plurality. There is a danger in applied theatre of imposing a linear narrative of transformation (particularly in terms of Boal's problem/resolution model) which operates as a top down approach, and can therefore be associated with cultural hegemony. Rowe refers to a 'stagnant backwater paradigm' whereby 'the emancipation of the individual, commonly valued within Western idealism, is promoted as the unequivocal goal of cultural interventions.' Critics of TfD urge us to ask what intervention means; intervene in what? and why? (Ahmed, 2002, 2004; Prentki, 2003)? What is the relationship between those who produce the intervention and those who are subject to it? While Prentki argues passionately for 'real participation, transforming communities into the subjects rather than the objects of their own development' through practices which draw upon 'indigenous knowledge' and the 'lived experience' of the participants, Ahmed worries that the mission to transform Third World communities through cultural intervention, ironically turns them into objects: 'judging the "other" according to the standard of development set by the "Developed"' (Ahmed, 2004).

For theatre practitioners, concerns about the passivity and object status of the 'other' as the recipient of TfD interventions is made more problematic by practices which involve 'trained' actors 'directing' indigenous communities. Such 'development' activities are ideologically problematic, perpetuating the ethnocentric values of the funders. The critique of interventionist practices, however, can run the risk of becoming self-defeating as Sheila Preston cautions: 'there is an argument that, because the dominant development discourse and its colonial history is inherently problematic, operating within this paradigm is inevitably so' (Preston, 2007: 229). Preston calls for the same kind of ethical practice as Denzin: 'a practice that enables theatre to be placed in the hands of ordinary people, who can use theatre to tell stories of their reality, to analyse and reflect through drama, to communicate and to explore the possibilities of change (in whatever way this is defined by a community) (Denzin, 2003: 232). The techniques associated with contemporary performance facilitate these kinds of practice through devising methodologies and which are open, flexible and responsive to the conditions, cultures, spaces and places in which the work is produced. The question of agency is fundamental, as Preston's model makes clear: 'agency is clearly located with those subjugated in their cultural world and change is ineffective, even dangerous if defined by an outsider' (Preston, 2007: 229).

This, however, raises questions about the role of the cultural artist and the status of applied theatre and performance as art. Thus the problems posed by the debates surrounding TfD are not confined to the stages of the Third World. There are related issues concerning intervention and evaluation in other educational and community contexts. What criteria and values are appropriate for judging the merits of the work? Should we be measuring its effectiveness in terms of the success of the intervention or its aesthetic merits? These issues are debated throughout the book in discussion of the political, social and educative implications of the different forms of performance featured and their aesthetic qualities. Denzin is helpful here, having rethought the relations between performance, cultural process, ethnographic praxis, hermeneutics, scholarly representation and the politics of culture. Throughout this study, then, I draw upon Denzin's model of performance ethnography to produce a discourse which is critical, reflexive and, where appropriate, performative.

Reflections on the present

In the twenty-first century, the conditions in which Brecht staged his critique no longer obtain:

> not only has the post-modern critique of the humanist subject undermined confidence in the very human agency on which social actions depend, but world political events in an age of 'total television' coverage seem to outpace all adequate means of response. To speak now of cultural intervention through theatre is also to speak of the resistance encountered by and within these very acts.
>
> (Colleran and Spencer, 1998: 2)

Kershaw makes a related point:

> the mediatization of society disperses the theatrical by inserting performance into everyday life – every time we tune into the media we are confronted by the representational styles of a performance world – and in the process the ideological impact of the performance becomes even more diverse. Moreover ... as performance proliferates, the radical in performance becomes harder to pinpoint.
>
> (1999: 6)

One of the key problems confronting practitioners concerns the tools of the trade. Digital media has transformed representations of reality and the screen rather than theatre functioning as a mirror of life. Practitioners of applied theatre will almost inevitably encounter this in their work, particularly with young people where invitations to respond to a stimulus, question or problem through performance will often produce soap opera dramatization or game-show debates. The performance vocabularies of postmodern youth have been constructed through the media; television, computer gaming and digital representations have, ironically, become the source to be copied. Thus rather than art representing life, young people draw upon mediated versions of 'reality' in their imaginative and creative acts. For example, in one of C&T's projects, the animateurs working in schools on a theatre project entitled *Lipsynch* found themselves working with highly skilled students, many of whom, it was revealed, practised lip-synching in the privacy of their bedrooms as a pleasurable escape into the fantasy world of music theatre (Sutton, (2009).

New techniques are needed to represent new realities. The practices featured in this account tend not to use the actor-based techniques that characterized many Western theatres during the second part of the twentieth century. The 'gestic' performance of the Brechtian actor has developed into something more complex as appropriate to our understanding of identity and performance in the twenty-first century. As various commentators have observed, theatre and media are involved in a dynamic dialogue of remediation (Auslander, 1999; Bolter and Grusin, 2000; Lehmann, 2006); as Lehmann notes with reference to Auslander:

> when film and then television first emerged they 'remediated' theatre, modelling themselves on theatre and on dramatic structures ... When contemporary experimental live performance now uses or references media, it is partially 'remediating' film and television but not in order insidiously to 'replicate' them to maintain its legitimacy ... but in order to probe their status and impact on us in a self-conscious manner – including their history of remediating theatre.
>
> (2006: 13)

Different kinds of performance have challenged the conventions of 'mimetic acting' (Kirby, 1972): 'It is born out of a different intention than wanting to be repetition and double – however, differentiated, condensed and artistically formed – of another reality' (Lehmann, 2006: 36). Indeed, Lehman moves on to suggest that 'the real of our experiential worlds is to a large extent created by art in the first place' (37). Thus while realism can be seen to be confirming and stabilizing in its constructions and re-presentations of gendered and cultural identities, post-dramatic performance offers a different kind of reflection and framing. Out of this space the concept of performativity has emerged as self-reflexive activity in a perpetual state of becoming; or as Pollock puts it: 'performativity is what happens when history/textuality sees itself in the mirror and suddenly sees double; it is the disorienting, [the] disruptive' (cited in Denzin, 2003: 10). Moreover, as Denzin reminds us, we need to be mindful of Judith Butler's assertion that 'every performance is an original and an imitation' (10). Theatre's 'double', to use Artaud's terminology, is self-reflexive; thus, reflects Denzin, 'even the imitation is an original, a transgression. Further, every performance becomes a form of kinesis, of motion, a decentering of agency and person through movement, disruption, action, a way of questioning the status quo' (Denzin 2003b: 20).

Cognitive theory offers a way to reconceptualize these complexities concerning relations between art and life, the dynamics between performer and audience and the production of meaning through the processes involved in applying performance. Even the distinction between active and passive spectators is challenged through this analysis because, as McConachie explains:

> it is unlikely that formal differences in the degree of theatricality have much to do with the political efficacy of certain kinds of theatre. Although Brechtian theatre may indeed pack a certain kind of political punch, it is not due to the so called 'alienation effect' ... there is no foundational cognitive distinction between 'active' and 'passive' spectators. We are required to move in and out of frames.
>
> (2008: 20)

At the very least there is evidence that the individual observing the actions of the other responds instinctively, embodying and conceptualizing the action through the activities of the brain. The observer may not move in responding to the actions of the observed, so appears to be passive physically but the neurons mirror the activity 'as if' they have been experienced (Gallese, 2001; Rizzolati et al., 1999). There is some evidence that the mirror neuron system is involved in understanding intentions (Iacaboni et al., 2005), in emotions and empathy (Singer et al., 2004; Wicker et al., 2003) in language, imitation and theory of mind (Arbib, 2006). All of these are important factors in social behaviour and cognition and transform our understanding of the spectator's perception of, and responses to, theatrical events. In particular, cognitive theory problematizes the notion of the 'passive' spectator as the consumer of 'pure' art. All spectators are both passive (in the sense that their responses are spontaneous) and active (as their responses will be physically experienced as imaginatively 'felt'). Moreover, they are all involved in cognitive 'blending' whereby knowledge of the 'real' through the spatiality, temporality and materiality of the here and now of the experienced performance environment interacts with our understanding of the' not real' of the imagined and performed. Thus cognitive theory offers a valid framework for conceptualizing the processes of participation, embodied learning, empathic engagement and meaning making in the practice of applying performance.

Principles of applying performance

In the course of my research for this book and in the selection of case studies, I developed a taxonomy as a means of defining and evaluating the practices observed and discussed. This involves seven principles, otherwise known as the seven 'p's and these proved helpful in relation to the questions I identified concerning the role and function of the practices I defined as 'applied performance'. Practitioners were invited to respond to the categories and identified their work in relation to the principles. These are presented as inductive rather than prescriptive, while they also engage in dialogue as part of the weaving of mind, body, world involved in cognition and participatory performance.

2.1 APPLYING PERFORMANCE: PRINCIPLES AND A COGNITIVE PARADIGM OF PRACTICE

1   Pedagogy

Applied Performance will have a purpose beyond entertainment and the production of an artefact for public consumption. It is not only the fact that the performance is produced in educational and community contexts, but it is its purpose (pedagogical/political/facilitatory) which distinguishes it as *applied* performance. Thus a key question we have to ask of all such work is, what is it for? In contemporary performance praxis, traditional dualisms are challenged between theory and practice, while form is inextricably related to content. Thus, in applied performance it is important to consider the political, social and educative implications of the different forms of contemporary practice discussed.

Drawing upon theories of social, critical and 'enchanting' pedagogy (and the concept of socially shared cognition), the book questions and explores the purposes of applied performance, developing Thompson's argument that one of its defining features is a commitment to *affecting* change. Using performance methodologies in social, educational and community contexts creates environments in which the participatory subject actively engages in the process of knowledge and identity production. The developing dialogue between educational theorists, psychologists and cognitive, affective and social neuroscience is transforming our understanding of how learning occurs. Recognition of the dynamic relations between emotion and cognition (Immordino-Yang and Damasio, 2007), the interplay between body and mind (Damasio, 1999, 2003, 2010) and the relationship between nature and nurture in recognizing the importance of the social environment in knowledge formation (Immordino-Yang and Damasio, 2007; LeDoux, 2002; Pinker, 2002) are all insights with profound implications for pedagogic theory and practice. Understanding the extent of the brain's plasticity and its consequent susceptibility to environmental factors in conjunction with discussion of the role of emotions on the brain and body (Damasio, 2003) has contributed to a turn to affect in educational theory. 'We feel therefore we learn' is the title of an article by Immordino-Yang and Damasio (2007), exploring the role of affect in education. Developing this work in a 2010 article, Immordino-Yang considers an educational revolution to be 'imminent' due to what she describes as the 'profound implications' of neuroscience on education (102): 'Neuroscientific evidence suggests that we can no longer justify learning theories that dissociate the mind from the body, the self from social context'(101).

Joseph LeDoux's concept of the 'emotional brain' is a compelling account of the relations between experience, emotion, memory and learning and has significant implications for both pedagogical and performance theory. As Rhonda Blair has summarized, 'since every experience our brain records changes our synapses, the way our synapses are "wired" is the result of learning of all kinds-cognitive, sensory and kinesthetic' (Blair, 2008: 20; LeDoux, 2002: 68). The extent of the brain's plasticity in responding to environmental and experiential stimuli is evident in the well-documented changes observed in the cortices of musicians. Enlargements in the auditory cortex, as well as those associated with the hands (in string players and pianists), have been shown to correspond to the age and extent of practice (Hyde et al., 2009; Trainor, Shahin and Roberts, 2003). Research into the effects of musical training on children indicates the significance of these findings for educational theory; as well as children responding differently to hearing music (with changes observed in structural brain development), musically trained children demonstrated improved verbal memory, literacy, visiospatial processing, numeracy and IQ in comparison to untrained peers. Research with adult musicians and non-musicians has produced similar findings:

> The results suggest ... that the effects of musical experience can be seen early in development. They also suggest that although the effects of musical training on cortical representations may be greater if training begins in childhood, the adult brain is also open to change.
>
> (Trainor, Shahin and Roberts, 2003)

These results have been discussed in terms of the 'potential benefits of early musical training' as well as 'potential benefits of musical experience in aging' (Trainor, Shahin and Roberts, 2003; Fujiola et al., 2006). What these music case studies demonstrate is a clear relationship between physical action and cognition.

The changing conception of learning and the potential role of the arts in developing new pedagogies is evident in a range of contexts. The reformation of museums and education as discussed in Part II, for example, coincided with a spate of 'unusually upbeat publication titles' from the UK government (Barnes, 2007): 'Expecting the Unexpected' (OFSTED, 2003); 'Creativity: Find it promote it' (QCA, 2003/2005); 'Excellence and Enjoyment' (DFES 2004). These are cited by Jonathan Barnes in a paper arguing for the importance of music in the primary curriculum and using cognitive neuroscience and psychology to make his case for 'brain based/mental and physical well-being' (2007). Cathy Davidson makes a strong case for a revolution in education and the workplace in her accessible and forward-thinking study: *Now You See It: How the Brain Science of Attention Will Transform the Way We Live, Work, and Learn* (2011). The potential of theatre and other creative arts practices to contribute to this revisioning of learning is summed up by Stephen Di Benedetto:

> recent scientific discoveries about brain function open up the possibility that we can think about the nature and value of theatrical practice by way of lived experience. Theatrical and other artistic creations capture

the attention of the neural networks of the body and make real experiences that might not be accessible to our everyday interactions, Through art we are able of offer experience and knowledge that *change* the attendant at his or her core.

(2010: 29)

This capacity to effect change through experiential and sensorial mediums such as theatre and music is anticipated in Schiller's notion of 'enchanting pedagogy' which points towards contemporary understandings of embodiment, cognition and the possibilities of learning, healing and transformation through the processes of applying performance (Trimingham, 2010).

In *Performance Ethnography*, Denzin provides a particularly succinct evocation of the knowledge and understanding performance provokes and which underpins the pedagogical principles of applying performance:

> Knowing refers to those embodied, sensuous experiences that create the conditions for understanding ... performed experiences are the sites where felt emotion, memory, desire and understanding come together.
>
> (2003: 13)

2   Process: praxis and poesis

In applied performance, the process of making work is often as important (and in some projects might be the most important element) as the artistic artefact. Brecht may have repeatedly said that the proof of the pudding is in the eating (1964), but in applied performance, proof is measured rather differently and the process of making the pudding can be as important or more important than its consumption. How can this process be measured and what are the implications for the evaluation of applied performance?

The turn to affect in applied theatre, involves a dialogue with a body of theory which speaks to process as a concept that 'arises in the midst of *in-between-ness*: in the capacities to act and be acted upon' (Gregg and Seigworth, 2010: 1). The discourse of affect is a language which conceptualizes the visceral, the experiential, the atmospheric: the *'forces of encounter'* to use the terms of affect theory (2). How a process *affects* participants is an important criterion for evaluating applied performance and affect theory provides a vocabulary through which to do so, referring to 'the intracellular divulgences of sinew, tissue, and gut economies, and the vaporous evanescences of the incorporeal (events, atmospheres, feeling-tones)'. The terms used to account for affect connect, touch and interact with the performance practices defined as applied and social theatre: 'performance(s) that can transform the practitioners, the participants, and the public's existing knowledge and experience' (Schechner and Thompson, 2004: 13).

Transformation for participants in applied theatre and performance is generally associated with the processes which culminate in the performance.

Process thus functions differently to rehearsal, affecting participants through activities which engage them cognitively and physically. Thus affect is inextricably related to cognition in the development of conceptual understanding. Drawing upon the work of cognitive linguists Lakoff and Johnson, McConachie explains that 'cognitive concepts arise, fundamentally, from the experience of the body in the world. As neural beings trying to survive in our environment we make meaning with certain "spatial relation" and "bodily action" concepts' (McConachie, 2008: 39; Lakoff and Johnson, 1999). Thus the crawling infant learns the 'source–path–goal' concept by moving from one point to another, as well as the spatial concept of 'forward/back' and 'balance' as they move through 'cruising' to toddling. Our sense of our bodies develops in conjunction with language acquisition and is a source of metaphors for thought and meaning, shaping our development of language, consciousness, reason and values: 'the body; a cognitive unconscious to which we have no direct access; and metaphorical thought of which we are largely unaware' (Lakoff and Johnson 1999: 7).

In Mark Storer's work with teenagers, 'exploring the transition from childhood through adolescence and on to adulthood' which culminated in the stage show, *Fat Girl Gets a Haircut and Other Stories* (Roundhouse, London, April 2011), the programme note refers to some unusual rehearsal processes, such as crawling around central London in laundry bags! Storer's methods can be seen to enable the teenagers to perceive the world in a new way, to engage differently with their environment through exercises designed to facilitate different perceptual experiences, whilst such activities also return them to modes of being associated with the pre-verbal and play-based aspects of child development. Indeed, this can be seen as corresponding to Alva Noë's concept of 'action in perception' whereby children develop sensory motor understanding through physically and creatively engaging with their environment (Noë, 2004). Storer's work, as discussed in Part II, engages in dialogue with applied theatre and performance as these rehearsal processes indicate. He refers to a 'journey' which has been 'unusual, unexpected and beautiful'; the source being the teenagers (their experiences and stories), the path consisted of eighteen months exploring 'different ways of working' (to include creating a mermaid out of lettuce leaves and making outfits out of paper), while the goal was a spectacular and moving staged performance facilitating dialogue between adult and adolescent perspectives.

Process, moreover, is ongoing after the event; in applying performance, legacy is important as a manifestation of change. This can take a number of forms and moves well beyond boxed artefacts in archives and teaching packs for schools. Part III features a living archive and a participatory performance project which used the archive as source and stimulus for performance. Discussion of process, however, and its relation to 'product' brings us to debates about aesthetics and ethics and the relations between *poiesis* and praxis. Derived from the Greek term and defined variously in terms of 'making' or 'production', poiesis has been used across arts and sciences to refer to processes involving transformation from one state into another. For Heidegger, in an oft-cited essay, poiesis is described thus:

> the rising of something from out of itself, is a bringing-forth. Phusis is indeed poiesis in the highest sense. For what presences by means of phusis has the irruption belonging to bringing-forth, e.g., the bursting of a blossom into bloom, in itself. In contrast, what is brought forth by the artisan or the artist, e.g. the silver chalice, has the irruption belonging to bringing-forth, not in itself, but in another, in the craftsman or artist.
>
> ([1977] 2003: 252)

For Erika Fischer-Lichte, the term 'autopoiesis' is used in conjunction with the 'transformative' potential of performance which lies in its capacity to trigger liminal and embodied experiences: 'Essential to this project and to the shift from art object to art event, is the collapsing of binaries, headed by that of subject and object, or in the case of performance, spectator and actor' (2008: 8). Thus, for Fischer-Lichte, an 'autopoetic system' is both 'producer and product'; 'the spectators become increasingly aware that meaning is not transmitted to but brought forth by them' (150).

This 'performative turn', to use Fischer-Lichte's term, converges with the changing direction of applied theatre and the shift from effect to affect as signposted in the subtitles proffered by Jackson (*Art or Instrument?*) and Thompson (*The End of Effect*). Indeed, applied theatre and performance, one might argue, provide an even more compelling example of this dynamic as the interactions between performers and participants physically collapse the boundaries between spectator and actor, subject and object; the conditions in which applied theatre is undertaken are associated with liminality and transformation. However, there are questions to be asked about whether this constitutes aesthetic experience, in Fischer-Lichte's terms:

> While I will label those liminal experiences aesthetic which make the journey the goal, the liminal experiences which use the journey to reach 'another' goal are non-aesthetic. Such goals could consist of a socially recognized change of status; the creation of winners and losers or communities ... That is to say, aesthetic experience concerns the experience of a threshold, a passage in itself; the very process of transition already constitutes the experience. Non-aesthetic liminal experience concerns the transition *to* something and the resulting transformation *into* this or that.
>
> (2008: 199)

This bears a paradoxical relation to the Aristotelian understanding of poiesis as goal-orientated (referring to doing or producing something which has an end outside itself and is not fulfilled until this is complete), in contrast to praxis, which is defined in relation to 'energia' as 'doing' without an external goal where the orientation and satisfaction has an ethical dimension; that is, praxis requires virtue (knowing which practical activities are worth pursuing as well as requiring the skill to produce them). Poiesis, however (in the Aristotelian sense), only demands the skill to deliver the practical activity. This conceptual dichotomy has also informed discussions of politics deriving from the work of Hannah Arendt and Jürgen Habermas. Arendt's conception of politics in terms of 'purposeful performance' involves a distinction between 'purposive action' (praxis) and productive activity (poiesis) where praxis is also associated with a moral objective. Arendt also distinguishes between 'work' (techne) and 'interaction' (praxis) so that poiesis (productive activity) is associated with technical expertise (as one form of knowledge), while praxis involves 'phronesis' a form of practical wisdom concerned with 'the capacity for determining what is good for both the individual and community' (Melaney, 2006: 467).

In this formulation, we might consider applied performance to have more synergies with praxis than poiesis and we might also argue that the instrumentalism Fischer-Lichte associates with the non-aesthetic is allied to '*auto*poiesis', where automatism, the third stage in human production, is problematized as being 'outside the range of willful and purposeful (human) interference' (Arendt, 1958: 151). However, rather than conceiving of all instrumentalism negatively, I suggest that applied performance challenges these dichotomies and demonstrates a dialogue between poiesis and praxis. Poiesis (retrieved and reconceptualized by Heidegger) exists at a threshold, in the liminal and transformative space we associate with the 'making' activities of applied performance, which, however, are part of 'purposeful performance' as praxis where the means and the ends of performance are moral, ethical political and pedagogical. In this conception, instrumentalism can be regarded positively as a creative force, an 'energia'. Indeed, in much of the work I will discuss, social engagement and aesthetics are inextricably related; some of the work might even be defined as 'public art' where the relationship between artist and audience becomes the art work (Kwon, 2004; Lacy, 1994).

3 Play

Play-based methodologies are fundamental to the work defined as applied performance and theories of play inform my analysis of the processes involved. The ludic nature of play is, moreover, a feature of Josephine Machon's concept of *(syn)aesthetics*, offering a 'redefining' of 'visceral performance' (Machon, 2009). Machon draws upon Immanuel Kant's '*free play* of imagination' ((1999: 194); Machon, 2009: 5; emphasis in the original) which Susan Broadhurst has summarized as a 'pleasure that depends ... on consciousness of the harmony of the two cognitive powers *imagination* and *understanding'* (Broadhurst, 1999: 28; my emphasis). These two terms are critical (and creative) impulses, connecting performance theory, cognitive science and the field of applied and social theatre.

'Play' writes McConachie, 'is fundamentally an emotion, a neuronal and chemical system in the mind/brain' (McConachie, 2008: 51). The relations between play and the imagination are of critical importance in discussions of cognition and performance (Blair, 2008; Lutterbie, 2011; McConachie, 2008). In Fauconnier and Turner's *The Way we Think*, imagination is conceived as the 'central engine of meaning' (2003: 15). Conceptual blending is part of children's play-making activities, the complex ludic processes which are the building blocks for making meaning and developing inter subjectivity. Playworkers refer to a liminal, inter-subjective space they term 'the ludic third', situated between players, playworker and participant (and between therapist and child).[2] This third space can also be seen as existing within the practice of applying performance. It is an in-between zone, occupied by practitioners and participants in the act of making participatory performance (the space inhabited by Storer and his teenage performers in rehearsal as they explored constructions of self and inter-subjectivity, using vocabularies and methods drawn from live art and its interdisciplinarities). Theories of play conjoin the competing discourses of philosophy, linguistics, psychoanalysis, phenomenology, cognitive studies and affect theory.

Since Huizinga's seminal study (1971) play theorists have endeavoured to define play. Sutton-Smith's *Ambiguity of Play* offers a comprehensive overview of play forms (to include behaviours, social playfulness, vicarious play, performance, festivals and risk-taking activity) but discussion of the relations between art and play is undeveloped. The historical perspective developed by Nagel (2002), charts the development of the dualisms which position play as other to legitimized activity. Although Aristotle and Plato both write of play as an activity confined to children (*paidia* and *paidia tinas*), the value of play can be seen in Aristotle's perception that 'the practice of science emerges only when leisure is available' (Politis, 2004: 30). Nagel credits Nietzsche as the play theorist conceiving of play as a philosophical Other where the sensual, irrational Dionysian excess is set against rational Apollonian thought. Nietzsche's, *Übermensch* is one who plays, rebels and redefines, while for Derrida, play is similarly subversive in its potential to destabilize and decentralize meaning (1998)). Huizinga conceives of a 'magic circle', a temporal order differentiated from everyday life, while for Schechner the 'underlying ground of play is ever present' and in 'dark play' the distinction between play and not play are blurred (2003). The Bakhtinian notion of carnival is also associated with the subversive potential of play as 'events [which] may have cognitive, emotional and cultural consequences' (McConachie, 2008: 54). Play is a slippery concept, refusing to be defined or constrained by the various taxonomies which endeavor to conceptualize its range of activities. Applied performance is similarly flexible, fluid and hybrid, drawing upon a range of play-based practices to facilitate social engagement. The taxonomy developed by Callois (building upon and disputing Huizinga), and much cited in game theory, posits a continuum between *paidia* and *ludus*, or free-play and rule-bound gaming, anarchy and discipline. Whilst the Dionysian aesthetic might be deemed to be more appropriate to the playfulness of applied performance practice (as sensual, bodily, primal and festive), the four patterns of play identified by Callois can all be seen to feature variously in live art and socially engaged practice: *agon* or competition; *alea* or chance; *mimesis* or simulation; *ilinx* or sensation.

A resurgence of interest in play is one of the features of the turn to affect in twenty-first-century performance. Live art, socially engaged practice and relational aesthetics engage in dialogue with play theory to explore relations between the arts and wellbeing. This has informed cultural policy in the United Kingdom as funders increasingly prioritize the impact agenda, requiring and rewarding evidence of social value in arts practice. Similar shifts throughout Europe and the United States are tracked in Shannon Jackson's *Social Works: Performing Art, Supporting Publics* (2011).

The practitioners featured in this study recognize the value of process-centred arts practice, prioritizing interaction and intervention over product; although the value of this work is often difficult to quantify, the dialogue between theories of play, cognitive science and affect offers a means of conceptualizing and evaluating performance in social and educational contexts. In writing about applied performance my hope is not only to disseminate and inspire innovative practice and to facilitate dialogue between practitioners, but to offer perspectives and paradigms for conceptualizing practice which might be used to validate the social and aesthetic value of such activities.

4 Presence

'Since the mid to late 1990s', Melissa Trimingham observes, 'it is hard to find any commentary on live performance that does not subscribe to the power of the phenomenological lived experience of the event, as opposed to its "representational" or symbolic intentions'(Trimingham, 2011: 66). Applied performance engages participants in a lived experience which requires us to be in the here and now (the time/space of performance). Whilst the concept of presence has been a subject of considerable debate in performance theory as well as being the focus of a transdisciplinary international collaborative research project ('Performing Presence from the Live to the Simulated'),[3] temporality continues to be an important principle of applying performance, with a number of practitioners using the same phrase in their references to 'being in the room' aware of the different energies of participants and the relations between performers and participants as they engaged in the 'moment'.

Like play, presence is an elusive, slippery concept, often cited by practitioners as important, but difficult to pin down conceptually. There is a danger of playing with a seductive illusion of a temporality which is pure and 'real' by virtue of its 'nowness'. Moreover, its elusive ephemerality offers a convenient escape route for the writer struggling to demonstrate efficacy or value in work which has disappeared. Whilst concepts of utopia (Dolan, 2006) and the sublime (Merleau-Ponty, 1962) offer a vocabulary for discussion of the atmosphere, environment, emotion and experience which are associated with the ecstasies of liveness, there is no proof of the taste of the pudding, once it has been eaten. Hence Rebecca Schneider's series of searching questions about the live and the present:

> Is the live really only a matter of temporal immediacy, happening only in an uncomplicated now, a 'transitory' present, an im-mediate moment? Is a 'maniacally charged present' not punctuated by, syncopated with, indeed charged by other moments, other times? That is, is the present really so temporally straightforward or pure-devoid of a basic delay or deferral if not multiplicity and flexibility? Does it not take place or become composed in double, triple or multiple time – especially if performance and the 'sedimented acts' that comprise the social are already a matter of 'twice-behaved behaviour'?
>
> (2011: 92)

In applying performance, presence remains an important concept, inextricably related to the equally vexed concept of liveness. Whilst different temporalities are engaged 'in the room' and 'in the moment' they can be understood in terms of the liminality, the 'ludic third' which is the 'no/where' of the now and here. As I have written previously, Stein's work moved increasingly towards musical techniques of composition (voices in counterpoint, elevating sound over sense) while recent work in the field of music cognition offers a means of reconceptualizing the presence of performance through analysis of the interrelations between past/present/future in our perception of melody.

Discussion of presence in applied performance begs further questions about how we perceive and experience being in the room; moreover, if this liminal space is transportative, where, precisely do we go? Theories of affect in conjunction with cognition are a means of conceptualizing the temporal frameworks of live art which the practices discussed draw upon, as well as exploring the experience of the spaces we access through the processes and activities involved in applying performance.

5   Participation

In contemporary performance the boundary between spectator and actor is challenged. Practitioners of applied performance create work which involves spectators actively engaging with the work produced, generally through participation or other forms of interaction. This raises a series of questions to be addressed to applied performance projects: What is the nature of participation? On whose terms? Are the relationships horizontal or vertical in terms of power?

In the process of 'applying' performance, the relations between audience and performer are redefined. Drawing upon Bourriaud's relational aesthetics ('an art taking as its theoretical horizon the realm of human interactions and its social context') as well as critiques of participatory practice (Claire Bishop, 2007), this study explores the importance of participation in the production of meaning (and embodied cognition), understanding and knowledge. Whilst participation is defined as a principle of applying performance, in some modes of practice, participation becomes the performance and this is the focus of Part III. My discussion of participatory practice is indebted to McConachie's work on spectatorship. Although McConachie does not examine contemporary forms of performance, his analysis can be extended to encompass contemporary performance practices. Cognitive science has sought to understand 'how the embodied mind of this brain responds to the world, which includes other material human bodies with minds/brains and the rest of material existence' (2008: 6). In particular, cognitive theory has reconceptualized our understanding of empathy, social interaction and group behaviour. Hence the usefulness and relevance of this theoretical perspective to my discussion of how applying performance *engages* participants.

6 Performance

What is the artefact in applied performance? What are its outcomes and how are these measured? A commitment to a performance outcome emerged as a defining feature of the practice featured in my research, although this took a number of forms. For some, the performance was the culmination of a process, a dissemination and sharing of the work undertaken; concern with finding an appropriate form as well as attention to the aesthetics of the performance event was also a shared objective. Whilst the outcomes are performative, they do not necessarily involve a public performance, as such. For C&T, digital media and interactive websites function far more frequently as outcomes than performance events for audiences. This is a means of disseminating and engaging wider audiences for work conceived and developed in non-theatre spaces, using, for example, mobile phones as means of engaging participants in the liminal space of intermediality. This practice is at the other end of the play continuum, using gaming technologies in conjunction with the physicality of live performance to engage participants in dialogic and embodied exchange and encounters.

A wide range of performance is featured in this study, ranging from displays in schools to installations in galleries, museums and immersive environments through to public performances on beaches and in theatres. Performance is part of a process of transformation and is an integral feature of the work discussed. In practices associated with live art, or forms described as site/place responsive, participatory and socially engaged, the dualisms between process and performance are not recognized or relevant. As in the concept of embodiment, an *integrated* approach is needed to assimilate: 'the dynamics of blending that involve attention, memory, empathy and heightened emotions' (McConachie, 2008: 19).

7   Pleasure

The final principle of applying performance is pleasure. For Barthes, bliss is 'unspeakable' and the pleasure of experience is conveyed in the pleasure of writing. (1975). Simon Shepherd's *Theatre, Body and Pleasure* talks of a different kind of embodied engagement through the felt pleasures of performance, the physicality of the body and theatre as 'an art of bodies' (2006, 5). In cognitive theory, feelings are 'emotions made conscious' and this provides an important link to theories of affect. Applied theatre scholarship recognizes and embraces the importance of affect but this is often conceived in conjunction with transformation. However, theories of affect have implications for our understanding of aesthetics and what is sometimes perceived as the false binary between aesthetics and ethics (as discussed in Part III). For Barthes, utopian performativity involves a psycho-physical pleasure which I recognize from my personal archive of performance memories, the 'moments of being' that have stayed with me as formative or transformational, enabling me to perceive differently (to include Bobby Baker's *Drawing on a Mother's Experience* in Prema Arts Centre, 1993; Deborah Warner's *The Tower Project* in 1999; and Mark Storer's *Fat Girl* in 2011).

As Sara Ahmed has observed in her account of 'Happy Objects':

> We are moved by things. And in being moved, we make things. An object can be affective by virtue of its own location (the object might be *here*, which is *where* I experience this or that affect) and the timing of its appearance (the object might be *now*, which is *when* I experience this or that affect). To experience an object as being affective or sensational is to be directed not only toward an object, but to 'whatever' is around that object.
>
> (2010: 33)

Isobel Armstrong's *The Radical Aesthetic* addresses the importance of a reading of the emotions to aesthetic discourse, arguing that 'the constitutive nature of affect has been ignored or bracketed in contemporary theory because of its seeming resistance to analysis' (2000, 13). 'The emotions', she continues, 'should be included within a definition of the rational rather than fall outside it.' Tony Jackson addresses similar concerns: 'What *is* the aesthetic power of the medium through which the work is undertaken – and why does it matter? (Jackson, 2007: 2). Both Thompson and Jackson argue that the supposed dichotomy between an aesthetic and an instrumental theatre is a false one; Thompson passionately advocates a 'commitment to pleasure, passion and enjoyment as a starting point for a political – aesthetic practice that acknowledges the importance of our affection for others as a stimulus to social change' (Thompson, 2009).

The embodied nature of the experience of affective practice is encapsulated in Thompson's description of applied theatre in contexts of conflict: 'the sheer physical enjoyment and energy that these projects can elicit, make them potential examples of the enactment of beauty – *a performance of beauty* – moments that make the heart beat faster, and people start searching for 'something of the same scale' Thompson, 2006: 56). This connects to the powerful writing of Hélène Cixous: 'when we feel and there is not yet a name for it, the heart catches fire' (Cixous, 2005: 188). For Cixous, 'writing moves at the pace of hand' and I am reminded of the jubilant speed of my writing on the tube as I returned home from seeing Storer's *Fat Girl Gets a Haircut and Other Stories*, enjoying the pleasure of writing about an experience which escaped definition (to be or not to be 'applied') but which clearly moved its audience, deeply and profoundly, through a combination of aesthetic beauty and affecting content.

It is in this liminal, intermedial space that this book really begins.

Part II
Practices

3
Performing Lives

3.1 AUTOBIOGRAPHY AND APPLIED PERFORMANCE

In autobiographical performance, the self is source and the body speaks; situated at a threshold (as a discourse of remembering and becoming) autobiographical performance is a means of articulating, exploring and interrogating identities and subjectivities through strategies which use the visual, physical and kinaesthetic to stage experiences and perspectives that have struggled to find voice through other forms (Heddon, 2008; Phelan, 1993). Since the 1960s experimental performance and feminism have engaged in productive dialogue, developing new vocabularies to articulate hidden histories and gendered experiences as the personal became political and public. Carolee Schneeman's 1975 performance, *Interior Scroll*, involved her pulling a roll of text from her vagina, a powerful intervention and a statement and materialization of Hélène Cixous's declaration that women should 'write the body' (1976). A wide range of performance artists use autobiographical material in their work, finding an appropriate form for personal content: Laurie Anderson, Annie Sprinkle, Holly Hughes, Rachel Rosenthal, Lenora Champagne, Peggy Shaw and Lois Weaver, to name but a few. In the United Kingdom, similarly, performers such as Bobby Baker, Leslie Hill and Helen Paris use solo performance to stage their experiences as women, while others use autobiographical performance to explore marginalized sexuality or race, such as Robbie McCauley, Tim Miller, Ron Athey and Adrian Howells.

Autobiography is also associated with the performance of place and practitioners such as Phil Smith, Mike Pearson and Michael Shanks perform lives through durational or site specific forms of performance. Definitions of autobiographical performance, moreover, extend to forms in which the lives of others are staged through contemporary modes of practice; verbatim performance, reminiscence theatre and playback are also a means of engaging with 'real' lives through performance. The appeal of autobiography, however, as numerous theorists have demonstrated, is often predicated on a paradox as it is also a fiction, a construction and performance of the self as narrative

(Heddon, 2008; Smith and Watson, 2002). If 'authenticity' is attributed to this 'body' of work (and bodies at work), it is not a result of mimesis, but emerges from the spectator's felt response to the experience of liveness, being in a shared space and being affected by the haptic, visceral qualities of work which can 'touch' them (sometimes literally). Our embodied responses involve us in empathic engagement, a process conceptualized through cognitive science and mirror neuron theory: 'Like a mirror image, the same sets of neurons are activated in an observor as the individuals actually engaged in an action or the expression of an emotion or behaviour ' (Berrol, 2006). Thus, as Peter Brook observes, 'as one person enters something that is thought to be his deepest subjective experience, there can be an instant recognition, a shared understanding between everyone else who is watching (Brook, 2005).

The body in performance is not, however, unmediated and even when we witness its mutilation (as in the work of Orlan or Marina Abramović), we are conscious of the performer's object status. We are moved to empathize through witnessing what is often unspeakable: acts of pain which affect us as both real and performed. Our engagement is both embodied and distanced as we remain conscious of ourselves witnessing the reality of the physical and emotional pain of the other. As Erika Fischer-Lichte has written, 'by emphasizing the bodily being-in-the world of humans, embodiment creates the possibility for the body to function as the object, subject, material and source of symbolic construction, as well as the product of cultural inscription' (Fischer-Lichte, 2008: 89). Thus autobiographical performance is a compelling and powerful medium with the potential to effect transformation, a term used by performance theorists such as Fischer-Lichte as well as applied theatre scholars such as Thompson (2009), Nicholson (2005, 2011), and Kershaw (1999).

Contemporary autobiographical performance is conscious of itself as representation; as Dee Heddon perceives: '[the] relationship between performer and spectator does set this mediation of experience apart from other modes. Though it is no less mediated, its different form of mediation enables a potentially different impact that can be capitalized upon strategically' (2008: 6). Performers of international repute, such as Suzanne Lacy and Mierle Laderman Ukeles, create socially engaged work which positions itself on a continuum between life and art, challenging divisions between the political and aesthetic, the personal and the public. Examples are Lacy's installations and performances on youth and public policy during the 1990s as well as *The Crystal Quilt* (1987), a participatory project involving 430 elders which explored and challenged media representations of ageing as well as public perceptions of older people. Ukeles' 1969 'Manifesto for Maintenance Artwork' challenges the binary oppositions between art/life, nature/culture and the private/public, while her practice seeks to merge everyday life and performance art. Thus, in *Touch Sanitation* (1978–1984) she famously shook hands with the 8500 employees at the New York Sanitation Department, thanking them for their work, while her celebrated 'work ballets' bring together individual workers (and the vehicles, props and materials they use) from community services and maintenance industries in a choreographed blend of interventionist, celebratory and spectacular performance, a collision of life, work and art. For these practitioners, public participation in performative interventions is the work of art. One of the clearest examples of this is Ukeles' 2008 mixed-media installation commissioned for the Contemporary Jewish Museum in New York as part of an exhibition in which seven contemporary artists were invited to respond to the book of Genesis. The environment created by Ukeles reflected upon the Cabbalistic account of the creation, whereby God's contraction to make room for the universe involved a shattering of vessels which, according to Jewish practice, can be symbolically repaired through the doing of good deeds (*tikkun olam*). This was the inspiration for Ukeles' work: *Tsimtsum / Shevirat Ha-Kelim: Contraction / The Shattering of the Perfect Vessels* → *Birthing Tikkun Olam*. Visitors were invited to participate in the making of the artwork by contributing a piece of themselves. The invitation to participate and the accompanying story formed the core of the artist's concept:

Dear Visitor, Dear Person,

Welcome! I invite you to come into this artwork, wherever you are. Look in the mirror. Please. Find yourself in the mirror. Who do you see?

Genesis 1 DAY 6 tells you that the image reflecting back at you is a likeness of the Eternal Creator of the world. The image that you see is sacred. You are unique in all of creation …

Yet, sacred Being is not enough. There is *Tikkun* work to be done. *Tikkun* is Hebrew for 'heal,' and even 'transform.' '*Tikkun* work' means that you can heal, restore, re-invent, re-create, even transform something in the world that is degraded, broken, hearts that are shattered.
My artwork is incomplete. I need you! I left the core of my installation space in the museum empty; its vacancy beckons you to take your place within it, to inhabit it. I invite you to participate in making it whole. How? I ask that you take up the unfinished work of my art by creating your own project of *Tikkun*. You come up with it. You decide. You commit. That comes out of your enormous freedom to create, not mine. You can expand this artwork, so that it becomes alive out in the world.[1]

Two forms of participation were invited. The first involved completion of 'a special AGREEMENT', using writing or drawing to produce a plan which was returned to the artist and formed part of the final artwork as part of the BOOK OF AGREEMENTS AND COVENANTS. The other means of participation involved signing up for one of the three 'DAYS OF TRANSFER AND

EXCHANGE', public events in which the artwork transformed through the contributions of participants as collaborators:

> I will give you one of these two-sided mirrors to take out into the world: the side with your image will light your way as you create your *Tikkun*, while the second side captures the sacred images of Others. In exchange, you agree to fill out and sign the *INDIVIDUAL COVENANT* attached to the back of the mirror. This will be a covenant between you, the participant, and myself the artist of this artwork. The mirror becomes a material token of exchange between us, as you accept your role as covenantal partner. Your filled-out *INDIVIDUAL COVENANT* will be transferred to hang in the place of your mirror. As *COVENANTS* begin to fill the space, the higher mirrors will be moved down to be brought into play. This flow of light, *COVENANT*, and *Tikkun* into the world will transform the artwork. Eventually *INDIVIDUAL COVENANTS* will replace all the mirrors.

The installation was developed over a period of seven months and as the mirrors were replaced by the paper covenants, the exchange functioned as the performed action, a material realization of Ukeles' concept of maintenance art as social ex/change as visitors made a contractual agreement to perform a good deed. Thus, in this example, process becomes performance while the relations between self and other and the private and public are playfully interrogated. The installation itself, moreover, with its changing composition of mirrors and paper created a moving physical display of the repairing of the world.

Autobiographical performance is also an appropriate medium for exploring memory and trauma as it shares similar textual and performative qualities. For Daniel Schacter 'memories are records of how we have experienced events, not replicas of the events themselves ... we construct our autobiographies from fragments of experience that change over time' (Smith and Watson, 2002: 9). The discourse of trauma as the 'missed experience' (Caruth, 1995) finds expression through what Machon describes as '(syn)aesthetic performance' in the work of, for example, Linda Montano, Meg Stuart and others (Machon, 2009). Thus, in autobiographical modes of performance, memory, trauma and unspoken aspects of experience find expression through a performative mode of consciousness which is fluid, mobile and ephemeral, a process of becoming which makes it particularly appropriate as a medium for working in social, community and educational contexts.

Applied theatre involves direct encounters with individuals and groups in a variety of working contexts. Making performance with, and for, a client group therefore involves working with real lives. This chapter examines a variety of strategies for making performance using autobiographical material as its source. It considers how contemporary performance techniques can be used to explore identity formation. This involves

Figure 1 Mierle Laderman Ukeles, *Participate*, 2008. Contemporary Jewish Museum, New York. Photograph by kind permission of Bruce Damonte

individuals and groups generating their own stories and experiences as a basis for performance, using themselves as a stimulus. The work featured illustrates how the realities of inner and outer lives can generate a range of performance possibilities. A series of questions are addressed through the work discussed:

What identities can be explored/recovered through performance?

How can performance facilitate memory and how can memory facilitate performance?

What are the relations between selves and others (I's and eyes) in perform-ance encounters and how can a cognitive approach facilitate understand-ing of these processes?

How can we understand authenticity in these contexts?

What are the ethical implications of using performance as a means of engag-ing with autobiographical experiences?

What are the implications for documentation as a means of remembering performance?

The chapter begins with an autobiographical account by a live artist who brings a personal perspective and a different voice to my study, as appropriate to the content of this chapter. This is a playful and performative account of a contemporary artist's experience of institutions and contexts which can be challenging and even hostile. Her endeavours to navigate an alienating environment and the ensuing interactions she facilitated offer an alternative pedagogy, whereby learning is enacted outside of classroom spaces through encounters with the other of live art. I continue by considering how performance can facilitate memory as a medium which is sensual, material, immersive and live but which is also transitory, ephemeral and partial. Here I bring into dialogue Indian aesthetics and cognitive neuroscience in my discussion of 'posttraumatic theatre' with reference to a performance storytelling project with victims of the 2004 Indian tsunami. A further section continues discussion of memory with reference to projects using performance in relation to dementia. Discussion of the making of memory and identity continues in a section on intergenerational work between schoolchildren and elders where performance provides a liminal space 'in-between lives' for exploring connections between histories and cultures and to develop empathic and embodied understanding of the lives of others. The final section, 'Making it Real' explores the vexed issue of authenticity in what I refer to as theatres of affect. The examples here are a multi-sensory performance installation exploring the experiences of those seeking refuge in the United Kingdom (London Bubble's *My Home*) and Mark Storer's devised piece with teenagers, *The Fat Girl gets a Haircut and Other Stories*. I will argue that contemporary performance offers possibilities for playing with and renegotiating identity, moving beyond memory, and recovering and transforming experiences through a radical and transformative aesthetics.

I begin with an autobiographical account by a practitioner, Helen Bryant. I asked her to contribute a piece of personal writing about her experiences of working as a live artist at a secondary school in Hull. Whilst so many accounts of applied theatre projects celebrate the making process and positive outcomes, Bryant's persona of the alien encapsulates what is also a familiar encounter for the contemporary artist seeking to provoke dialogue, to facilitate different perceptions (by offering alternative ways of 'doing') and, where appropriate, to intervene in institutional contexts to promote change. Bryant depicts the bewildered and vulnerable practitioner, navigating foreign territory and speaking a different language. Bryant's interest in working with autobiographical personas, her commitment to play based methods and her understanding of performance writing provoked me to offer her alien a voice and a home.

*   *   *

The alienated alien: an autobiographical account by a performance artist on her experience of applying performance

By Helena Bryant

The Zero Suit of Invisibility, and other adventures
I woke on the island, with a memory of drifting, of being at sea ...
Marooned. 51° 28' N

Here I am, marooned on an oval pile of cobbles, approximately 8ft by 4 in a gallery space next to a children's play area, in the middle of a park in Bermondsey, South London. I am dressed shabbily, and sport a fake beard, to approximate the archetype of the shipwrecked mariner. I have a tattered book, in which I have begun to transcribe some memories, and am periodically reading from Robinson Crusoe, by Daniel Defoe. But my peace is disturbed by three girls who would like something different.

Hello!' they call. 'Hello! hello! hello!' I am fully aware of them, but do not break my pretence of isolation and respond to or acknowledge them, although it is obvious I know they are there. They are determined to break me, in my enforced isolation, and properly catch my gaze. They begin to describe what my purpose might be, what the conditions of the game are that I have set. 'OK. If you're sitting on rocks and you can't speak ....' '...', but they can't go further with the logic of the game to know what the next move should be. They move away and then return, circling me and whistling, and calling out again 'hello! hello! hello!, WE'RE HEEEERE ....' 'HELLLOO!' 'Can I throw this at you?' (How sweet that she should first ask permission before chucking it at me.) I don't respond. Now they dance at the end of my island, mimicking karate chops, determined to foster a reaction that makes me acknowledge their presence.

The girl with the screwed up piece of paper then throws it at me – it happens to land directly in my notebook. I carry on writing without looking up. It seems antagonistic not to answer the girls questions. 'You're evil', they say next. 'Can't you talk? You're evil.'
'Touch her leg', goads one. 'Knock , knock. Bash her on the head.'
'She doesn't speak English. She speaks pirate. That's why she doesn't reply.'
'Hello ......? Hello ......?' The girl prods me. One of the girls turns to another of the artists who are present with their works in the gallery, 'You're a nice lady, Emma', she says. 'And NORMAL. She's not. She's deaf'

Why won't I engage? Of course, they are forcing me to engage with them, but I have to do so while maintaining my fiction of being alone, marooned, stuck on my island and miles form anywhere. And although they acknowledge that I am playing a part ('she's acting', says one to the other); nonetheless, they become frustrated and want in some ways to take more part in and influence my 'game'. The repeated direction to bash me on the head, from one girl to her friend, thankfully, isn't carried out.

They leave me be, soon after, and I consider the provocations between us. Somehow their small transgressions in the gallery (prodding the artwork, harassing the artist) were tolerated. I think they too were playing or acting, running away when they felt that they had stepped too far, but returning to try the taunt again, because it was all just a game, and they wanted to have another turn. And was my self-alienation provocative? Had it challenged them? And if so, was there a purpose to this? I return to my books. To my memories, and to those of Robinson Crusoe.

Kingston Upon Hull 53° 45′ N

'Had I the sense to return to Hull, I had been happy', says a plaque in the Queen's Gardens in Hull, paraphrasing Defoe's hero as he reflects on whether or not he should have gone home instead of to sea again. Had he done so, he would not have become castaway. But also, there would be no story. No adventures. Which I suppose doesn't appeal to the young. And so, instead, he tells us 'my ill fate pushed me on now with an obstinacy that nothing could resist.'

Had I had the sense never to go to Hull, I might have spared myself some suffering. It had felt a little like being deported, or being sent to Siberia. I was stationed there in a secondary school, as one of a thousand artists going into a thousand residencies in the Year of the Artist (2000–2001). Only a few years out of art college, with everyone believing that art could make a difference, I wanted to see what I could do.

Hull is not really so different to towns I knew, but I was an outsider. And in many ways, being an artist puts you on the outside, anyway. I looked different, both in how I appeared and the way I looked at things. People saw this, and commented. What had brought me there? What was I doing? Someone even asked me in the street if I was a missionary. Better still, as I wheeled my boxed up studio equipment into the school, one of the children asked me if I was a magician.

Some of the keys aims of the residency were:

'to demystify the artistic process and show the many roles an artist assumes in the development and exhibition of their work.'

And also,

'to engender the experience of the infectious outsider so, with the demystifying, there is also the contaminating and the opportunity to explore new relationships and challenge the systems within education which are designed to be stable ....'

The school was located in and served the needs of a sprawling and impoverished council estate on the outskirts of the city. The building, the grand last stand of a deluded council architect, looked like a spaceship. It was shaped like a cross between a bullet and a blancmange, with an exterior of glass and metal. Its claims of being 'vandal proof' had been disproved by the local youth within weeks of its opening. The building's interior was bathed in a yellow glow, with interior rooms starved of daylight, and series of interior windows making a line of vision from classroom to classroom to classroom. The corridor system, like a giant electrical circuit, had no dead ends. Throughout the day a pair of teachers would circum-navigate the corridors trying to catch the students absent from lessons, who lurked in throughways and unused space and hiding places, preferring to stay inside the building and play a game of cat and mouse than to find a place to be undisturbed in the outside world.

My allocated studio was a greenhouse conservatory next to the central courtyard garden that students had long since been banned from, due to their proclivities for breaking things. The space showed the evidence behind this, its sloping roof full of cracks like spiders webs, scars and fissures from the impact of assorted missiles thrown on to it, and which let in the rain. People could peer down as they walked along the corridors above, to see the artist at work. I erected a shed inside my space to protect from the cold and rain, and would hide in it daily, wondering what on earth it was that I was meant to be doing.

My original proposal had involved the fictitious trading company of 'PROTECH+' whose business was the manufacture and experimentation of 'Emotional Defence Wear', and 'strategic advancements into the safety of expression'. I had wanted to be based in the science department, where I would research and develop products, drawing others into the process, and then test them out in different places around the school, through performances. I was chosen on the strength of this proposal, and through an interview panel. The panel had all thought me a suitable artist in residence for the school except for, as it turned out, the school representative, their head of art. He didn't like or understand me particularly well, and I recall that, throughout the interview, he could barely look me in the eye.

The residency was problematic from the start. As I arrived, the school had failed an inspection and was being put on special measures. My police check hadn't yet come through, and no one was sure whether or not I could even be there. Before accepting the commission, I had anticipated that the teachers at the school would collaborate with me in the design of activities, but upon arrival it became clear that there was no time in their schedules to spare for this, and I was expected to just go about my business and make things happen.

Feeling railroaded into accepting my placement, and having things of greater priority to attend to, the head of art made no attempt to broker a relationship between me and the science department, or anyone else there. The majority of staff had no idea why I was there or how what I did was art, and just thought I was weird. I struggled to find a structure through which I could include the staff and students in my activities, and became paralysed through self-doubt and loneli-ness. This in turn led to the impression that I was just dossing around. I felt out on a limb and anxious that to become an 'infectious outsider' and 'challenge the systems within education which are designed to be stable ...' might be a dangerous thing to do, as the school seemed unstable enough.

Eventually the courage came to me for invention and intervention. Fashioned from a special silver coloured 'zero' fabric that would let nothing in and nothing out, I made myself the 'Zero Suit of Invisibility'. This suit would allow the wearer to wander around almost imperceptibly. It would install a barrier to the world. It would be as though they were there, but not there, at the same time.

I paid for a train ticket for a fellow artist friend to come and help as camera operator, bodyguard and moral supporter. We wandered around the school, and she filmed me being 'invisible'.

It hadn't fully occurred to me before, but wandering around this spaceship school, covered head to toe in a silver suit, I looked like an alien stowaway. And to the errant pupils also wandering the school instead of gong to lessons, I had magnetic appeal. They saw me. They followed me. When I escaped them, they hunted me down. They wanted the alien caught. We captured this on video.

'WHO ARE YOU? WHERE DO YOU COME FROM?' shouts out one of the congregation. They have surrounded me and I am backed into a corner next to the music suite. I am lying on the floor, responding to the threat by playing dead. 'I think I can talk to it', says another. 'She's shaking', says one of the girls. 'She's an artist', says my minder. 'Ah, bless her', says the girl. One of the boys approaches and leans over me, peering down. 'What are you doing?', he asks.

Ten minutes later, and I've escaped the throng into an unused classroom, and have struck up a conversation with a handful of the pupils. I begin to explain how I've made my suit from special fabric so I can be invisible and protected, and they're asking me questions. But now a teacher walks in and the children are caught. They try to run away.

'Come here will you, don't even try to walk away', he instructs. 'Why aren't you in lessons?' They mumble in futile attempts to explain something. 'GET BACK TO YOUR LESSONS, NOW!'

And the pupils leave the room, and then the teacher leaves the room, with not a word to me, the powers of my suit seeming to have worked very well on him.

To be fair, the teacher knew that I was meant to be invisible, and was playing along, intervening without acknowledging me partly as a way of trying to assist me. And caught on camera it's very pertinent and funny. But this non-engagement of the staff with how the pupils were seeing me, and how they reacted to an alien in their midst, was a very accurate portrayal of my experience.

The following day, I played the unedited footage in the staffroom, which caused some mirth, but opinion was divided as to if it was any good. I was summoned by the head, who advised that my performance had been disruptive. He had had many complaints. The students following me had been noisy. I had managed in some ways to alienate myself further.

I continued at the school for several months longer, forever identified as the woman in the silver space suit. I delivered or got involved with many other activities there, but relationships with the head of art did not improve. An evaluation

report outlined lots of things that should be learnt from, and the end of term saw
my salvation, and a return to London.

* * *

Whilst the formal evaluation of this project may have been somewhat critical, it is worth pausing to reflect on the criteria for success and the learning
involved in this process. The teacher instructing pupils to return to their
lessons (which, as Bryant acknowledges, may well have been performative)
appears to be oblivious to the lessons being learned through the encounter
with Bryant as an alien other in the school environment. Personifying difference, she assumes an object status which enables her to physically mediate between the real and imaginary. She lies on the floor ('playing dead'), a
poignant, yet strategic move, signifying vulnerability and a potential victim
status. This invites curiosity from the pupils ('I think I can talk to it' and
'what are you doing?'), as well as empathic and sympathetic engagement
('she's shaking' and 'bless her' in response to the declaration of her artist status) as the pupils move (conceptually, physically and emotionally) through
their engagement and interaction with this strange persona. Relations may
not have improved with the Head of Art while the considerable potential
to develop the work through, for example, explorations of bullying or
cultural difference (in ways which might offer refreshing alternatives to
the often bland educational diet of theatre in education performances and
workshops) were not realized. The physical presence of the live artist in
this context creates opportunities for embodied engagement with the work
and the issues explored. Moreover, Bryant's persona, as a manifestation of
her personal and professional situation and experience within the school
had integrity, honesty and involved an element of risk taking, all of which
are features which contribute to the power and conviction of performance
which draws upon real lives. For some, Bryant's intervention may have
been perceived as threatening or distracting, particularly in the context of
a school in special measures where risk taking may not be compatible with
a performance management agenda. For the pupils, however, the alien's
interventions involved them developing new understandings of relationships through their experience of living (within the school environment),
learning and playing with a live artist.

3.2 ACTS OF RECALL: MEMORY, IDENTITY AND POST-TRAUMATIC PERFORMANCE

The relations between performance and memory have been discussed by a range of performance theorists (Auslander, 1999; Phelan, 1993, 1998; Schneider, 2011). For Phelan, performance's only life is in the present and it cannot be recovered. The challenge for documentation, she suggests, is to bring into being 'a full seeing of the other's absence, a seeing which also entails the acknowledgement of the other's presence' (Phelan, 1993: 149). In a subsequent study she argues that a preoccupation with 'the perils of preservation' means 'we have created and studied a discipline based on that which disappears and that cannot be preserved or posted ... the challenge before us is to love the thing we've lost' (1998: 11). In its determination to preserve, performance studies, according to Phelan, has become preoccupied with diagnosis and 'the careful recitation of the facts of the event'; only recently, she maintains, has the field begun to focus attention on '*curative interpretation, to the affective and ideological consequences of performance events* ... such interpretations, which are always re interpretations, help us move past the time of the diagnosis' (Phelan, 1998: 7; my emphasis).

For the field of applied theatre, of course, the 'affective and ideological' potential of performance is the focus of its practices and research. Whilst cognitive science challenges the psychoanalytic paradigms Phelan draws upon, her conception of trauma as being 'untouchable' and 'beyond representation' creates further synergies between performance and memory as discourses which rupture the symbolic order of language and culture: 'The symbolic cannot carry it: trauma makes a tear in the symbolic network itself' (Phelan, 1998: 5). The problem here, I suggest, is the psychoanalytic model and its limitations.[2] The cognitive approaches deployed in this book offer a means to conceptualize the relations between memory, theatre and trauma through an account of performance processes which, I suggest, move its audiences beyond trauma. As McConachie's work on spectatorship demonstrates, insights from cognitive science suggest empathy and emotional responses are more significant than semiotics to the spectator's experience. McConachie challenges Auslander's 'continuum' and its supposition of synchronicity between live and mediated performance.[3] Drawing upon the philosopher Noel Carroll, McConachie argues persuasively that 'we process liveness differently from landscapes' (McConachie, 2008: 57–8).

Virginia Woolf captures the ontological dimension of memory in her phrase 'moments of being' which refers to the non-linear temporality and non-representational quality of remembering and its 'felt' qualities (Woolf, 1985). According to Gerard Edelman, for example, memory involves diverse perceptual and sensory systems, variously distributed: '[memory] is in some sense, a form of constructive recategorization during ongoing experience, rather than a precise replication of a previous sequence of events ....' (Edelman and Tononi, 2000: 95; cited in McConachie 2008: 33).[4] As McConachie has suggested, the experience of theatre involves what Edelman refers to as 'the remembered present of consciousness' (2008: 35), a concept which is particularly pertinent to the temporality of contemporary performance and associated notions of presence as well as to the discussion below of dementia.

Much of my discussion revolves around a performance storytelling project with victims of the 2004 Asian tsunami. In this context, testimony and trauma are part of the process of generating performance. My analysis considers how the aesthetic concept of *Rasa* in Indian cultures can be explored from the perspective of cognitive studies (and in relation to the 'emotional systems' identified by Ciompi and Panseek and adopted by McConachie as part of his cognitive approach to spectatorship[5]), offering an understanding of the embodied practices involved in performance storytelling in this context. I consider how performance is used to evoke, explore and reconceptualize memory in relation to trauma.

In contemporary theatre, practitioners who stage memory are most frequently discussed in the context of autobiographical performance, a genre which has produced a body of research exploring the theory and practice of representing lives (Gale and Gardner, 2004; Heddon, 2008; Miller, Taylor and Carver, 2003). These accounts engage with issues of identity, subjectivity, authenticity and have been informed by two of the theoretical paradigms challenged by cognitive science, poststructuralism and psychoanalysis. Although many accounts of autobiographical performance draw attention to the construction of identity through performance, the staging of lives involves more than language. In performances involving spectatorial proximity where audiences are 'seen and heard' (defined by Anna Fenemore as 'visceral-visual' experience as opposed to 'optical-visual' performance), the act of viewing becomes 'existential' and 'intersubjective', to use Fenemore's terms, moving us through tactile and kinesthetic processes and sensations. Drawing upon Elaine Scarry's work, Fenemore explores the combination of pain and pleasure elicited through touch, somaticism and vision in what is variously described elsewhere as 'participatory' or 'immersive' forms of performance. Performance theorists perceive that proximity is a factor in provoking empathic engagement. As Simon Shepherd has argued:

> However imaginatively engaging they are, however kinaesthetically activated to the spectator, filmed bodies, computer generated images, are not physically present to, inhabiting the same space as, spectators.
>
> (2006: 143)

Mirror neurons are more likely to be engaged through the physical and often somatic activity which constitutes performance.[6] Contemporary theatre practice, as Di Benedetto has demonstrated, affects audiences through the provocation of the senses (Di Benedetto, 2010). Di Benedetto makes similar observations to Fenemore about the particular modes of engagement and perceptual experiences involved in what is often referred to as 'live art', but filters his findings through the lens of contemporary neuroscience to describe 'the reception and analysis of sensorial theatrical events'. Like Fenemore, he distinguishes between contemporary performance and what he refers to as 'traditional' perceptual experience which operates differently in terms of audience engagement. His rationale is that in contemporary performance the spectator cannot draw upon prior experience and expectations and is therefore thrust into sensually arousing instinctual responses. Whilst others might wish to question this division and its underlying assumptions and definitions, it is pertinent here, enabling us to explore the relations between performance and trauma.

It is generally acknowledged that trauma involves an event which is beyond representation as an experience that is not fully registered at the moment of impact and which affects the mind and body of the victim (Caruth, 1996; LaCapra, 1996). It has been suggested, nonetheless, that contemporary forms of theatre and art have the potential to engage in dialogue with trauma through sensorial, embodied and somaesthetic experience.[7] Coining the term 'post-traumatic theatre', and using Levinas's concept of the 'other' in conjunction with Cathy Caruth's study of trauma as 'a missed experience', Katharina Pewny considers how encounters can be staged in theatre after a massive violation, arguing that in some performances (with reference to the work of Christoph Marthaler and Meg Stuart), the audience's experience complements (we might say mirrors) that which is not being shown on stage. 'Post-traumatic theatre', Pewny suggests, 'operates from the wound, the violation', Caruth's 'missed experience' and, she argues, can 'transform traumata through the spectators encounter with the trace of the other'. 'I feel your pain', she suggests, 'is an utterance located on the spectators side towards the stage/the performers.'[8] A cognitive approach to the spectator's experience of this work would suggest that our ability to empathize with the traumatic experience of others is both effected and affected through 'mirroring'; this involves more than 'monkey see, monkey do', however, as McConachie has argued, with reference to simulation theory: 'embodying other's emotions, produces emotions in us' (2008: 67). McConachie's study, however, examines dramatic theatre (for the most part) and acknowledges that post-dramatic theatre operates differently, with 'narrative strands' rather than a 'through line' narrative. Although he maintains that spectators will still use similar processes to engage with performance, the cognitive operations maybe differently inflected (e.g., making use of 'iteration' in relation to narrative structures). The spectator's experience of contemporary performance, I suggest, will still involve 'mirroring' in responding to and embodying the movements, sound, rhythms and images which constitute the fabric of the performance, and their engagement will involve what McConachie describes as 'the dynamics of blending that involve attention, memory, empathy and heightened emotions' (2008: 19).

Similar processes appear to be at work in Jill Bennett's study of 'how the medium of visual art can register and embody affect' (2005: 7). Building on her experience of curating an exhibition on the theme of trauma and memory, the work discussed, she explains, engages with trauma whilst not being recognizably 'about' an event or experience. Her argument has synergies with Pewny's thesis as she considers trauma in art as an encounter within which the spectator can experience the sensual traces of the artist's 'post-traumatic' memory.[9]

> Under these conditions, the affective responses engendered by artworks are not born of an emotional identification or sympathy; rather, they emerge from a direct engagement with sensation as it is registered in the work. In this regard, trauma-related art is best understood as *transactive* rather than *communicative*. If often touches us, but it does not necessarily communicate the 'secret' of personal experience. To understand its transactive nature we need to examine how affect is produced within and through a work. And how it might be experienced by an audience coming to the work.
>
> (Bennett, 2005: 7)

In performance, however, the encounter is multi-sensual; bodily sensations can be transferred between stage and audience through the nose, skin and muscles as well as the eyes and ears. I suggest then, that contemporary performance, as a live and sensory medium is an appropriate form to embody affect. As such it can be used not only as a means of expression (or transaction) but also has the potential to transform experience through participatory processes in which memory can be remade, reconceptualized and rediscovered in different forms, whilst some aspects can be relinquished, as evident in the example below which explores how an experience of trauma was mediated through a performance process.

Touching trauma: Vayu Naidu's rasaesthetics and performance storytelling

On 26 December 2004, the world woke up to the devastating scenes of the Indian tsunami. Images of mud-swept landscapes, collapsed buildings, bewildered, weeping survivors in search of their families, dominated television and computer screens as the world's media sought to represent trauma and provoke a material response through contributions to an international relief effort. For UK-based performance storyteller Vayu Naidu, the tsunami was a transformative experience.[10] She was staying in South East India at the time the tsunami struck, visiting relatives in a village on the East coast highway close to the catastrophe. In the immediate aftermath, she joined the teams of rescuers supporting survivors, providing food, water, shelter and reassurance. The survivors urged those helping them to tell their story to the rest of the world and Naidu felt compelled to respond to this request by using her skills as a performance storyteller. Having returned to the United Kingdom, profoundly affected by the experience, she travelled back to the east coast in February 2005, to work with survivors, using storytelling to help those involved in the disaster (as victims and as support workers) to engage in dialogue about their experience and to help the process of recovery.

The story of the tsunami was relayed to the world through the media, but for most of the communities affected, word of mouth rather than the media served as the main means of communication. This was a natural disaster and for many victims was perceived as an act of God; these communities were traumatized not by war but by forces of nature and this made the experience particularly difficult to comprehend. Whilst physical and practical support were critical immediately after the tsunami, there were also psychological and spiritual needs to be addressed as a consequence of the damage to people's lives. This is where the Indian oral performance tradition had a role to play. As Susan Schwartz explains, 'Performance itself is central to the way the varied cultures within India understand their world, interact with it and thus produce an active dynamic' (Schwartz, 2004: 1). Moreover, she stresses the 'special status' of performance: 'it is through performative modes that the sacred becomes palpable in India' (6).

The art of performance storytelling derives from listening cultures. Although storytelling generally involves the performer narrating to an audience (most frequently as a group), the performer's physical presence involves a proximity and intimacy which facilitates kinaesthetic sensations: 'Vayu defines the core characteristic of her practice as something that occurs "in the moment", in response to a range of variables, including the *chemistry* with the audience and the energy of her own body' (Aston and Harris, 2008: 148).[11] Naidu's gestural style is a distinctive blend of ancient and contemporary forms of performance with traces of, for example, the Indian dance drama *Kathakali*, combined with contemporary forms of popular performance. In *Gesture and Thought* (2007), David McNeill advocates gesture and speech as part of a single communicative system. Although he is writing about the gestures of everyday life rather than declamatory gestures of some models of performance, his research connects with performance storytelling, and with Naidu's hybrid style in particular which incorporates 'everyday' gestures as part of a rich movement and speech vocabulary, mixing different dialects and dance/drama traditions and blending them into a form where gesture, body and speech work together, mutually and kinaesthetically. As McConachie writes, with reference to *Kathakali* traditions: 'separate performers vocalize the script while others dance the characters, the simultaneity and co-expressiveness of speech and gesture demands close coordination between the vocalized and the dancers in *Kathakali*' (2008: 87).

Naidu has used dancers in her theatre-based work in similar ways (as well as musicians), but in her storytelling in other contexts she works alone and movement, voice and gesture work as one.

For the tsunami, project, as in all Naidu's work, form was carefully sculpted to content to motivate the audience towards empathic engagement. My use of the term 'motivate' draws upon Fenemore's discussion:

> In *being motivated* 'experiencers' are able to experience some kind of associational or empathetic kinaesthetic impulse or sensation. 'Experiencers', thus are 'being moved' (bodily) by performer and event such that they begin to experience kinaesthetic sensations normally attributed to their own intentional acts of moving, touching or seeing.
>
> (2003: 112)

What Fenemore is describing here are processes which we can conceptualize through cognitive neuroscience; mirror neurons are the scientific basis for the experience she describes: 'certain somaesthetic sensations can be developed where kinaesthetic sensations of movement can begin to exist *without* touch or direct physical manipulation.' Thus, Fenemore concludes '"Experiencers" then, can experience *visual* matter *muscularly* and be moved by visual input' (113).

This, I suggest, corresponds to the felt response Naidu's storytelling evokes.[12] For this project, Naidu's cultural background as a woman from southern India (her career as a performance storyteller developed after she came to England in the late 1980s) and her personal experience of the tsunami enabled her to engage empathetically from her characteristic position as someone who situates herself 'in-between' Eastern and Western cultures, past and present, fact and fiction: As Aston and Harris have observed, 'Vayu describes her work as "*intracultural*" and as a performance practitioner, she might easily function as a "case study" for discussions of Diaspora subjectivity and 'cultural hybridity' (2008: 140). As a storyteller, Naidu occupied a liminal position; the majority of Indian storytellers are male, and '*will not let you enter their fold because there's so much sacredness involved*' (Aston and Harris, 2008: 140).

The tsunami project, however, involved storytelling in a different context as a form of participatory performance and of applied theatre. Although Naidu's previous work had involved her working in community and educational contexts, this was her first experience of a cultural intervention in a traumatized community. In India, both storytelling and performance play an important cultural role: As well as being 'sacred' and patriarchal, the teaching of storytelling involves pedagogical practices which appear to be based on the principles of embodied cognition:

> The 'guru' would provide ... lessons by example, which the student would absorb, copy, and rehearse until the teacher was satisfied ... when

the transmission is experienced physically, as sound enters the body through the ears and movement is physically internalized, it is more active, more engaged, and it is immediate, that is, unmediated.

(Schwartz, 2004: 5)

In this description of a learning process, some of the fundamental principles of cognitive neuroscience are implicitly understood – that is, the ways in which learning is embodied: as Schwartz recognizes, 'Those who learn physically learn differently and experience their knowledge differently as well. It becomes ingested' (5). This understanding has important implications for the workings of memory which, as Mark Johnson has argued, is dependent on non-representational and embodied 'cognitive concepts'; this means, as McConachie has summarized, that 'concepts are not inner mental entities that represent external realities. Rather, concepts are neuronal activation patterns that can either be "turned on" by some actual perceptual or motoric event, or else activated when we merely think about something' (2008: 39). Non-Western spectators, as McConachie has speculated, would use 'the same cognitive concepts to anticipate and construct their dramatic narratives'. However, their 'schemas' would also 'import' culturally specific 'notions of time, space, human-divine relations, and other materials' (166–7).

While the neuroscience of empathy helps us to understand how the act of performance works on an audience through a process of embodiment, the concept of *Rasa* in the pan-Indian tradition is also a means of conceptualizing this process. There are nine *Rasas* which are 'key emotional states' considered to be 'universally felt across all cultures' (Aston and Harris, 2008: 149): love, heroism, the comic, disgust, fear, anger, pathos, wonder and peace. There are some intriguing synergies here between contemporary theories of cognitive science and Indian aesthetics. Like cognitive psychology, *Rasa* challenges divisions between mind and body with paradigms of integration. As Lee Siegal explains: '*Rasa* is at once inner and outer quality of the object of taste, the taste of the object ... the psycho-physiological experience of tasting provided a basis for a theory of aesthetic experience which in turn provided a basis for a systemization of a religious experience' (1983: 43).

Richard Schechner has also studied and trained in rasic performance, incorporating it into his practice and developing the concept of rasaesthetics (Schechner, 2001).[13] The Rasic performer 'opens a liminal space to allow further play – improvisation, variation and enjoyment' (Schechner, 2003: 356). Crucially, the performer is both a self and a spectator of the self; s/he is not defined by character but, like the audience, is a partaker in *Rasa* and this is central to Schechner's conceptualization. Thus the rasic performer engages in a form of conceptual blending through a critical and creative self-consciousness. Schechner's concept of rasaesthetics is discussed in more detail in Part III.

There are some parallels between the concept of *Rasa* and the six emotional states identified by Luc Ciompi and Jaak Panksepp and used by McConachie as a basis for analysis in his cognitive approach to spectating (FEAR, PANIC, RAGE, CARE, PLAY, SEEKING). The synergies between both Eastern and Western paradigms can be seen to endorse their respective claims to universality. Whilst some of the terminologies are different (and translations also differ) 'fear' is common to both paradigms and PLAY is linked to the comic via 'social laughing' in McConachie (2008:106); SEEKING can be linked to heroism and love, while sorrow/pathos and disgust, which feature as *Rasa* but are not explicitly identified in Ciompki and Pansepp's systems, can be considered as part of the fear and panic networks. As McConachie explains, these are 'basic emotional systems' identified through neural circuits as provoking 'arousal' and 'affective consequences.'

One of the most useful explanations and discussion of the concept of *Rasa* is provided by John Russell Brown:

> The *Natyasastra* instructs actors to consider a *rasa* as the consequence of one of the nine dominant emotions or 'durable states of being'. 'Sensation' is probably the most useful translation of *rasa* for present-day use, both with regard to the actor being a person in a play and also – equally important in this acting manual – when speaking of an audience's reaction to an entire performance.
>
> (2005)[14]

Naidu refers to the *Rasa* as the 'emotional juice' of a story and it is this essence which is the basis for the audience's empathic response: the 'triggering of emotional resonances that suggest meaning' (Aston and Harris, 2008: 149). Moreover, as Aston and Harris summarize: 'the *Rasa* also provides the impetus or the *beat* of the narrative working through the performer's body and thereby also informing gesture, expression, pace and timing' (149).

A cognitive approach enables us to more fully engage with the processes involved in Naidu's project. She began by telling a story about a woman who has a story to tell about a huge event but no-one is listening (*pathos*). She told the story in English and the relief workers told it in Tamil. She felt that hearing the story in another language would act as a means of displacement. Her audience was drawn from two disparate cultural groups: the fishermen came from the lowest caste rural communities (many of whom were out to sea when the tsunami struck and lost wives and children who were working close to the shore to prepare for the catch), while the support workers and sympathizers tended to be middle-class women from urban backgrounds. The participants in the workshop were invited in groups to create the untold story and this was again performed in two languages. Although the stories told referred to the tsunami, the fictional framework enabled participants to articulate and explore their experience of trauma at a distance. The stories produced and subsequently performed contained a variety of *Rasa*. For some groups the focus was *anger* and *fear,* moving to *love* and *pathos* in remembering lives lost. For others, the narratives involved *heroism* and *wonder* and for many the dominant *Rasa* was *peace*. When the participants performed their stories in local villages, Naidu recalls the audience responses were different: the women cried (*pathos*), while the children laughed (*comic*). The storytelling, she explains, acted as a form of release, stimulating memory and facilitating healing.

Drawing upon Brecht, Bennett suggests it is possible for the empathic connections provoked through representations of trauma to combine affect with critical inquiry, so that the space between self and other is not eradicated but 'inhabited'; this avoids the simplicity and sentimentality associated with Brecht's 'crude empathy'. McConachie also makes the case for the rehabilitation of empathy, suggesting that: 'Brecht misunderstood the cognitive process of simulation ... the ability to simulate another's state of mind is usually prior to the kind of judgment that induces sympathy or antipathy' (2008: 76). Aston and Harris consider Naidu's storytelling in relation to both Stanislavski and Brecht: 'when you have to identify with an emotion you go back into your history, through your memory. That creates a process of reflection, the reflection creates what we call your interior landscape, your internal geography' (2008: 150). Naidu's technique, however, has more in common with Brecht, or rather:

> a postmodern re-working of Brechtian ideas ... the storyteller's persona functions as an 'anchor'; as a medium *between* the story and the audience. Vayu seems then to speak from a position that moves between 'inside' and 'outside' of the narrative, and she re-presents and comments on the characters in a manner that allows the audience a degree of identification with them, regardless of gender, but at the same time firmly maintaining a distance.
>
> (Aston and Harris, 2008: 151)

Whilst Naidu's use of two languages facilitated the critical awareness Bennett advocates in terms of critical empathy, there was clearly more at work in terms of cognitive blending. The spectators were conscious of Naidu as a storyteller, performing both a fictional narrative in which she represented a series of personas, moving in and out through different vocal registers and gestures while she was also 'present' in the here and now as Vayu Naidu, a storyteller whose form and content is the familiar made strange due to her gender (not male) and the hybrid nature of her style (Eastern and Western). She was also functioning as both 'social' worker and performer, a person who has engaged with her auditors, worked with them, listened to them and helped them. As experiencers and as participants, this audience was also blending the relations between their personal memories and the story being told as both collective and individual memory of trauma. The fishermen involved in this form of participatory performance used the performance vocabularies they were familiar with and their boat songs were incorporated into the storytelling. Through the stories they created, Naidu suggests, the fishermen were 'lifted from grief'.[15] As a consequence, they were able to return to their catamarans for the first time, taking Naidu with them; seven miles out to sea, they stopped the boats and engaged in prayer and songs. The sea was personified as a mother in these rituals: 'why did she let us down?' they lamented, yet the return to the sea was an important outcome of the project.

Naidu's account of the tsunami experience is reminiscent of Jill Dolan's concept of 'utopia' in performance and its implications for what might be described as a form of post-traumatic theatre. Dolan refers to 'the beginning (and perhaps the substance) of the utopian performative; in the performer's grace, in the audience's generosity, in the lucid power of intersubjective understanding, however fleeting' (2005: 62). McConachie agrees, but suggests that 'grace, generosity and intersubjective understanding are most likely to occur in the theatre when CARE is present to wrap spectators and actors together in communitas' (2008: 97). He could be describing Naidu's tsunami project and its *Rasa* of CARE.

3.3   Remembered lives and the continuous present: applied performance and dementia

The affective potential of contemporary performance as a sensual and interactive medium has generated a range of possibilities for applications in health contexts, as documented in Emma Brodzinski's account, *Theatre in Health and Care* (2010). Moreover, the capacity to enter into dialogue with the non-representational experiences of both memory and trauma has led to a range of activities using performance as a means of facilitating and exploring memory. Pam Schweitzer's work in reminiscence theatre in the United Kingdom is particularly well documented (Schweitzer, 2006). In this section, I focus on the applications of performance to dementia as a condition which, I suggest, can be understood in relation to memory, trauma and contemporary theatre practice. In *Post Dramatic Theatre* Hans-Thies Lehmann refers to contemporary performance as having 'the power to question and destabilize the spectator's construction of identity' (2006: 5). Trauma theory uses similar terminologies:

> Traumatic events ... breach the attachments of family, friendship, love and community. They shatter the construction of self that is formed and sustained in relation to others. They undermined the belief systems that give meaning to human experience.
>
> (Herman, 2001: 51)

This could also be a description of dementia, which is similarly a fragmentation of self, powerfully evoked by Melanie Wilson (as discussed in Part X 'Digital Transportations'). Dementia could be regarded as a form of trauma, although the experience for the family, friends and carers of the sufferer is a different form of trauma to the experience of the person with the condition. In this chapter, I draw upon my personal encounter with dementia through my experience of a relative with the condition. Anyone who has been personally associated with the dispersal of identity, anxiety and changes in personality that are symptomatic of dementia may well recognize and endorse the connection with trauma. What is important to understand, however, particularly in the context of care (and the possibility for intervention), is that dementia is a process that progresses through stages. Most performance work takes place in the context of a community or residential setting. By this stage, the sufferer is often in the later stages of the condition, having progressed through the loss of short-term memory to a point where they inhabit a form of continual present and this is the place where, it is suggested, dialogue can take place. The advice to carers in the early stages of dementia is not to draw attention to repeated conversations (one of the earliest and most frequently reported symptoms) as this creates anxiety for the person with the condition. Thus even in early stage dementia, there is a sense of meeting the sufferer in the place they are currently inhabiting and this can involve sustaining a form of fiction, or pretending to pretend. Thus recovery of memory is not an objective of intervention and this is something which student practitioners need to be alert to as some activities, carefully designed to stimulate reminiscence can be potentially distressing. A further factor, however, which is fundamental to understanding and caring for the person with dementia is remembering and respecting both their previous and current identities. Thus the former head teacher may continue to dress in a suit in the day care centre, while the retired organist continues to sing hymns (musical memory is one of the last faculties to be lost).

Remembering to forget: a trip down memory lane

It is Boxing Day 2010 and my relative, who is staying with us over the Christmas period, asks when it is Christmas day. The children sitting at the breakfast table are clearly not sure how to respond. She is told in a gentle but matter of fact way that it was yesterday. 'Oh', she responds, 'I don't remember.' A now familiar look of bewilderment and confusion is evident in her face, so I remind her of the photo frame we bought for her. She relaxes immediately, remembering that it also functions as an alarm clock and woke her that morning. She returns to her room and brings the clock with her to show us all (again). The photo is monochrome and shows her with her late husband and children in a garden. She is not sure where it is taken but she thinks it is Rochester, where she was brought up and she begins to reminisce. We live 45 minutes' drive from Rochester and decide, on impulse, to visit as she seems interested and animated when we talk about it.

It is a grey, cold winters day and the Rochester streets are quiet in the aftermath of Christmas. The Medway towns, once thriving, are now part of a regeneration project, benefiting (albeit slowly) from the proximity to London and being on the train line to the 2012 London Olympics stadium. The demise of the dockyard in the 1970s and the crisis of the manufacturing industries during the 1980s recession have contributed to what my relative describes repeatedly as the town's sadness. We identify (with difficulty) the street corner where her parents' shop once stood. The changed windows and converted buildings nearby defamiliarize it. Throughout the visit, however, her memories appear to be vivid. She recounts the tragic accident at the dockyard when a school-girl was hit by a bus. She remembers the policeman whose day job was to conduct traffic before traffic lights replaced him. And she remembers the various shops of her childhood, most of which no longer exist as we walk up the High Street. We go into an Italian café for coffee (which is my idea) and I try to encourage her that the café and the presence of various food outlets is a sign of regeneration. But she seems to resent the presence of the Italians in her home town (even though the coffee is excellent). I am, nevertheless, thinking about the impact the trip has had on her as a means of stimulating memory – like a piece of durational performance, she has walked through the streets of her past and remembered them, whilst also being aware of her current situation as a visitor, several decades later. I am even wondering about the value of this kind of activity as a form of reminiscence theatre when she turns to me, panic stricken and asks about the whereabouts of her dog. I have to explain that he is at our house with our children. She asks how he got there and I have to remind her that he travelled with her in the car when she was brought to our house. For the first time, she draws direct attention to her condition and tells me (with a terrified look on her face) that she is worried about her memory. I can only reassure her not to worry, whilst regretting our decision to make a visit which appears now to have caused her so much anxiety. Returning home (and expressing surprise again at the presence of the dog), she goes to the piano and begins to play – just as she used to.

As her condition has worsened and her personality changes, we continue to tell ourselves that it is the illness which is changing her. But we have learned to meet her where she is, inhabiting the provisional temporal space which is her reality. I am not sure whether the events of that day triggered some form of short-term memory crisis as she had so clearly been enjoying remembering and, I suspect, found the experience of being able to remember reassuring. Coming back to the present, in the Italian café, was clearly traumatic as she so clearly experienced and articulated an existential and ontological crisis; 'I am I because my little dog knows me', wrote Gertrude Stein, a repeated refrain in her writing (in different configurations), initially derived from a fable about a woman whose identity depends on her appearance and who needs her dog to verify that 'when I am I my little dog knows me' after her clothes are stolen when she falls asleep by the wayside.[16] In this phrase so much is encapsulated: the destabilizing of identity and language also involves a turn to audience (for recognition), anticipating the post-dramatic as well as articulating the concept of the continuous present, which is of course the temporality of theatre. It is in this space, I suggest, that exchange can take place between the neuro-divergent consciousness of the dementia sufferer and the neuro-typical world of those on the outside. Trauma, dementia and post-dramatic theatre have the capacity to 'destabilize the [experiencer's] construction of identity' (to use Lehmann's and Fenemore's performance terms). Thus, it would appear, that the presentness of contemporary performance and its capacity to provoke the senses might mean that it is possible to engage in dialogue with the experience of dementia and even to represent it.

Good medicine: multisensory performance and affective science in Spare Tyre's *Once Upon a Time*

Several companies and practitioners are exploring the potential value of contemporary practice with dementia sufferers (Magic Me, Melanie Wilson,

Entelechy Arts). Here, I focus on *Once upon a Time* (2010), a work in progress by the London-based theatre company, Spare Tyre. Since its origins as a Feminist Theatre company, Spare Tyre have sought to work with voiceless communities and to challenge prejudice through participatory projects with a range of groups, including women who have experienced sexual violence, adults with learning disabilities and older people aged 60 plus. Over the last 15 years they have developed expertise in working with the over-sixties, creating projects which 'aim to connect participants back to social networks, confronting alienation through theatre'.[17] A core feature of their work is the use of multi-sensory techniques and interactive media to engage participants through highly visual, aural, tactile, aromatic and kinesthetic stimuli. Productions such as their devised piece *Feeble Minds* (2009), their version of *Timon of Athens* (involving artists with learning disabilities as well as artists aged over 60) are richly textured, creating atmosphere and energy through 'affective' sensual environments which stimulate visceral responses. An outdoor version of *The Trojan Women* (2011) used physical and popular modes of performance to explore and celebrate sexuality in the over-sixties. The company's work is informed by research through collaborations with health professionals. *Still Life Dreaming* (2011), a Wellcome Trust funded production, draws on cognitive ageing research undertaken through the Lothian Birth Cohort study,[18] exploring life stories from the participants and scientists. A commitment to advocacy is underpinned by an understanding that change happens through the process of making and experiencing art. Audiences are clearly moved by the integrity and passion of performances which express the felt experiences of the learning disabled: anger, disappointment and injustice as well as love and humour are powerfully articulated through the sensual language of contemporary performance. 'Theatrical performance', writes Stephen Di Benedetto, 'has the potential to change our experience of the world and therefore, the potential to change our ability to perceive the world in a new way ... sensorial perception is intrinsic to the power of theatrical representation to transform the human experience' (2010: x).

The company's understanding of embodiment is evident in their workshop methods and performance vocabularies. Workshops explore perception by, for example, inviting responses to a range of abstract visual stimuli, which then serve as a basis for devising. Touch is often a starting point for workshops and for developing stimuli into performance. Participants describe holding exercises as part of the process of generating community; performers interact with each other by gently stroking faces, holding the gaze physically as one performer supports the other's head in his hands. This is extremely moving to watch, touching the audience as we attend to the intimacy of the action through embodied simulation; as Di Benedetto explains in his discussion of witnessing touching on stage, 'we receive the information by way of our gaze; however, mirror neuron response ensures that neurons will fire and stimulate the same part of the brain that would respond if we were the character being [touched]' (2010: 70). Fenemore also writes of the importance of touch in conjunction with the 'complex somatic processes and somaesthetic experiences involved in spectating on *being moved* by performer or performance ... These *states of sensing* rather than objectification or imaginative self-transformations are somaesthetic experiences in that they are not specifically located 'sensory perceptions' bound into an object, instead they are somatic interpretations of the *potential* to experience something' (Fenemore, 2003: 108–9). This sensory work in and through performance informs and is informed by Spare Tyre's workshop processes. The company's understanding of these modes of embodiment and perception enabled them to respond creatively to their experience of being confronted with people with high support needs in community care settings. This has led to the development of a multi-sensory person-centred approach to dementia (and which they clearly differentiate from their work with learning disability). Having encountered some obstacles to their work through assumptions that one size fits all in terms of learning disabilities and dementia, Spare Tyre embarked, somewhat intuitively on a quest to discover how they might engage in creative dialogue with dementia: 'we asked ourselves, if we create extreme sensory environments, will we get a response?' and this led to their work in Nightingale House in London (2010) a residential home for dementia sufferers.[19]

This is not reminiscence theatre, Arti Prashar emphasizes, as the work engages participants in the here and now, rather than in the past.[20] A pilot project at Nightingale House explored an interdisciplinary and multi-sensory approach which the company describes as 'layering touch, sound, taste, smell', using movement, lighting, projection, music and narrative as stimuli within a safe and immersive environment. The work is a collaboration with the interactive digital design company Genetic Moo. The artists, Prashar explains, participate as collaborators and not as tutors – being a 'fellow person in the room'. Dementia is understood by the company as a spectrum condition and they describe their approach as 'organic' as a means of responding to the complexities of the condition through a person-centred ethos. One of the principal outcomes of the project was the changed perceptions of the staff working with the participants: 'putting people into a creative environment means they are seen differently', says Prashar, while the work was also perceived as a means of 'unlocking' the world of dementia for a potential audience to enter into.

The project involved three 50-minute sessions. Although the company were advised that concentration spans were limited and unlikely to extend to a full session, the staff were surprised that attention was sustained by many participants for the duration of the workshop event. Each session began with composed music and a darkening of the space to create the immersive environment. There were generally a maximum of six participants due to the spatial considerations involved in accommodating wheel chairs and bed chairs for participants with limited mobility and to ensure quality of engagement.

The first week tested the broad spectrum of sensory stimuli to see how participants responded. A verbal and physical introduction generally involves a loose narrative based on a traditional folk story, designed to reach across cultures and engage participants emotively (a story loosely based on *King Lear* was used for the Nightingale House pilot). The story was broken down into short sections, using different sensory stimuli with extensive use of repetition. Staff observed a number of significant responses in residents, some of whom they referred to as being 'awakened' through the process. One example cited was a resident with no remaining expressive language who had given no indication of understanding receptively. Thus it was assumed that he wasn't able to understand verbal communication. He was witnessed becoming engaged with the story and when given an instruction, he communicated. Thus he became excited by the coloured torch portraying an image of the moon. Asked if he could paint the moon, he took the torch and moved it to recreate a version of the image.

A full range of sensory activities were involved initially, including an opportunity for sharing food. The experience of the first workshop was overwhelming, however (Prashar refers to it as chaotic), and participants were

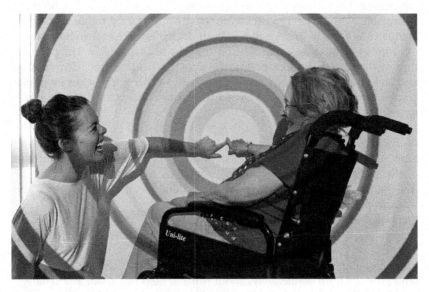

Figure 2 Helen Preddy and Heba Soliman in Spare Tyre's *Once Upon a Time* at Nightingale House, 2010. Photograph by kind permission of Arti Prashar, Artistic Director, Spare Tyre and Patrick Baldwin, photographer

invited in the second session to identify the senses they wanted to awaken and at which moment through a range of choices on what is described as a sensory journey. Although some participants had very limited physicality, they were moved into the environment so that they were able to benefit from proximity to the stimuli; Prashar describes twirling a lady in a wheel-chair around and around in the light of the projector screen; 'she owned that space', she reflects, and explains that one of their objectives was 'to make people comfortable to express what they want'.[21]

Whilst it is evident from the qualitative responses to Spare Tyre's pilot project that significant responses were elicited, the reasons for efficacy are more difficult to establish. Sensual performance can often trigger memory, as evident in Spare Tyre's work at Nightingale House, but recognizing the temporality of memory is fully understood by the company. As Rhonda Blair has summarized, 'Memory is now known to be an often unreliable or approximate process of neural pattern reactivation: the neural patterns that are activated to "retrieve" a memory are never precisely the same thing twice, because the brain changes at least minutely with each event' (Blair, 2008: xiii).

This is acknowledged in Spare Tyre's work; the participant responding to flowers with a memory of her wedding is 'a memory doesn't have to stay in the past', Prashar suggests. 'Is it a memory or a present state of mind? She was there – in that church – the memory is in the here and now – it's a happening – she's responding to her sense of the present.' Throughout my discussions with Spare Tyre the word 'emotive' was used frequently by the company as a key to understanding both the experience of dementia and as a means of facilitating expression on the part of the sufferer. The provocation of the senses through performance methods stimulates felt responses and this is endorsed by my association with similar approaches in similar contexts.[22] Paula Niedenthal offers a means of conceptualizing the affects observed at Nightingale House:

Individuals embody other people's emotional behaviour.
Embodied emotions produce corresponding subjective emotional states in the individual.
Imagining other people and events also produces embodied emotions and corresponding feelings.
Embodied emotions mediate cognitive responses.

(in McConachie, 2008: 66–7)

Autobiographical work, as numerous theorists have noted is not, at heart (and I use the term deliberately) about truth or facts but about an exchange, to use McConachie's terms. The sharing and rehabilitation of empathy and affect through recognition of the felt experience of the other. In working with (and through) dementia, presence and the present are crucial conditions for exchange. Immersive and multi-sensory environments can function as potentially transportative, liminal spaces facilitating interplay between real, imagined and remembered identities. The practitioner, as in Prashar's example of the wedding memory, needs to engage imaginatively and intuitively, meeting the participant and sharing the conceptual space they are inhabiting, however temporarily. For the participants, these interactions are also recognition of their identities (however fragile) – the 'I am I' because another 'knows me'. Thus the practitioner may function as performer and audience in these complex participatory exchanges. The pleasure in this mode of performance is located in play as emotions are embodied and the sufferer becomes cognitively engaged in a moment of being, a recognition and acknowledgement of their identity through interaction with another as well as the pleasures of partaking in an environment where imagination, memory and fantasy can be explored through synaesthetic means and where language, logic and rationality are delightfully suspended. This, I will argue in Part III is a neuro-divergent aesthetic, enabling participants and performers to perceive differently.

3.4 BETWEEN LIVES: INTERGENERATIONAL PERFORMANCE

In an editorial article (2006), Helen Nicholson refers to Joseph Roach's discussion of the interaction and interdependence between 'collective memory, history and performance', a continuum which is evident in the various sections of this chapter, exploring the participatory processes involved in making and embodying social and individual memory, cultural and personal histories and identities and subjectivities through performance. The politics of performing history and memory has been a theme of feminist performance theory (Gale and Gardner, 2004; Heddon, 2008) which engages in dialogue with applied theatre and performance. As well as a means of giving voice, autobiographical performance is a form through which we can understand and embody the perspectives of others. Intergenerational performance is being used increasingly to bring together different age groups, most frequently school children and their grandparents' generation in creative collaboration. The differences between the experiences of children brought up during the Second World War and their millennium grandchildren involve technological advances which have radically changed the way we think, communicate and learn. In short, these generations perceive differently, as the digital natives of the twenty-first century interact with a mediatized environment which we now understand as playing an important role in neurological development; the brain's plasticity is such that children's interaction with technology will mean they become wired differently to their parents and grandparents. The profound implications of this for education are encapsulated in the statement by Ramachandran: 'I predict that mirror neurons will do for psychology what DNA did for biology: they will provide a unifying framework and help explain a host of mental abilities that have hitherto remained mysterious and inaccessible to experiments' (Ramachandran, 2000). In section 3.4 on "Digital Technologies', this is discussed in more detail with particular reference to Jonathan Barnes's work, who draws on contemporary neuroscience to argue passionately in favour of an interdisciplinary curriculum for 8 to 14-year-olds as a means of developing what Daniel Goleman refers to as 'emotional intelligence'.

The gap between generations can generate indifference and intolerance, but to experience first-hand accounts of oral history which have local relevance can create an empathic response. The London Bubble's *Blackbirds* production in May 2011[23] involved primary and secondary schoolchildren collaborating with groups of elders, many of whom were at day care centres or in sheltered accommodation. Barnes is on the Board of Directors for London Bubble and Jonathan Petherbridge, artistic director for the company, cites his work as an important influence on the company, clearly informing the pedagogical approaches which underpinned the research and development stage of *Blackbirds*. Research at London's Imperial War Museum involved pupils accessing primary materials on the London Blitz, as they learned about evacuation, rationing, and worked closely with photos of the period and maps of bomb damaged areas, subsequently undertaking a 'Blitz walk' of vicinities most seriously affected. A single street (Mayflower) would eventually become the focus for the piece. As the children were drawn from the local area, this research had personal relevance and was one of the factors facilitating their engagement with what they understood as human history.[24] One of the most significant features of this project was the process of data gathering through interviews with the groups of elders. Schoolchildren from the ages of 8 to 17 participated in the collection of memories. Training was given on interview techniques, enabling the pupils to lead these sessions, understanding how to generate dialogue, developing listening and questioning skills. The result is an oral history resource archived principally on the London Bubble website, with some material deposited at the Imperial War Museum. These testimonies were the basis for developing *Blackbirds*, using interview material as a primary source for the development of the piece. Drawing on verbatim theatre techniques, recordings of the person giving the testimony were used in rehearsal as a stimulus for physical work and improvisation. The focus on Mayflower Street involved electoral roll research to discover the names and details of the families who lived in the houses. In productions of this kind, fact and fiction intermingle. This was not described as documentary or verbatim theatre, but as community performance by the company. Although a script was developed for the performance, rehearsal methodologies were the same as for devised work and a strong sense of ensemble was evident in the resulting performance. There was a clear concern for 'authenticity' in the methods used to research the piece and an awareness of the ethics involved in using material which refers to 'real' lives. The company describe this as 'telling the story of the area back to those who live there'.[25] One of the principal objectives of the piece, however, was not to re-present history (as a naturalistic slice of life), but to explore connections across and between past and present, old and young. Thus the piece travels through different phases, starting in the present, then moving to the past and back again as it follows the journeys of the various residents of Mayflower Street and the impact of the Blitz on their lives. One of the recurrent themes is the normality of the war for those who lived through it. Evacuation to the shelters became a regular part of everyday life and the action is repeatedly disrupted by the sirens sending families to shelters, whilst the account of the gradual impact on the houses in Mayflower Street as the Blitz continued is true to the evidence gathered during the research process.

In performance, *Blackbirds* moved between narration, direct address, acted scenes, structured episodically and employing physical movement sequences (a particularly powerful means of conveying that which could not be represented), leaving the spectator to use their imagination to fill in the gaps as the acoustic echo at Dilston Grove amplified the high decibels

Figure 3   London Bubble, *Blackbirds*. Photograph by kind permission of Steve Hickey and London Bubble

of bombs dropping (causing my nine-year-old in the audience to respond physically by cowering). Projections were effected through hand-held sheets as young performers stood behind the testimony of the elders. This was a performance which touched its audience not through physical proximity (although the spatial dimensions of the performance venue created an intimacy between performer and audience), but through an embodied response and a shared experience. The experience of the audience (who were sitting either on benches or on the floor) was clearly registered as a group response through shared gasps, sighs, laughter and, on occasions, jumping or cowering as rubble suddenly descended. The non-matrixed performance style was appropriate to the form and content and the non-trained performers, contributing to the integrity and honesty of the piece. I was reminded of Joseph Roach's comment that through performance, 'memory reveals itself as imagination' (Roach, 1995: 29).

Memories, archives and personal performance: The Women's Library and Magic Me

Roach's perception is also pertinent to my next example of intergenerational performance, as this featured autobiography and memory as source rather than stimulus material. *Moving Lives* (Women's Archive, London, April–June 2011) was a collaboration between Magic Me (a company specializing in intergenerational arts projects), the Women's Library, Mulberry School for Girls and a group of older women associated either with the library, Magic Me or various community groups:

> Working with writer and theatre maker, Sue Mayo, visual artist Ellie Rees, and a photographer, Kerry Clark, 'the participants explored the ways in which women archive their own lives, intentionally and unintentionally. What objects, documents and images hold our memories, and what do we do with them?[26]

Although intergenerational exchange was an aim of the library project,[27] the importance of personal testimony as a means of giving voice to identity was encapsulated by one of the participants, objecting to her representation by another: 'You're painting a picture of me which isn't the truth.' This comment was made towards the start of the process in response to an exercise that was contributing to the creation of a video diptych. By the end of the project, such concerns had dissipated and there was an understanding of memory as narrative and of identity as similarly flexible and malleable. As part of the final sharing, in a conversation over tea and cake, I reminded the teenager of her complaint about the way she had been presented by one of the Jewish elders participating in the project:

> I know I said that and it's like what I thought when we were doing it, but now we've done the whole thing it's different; I don't mind now I can see it up there (referring to the exhibition). That's how [name] saw me and that's different to how I see myself but that's like her point of view isn't it. I understand that. (PAUSE) But it's different now, anyway; there are lots of me's ... and different people see different ones and they're all real, sort of, you know what I mean?
>
> (Mulberry participant)

To which one of the other teenage participants responded, 'Maybe that's what Magic Me means ...' (referring to the name of the company running the project). This led to a conversation about the meaning of identity (as something which the individual can claim) and its relation to subjectivity and to discussion of nature and nurture as collaborative processes contributing to the complex notion of self. As a conversation between a group of women, two of whom were Jewish elders and the other two were Muslim teenagers, gender and ethnicity were clearly felt as determining factors in identity construction. Yet this project had changed their perceptions of themselves and others and it was clear that for all of them, the personal had become political. They all agreed emphatically that the archival work on the suffragettes, and Emily Wilding in particular (whose personal artefacts are housed at the library), had convinced them of the importance of the vote. One woman in her seventies first voted after a previous Magic Me Women's Library project, when she first learned about the suffragettes.

The collaboration between Magic Me and London's Women's Library, led by Mayo has been ongoing since 2004 and brings together elders from a range of contexts (a Jewish community group, some members who had been part of other Magic Me projects as well as individuals associated with the library) with pupils from London's Mulberry School for Girls (which is 98 per cent Bangladeshi).[28] In the 2011 project, six older women participated (five of whom had taken part in the project before). The older women were of Scottish, West African, Jewish, Indian, Guyanese and White United Kingdom origin. Nine Mulberry pupils were recruited from Years 9 and 10 of Bangladeshi (8) and Moroccan (1) origin. For Mayo, 'being surprised about somebody else' is at the heart of this work in a society which she describes as increasingly 'stratified': 'even in families, they often don't even eat together anymore', she observes, expressing concern about the increasing communication gap between generations. Mayo is realistic about not claiming 'more than can be achieved' through applying performance: 'you can change relationships, but you can't change East London.'[29] In the work I observed, however, the shifts in perception were significant as evident in the example cited above and in the project's evaluation document.

Mayo emphasizes the importance of creating appropriate conditions, in the room, to facilitate forms of exchange that may lead to change. Participants agree on a set of rules (which change each year as appropriate to the project and its participants):

> Confidentiality: what is said in the group, stays in the group.
> No use of mobiles unless there are special circumstances.
> Respect one another: think before speaking; don't interrupt or speak over someone; give everyone an opportunity to contribute; no rudeness or swearing.

The importance of these rules was evident in one of the early sessions I observed. One of the elders had a tendency to dominate conversation, while some of the teenagers would request toilet breaks when the elders clearly expected to wait (hence Mayo referred to the need to address the different energies in the room as one of the structuring principles for her workshops). In previous work, Mayo explained, some of the elders had a tendency to prioritize their memories, regarding their accounts of the Second World War as having more significance than the experiences of the teenagers. Mayo's exercises are carefully designed to ensure equality and genuine collaboration and 'connections'.[30] Participants begin, for example, by writing something about themselves that no one else knows on a Post It note. These are folded and distributed to the group as a lucky dip whereby the secret is read out and the person who correctly identifies the author selects the next Post It and so on. In a later exercise (and after various other games involving autobiographical material), a game of Dominoes is played with Post Its, making connections between what the group has found out about each other. Thus the teenager who said she wanted a love marriage in preference to an arranged one had her comment placed next to the Jewish woman who had celebrated 26 years of marriage, having married a man who converted to Judaism in order to marry her.

One of the most moving connections involved participants bringing to the workshop an object of personal significance, containing a memory. One teenager brought her Koran and found connections with the Hebrew prayer book of one of the elders. Another teenager brought in a framed poem by her late sister and spoke of her faith and the pilgrimage she and her family went on after her sister's death.

> Our own life stories were told through photographs, a baby blanket, a key ring, a shoe.
> A doll from one participant's experience of evacuation met a toy from the Telly Tubbies.
> The stories were of loss, love, fun and friends. Everyone felt confirmed by their markers of memory.
>
> (Mayo, 2011)

The memories of the group were contextualized in relation to each other and in relation to cultural histories through a timeline. Thus each memory was dated and significant events of that year were recorded, creating a chronology of remembered dates and events, significant to participants but which might appear to be somewhat arbitrary to an outsider. For each memory and event, a further Post It would indicate what survived (e.g., photographs, school reports, marriage/birth/death certificates and/or oral accounts). Thus 1997 was a year remembered for the death of Diana, a divorce, the birth of a sibling and the loss of a dog. The timeline started in 1942 when one of the participants walked over a bomb which failed to detonate and ended in the present, with the date of the project. This process of working with memory drew upon what neuroscience defines as 'explicit' (what we consciously remember) and 'episodic' memory (drawn from personal experience). A complex process was involved here, as the various activities of the project enabled participants to understand the relations between memory and imagination, whilst the transformations of memory were also a means of redefining identity and notions of the self. Cognitive theory provides a lens through which we can see how learning and transformation was effected through methodologies Mayo defines explicitly in terms of live art. As LeDoux explains:

> Much of the self is learned by making new memories out of old ones. Just as learning is the process of creating memories, the memories created are dependent on things we've learned before. ... [Memory is] *a reconstruction of facts and experiences on the basis of the way they were stored, not as they actually occurred.*
>
> (LeDoux, 2002: 96; my emphasis)

LeDoux also writes of memory as 'an imaginative reconstruction or construction, built out of the relation of our attitude toward a whole active mass of past experience' (2002: 177). Although the memories of the participants in this context were associated with objects and hence initially retrieved associatively, the working methods facilitated an understanding of memories as processes (rather than as objects for retrieval). The fluid form of memory as changing in content and substance according to context was evident in subsequent exercises where memories were retold in different formats and changing versions emerged. In one exercise, for example, participants were paired and asked to recount their object memories independently (and the relations between them were discussed) before repeating their accounts as part of a turn-taking exchange, developing episodic and fragmented narratives as their stories and voices were juxtaposed with each other. In performance, a range of stories were recorded and edited to provide a soundtrack of different voices, articulating different memories and experiences. With each rehearsal and repetition, the accounts were transformed, whilst it was also evident their authors were listening to and accommodating each other. This process of repetition and retelling in different creative formats is, in fact, analogous to the workings of memory:

> If you take a memory out of storage you have to make new proteins (you have to restore, or reconsolidate it) in order for the memory to remain a memory ... The brain that does the remembering is not the brain that formed the initial memory.
>
> (LeDoux, 2002: 161)

Understanding the archive as an act of reconstruction involving historical research (a form of semantic memory) and the imagination was also a feature of the project. The group worked with the contents of the pockets of Emily Wilding Davison (the suffragette who died when she fell under the King's horse in 1913) and the police statement accompanying her personal effects. These consisted of a tiny purse (with the impression of a coin clearly visible on the fabric, indicating the force of the horse's weight on her body), a return train ticket (the implications of which we discussed in view of

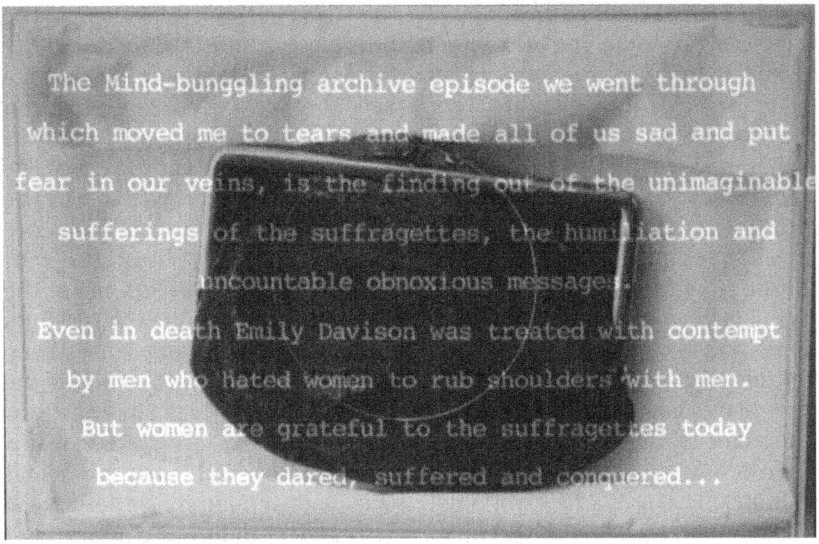

Figure 4 Moving Lives Group, Magic Me. Still from the video installation the group displayed at The Women's Library in May 2011. Photograph by kind permission of Magic Me. Image created by Moving Lives Group

her suicide/martyrdom), a handkerchief, a badge and a suffragette rosette. Having carefully arranged and photographed the items in relation to each other (to create an emotive picture), the group discussed and then contributed examples of their own personal effects to establish connections with the suffragette. Various travel tickets were compared with the 1913 version as well as a membership badge and various ID cards. These were arranged in relation to Wilding Davison's, creating a visual representation of the relationship between her personal effects in 1913 and the collection from this group of women in 2011. Finally, everyone contributed their purses which were arranged in various configurations until a preferred design was agreed (a circular design with Wilding's purse at the centre was eventually rejected in favour of a linear arrangement in size order, emphasizing the size and age of Wilding's purse in relation to the rest (and at the start or end of the line, dependent on the perspective of the viewer). All this was photographed and used in the exhibition. Throughout this archive section of the project, the emphasis was on exploring relations (similarities and differences) between the female participants in the project and this piece of archival feminist history. Many of the participants were visibly moved by the process and this contributed to affective learning as knowledge was gained through felt experiences which were also conceptualized through discussion and through the activities with the artefacts. The archive also contained some hate mail sent to Emily Wilding Davison as she was dying and this generated strong responses. For some, the proximity to these pieces of history and the ability to physically touch the items created authenticity, 'making it real', as one of the participants commented. For others, it was the process of exploring the relations between the items from history and their personal possessions which made this meaningful. And for some, the factual knowledge of the circumstances of the suffragette's death and the speculation generated by the return ticket enabled them to understand history as open to interpretation, a malleable and creative form, liberating it from the closure associated with the study of facts and dates. History was perceived as sharing some of the same qualities as memory – an 'imaginative reconstruction', to use LeDoux's terms, to which we can connect by drawing upon emotional, kinaesthetic and personal experience; that is, through applying 'live art', which is the term Mayo uses to describe her working methods and which she felt it was important to honour in the project. Working across art forms, she explains is a means of engaging the different energies of participants as a group and as individuals. Live artists working in social and community contexts need to be aware of what is in the room.[31] This understanding is crucial to the creation of an environment in which embodied cognition can be achieved.

Participants in this project clearly deepened their understanding of themselves as well as their relationships to a range of others. This was achieved through processes which drew upon autobiography, but avoided nostalgia. The process of condensing identity into forms of visual art was further developed in the creation of the video diptychs, referred to previously. Participants had produced poems (produced through a metaphor exercise) about themselves and another group member. Each individual was asked to choose a small section which 'accurately and potently explains you', Ellie Rees explained. Each participant had produced a visual portrait on an overhead projector (OHP) and this was used in conjunction with the phrase or sentence selected to produce the diptych. Plastic and wooden letters were used to create the words on the OHP with the requirement that the sentence had to fit on the OHP. The editing process required participants to focus on the essentials, choosing words which most pertinently and concisely conveyed and encapsulated their preferences for self representation.

> Those birthday and Christmas cards fly around you like a flock of birds, delivering messages from friends and families you love. And even though you sold your ring, the memory is locked in your heart.
> (Meryam, writing about Roberta)

> Your wooden treasure trove protects your memories, under the bed. Dreams come out of it like magic
> (Roberta, writing about Meryam)

> (Mayo, 2011)

Rees contextualized the practice through an introduction to conceptual art, looking in particular at the work of Louise Bourgeois, Tracey Emin, Cornelia Parker, Annette Messenger and Helga Steppan. This session, Mayo observes, 'helped the whole group to begin to form a common understanding that the art that they were making might not be narrative or naturalistic, but could express ideas and emotions powerfully' (Mayo, 2011). This is endorsed by the comment of an adult participant:

> *I've changed my mind about modern art after this. It doesn't have to be symmetrical. I look at it in a different light. Wonky wavy words looked nicer. I kept trying to put things in order.*
>
> (Mayo, 2011)

The project culminated in an installation for an invited audience, followed by a tea party (a tradition of the library project). The audience were invited to contribute to the processes and materials in the project thereby engaging conceptually and creatively in reflecting on collecting, memories, archives, identity:

> Our invitation asked people to bring with them an object that held a memory for them. On arrival, the audience were asked to bring their object to a table, where group members labelled them and heard a little of the story. Then audience members could be photographed with their object, in Polaroid, to take home, and digitally. These images were added immediately to the installation.
>
> ...
>
> *It made it that people brought their objects. They were the most forthcoming at the tables because they had brought something. It was personalized.*
> (Adult participant)
>
> (Mayo, 2011)

The discussions with the audience (as evident in the conversation cited at the opening of this section) engaged with the themes of the project, exploring connections between histories and 'life-stories attached to gifts, souvenirs, travel tickets and items of clothing'. The dynamic relations between memory and learning and the ways in which this contributes to the construction of identity were evident.

The process and performance demonstrated the validity of LeDoux's perceptions:

> Learning, and its synaptic result, memory, play major roles in gluing a coherent personality together as one goes through life. Without learning and memory processes, personality would be merely an empty,

impoverished expression of our genetic constitution. Learning allows us to transcend our genes.

(LeDoux, 2002: 9–10)

Above all, the group engaged (through live art practices) in a conceptual and embodied understanding of memory and identity as a creative process, as encapsulated by Elizabeth Wilson:

> So memory neither produces something completely new, nor simply reproduces something that already exists. Instead, memory is 'literally manufactured' ... within or between already existing schemata. Memory is never the re-presentation of an element stored elsewhere; it is always an 'imaginative reconstruction', a constant variation without a discrete origin.
>
> (Wilson, 1998: 173)

3.5 MAKING IT REAL THROUGH APPLYING PERFORMANCE

Cognitive science investigates the relations between brain and body, arguing that our emotional and intellectual lives develop from our biology. The concept of self in terms of source or origin is challenged through conceptions of self (like memory) as fluid, mobile and multiple. For LeDoux, the self is described as a 'dramatic ensemble', 'not real, though it does exist' as 'the totality of what an organism is physically, biologically, socially and culturally' (LeDoux, 2002: 31). For Damasio, similarly and crucially, the mind is described as 'a process, not a thing' (1999: 183). Thus, in cognitive science the self is conceived as being like an autobiographical narrative: Damasio refers to a 'lived past and anticipated future' emerging from 'the gradual buildup of memories of ... the objects of the organism's biography' (Damasio, 1999: 196; cited in Blair, 2008: 66).

Imagination and emotion are similarly conceived in a synchronous rather than dichotomous relation to rationality. As Blair has written in relation to actor training:

> imagination is the result of the brain's evolutionary development and is essential to the fact of our physicality, not just our psyches. Actors consistently get at imagination by engaging the senses, e.g. the visual, aural, olfactory, and kinesthetic; we get at imagination and attention through the body ... Imagination, in not just its psychological, but also its physical dimensions, is a basic component of consciousness.
>
> (2008: 62)

Damasio is one of several neuroscientists to explore cognition and consciousness in terms of narrative and image construction:

> Consciousness begins when brains acquire the power, the simple power I must add, of telling a story without words, the story that there is life ticking away in an organism, and that the states of the living organism, within body bounds, are continuously being altered by encounters with objects or events in its environment ... Consciousness emerges when this primordial story – the story of an object causally changing the state of the body – can be told using the universal nonverbal vocabulary of [neural and chemical] body signals. The apparent self emerges as the feeling of a feeling.
>
> (1999: 30–1)

Damasio conceives of consciousness as deriving from 'the unified mental pattern that brings together the object and the self'. Psychoanalytic paradigms (also dependent on narrative formulations) are undermined as divisions between the unconscious and conscious are challenged.

As McConachie has argued, the 'truth' claims of several aspects of theatre and performance scholarship (particularly work which is informed by psychoanalysis and semiology) have been called into question by cognitive theory: 'Most cognitive scientists would agree that language has a role to play in the construction of thought, but its role derives from the embeddedness of language in the workings of the mind/brain ... in the making of meaning' (McConachie and Hart, 2006: 3). McConachie draws on cognitive theory to posit image schemas as conceptual developmental processes in the mind/brain prior to language. As the child explores the environment, their kinesthetic experiences and encounters create a series of conceptual paradigms, functioning as building blocks for negotiating, problem solving, action and agency. These conceptual systems, as Lakoff and Johnson have argued, are metaphorical in nature: 'metaphor is pervasive in everyday life, not just in language, but in thought and action ... our concepts are what we perceive, how we get around the world and how we relate to others' (1999: 3). Thus cognition, emotion and physiological processes are interconnected neurologically, while the ubiquity of metaphor and its centrality to our perception, experience and conceptualization involves us in Damasio's story making (with and without words) as a means of making sense of who we are – biologically, physically, kinaesthetically, socially. In the construction of metaphors and Damasio's stories, we are often involved in exploring ontological concepts at a profound level.

This chapter concludes with descriptions of two projects exploring lives and realities through a process of making and performing stories with and without words. The first (*My Home* by London Bubble) might be considered to fall outside of definitions of applied theatre and performance as a scripted piece made with actors for an audience. However, for my purposes the company's work is relevant, as the programme note to *My Home* makes clear: 'we have thought long and hard about how theatre is accessed these days – by who, and for what reason – and this has led us to a belief in making theatre both for, and with, people of all ages, to try and make it useful, to try and make it relevant, and to try and make it outside of black boxes.'[32] This particular piece is an example of the interplay between practices which are participatory and socially engaged (and might be deemed 'non-aesthetic' in Fischer-Lichte's terms) and aesthetic theatre for audiences.

My Home, directed by Karen Tomlin, responded to the alienation of Londoners through a series of multi-sensory installations in a series of houses in 2006. Stories were gathered through interviews with people from Polish, Vietnamese, Kurdish and Somali communities, all of whom were asked to talk about what home meant to them. 'Alienation is related to a sense of not knowing about, or connecting with, others', the Director writes, '*My Home* aims to look at some of the stories that people have to tell to try and make this connection a little closer.'[33] These connections were created through a performance contextualization. The script was verbatim, using interview material, while the staging of the piece in London houses was a further means of creating authenticity.

Home truths: London Bubble's *My Home*

In *My Home*, the use of a verbatim text and the staging of the piece in three different houses might be deemed to be strategies associated with the illusion of authenticity. This was in counterpoint to the to production's staging strategies. As Petherbridge explains, although the company wanted the audience to accept that the performers were speaking the words as if they were occupants of the domestic environments they were inhabiting, the actors were also aware of themselves as 'channels', or vehicles for personal testimonies, delivering text which was owned by the person whose life the actor was representing. The ethics of verbatim performance have been extensively discussed (Hammond and Stuart, 2008; Martin, 2010; Paget, 1987), but in this conception what was involved for performer and audience was a process of cognitive blending whereby we are aware of the actor representing another whilst simultaneously participating in the illusion of the fictive performer being the person represented in the here and now. The design also framed the performance as both real and fictive. Thus the audience was aware that the performers did not really belong in the house

Figure 5   Sarah Hobson in London Bubble's *My Home*. Photograph by kind permission of Steve Hickey and London Bubble

and that the rooms were constructed environments. The rooms themselves were designed to provoke a physical and embodied engagement with the space. When the audience arrive, a 'Somali Man' leans out of a window and throws down the door keys, inviting the audience to let themselves in. Once inside, the door closes behind the audience and 'the dark space lightens to illuminate photos on the wall.' Thus we move from a staging which we might associate with site specific performance to something more theatrical and naturalistic. The Somali Man joins the audience to talk about his 'special home' as if it is the one they are in, but his description of the white walls, the balcony and the large garden with sea views and which is full of fruit (and which he throws at the audience) is manifestly not a reference to this converted house in Camberwell. Various staging devices also ensure that the audience's disbelief remains intact, whilst aromas provoke their sensual engagement in ways which we also associate with contemporary modes of performance. Cigarette smoke lingers as the audience hear the voices of three Polish men in the living room, but on entering they discover the voices emanating from a chair, a tea cup and a radio. This mode of surprise and estrangement creates awareness of and draws attention to the construction of these stories and the nature of our engagement with them so that in this example, encounters with objects change consciousness (to use Damasio's terms). Some scenes were created wholly through sound such as the recording of a baby being bathed behind a closed bathroom door. The audience's presence as groups of twelve individuals also acted as a framing strategy, being aware of themselves within a large group in small and intimate spaces whilst also being aware of the responses of others. Many of the staging strategies are those we associate with immersive installation and one-to-one performance, but the organization of the group prevented the audience from becoming submerged in illusion. Moving around the house made the audience conscious of their role as spectators and participants, encountering something which is staged. Indeed, to some extent, the house corresponded to an exhibition and the performers were exhibits, objects which, like the teacup, were vessels for communicating the stories of others. However, the experience was also one which was moving and affecting, engaging the audience in critical empathy. In the bedroom, a girl described her transition to adulthood. Nostalgia was avoided as the performer was so obviously not the originator of the story, but an adult, partially dressed in the clothes of her childhood. In the white Kurdish bedroom, the actress, 'like a child in a bunk bed', spoke of her experience of arriving in England. As she climbed out of bed she revealed her white socks. The speech moved into adulthood and she dressed accordingly layering her clothes according to her age and her experience of changing cultures. The truths in this piece emerged not from a sense of association with the origin of the stories (as they were so obviously removed from this context), but through the visceral and visual experiences which create embodied engagement. The house and the performers were situated in a liminal space between the real lives they were representing and the everyday which the audience, to some extent, brought to the performance as participants in the presentation of the environment and its atmosphere. In the Polish woman's room, the audience sat on boxes as the performer set out tea, apples and honey offering them out as she talked about her memories of the orange carpet of her home and unfiltered cigarette smoke. In this private yet public space, the audience were invited to make connections with the lives and the experiences of these people and it is in this sense, hearing the stories of hardship, alienation and the difficulties of moving from one home to another that they engaged with issues of citizenship – not in an abstract sense as in an issue-based piece but on a much deeper level. The audience learned about the traditions, rituals, habits, tastes and smells of the different homes represented by the performers in the production. This involved an empathic engagement through the provocation of the senses, but the empathy experienced was also (and simultaneously) critical as the audience remained conscious of the feeling of themselves being moved, and the strategies used to solicit their responses.

The true real: Mark Storer's *Fat Girl Gets a Haircut and Other Stories*

My final example in this chapter is a piece made with teenagers by Mark Storer, exploring 'the transition from childhood to adolescence and into adulthood' (programme note). This was performed at the Roundhouse in 2011 after a two-year development process which included 'crawling around Trafalgar Square in laundry bags, creating a mermaid out of lettuce leaves and making outfits out of paper'. All the stories are 'true' according to the programme and these are described as 'the heart of the show'. Most of Storer's work is devised, often site responsive and collaborative. It is generally also autobiographical, using the lives of the participants Storer works with as a stimulus.

I have selected Storer's piece to end this chapter for a number of reasons. Firstly, Storer's work is profoundly affecting (Nicholson, 2011); this is achieved through a relationship between form, content and process. Storer has previously worked in settings ranging from working men's clubs to hospitals (with children on a renal ward) and although his work has been written about previously in the context of both site-specific and educational performance, he is absolutely clear that his priority is to create high-quality art. In this production, the performance took place in a theatre and this was one of reasons for its selection, as I wanted to feature a staged piece within my range of examples.

The piece was performed but not acted. Occasionally a performer would stumble or hesitate, a reminder to the audience of who the performers were. The style of delivery was similar to companies such as Forced Entertainment who have, paradoxically, perfected the art of non-matrixed acting. It is, however, extremely difficult to achieve, particularly for student performers. It involves understanding how to be 'in the moment', acknowledging the relationship with the audience. Storer's process was clearly play-based, using a series of exercises and experiences to explore identities within liminal environments. For Storer's teenagers, an understanding of multiple selves and of subjectivity in terms of narrative appears to have been endemic to the process.

As the piece opened ('I let you look at me') the performers drew attention to themselves, entering from the back of the auditorium and moving slowly forward from our space towards the stage on which was positioned a white sheet surrounded by pristine plastic tomato ketchup bottles. A boy crouching was ritualistically splattered by the ketchup. I was reminded of Bobby Baker's *Drawing on a Mother's Experience*, in which she used black treacle to signify post-natal depression, wrapping herself in the sheet, foetus-like, and rolling off at the end of the show. Ketchup, of course, like Baker's black treacle and Finley's chocolate and honey is metaphor laden, so whilst this may be creative borrowing (and Bobby Baker was involved in workshops as part of the process so it was clearly a formative influence), it is powerful in ways that so many Baker imitations are not. Ketchup is associated with childhood, a sweet and happy substance according to my children when I ask them what it signifies. Yet its colour and texture are also associated with blood and wounding. It simultaneously connotes pleasure and pain and thus the ketchup-splattering moves from fun play to deep play and then to something more disturbing as the messy play became increasingly violent. The boy's body, crouched and foetus-like, appeared to be battered by the blood-red streaks. He was wrapped in cloth and rolled off – as object and subject. This opening sequence may have been what provoked my partner's comment at the end of the show: 'It knocks the spots off all those little improvs about bullying.' This may or may not have been a reference to bullying as it worked on a more ambiguous level, permitting a range of readings and responses. Difference and humiliation were one of the central themes: 'there is a fat girl in our story and she cut her hair many years ago. Our fat girl today could be a boy. Much better that she cut her hair of her own volition than cutting it because of the taunts and hurtful jibes of others.'[34]

A series of selves, identities and memories were explored. Each performer appeared to be telling their own story as there were 11 performers and 12 stories. The association of each story with a performer created a strong sense of empathy as we responded to their honesty and vulnerability through what appeared to be very open and sometimes raw material. Caged birds featured prominently in circulating projections and some breathtakingly beautiful shadow puppetry. Two 'swallow' scenes, explored repressed emotion, entrapment (through images of containment) and the desire for freedom. The pleasure and pain of the show involved laughter as performers played with wigs, masks and mirrors, leading to a pig dance under the story title 'Infidel'. This was visual object theatre, designed by Alexa Reed, a visual artist whose work, like Storer's, 'crosses between theatre, live art and installation'. Bauhaus-inspired references created the enchantment Schiller called for. In 'The Boy who cried for the world cries', the performer wore a paper costume which was then immersed in a pool of water. An awakening to sexuality was explored in 'My Body, My Secret', which referred to the children's party game of eating apples (in pairs and blindfolded), without dropping the fruit. This game, played between a boy and girl, evoked emergent sexuality with beauty and simplicity: 'if kissing is a game, then what is love? If life is a game, where do we start? And how do we finish?' Although the strength of this piece was the stories themselves, the staging reflected and complemented the beauty of the autobiographical narratives. The climax of the show was arguably the most moving. 'How to make a paper Daffodil' told the story of a child's loss of her mother: 'I made paper daffodils in nursery. They were made with egg cups and paper. I made them for her. It was the last Mother's Day we had'. The story was told as a monologue, using a memory box as a focus. As each item was affectionately and poignantly revealed to the audience, family photographs were projected around the circular auditorium, culminating in a picture of a very frail mother with her daughter in a garden. This, we were told, was the last photograph taken. In the final moments of the piece, the performer entered the large bird cage which had descended and exchanged her dress for her mother's. As the bird cage ascended, an antique-looking paper wedding dress was flown down. Lighting contributed to the provocation of emotion in this sequence. According to Kandinsky, 'shades of colour, like those of sound are a much finer texture and awake in the soul emotions too fine to be expressed in words' (2006: 82). Words were certainly powerful in this piece, but colour and sound were equally part of the palette of emotional textures. Lighting and colour were used, as in Wilson's theatre, to transform objects and the dress became, as if by magic, the ghostly and beautiful evocation of presence and absence through memory.

In this production, the aesthetics of the piece were inextricably related to the process and to its pedagogy. Storer's work has integrity because it emerges so clearly and visibly from the participants whose material is transformed through a play based process into something fusing poiesis and praxis – Schiller's enchanting pedagogy.

4
Placing Performance

4.1 PLACING APPLIED PERFORMANCE

> it is not a matter of choosing sides – between models of nomadism and sedentariness, between space and place, between digital interfaces and the handshake. Rather, we need to be able to think the range of the seeming contradictions and our contradictory desires for them together; to understand, in other words, seeming oppositions as *sustaining* relations ... Only those cultural practices that have this relational sensibility can turn local encounters into long term commitments and transform passing intimacies into indelible, unretractable social marks – so that the sequence of sites that we inhabit in our life's traversal does not become genericized into an undifferentiated serialization, one place after another.
>
> (Kwon, 2004: 166)

In this chapter I consider how site, space and place feature in the theory and practice of applied performance. I explore the relational sensibilities characterizing this work (in terms of place as a process of making, embedded in a dynamic and mutually constitutive relationship between the physical and social environment) and challenge the dichotomies associated with site and place.

Site-specific art moves performance beyond theatre spaces and galleries and is defined by Nick Kaye as a medium which consists of 'exchanges between the work of art and the places in which its meanings are defined' (2000: 65). The complex and shifting dialogues between performance and site/space/place, and the abundance of practices exploring and interrogating these relations has been discussed and debated by a wide range of scholars (and practitioners) from different disciplines: in performance, scholars such as Jen Harvie, Dee Heddon, Kathleen Irwin, Gay McAuley, Mike Pearson, Heike Roms, Cathy Turner and Fiona Wilkie converse with contemporary art historians and critics such as Miwon Kwon and geographers such as Nigel Thrift and Doreen Massey as well as anthropologists such as Kathleen

Stewart. Fiona Wilkie's essay 'Mapping the Terrain' discusses her survey of site-specific performance in Britain from 2000 to 2001 (2010). She identifies popular sites as parks/playgrounds; workplace buildings/sites; churches; galleries/theatre building environs; museums and grounds; beaches; tunnels, shopping centres, hospitals and castles. Many of these sites are public or cultural spaces, associated with particular communities or institutions. A variety of practice has been variously conceptualized and categorized as site responsive, site sympathetic, site generic, environmental art, context sensitive or specific, landscape theatre, place responsive etc. Within these critical and practical configurations and engagements there is, as Pearson notes, a movement from 'fixity to mobility, from architectonic to peripatetic ... from expositional to relational modes' (Pearson, 2010: 8).

The synergies between site- and place-responsive performance and work defined as applied theatre is evident in Jen Harvie's appraisal: 'Site-specific performance can be especially powerful as a vehicle for remembering and forming a community for at least two reasons. First, its location can work as a potent mnemonic trigger, helping to evoke specific past times related to the place and time of performance and facilitating a negotiation between the meanings of those times' (2005: 42). A number of practitioners and companies have produced work which is site or place responsive and socially engaged. Building on the pioneering work of Brith Gof and Welfare State International, UK companies such as Emergency Exit Arts, and Walk the Plank, produce work which uses spectacle as a means of community celebration, drawing upon historical, cultural and contemporary associations in their work in public spaces. Companies such as IOU, Red Earth, Wrights and Sites, and Lone Twin engage in various ways with site and place as source/stimulus and as community engagement. Gay McAuley's typology is particularly pertinent as she explores the potential of site as a means to change the spectator's engagement with and perception of a particular place, whilst she also alerts us to the ethics of place-responsive performance, 'locally based spectators experience an enhanced kind of creative agency in that their knowledge of the place and history may well be deeper than that of the performance makers, and they will continue to frequent the place after the performers have left' (2007: 9).

For practitioners engaged in work that is participatory and socially engaged, the emphasis shifts from landscape (or what Kwon refers to as a 'phenomenological or experiential understanding of the site') to the lived experiences of the inhabitants within the places of performance. This often involves working in institutional or historical contexts, re-animating derelict sites through live art or producing performance in the context of working environments (industrial or social). A pioneer for this work might be seen in Deborah Warner's 1999 Euston *Tower Project*, which reclaimed the empty offices of a vacant London tower block to create an enigmatic blending of site-specific and installation art. Abandoned rooms (with a Marie Celeste quality) contained elements of office furniture (a filing cabinet left open, a phone off the hook and a fax machine churning out *Paradise Lost*), while bizarre encounters with virtual sheep in corridors and angels in windows left the spectator (required to experience the journey in isolation) with a profound sense of estrangement as the spectacular views of the bustling city were seen from a very different perspective within the surreal world Warner created. This was not participant-centred or socially engaged work, but live art was used to re-animate the site and to shift our perceptions of, and engagement with, a profoundly symbolic space. The industrious business environment was transformed into a ghostly, haunted place; its previous inhabitants had presence through absence, evoked through the chairs and objects left in transition in the space between departure and return and we were left to question what it is all for. This project subsequently migrated to Perth and New York, an example of the mobility of site-responsive work and its chameleon qualities.

Whilst Warner's project might be considered in relation to the second category of Kwon's paradigm as social/institutional (whereby site work is redefined in more public contexts, rather than being purely physical or spatial in orientation), various practitioners can be seen to have developed similar models which are more overtly socially engaged as well as being site-specific or site-responsive. Kathleen Irwin's 'found-space' projects in Canada, for example and particularly, *The Weyburn Project* (2002) which was set in a disused wing of the old Saskatchewan 'Mental' Hospital in Weyburn (now the Souris Valley Extended Day Care Centre). Irwin's work with Nowhere Productions explores the potential of site in terms of time, space and community. Drawing on oral history as well as various publications and archival research, this project explored the history of mental health treatment (the hospital was pioneering in its use of 'work and water' treatments in the early twentieth century and its drug-based experiments, particularly LSD). The devised performance involved an evocative journey through a phantom site, where the stories of former patients, family members, doctors and nurses were articulated through visceral performance as the audience were able to 'see, hear, smell and touch the evocations and impressions presented by installations, performers, spoken words, live music and most of all through the sounds and silence of the building itself' (Weyburn, 2002). This was politically committed art, an event which was designed to intervene in the site and the history it represented; the performance used live art to engage in dialogue with the building:

> The architecture and monumentality of the building is not mute on notions of utopianism and modernity; it is a graphic articulation of an edenic social project driven by paternalistic systems of governance. The building's deterioration and decay frame the discourse differently. Is it a monolithic marker of a failed project of modernism? Such an

ulterior reading suggests binaries of self-expression/institutionalization, self-determination/control that were the immediate concerns of the 'inmates' and reflect the concurrent emergent issues that define the post-modern period.

(Irwin, 2002)

Projects such as Martha Bowers's *The Dream Life of Bricks* (discussed in Part III), are similarly conceived to create experiential performance events through embodied engagement with sites and places: reconfiguring the histories they house, exploring the memories they contain and the complex relations between ourselves and the physical or built environment. Above all this work is a means of 'remembering and forming communities' to use Harvie's terms. As such, the work moves into Kwon's 'discursive' realm, engaging with the politics of place, the cultural, social and personal histories which are blended through performance with myths, dreams and memory as part of the complex textures of site-related work.

For many practitioners, site-responsive work is also participant centred. Mark Storer's 2004 *Visiting Time* (a participatory piece at a working hospital in Dorset) and his 2007 *Boy Child* (in a wing of the former Admiralty Underwater Weapons Establishment in Southwell Park, Portland, Dorset) have been described by Anna Ledgard as 'site-specific' and 'pedagogically engaged' (2010). As Ledgard and Nicholson have noted in their accounts of his work, Storer's practice defies categorization as he moves between and beyond live art, performance and applied theatre (Nicholson, 2011). Both pieces discussed by Ledgard were funded by the Arts Council, England, and the Wellcome Trust and both involved a collaboration between Ledgard as producer and educationist and Storer as performance maker. *Visiting Time* involved working in conjunction with health professionals and patients. The participants were cast as 'patients' and invited (in groups of five) to an 'appointment':

> They were tagged and swabbed, and led by performers, all clad in pyjamas and pillow-head masks, through a working hospital, encountering along the way a series of performance installations. In one a 'pillow-head' figure, limbless, trapped in a cotton-wool cocoon, attempted to keep a balloon in the air ... In the lecture theatre a scientist asked the audience the enigmatic question: 'How can I make a snowball when my hands are always hot?', referring to a condition associated with cystic fibrosis.
>
> (Ledgard, 2010)

The difficulties of working in the context of a functioning hospital and the ensuing affects of Storer's interventions for those he is working with are also discussed by Nicholson in her moving account of *For the Best,* a performance piece Storer developed in conjunction with his experiences of working with children in a renal unit. The influence of *Visiting Time* on the later piece is clear, not simply because of the hospital context, but in the visceral qualities of the performance which engage audiences physically and emotionally; the beauty of Storer's imagery where objects speak louder than words and the embodied engagement his work facilitates through a personal practice which makes no distinction between the participatory and creative elements.

In *Boychild*, Storer and Ledgard worked with boys from Portland Young Offender's Institution exploring their experiences of incarceration and pubescence. The site for this piece was to some extent, extraneous for it was chosen as an appropriate environment for performing the material Storer and Ledgard were developing, rather than being directly associated with the participants (i.e., this was not a 'lived' environment for those involved). This is in keeping with Storer's interest in transforming or transgressing space; the changing of the space from 'literal' to 'dramatic', from 'expected' to 'unexpected' (Ledgard, 2010). Storer's work has the ludic and magical qualities of Robert Lepage and the visual and compositional strength of Robert Wilson. Ledgard describes how he encourages participants to perceive differently by defamiliarizing the environment, changing the layout, introducing 'symbolic' objects or 'disrupting' the space, to facilitate new kinds of engagement. Storer's work can be seen as context responsive whilst being situated between applied modes of performance and live art.

Space and place in applied performance

Applied performance is ambulant and peripatetic; it is often situated outside of the black and white boxes of buildings based theatre and adjacent to the production activities on company websites where education, outreach or participation are identified as separate categories, differentiating a company's work in educational, social and community contexts from its mainstream production activities. This means that applied theatre is often defined as 'other' in relation to the performance work of many companies (exceptions are those companies whose work is focused on applied theatre and performance). Sue Mayo of Magic Me recounts how a performer once protested vehemently, 'I don't do workshops', and was pacified by a director who introduced Sue as the 'workshop person'.[1] Indeed, the workshop is often regarded as the place of applied performance, a place where things are made, but which is not a site of production per se. Whilst applied theatre scholars challenge such misconceptions and divisions, the turn to site in performance studies has led to new understandings of many of the practices associated with applied performance. Although it is clear, as Sally Mackey and Nicholas Whybrow argue, 'that both site and place have, in a sense always been integral to applied practices' (2007), research across and within a range of disciplines, particularly geography (Cresswell, 2004; Massey, 2005; Relph, 1976; Tuan, 1974, 1977); anthropology (Low and Lawrence-Zuniga, 2003); philosophy (Casey, 1993);

and phenomenology (Merleau-Ponty, 2002) have contributed new understandings of space and place in terms of process. The relations between the two concepts continue to be debated and performance studies has been one of several disciplines contributing to the burgeoning research in this area. Place is most frequently associated with stability and fixity. The traveller lost in Descartes's seventeenth-century forest is advised 'not to wander from side to side, far less remain in *one place*, but proceed constantly towards the same side in as straight a line as possible, without changing their direction for slight reasons ... for in this way, if they do not exactly reach the point they desire, they will come at least in the end to *some place* that will probably be preferable to the middle of a forest' (1924: 25). Descartes anticipates much subsequent writing on space, place and cognition in his use of theatrical metaphor. In his nine years of wandering, he states, 'I did nothing but roam from one place to another, desirous of being a spectator rather than an actor in the plays exhibited on the theater of the world' (27). Twentieth-century phenomenology (particularly in the writing of Merleau-Ponty) challenges such distinctions, suggesting that meaning is made (embodied) through our physical relations with the material environment. Thus the traveller is an actor, producing meaning through his physical and social interactions.

In *The Practice of Everyday Life* de Certeau famously distinguishes between place and space:

> Space occurs as the effect produced by the operations that orient it, situate it, temporalize it ... in relation to place, space is like the word when it is spoken, that is, when it is caught in the ambiguity of an actualization, transformed into a term dependent upon many conventions, situated as the act of a present (or of a time), and modified by the transformations caused by successive contexts ... *space is a practiced place.*
>
> (1984: 117; emphasis in original)

The reference here to the 'word' is indicative of de Certeau's distinctive blend of psychoanalytic and poststructuralist theoretical perspectives. For de Certeau, the story functions to 'authorize' or to '*found*'; it 'opens a legitimate *theater* for practical *actions*' (117, 125; emphasis in original). The movements of actors/pedestrians, 'spatialize' as they engage in the 'rhetoric of walking': 'a law made into a story and historicized ... recounted by bodies' (149). As urban practitioners walk, they 'write' text through the movement of their bodies but cannot read it, creating 'networks' of writings, multiple and polyvalent, 'a manifold story that has neither author nor spectator' (93). Place, in this conception, is other to space; it becomes 'dreamed', a desire, an imaginary realm: 'to walk is to lack a place. It is the indefinite process of being absent and in search of a proper. The moving about that the city multiplies and concentrates makes the city itself an immense social experience of lacking a place' (103).

Drawing upon his psychoanalytic influences, de Certeau conceptualizes place in similar terms to memory:

> A memory is only a Prince Charming who stays just long enough to awaken the Sleeping Beauties of our wordless stories. *'Here*, there used to be a bakery.' *'That's* where old lady Dupuis used to live.' It is striking here that the places people live in are like the presences of diverse absences. What can be seen designates what is no longer there: 'You *see*, here there used to be ...', but it can no longer be seen. Demonstratives indicate the invisible identities of the visible: it is the very definition of a place, in fact, that it is composed by these series of displacements and effects among the fragmented strata that form it and that it plays on these moving layers.
>
> (1984: 108)

In de Certeau's psychoanalytic paradigm, place is conceived as 'other' in relation to space. Indeed, as in various other configurations, place is associated with the feminine, the m/other (as well as bodily experience and sensation: 'I feel good here'):

> how about the female foetus who is from this very moment [the mirror stage] introduced into another relationship to space ... what counts is the process of this 'spatial captation' that inscribes the passage toward the other as the law of being and the law of place. To practice space is thus to repeat the joyful and silent experience of childhood; it is, in a place, *to be other and to move toward the other*.
>
> (1984: 110)

Thus space, for de Certeau, is associated with the urban, the symbolic (and masculine) order of language and law, while place is the feminized other. 'Thus begins the walk that Freud compares to the trampling underfoot of the mother-land' (110).

As various feminist critics have argued, place is too readily equated with the maternal, the unconscious, the imaginary and nature (Grosz, 2002; Haraway, 1989; Irigaray, 1992; Massey, 2005; Rose, 1993, 1996), while the production of space and spatial knowledges is associated with masculinist authority. The evocative title of Rose's 1996 article, challenges the dominant sexualized paradigms: 'As if the mirrors had bled: Masculine dwelling, masculinist theory and feminist masquerade.' Drawing on the work or Luce Irigaray and Judith Butler, Rose produces a piece of performative writing which experiments with multiple voices to articulate different identities, challenging distinctions between real and imagined space. In 'Making Space for the Female Subject of Feminism', she has argued that the 'process of representation is central to everyday space and to the en-gendering of subjects in that space' and urges geographers to be aware of 'the female subject of feminism [which] is not to be able to name a specific kind of spatiality which she would produce; rather it is to be vigilant abut the consequences of different kinds of spatiality' (Rose, 1995: 354).

For Elizabeth Grosz, the problem is the need to 'reveal the masculine inherent in the notion of the universal' (2002: 300), as a means to expose the gendered coding in the conception of the city as 'body-politic' into which the individual feminine body is subsumed. Grosz also critiques Lefebvre's concept of the production of space, challenging the humanist principles underpinning models of the city as extensions or productions of the human subject. She problematizes models of the city as a projection of the body and the positioning of women in the disjunction between body and map, as well as totalizing views of the body and city as fixed and unchanging. The model Grosz proposes involves a dynamic relationship between the body and city, an 'interface' with connections and temporary forms of 'co-building' (2002: 301). As I will show, there are synergies here with the cognitive approaches explored in this chapter.

The theatrical challenge to Peter Brook's notion of the 'empty space' in theatre has been led by semioticians and feminist critics, drawing upon poststructuralist theory to develop a vocabulary for analysing performance as a series of referents and relationships. Thus *space* in theatre criticism is frequently understood in terms of the *mise-en-scène* and a 'reading' of performance involves understanding all the elements of composition. Performance in non-theatre spaces can be similarly analysed in these terms through a deconstruction of the elements of composition to examine the making of meaning. De Certeau, however, has also been useful for feminist and performance theorists as he regards the practice of everyday life as potentially subversive, resisting the regulated structures of power. Hence his relevance to applied theatre and interventionist performance practices. Thus space and spatial relations are conceived in terms of constraint; de Certeau's notion of the relations between 'strategy' (associated with organizing systems of authority) and 'tactics' (the means to resist or find alternatives) gives value to the ordinary and the vernacular as subversive. There are, he suggests (in a passage which reminds me of Boal) '[i]nnumerable ways of playing and foiling the other's game ... that is, the space instituted by others, characterizes the subtle, stubborn, resistant activity of groups which, *since they lack their own space*, have to get along in a network of already established forces and representations' (de Certeau, 1984: 18). Space here is presented as a structure to be inhabited or resisted. It is not fixed, however, as it can be unmade: 'A practice of the order constructed by others redistributes its space; it creates at least a certain play in that order, a space for maneuvers of unequal forces and for utopian points of reference' (18).

Although space refers to the architectural and structural aspects of a physical environment, it is also 'situated' to use Merleau-Ponty's terms, an 'embodied HERE' (1962: 17/14). The body remains central to this perception of space, functioning like speech or words as the maker of meaning, creating syntax in its routes through space. De Certeau's account associates place with lived experience (and I am surely not alone in pondering why place isn't practised space?). Like space, place is something which is also made but whereas space is practised or effected through the performance of bodies and objects (the means whereby the position of things becomes possible), place is created, at least in part, through affect – a concept which has been embraced by applied theatre scholars and practitioners but which is missing in de Certeau's account. Cameron Duff argues that de Certeau's account 'has largely ignored the *felt* and *affective dimensions* of city life ... To experience place is to be *affected by place*, just as it involves an active reckoning of the tactical opportunities and practical resources places invariably present' (Duff, 2010: 881).

A cognitive perspective offers a means of reconceptualizing the relations between space and place, challenging psychoanalysis and poststructuralism through scientific paradigms whilst also engaging in productive dialogue with phenomenology. In *Philosophy in the Flesh*, Lakoff and Johnson set the scene: 'Our sense of what is real begins with and depends crucially upon our bodies, especially our sensorimotor apparatus, which enables us to perceive, move and manipulate and the detailed structures of our brains, which have been shaped by both evolution and experience' (1999: 17). Language, in the context of cognitive science, emerges from and is embedded within the workings of the mind/brain. As Blair has summarized: 'language arises directly out of our physical beings: consciousness, reason, and language are a direct manifestation of our bodies and the sense we have of ourselves as bodies' (Blair, 2008: 17). Thus in terms of cognitive science (although its relationship with phenomenology continues to be debated), we are not merely subject to but have agency in our embodied engagement with the world and the 'production of place' can be regarded as part of this process.

In this chapter, I will explore through a series of case studies how place can be conceived as an embodied activity and as a way of being in the world (rather than a fixed location), as practice (the production and performance of locations, identities) and as transformation (changing our perceptions and understanding of the lived environment). I will examine the interplay between space and place through performance as a means of transforming space into place and place into space.

Site and place

Site and place are also integral to visual and live art practices which have moved beyond the clean quiet cubes of gallery spaces, to question who art is for, where it can be staged and to explore the experience of spectatorship. As Leslie Hill and Helen Paris have asked: 'what is the place of this kind of work in this kind of place'? (Hill and Paris, 2006: 9). Live art and applied performance are situated on a continuum in which place, the body and human activity are interconnected; what distinguishes one practice from the other is the nature and function of the artefact and the relationship between performer and spectator. Writing about 'new genre public art' (a variant of applied performance and live art in the United States which seeks to 'push the boundaries of public art as we have come to know it and engage the public in a dialogue about the place and meaning of art in our daily lives'), Suzanne Lacy suggests 'what exists in the space between the words "public" and "art" is an unknown relationship between artist and audience, a relationship that may *itself* be the art work' (1994: 20). Aesthetic paradigms are challenged through practice which 'shifts the focus from artist to audience, from object to process, from production to reception and emphasizes the importance of a direct, apparently unmediated engagement with particular audience groups' (106). These relationships are, however, mediated through curators and the institutional contexts in which the work is situated, as discussed below. However, the attraction of non-gallery, non-studio and non-theatre spaces is conceived by Lacy and Kwon as the encounter with 'real' people in 'real' places.

The concept of site in theatre and performance has been discussed by a number of theorists and practitioners (Etchells, 1999; Irwin, 2009; Kaye, 2000; Lavery, 2007; Pavis, 2003), but for my purposes, the work of Mike Pearson has been particularly influential, perhaps due to Pearson's experience as a practitioner working in social and community contexts. Pearson's definition of site is broad ranging (encompassing site-determined, site-oriented, site-referenced, site-conscious, site-responsive, site-related and other permutations) and establishes the contextual landscape in which the work discussed here is situated:

> I suggest that the conventions and techniques of the auditorium may be inappropriate or inadequate to the task of addressing 'site.' And that site-specific performance is other than a transposition and modification of stage practices. If the stage is essentially *synecdochic* – in which limited resources stand in for a complete picture, as when a chair and tables suggests a domestic scene – site is frequently a plenitude, its inherent characteristics, manifold effects and unruly elements always liable to leak, spill and diffuse into performance ... Although the stage is a site of imagination and site is always inescapably itself, site may be transformed by the disruptive presence of performance seeking a relationship other than that of a ready-made scenic backdrop against which to place its figures.
>
> (2010: 1–2)

Analysis of the relationships between artists and participants in the performance of site and place has been informed by phenomenology's reconceptualization of subject–object relations and the challenging of mind/body dualisms. Merleau-Ponty's embodiment theory and phenomenology of the senses ([1962] 2002, and 1974, Heidegger's concept of *dasein*

(1977) and Bourdieu's notion of habitas have all informed current conceptions of place in terms of fluidity, a constant process of making and being: 'places are constructed by people doing things and in this sense are never "finished" but are constantly being performed' (Cresswell, 2004: 37).

Problematizing place

According to Heidegger, 'we do not dwell because we have built, but we build because we are dwellers' (1977: 326). Place has been defined as space(s) 'which people have made meaningful' (Cresswell, 2004: 7). Performance contributes to this process through the creation of events which, in various ways, draw upon histories, cultural and personal memories, identities (in flux) and the journeys that move us between places, contributing to the understanding which distinguishes one place from another. During the writing of this chapter, Japan was struck by a huge earthquake, followed by a tsunami. My writing about place was against a backdrop of images of displacement – devastated homes and communities and the endeavour to construct shelters as temporary homes in the face of adversity. Humanist conceptions of place may have been subject to feminist and poststructuralist critiques as patriarchal, domestic and universalizing (Rose, 1993), but the making of place is something we continue to 'do'. The earthquake, tsunami and the ensuing nuclear disaster in Japan were occurring alongside the escalating conflict in Libya, where the negative aspects of place making were staged: 'Territorialism, introversion, defensiveness and boundary-making that excludes difference can be all too familiarly depressing signs of more negative practices associated with located or local place' (Mackey and Whybrow, 2007: 6).

Although place is often perceived in terms of stability ('there's no place like home') and rootedness, the boundaries constructed to distinguish one place from another and the factors associated with belonging to a place are also associated with nostalgia, parochialism, exclusion and violence. In discussing place, we also need to be conscious of the related conditions of placelessness and displacement. Performance can also be implicated in this process. The arts industry, as Reid and Smith have observed, has made a significant contribution to regeneration projects such as the Lower East Side in New York City, promoting the gentrification process associated with urban renewal which, however, increases property prices and causes the displacement of the poor:

> Gentrification, [protestors] argue, is *not* for the good of all and is *not* a progressive development from the perspective of the community and its residents. For them, it means homelessness, displacement, expensive and inaccessible housing, and a challenge to their cultural diversity, practices and tolerance that have been a mark of their neighbourhood.
>
> (Reid and Smith, 1993: 199; cited in Cresswell, 2004: 95)

In the United Kingdom, conversions of industrial buildings into art centres and studios (e.g., Arnolfini in Bristol) are part of a process of urban renewal, while construction of flagship galleries in areas of cultural deprivation (e.g., Baltic and Sage in Newcastle and Gateshead and Turner Contemporary in Margate) are similarly designed to contribute to regeneration and to promote social inclusion through widening participation in the arts. Regeneration has been defined by the Department of Media, Culture and Sport (DCMS) as 'the positive transformation of a place – whether residential, commercial or open space – that has previously displayed symptoms of physical, social and/or economic decline' (DCMS, 2006). A subsequent definition from the Department of Communities and Local Government (CLG) considers regeneration as a set of activities that '*reverse* economic, social, and physical decline in areas where market forces will not do this' (2008; my emphasis). Regeneration, however, may mean displacement for some as evident in, for example, the Kent coastal town of Whitstable, which in the 1990s became a fashionable watering hole for Londoners, many of whom bought second homes or relocated and commuted to London. Fisherman's cottages were transformed into boutique accommodation, the harbour became home to award-winning restaurants, and the high street was revitalized, earning the label 'Notting Hill-on-Sea', although butchers, grocers and local crafts shops survived as part of the heritage attracting commerce. Londoners came to Whitstable for the local, the quaint and the historical so preservation, renovation and tourism drove the local economy. Property prices escalated and the once derelict beach huts were suddenly a sought after commodity. With Whitstable transformed into a fashionable town (complete with new arts centre) featured in Sunday newspapers, the rising costs of housing and the associated effects of gentrification have contributed to social migration, leading to increased populations in rural Thanet (Margate, Broadstairs and Folkstone) as the less affluent moved further down the Kent coast.

In Margate, a culturally-led regeneration strategy, based on the premise that 'culture' can function as a connector of communities, defined its first priority as 'place making and place shaping.'[2] Thus the MRP (Margate Renewal Partnership) defines place in terms of politics and cultural policy, a reminder that 'place', as Cresswell notes, 'is invested with meaning in the context of power'. In Margate, however, a sustained campaign and a range of participatory arts projects have begun a process of transformation in which we see a different politics of place, as practiced, performed and lived. A figurehead and public voice for the regeneration of the town is the artist Tracy Emin:

> *Every time I come here something has gone, something is missing. This time it's the scenic railway. Another time it's the big wheel. After the storms of 87 it was the pier. In the Eighties it was the entire Lido complex. Every single time I come something has been burnt, destroyed, fire bombed, boarded up,*

demolished or just completely forgotten about and left to go in to a tragic state of disrepair.

It's strange to witness the death of a town. In some ways there is a melancholy romance. It's like the tragic set of a film, but the sad thing is that the star is Margate. Margate has become Britain's tragic Norma Desmond from Sunset Boulevard, almost nothing can save her.

I never imagined in a million years that, at the age of 44, I would be sitting in my car, staring out of my window, thinking these thoughts. As a child Margate had magic. It had charisma. It had a sense of humour. But it also had incredible architecture, thousands of holidaymakers, day-trippers, beauty competitions, a thousand fish-and-chip shops, a harbour full of hundreds of brightly coloured fishing boats and an incredible Victorian funfair.

All of this had the backdrop of some of the most beautiful sunsets in the world. And that is not an exaggeration. Turner painted enough of them. And if you study Turner's seascapes, in many of his miscellaneous seascapes, imaginary seascapes, the sunset you most definitely see sets in Margate. There is something about this place which is so shaggable. It lends itself to raunchy. It makes me feel sexy being here. Even with the depression of everything falling down, everything collapsing, the sexiness of Margate overrides any of that kind of depression. Kiss Me Quick is an understatement. I sit here feeling very, very sad.

I want someone who is a giant to come along and treat Margate like their very own special model village. I want them to return Margate to its man-made majestic beauty. I want them to lovingly recreate the scenic railway and the big wheel. Make Dreamlands a place possible for teenage lovers to have dreams, the Teddy Boys to whirl on the Wurlitzer and Mods to dodge with their girlfriends on the dodgems, the Victorian promenade to be graced with beautiful, wrought-iron railings.

I want the giant to flick the switch on the battery box and Margate's summer lights to twinkle and dance between every guesthouse and hotel. I want all the boarded-up hotels and guest houses to be opened up and come alive again. Tiny figures to be placed at the Lido swimming pool. The giant bends down and nimbly, with thumb and forefinger, replaces the 30ft diving board.[3]

Margate is one of several south-eastern coastal towns to have suffered long-term decline since the 1970s. Once a popular seaside resort, Margate's identity and reputation withered under the changing tourist gaze, which regarded traditional British resorts as unfashionable in the context of glamorous foreign destinations made possible by cheap travel and package holidays. The demise of the fishing and shipbuilding industries also played a role in Margate's fading fortunes. A struggling economy, high levels of unemployment and a changing demographic through the inward migration of disadvantaged and transient groups, occupying redundant holiday accommodation has contributed to the town's decline. The decaying and redundant physical infrastructure so lamented by Emin testifies to the forces of globalization, eroding local culture as empty car parks replaced elegant Edwardian architecture, boarded-up shops, derelict arcades, charity shops and fast-food outlets dominate the seafront, looking on to the golden mile of sand for which Margate was once famous. Arsonists forced the closure of the iconic Dreamland funfair, the big wheel which used to dominate the skyline was sold and disappeared, piers collapsed and the decaying art deco lido is a haunt for dereliction photography, a ghost of its former glory.

Emin is often referred to as Margate's 'daughter' having spent her childhood in the coastal town. Her public laments for the loss of its history and identity powerfully articulate the subjective and emotional attachment which creates a sense of place (Agnew, 1987). Whilst some critics might regard Emin's tributes as nostalgia, the salt and tears of Emin's art work and media statements personalize the politics of place making as policy. Emin's celebrity status and association with the local have been a distinguishing feature of the regeneration project in which the coastal community has had a powerful voice, campaigning against the destruction of the fire-damaged Dreamland (and the proposals to turn it into a shopping centre).

Doreen Massey's conceptualization of place, questions the critique of globalization as the villain in the narrative of the erosion of place. Challenging notions of authenticity and identity (implicit in Emin's accounts) which posit the fixity and rootedness of place (as history) against the fluidity of the global economy, Massey argues, overlooks the specificity of people's experiences of capitalism and mobility. Massey discusses place in terms of 'routes', in preference to 'roots': 'Identities are relational in ways that are *spatio*-temporal (Massey, 2005: 192). For Massey, 'the practised making of the identity of place – a *global* sense of place' and 'the construction of a place-based politics' is 'not restricted to the immediate or the local' and challenges the time/space compression associated with globalization:

> Space is as much a challenge as is time. Neither space nor place can provide a haven from the world. If time presents us with the opportunities of change ... then space presents us with the social in the widest sense: the challenge of our constitutive interrelatedness – and thus our collective implication in the outcomes of that interrelatedness ... and the ongoing and ever-specific project of the practices through which that sociability is to be configured.
>
> (2005: 195)

Massey's perception of twenty-first-century place and space resonates with two community projects in Margate, both commissioned by Artangel which were developed and performed during the first phase of the regeneration process.

Changing places: public art and performance in Margate

Towards a Promised Land involved the innovative photographer and conceptual artist, Wendy Ewald, documenting her work with child migrants in Margate. The project was not confined to asylum seekers, however, but included British children who had relocated to the town. Ewald was struck by the ever-changing pupil population at local schools and decided to develop a project which would explore the children's experiences of dislocation and relocation: 'So I decided to develop a project with the broad idea of what it is for the kids to start their lives over, whether fleeing war torn places or being moved by parents from one part of the country to another' (Ewald, 2006: 141). Ewald's work as an educator and photographer has a pedagogical orientation as she teaches children how to use photography to explore their experiences and perceptions of place, community and identity. In Ewald's work the relations between photographer and subject are blurred as she encourages participants to become artists and authors: 'I taught them to use a Polaroid camera and positive/negative film, which is quite complicated. They had to measure the distance between themselves and their subjects, and carry buckets of sodium sulphite in which to dip

Figure 6   Uryi, Towards a Promised Land, Margate, 2010. Photograph by kind permission of Wendy Ewald

the negatives. This slowed down the process and gave them time to think about what they were going to photograph' (2006: 144). Through this process, the participants were able to explore their developing relationship with the new environments in which they were situated, creating new identities of/through emplacement. Self-representation and relations to the 'other' of Margate and its inhabitants were playfully negotiated as the children were conscious of positioning themselves as the perceiving author/subject looking through the view finder at the environment which is both the observed other and a temporary home where new identities and futures can be created: 'They took pictures of what they noticed – an extraordinary thing considering that they were in a place that didn't acknowledge them – didn't know who they were – and without themselves really knowing where they were' (Ewald, 2005).

The photography workshops provided a liminal space in which identities, subjectivities, histories and futures were playfully explored. Thus the children were involved in the conceptualization of place through a creative act of making. The different responses of the four groups is indicative of the social, cultural, gendered and familial variabilities which constituted the individual subjectivities of the participants as makers of meaning. As subjects the children were both positioned by and taking up positions as human actors engaged in a way of experiencing the world. Although there were connections between the children's experiences of displacement (e.g., some of the children were seeking refuge from war zones, including a child whose family escaped from sectarian violence in Northern Ireland, while others had fled from domestic violence or threats of violence), Ewald became increasingly conscious of the differences in their perceptions of, and responses to, the process of place making. Participants were drawn from a local primary school, a secondary school, asylum seekers at the Nayland Rock Hotel (where families were held until their applications had been processed and which was subsequently the setting for the hunger strikes of asylum seekers prior to eviction) and a centre for housing unaccompanied immigrant minors.

All the children were involved in the same workshop process. Ewald began by creating photographic portraits of the children, facilitating their involvement through Polaroid tests 'so they could suggest changes before I shot the final photograph' (2006: 144). After teaching the children some principles of photography, she asked them to identify objects they'd brought with them on their journeys so these could be photographed for the installations. This, she observes was easier for the British children who generally brought toys as personal precious objects which had travelled with them. For the asylum-seeking group the objects were more practical – suitcases or clothes – and some were unable to identify anything; one of the asylum seekers 'made pictures of the Orthodox icons he and his mother arranged in a holly shrub just outside the hotel' (Ewald, 2005). In this phase of the work, the children were also 'photographing their surroundings as well as their dreams and stories, if they wanted to' (Ewald, 2006: 145). Here some differences were also apparent; while many of the British children produced maps to visualize and conceptualize their journeys, depicting where they had come from in relation to Margate, the refugee children did not engage in mapping, inhabiting a continuous present with little sense of history: '[these] kids drew different things ... They talked about their journeys but they didn't make maps of them ... For most of the kids there was no map to make of where they actually were, because they didn't really know' (145). There were also differences between the children with their families at the hotel and those at the centre who were 'tense and deeply uncertain' but wanted to go to school and learn English: 'With these kids, I felt a sense that something was always about to happen; everyone was on edge all the time' (146). This group of children, however, told their own stories in contrast to the family-based children whose parents spoke for them. Although many of the immigrant children in both groups had limited English and took longer to teach, Ewald described them as more confident, sophisticated and worldly than the British children; the latter, she speculated, seemed to be complicit with the family's need for change and seemed to carry a burden of responsibility, often perceiving themselves as needing to change behaviours in the new environment. For both groups, however, the workshops were an opportunity to recreate personal histories:

> Uryi had brought almost nothing with him from Belarus, not even the kind of snapshots most of us keep to enliven our personal histories and transpose our memories, the way snapshots usually do, into the present tense ... Since visual evidence of their former lives existed only in their imaginations, the children saw our workshop as an opportunity to reinvent themselves by making new photographs. They were free to tell the stories they wanted to tell, without fear of the immigration authorities scrutinizing them for incriminating biographical details ... Uryi said he hadn't dreamed since leaving Belarus; he wanted to make photographs of a 'police dream' he'd had back home. In the dream he and a friend witnessed a bank robbery. His friend was shot by the robbers, but Uryi was able to capture the robbers and take the money back to the bank.
>
> (2005)

Ewald edited transcripts of interviews with the children and worked with them to select texts to write on Mylar sheets over the photographic portraits. These were then made into huge banners to hang around the city. The performative element of the project was carefully staged, as Ewald sought to establish a gradual process of community engagement: 'The refugees', she observed, 'were resented by the townspeople, and their presence largely ignored. They were, in too many ways, non-entities' (2005). Ewald wanted to make the immigrant communities visible as well as wanting the disparate social groups within Margate to embrace the project: 'We were aware of the tension that the presence of the asylum seekers caused.' In July 2005 a series of banners were hung along the chalk cliffs of the sea wall. Several months later, in May 2006, more banners were hung at locations the children had chosen around the city centre, including Dreamland. The children's work was exhibited at the Outfitters Gallery in the town and they were invited to return to Margate to see the banners and visit the display. A final stage involved a performance event as part of another Artangel project: *Exodus* (comprising a film, 'combustible sculpture' and CD of plague songs). This took the form of a community celebration, 'Exodus Day': 'dramatic moments in the film realized as a public event on 30 September'. In Margate's central shopping precinct, Pharaoh Mann opened the proceedings with his victory speech. In Dreamland, a 25-metre sculpture of Waste Man, containing 'the unwanted detritus of consumer society' was burned at dusk. The event concluded in the Winter Gardens with a cycle of specially composed *Plague Songs* featuring local singers and musicians.

Traces of the performance remain in Margate in the form of the banners. For Ewald and the participants, the project survives in other ways, as memories of a hugely significant experience. The children were provided with photo albums 'as keepsakes of their first days in a new country. The albums had blank pages to accommodate images of the future. We shared a hope that the pages would be filled with photographs of the children and their families as they became integrated.' Ewald has written poignantly of the aftermath of the project, her visits to some of the children in their new homes and the positive changes in the participants when they returned to Margate for the exhibition event. She also records the story of Uryi (who, she suspects, was deported) as well as the various responses of the Margate communities to the different aspects of the project. Whilst many of the responses were positive, one of the installations by a South African Muslim student at a local school was burned after the 7 June 2005 bombings in London (just prior to the exhibition) while another portrait was vandalized with eggs and red paint. Overall, however, the project demonstrated the potential of performative art to create change through the process of place making. This project is one which explored place in terms of Massey's routes, unsettling the rootedness of some of the town's inhabitants:

> One local shopkeeper explained that the project was important because Margate is made up of so many different people. She thought that people grumbled about change, but once they understood something new, they welcomed it. The local librarian said the banners helped people to think about Margate in a different way. She was pleased that the arts were being used to change people's perceptions. Tulie, owner of the Joke Shop and a self-styled community leader said it was wonderful the banners were so

public, so everyone could enjoy them. 'The children are our future', she said, 'and even though the banners are black and white, they brighten up the place.' But others have questioned the use of black and white images and the fact that the kids aren't smiling. They asked, 'Is this another grim image of Margate?'

(Ewald, 2006: 152)

Margate has continued to change through a high profile and controversial regeneration project. This is evident in the development of the Turner Contemporary Gallery – a symbolic landmark building on the seafront, while a compulsory purchase order secured the future of Dreamland and its Grade II listed scenic railway as a heritage amusement park. Emin welcomed the news, as did the campaigners for Dreamland; but some salt and tears remained for Margate. The 'phoenix rising from the ashes', as Emin has described its regeneration, is a two-headed beast, consuming and commodifying place as the heritage industry ensures its survival. Margate has slowly transformed from a derelict wasteland haunted by the relics of its former glory to a thriving cultural backwater where contemporary art making flourishes against the backdrop of Turner's sunsets. Place is again being made and remade.

Contesting place: shifting theoretical positions

Space, place and site remain contested terms. During the 1970s, human geographers (Yi-Fu Tuan, 1977, and Edward Relph, 1976), moved discussion of place beyond location towards a philosophical and phenomenological understanding of place as perspective – an idea, an attitude and above all, as a way of 'being' in an environment. Tuan and Relph both compare place with space, suggesting a continuum linking place/experience to space/abstraction. For Tuan, place is 'pause', where an 'affective bond between people and place' can develop, while space is discussed in terms of movement and action (Tuan, 1974). Relph's account draws on phenomenology and Heidegger's philosophy to conceive of place as a form of consciousness:

> The basic meaning of place, its essence, does not therefore come from locations, nor from the trivial functions that places serve, nor from the community that occupies it, nor from superficial or mundane experiences ... The essence of place lies in the largely unselfconscious intentionality that defines places as profound centers of human existence.
>
> (1976: 43)

Whilst radical and cultural geographers have challenged the essentialist thrust of humanistic theory and its assumptions of universality, pointing to the social construction of place and the performance of gender, class and race which define emplacement or displacement, phenomenology has, nevertheless, destabilized the dichotomies underpinning Western philosophical discourse and established notions of synchronic space and diachronic time. Merleau-Ponty's sensual phenomenology positions the perceiving body centre stage, at the heart of an epistemological and ontological framework that collapses subject/object distinctions. Edward Casey's theory of place conjoins phenomenology with Bourdieu's practice theory and 'spatiality', whereby the gendered and socialized knowing body experiences and learns through embodied interaction so that understanding develops through the sensual, emotional, kinaesthetic and spatial faculties as well as through language.

Contemporary performance makers, I suggest, contribute to the process of making space meaningful through practices which explore (and challenge) how we experience the environment we inhabit. In *The Provocation of the Senses in Contemporary Theatre*, Di Benedetto argues that sensorial perception is fundamental to the transformational potential of contemporary performance. In contemporary performance, he suggests, and in contrast to 'traditional perceptual experience', the spectator cannot draw upon prior experience and expectations and is therefore thrust into sensually arousing instinctual responses (Di Benedetto, 2010: 321–2). Applied performance draws upon these vocabularies, moving beyond the experiential forms of practice emerging from visual and live art to engage in the making of place and spatiality through activities which involve an experiential encounter between performative selves and others: the spectator/participant's position is being constituted through the encounter with the performance situation and the performers. In this encounter there is often a transfer of bodily sensations (visual, auditory, olfactory, tactile, etc.) which affects the participants, creating a felt exchange, an embodied experience. Thus in site responsive work, where space is made meaningful as place through encounters between performers and spectators/participants, there is potential to transform our perceptions of the performed environment, as evident in *Towards a Promised Land* and the examples which follow.

Drawing on de Certeau, Cresswell describes practice as 'a tactical art' playing with the found structures of place:

> place is constituted though reiterative social practice – place is made and remade on a daily basis. Place provides a template for practice – an unstable stage for performance. Thinking of place as performed and practiced can help us think of place in radically open and non-essentialised ways where place is constantly struggled over and reimagined in practical ways. Place is the raw material for the creative production of identity rather than an *a priori* label of identity. Place provides the condition of possibility for creative social practice. Place in this sense becomes an event rather than a secure ontological thing rooted in notions of the authentic. Place

as an event is marked by openness and change rather than boundedness and permanence.

(2004: 39)

Place as event is a useful concept in conceptualizing the relations between space, site and place. The French urban theorist Henri Lefebvre distinguishes between abstract space (absolute space) and lived and meaningful spaces (social space) (Lefebvre, 1991). Social space would appear to be close to the definition of place in Cresswell's account. As Cresswell notes, 'the majority of writing on place focuses on the realm of meaning and experience. Place is how we make the world meaningful and the way we experience the world' (2004: 12).

Theorizing of place terms of process, making and event has challenged the binaries of local/global and space/place; place is conceived as fluid, liquid and porous and boundaries are replaced by liminal forms. The 'deterritorialization of the site' Kwon observes, has displaced what she refers to as 'place bound' identities. Yet some tensions between site and place remain in theoretical accounts:

> Current forms of site oriented art, which readily take up social issues (often inspired by them) and which routinely engage the collaborative participation of audience groups for the conceptualization and production of the work, are seen as a means to strengthen art's capacity to penetrate the sociopolitical organization of contemporary life with greater impact and meaning. In this sense, *the chance to conceive the site as something more than a place* – as repressed ethnic history, a political cause, a disenfranchised social group – is an important conceptual leap in redefining the public role of art and artists.
>
> (Kwon, 2004: 30)

But the concept of place here (and Kwon's reference to site being 'more than' place) and its relation to site is something I want to call into question. Place has been rehabilitated; having been regarded in parochial terms as the poor relation of site, place has been revisited by geographers as worthy of regeneration. No longer conceived in terms of fixity and territorialism, place has been reconstituted. Massey encourages us to think of place in terms of bodies, objects, narratives and energies. As the work featured in this section demonstrates, we have arrived at a meeting point between site-specific art (emerging from the disciplines of art and theatre as a response to and rejection of the commodification of art/theatre as object/product within the cultural industries) and applied theatre – a causeway where a range of disciplines intersect: contemporary art, public art, performance art and 'applied' performance.

The remainder of this chapter consists of three case studies. The first, a piece exploring the global/local themes, has been described by its maker as a 'cheat of the usual site-specific procedure', in that it is portable, touring to a range of venues all over the world. *Of All the People in All the World* by Stan's Cafe interrogates the relations between space, site and place in its form and content whilst it also challenges distinctions between applied theatre and performance as a piece which has moved effortlessly between educational and social contexts. Moving from international to national, my next case study explores a collaboration between a performance art company, Reckless Sleepers, and the National Museum of Scotland. Temporal boundaries coalesce through a process which brings the past into the present through the exploration of objects and environments, whilst it also creates new paradigms for museum performance. The focus narrows as I feature a project which might be considered to be 'local' in orientation, confined to the specifics of place – another coastal town in Kent. *Pebbles to the Pier* by Accidental Collective is an account of the practice of place through live art.

4.2   STAN'S CAFE: *PLAGUE NATION/OF ALL THE PEOPLE IN ALL THE WORLD*

Each grain of rice = one person and you are invited to compare the one grain that is you to the millions that are not. Over a period of days a team of performers carefully weigh out quantities of rice to represent a host of human statistics

○ the populations of towns and cities
○ the number of doctors, the number of soldiers
○ the number of people born each day, the number who die
○ all the people who have walked on the moon
○ deaths in the holocaust.

The statistics are arranged in labeled piles creating an ever-changing landscape of rice. The statistics and their juxtapositions can be moving, shocking, celebratory, witty and thought provoking.

(Yarker, 2007)

Figure 7   Of All the People In All The World at the Nagy Britmania Supernow Festival, Budapest. Photograph by kind permission of Graeme Rose and Stan's Cafe

First commissioned in 2003, *Of All the People in All the World* (*OATP*) and
its schools version, *Plague Nation*, is both site and place responsive as it
is nomadic, self-assembling and adapts to the social, spatial cultural and
historical context in which it is situated. Indeed, it could be argued that
whilst this is site orientated, it is not site specific as it is so readily adapted
to multiple locations. This is a form of 'mobilized' site specificity, to use
Kwon's terms, which is not location bound. As Kwon notes in her critique of
the terminologies, ideologies and practices of site specificity, these forms are
becoming 'more and more unhinged from the actuality of the site' (2004:
30). Indeed, adopting Kwon's terminology, the project can be seen to 'find
new meaning[s] and gain critical sharpness through recontextualizations'
(2004: 52). Many of Kwon's questions and concerns about the 'displacement' and the 'discursive virtualization of site' through the 'invocation' of
audience specific, community specific and socially engaged public art (2004)
are productively addressed in what is often branded 'The Rice Show'. In her
three paradigms of public art, Kwon identifies a series of shifts:

> From aesthetic concerns to social issues, from the conception of an art
> work primarily as an object to ephemeral processes or events, from preva-
> lence of permanent installation to temporary interventions, from the
> primacy of production as source of meaning to reception as site of inter-
> pretation and from autonomy of authorship to its multiplicitous expan-
> sion in participatory collaboration. While these shifts represent a greater
> inclusivity and democratization of art for many artists, arts administra-
> tors, art institutions and some of their audience members, there is also
> the danger of a premature and uncritical embrace of 'progressive art' as
> an equivalent of 'progressive politics'.
>
> (2001)

The promotion of distinctive urban identities through public art risks participating in the 'heritage industry' and a branding exercise whereby cities
are redefined as 'cultural commodities', whilst the interests of the artist are
also well served, as a contributory factor to the city's 'unique' 'distinction'.
As Dennis Kennedy has written in his reflections on the globalization of
Shakespeare, we inhabit a world 'where the individual is valued mainly as
shopper and where difference is simply another market obstacle for Coca-
Cola to overcome' (1988: 188). These ideologies are, however, destabilized
as Yarker's infinitely flexible cartographic dramaturgy emphasizes both
sameness and difference, providing a critique of cultural homogeneity and
corporate capitalism (we are all but grains of rice and McDonalds is a feature
of almost every urban environment) as well as emphasizing cultural differences visually and cognitively: the rice piles graphically illustrate statistical
contrasts, providing an insightful commentary (through the organization of
the statistics) on the relations between different countries, continents and

cultures. Thus the installation actively explores the relations between space and place as something which is constantly in the process of making.

Whilst Yarker's recipe is simple, the piece is profound, working on a number of levels. It explores the relations between the individual and their environment and the situation of the individual in relation to 'all the people of all the world.' Amongst other things, it is a project exploring place; the place of the individual in the world and their relationship and situation (represented visually) to others.

For Yarker, the initial inspiration was a consciousness of being in the world – wanting to explore the relations between microcosm and macrocosm: 'sensing our place on the lip of a vast landmass, was certainly part of it. Two years later, we were again on tour, this time watching real cities become model cities and model cities become real cities ...' (Yarker, 2005a). This sense of being situated in relation to the vast landmasses of other countries and cultures is powerfully and poignantly visualized through the spectator's consciousness of his/her position in relation to the piles of rice representing statistical data on social, historical, geographical and cultural topics. Walking through this cartographic terrain, we are experiencing place:

> To be in the world, to be situated at all, is to be in place. Place is the phenomenal particularization of 'being in the world'. A phrase that in Heidegger's hands retains a certain formality and abstractness which only the concreteness of *being in place*, i.e., being in the *place world* itself, can mitigate.
>
> (Casey, 1993: xv)

In Yarker's performance installations, moreover, we are aware of all the places as well as the peoples of the world through what can be considered as socially shared cognition:

> To say that cognition is socially shared is to say that it is distributed (among artefacts as well as people) and that it is situated in time and space. Because it is distributed, and its assembly requires the active engagement of those involved, it is to some extent constructed.
>
> (Brown and Cole, 2000: 198)

There have been over 50 performances of *OATP*, each of which is specific to a time and place. Active engagement is required of performers and spectators; the performers conduct the research, construct the installation and interact with the audience in a constant process of performance and place making. The spectator is a pedestrian, walking through the installation and engaging cognitively and emotionally with the statistical data and rice artefacts: 'The range of subjects addressed in the performance ensured that anyone who paused to explore the rice piles found connections with their personal areas of interest' (Stan's Cafe, 2003).

The responses of the audience, moreover, are culturally specific. Kerrie Reading, a Stan's Cafe associate artist who worked in the Salisbury, Oldham, Bucharest, Washington DC and Birmingham 2008 versions, explains the dynamic relations between space, place, audience and the shaping of the installation:

> The space will inform the piece, the space and the piece will draw the audience in and the audience inform the space.
>
> Salisbury Cathedral for example – many of the audience were visitors to the Cathedral and happened to stumble across the rice. The rice made its way into the sermon on the Sunday. The piles became something different because of the religious connotations attached to them – informed by the space and informed by the meaning some audience members decided to attach to it because of its location.
>
> Bucharest was a difficult space, it was a liminal space anyway, which gave it less authority. It didn't really have set opening times, people came to see it before and after another show that was happening ... it developed as a piece and responded to its locality. Bucharest – poorer country. The rice was seen as a food product. The question 'Why not pasta?' was asked – A religious/cultural significance.[4]

In Bucharest, Yarker observes, a lack of 'authority' in the setting was key to the success of the piece in this context: 'The show addressed many issues arising from the authoritarian rule of Romania's Communist era and outstripped the contemporary school textbooks in speaking of uncomfortable historical facts. To be outside local authority was what helped to give this performance much of its power.'[5] Another performer, Nick Walker, commented on the complexity and risk of the politically volatile environment for the Budapest show with armed guards on the door:

> 'Last October', said our fixer, Gabor, 'people were being shot in the face with rubber bullets outside this venue. I hope that doesn't happen while you're here.'
>
> 'Yes, we hope that doesn't happen either', he deadpanned.
>
> (Yarker, 2007)

Performed in the Museum of Ethnography the statistics featured 'immigration, diaspora, children's health, and the 1956 revolution, navigated via culture, transportation, and cheap gags. The cast (Hungary and its neighbours) came in 50 kg "hernia" bags, and if some were kicked over the floor, it was for the most part accidental' (Stan's Cafe, 2007).

The piece has to adapt itself to the various architectural structures in which it is situated (cathedrals, post-industrial spaces, art galleries, museums, a railway station, marquees, office complex and university bookshop). But this is not a 'cheat', as place making is part of the process; place 'as space made meaningful by human actions' (Van Erven, 2007: 27). There is contiguity between context, site, place and space, and each performance belongs to the physical conditions in which it is created; collaboration with the local community and research within the locality influences the shape of each piece as well as topical issues. In Mannheim, for example, the performance coincided with the election and results were illustrated as they were announced with performers adding grains of rice corresponding to votes to each party political pile. As Reading has commented from her experience as a performer:

> It feels new and fresh at each site, even though we go through the same process it can never be the same twice. The space and its shape have a huge impact, as do the performers as each person brings their personality and interests to the piece. Old favourites come out, yet new narratives are explored at each venue. Audience will offer suggestions and the place offers suggestions through its history.[6]

In her comments on the Salisbury Cathedral staging, she refers to a diverse and cosmopolitan audience 'each looking for themselves in the piles':

> An interesting dynamic and alteration to the piece was the soundtrack the Cathedral unintentionally offered, in the form of music, bells and prayer. The latter was conducted over microphones and politely everyone was asked to remain still and silent as this was delivered. Looking out at the sea of people carefully positioned by 'Child soldiers', 'Refugees', and 'People killed in fighting in Kingston, Jamaica' felt poignant.
> ...
> Over time we learnt how best to use our allocated space, which, ironically considering the vast size of the cathedral, was quite limited, especially once we took into account access points. Small piles didn't work in the centre of the transept as visitors are so busy marvelling at the ceiling they don't see where their feet are going. Small piles didn't work by the exit door as they got blown around by gusts of wind. We stuck to choosing large piles and building around them, which worked well until the final day when '*X-Factor* Viewers' were stepped on and in recoil 'Millionaires in the World' got a kicking.
> As we settled in we felt able to be more playful with the placement of our statistics. Execution statistics were carefully placed behind a railing, a flat tomb provided a good platform for more statistics and 'The Population of Surprise' hid behind a pillar.
>
> (Stan's Cafe, 2010)

While rice was chosen as the most practical material to work with in the representation of human statistics (Yarker had also contemplated sand and salt) it is also deeply symbolic. The grain of rice representing a person and human statistic has a poignancy by virtue of its shape and size (identical, uniform and seed-like – even embryonic) and the associations of rice with poverty, deprivation, survival, subsistence, human needs and rights. In some versions of the installation a single grain of rice, representing an individual is set in stark context against a mountainous statistic. There's an interesting paradox here, however, as individuals are measured and counted en masse; it is not possible to count the individual grains, so the individual is abstract and generalized, as in de Certeau's bird's-eye perspective on the city, or a Lowry painting.

Simon Parry explores the piece in its various versions from the perspective of citizenship education. Drawing upon Martha Nussbaum, David Harvey and Henri Lefebvre he considers how the installation stages the world 'not through an appeal to an abstract notion of shared humanity, but through spatial practices which strive to represent humans in global space without disregarding inequalities, differences and similarities' (Parry, 2010: 318). Parry's discussion of *Plague Nation*, the title of a schools version of the project,[7] considers how participatory performance engaged the students in understanding human and social geography, health and ethical issues as well as the relationship between themselves and the diverse others they are constructing and staging through weighing and placing the rice piles. Parry's insightful analysis (from his perspective as a Wellcome Trust funder and performance scholar) alludes to the embodied nature of the learning and performing processes engaged; referring to Lefebvre's notion of the 'affective kernel' which incorporates the emotional and imaginative experiences of the citizen or performer: '*Plague Nation* paradoxically offers an understanding of human health in global terms not by encouraging an emotional connection with other humans but with piles of tiny identical objects' (326). Abstract statistics and illustrations in textbooks and on virtual learning websites provided useful information and facts, but *Plague Nation* was a means of materializing the data, facilitating embodied cognition:

> Statistics presented ranged from the number of children in the school who have sandwiches for lunch to the number of children who die every day in the world from malaria. It is difficult to imagine what it means when you read in a newspaper that 15 million people died last year from infectious diseases but when you can see this number, when you can touch it, see individual grains and compare it to the population of your home town, it suddenly becomes a very real and moving figure.
>
> (Stan's Cafe, 2005)

'Real' and 'moving' are key terms as this is how the project made meaning, transforming and materializing abstract data into something tactile, visual and experiential. Topics featured in the installation range from human rights to aspects of popular culture with each mound of rice and statistic, offering considerable food for thought:

> People who die each year from infectious diseases, 15,000,000
> All the 10–14 year olds in Bristol, 22,871
> People aged 9 and over in Birmingham, 5370
> Children under 5 killed by diarrhoea causing disease in 2011, 3,000,000
> Applications to Big Brother, 10,000 (twice deaths in the world from TB – 5000).
> Asylum seeker applications for 2002, 85,865, set against those granted, 9444.
> Children who will die this year from diseases for which there is a vaccine, 2,000,000, and children saved by immunization, 3,000,000.
> Runners in the London Marathon with the name Smith, 463.

Parry also comments on the transformative potential of visual spectacle. Seeing the world and humanity represented in this form as grains of rice offers new perspectives on a whole range of political, environmental, health and ethical issues.

As a schools' project, emerging from and in conjunction with one of the company's mainstream productions, *Plague Nation* demonstrates developing synergies between the company's production and educational work. This continuum is a feature of many of the companies featured in this study. Yarker's perspective on the company's work in schools is also consistent with the practitioners interviewed: 'refusing to compromise on quality and continuing to treat all their collaborations as fellow artists' (Dimsdale, 2008). Thus in *Plague Nation*, the pupils (from two schools in Birmingham, one in Bristol and one in Nottingham) were the researchers and performers, investigating statistics, measuring the rice and interacting with the audience who visited the installation.

Of All the People in All the World explored a wider range of statistics as part of a performance of place. The World version in Stuttgart's Wagenhalle, two years after the first version of the installation, involved a series of shifts to adapt the show to such a huge space. 'Whole countries could now be placed side by side', Yarker explains, while the company continued 'to mix global issues with local references' setting the mountainous statistics representing major historic events against the 'smaller domestic numbers'. Yarker was concerned to sustain the playful tone, to prevent a 'graveyard' of death statistics: 'we wanted jokes along with the shocking' (Yarker, 2005b).

There is, however, something else at work as the individual sees/reads themselves in the rice and this was brought home to me by my personal experience of the 2008 World version at the A. E. Harris factory in Birmingham. This was the second staging in Birmingham but the first time at the A. E. Harris factory,[8] a presswork and tool making company in

Birmingham's Jewellery Quarter. Stan's Cafe used a vacant section of the site, consisting of shop floors, tool rooms and offices, enabling them to design the piece as a journey, moving the audience through the Americas, Europe, Africa and Asia; 120 tons of rice represented the 6.7 billion world population:

> One room contained three piles representing the population of the world in 1 AD, 1500 AD and 1900 AD. These were made more sculptural through the use of theatrical lighting which slowly cross-faded over and between the piles. The largest pile in the rest of the show represented the 1, 148, 000, 000 inhabitants of India.
>
> We also tried out a new approach in this version, where in a small side room we represented a range of individuals and small groups who had been involved in famous events – moments of tragedy, discovery, celebration, protest or exploration. A further new feature introduced was a website, thericeshow.com, which collated the webcast tannoy announcements, twitter feeds and any visitors' photographs posted on Flickr. This new site gave us the opportunity to have an ongoing digital dialogue with audience members and those unable to visit.
>
> (Yarker, 2007)

I visited the Birmingham installation with my father, a retired production engineer who had spent his childhood and working life in Birmingham and for whom the factory setting had particular personal significance. Having lived through the manufacturing crisis of the 1970s, the empty workplace resonated with him, while the similarities to his working environment created an emotional and cognitive connection with the place. For him (and presumably for others bringing similar experiences to the installation), the physical environment triggered memories of the life and death of the manufacturing industry in the region (known as the Black Country). The story of BSR is typical of many others (with similarities to the context in which *The Dream Life of Bricks* was created, a site-responsive production discussed in section 4.3 in which the history of the New England Sprague Electric Company is raw material for the performance). It was 1977 that saw the beginning of the end for his company, BSR, who made record decks.[9] Although this was a year of peak production, the writing was on the wall. The Prime Minister James Callaghan visited one of the sites, meeting a 17-year-old 'Miss BSR', shortly before the general election and a Government enforced wage freeze. BSR progressively shrank, from five factories to one, as the pound strengthened against the dollar, devastating orders, while competition from manufacturers in the Far East also caused orders (particularly from the United States) to fall dramatically. By 1979, most of the workforce were on short time, followed by four-day working, redundancies and then a three-day week for the remaining 8000 employees; 2300 redundancies were announced in 1980 (1700 at the company's Scottish site); after a temporary lull in 1981, the Black Country workforce of 5000 faced catastrophe. In 1982, one site closed completely (1100 jobs) and the others gradually followed suit with 800 redundancies at other sites and the remaining workforce (2500) transferring to a single surviving site; 10, 000 employees lost their jobs over a five-year period – 10,000 grains of rice would have been needed if this story had been represented in the A. E. Harris installation – 10,000 families experienced the consequences of redundancy, while others, like my father, lived with the threat of redundancy (and the consequences of being a survivor where each relocation meant the loss of someone else's job). In the context of a general recession, this was disastrous for the area; the weekly queues to sign on grew longer and longer as BSR and similar companies floundered. The last record deck was made in 1984 as the company merged with a business in Hong Kong, eventually changing its name and producing parts for computers.

My father was drawn to the small annex which he referred to as the 'tool room', noting the etchings on the wall, remnants inscribed by the draughtsmen who worked here. This, he explained was where drawings were laid out and checked and the marks on the wall were a familiar code. The tool room in the installation was a small space housing Yuri Gagarin (in Vostok) and represented by a single grain, set against a small pile of rice representing people currently on the international space station with another pile for those who have walked on the moon. Yet, as space rockets were launched and men walked on the moon, Birmingham struggled to survive a recession with the decline of its manufacturing and motor industries. Local history is juxtaposed with international history; a shrinking economy and struggling workforce is contrasted with the thriving multibillion-dollar space industry. The connections and poignant ironies might not be evident to all, but for those familiar with the history of this place, the installation is framed and understood in this context. Local history is a lens through which the contents of the installation are seen and felt. The engagement of my father as a spectator was 'embodied',[10] as he drew upon the memories of his working life, the three-day week, the ongoing threat of redundancy, factory closures and restructuring, the relief and guilt of the survivors as they migrated from one factory to another until only one factory remained. There are ghosts of the past in the fabric of the building and a haunted beauty to the installation as a whole. Parry speaks of the reverence of the performers, the respect and dignity demonstrated to the place they occupy as if they are conscious that they represent lives that have been lived here:

> On one level, there is no performance, no transformation, all you see are some adults and young people arranging and patrolling piles of rice and nothing or no-one, apart from the minimal labels on the piles, is

pretending anything. On another level the performers' uniforms, their careful behaviour and attitudes of awe and reverence position the piles of rice as things of value, maybe artefacts in a museum or rare creatures. They play with the paradox that certain humans can be sold for more than others, more productively commodified in their plastic packaging, by selling five grains of rice for 50 pence.

The reflexive nature of the performance is enhanced by its playfulness and the invitation to laugh at the incongruities of its more heterotopic aspects. The performers inhabit their roles with a certain lightness more akin to live art or some street theatre than with the level of transformation required by more conventional theatre.

(2010: 329)

The performers responded to questions from the audience but appeared detached, moving and functional objects in the installation, anonymized through their brown industrial coats. Reading describes the performer's experience:

As you discussed with the A. E. Harris space, a lot of the audience (particularly local audience) were intrigued by the industrial site and many conversations with audience members involved a discussion about their relationship with the space directly, or the industrial past of Birmingham. The sheer size of this version (both the space it occupied and the fact that it was the world version – the first and only one in the UK) required multiple performers at all times, and this allowed roles to be explored to a greater depth, they didn't need to be rushed, I could take my time, I often allowed myself the time to be a cleaner, simply occupying the space and sweeping, brushing, erasing feet marks. This became integral to the role as it was so vast and 10 by 10 metre square piles needed a lot of maintenance! There was the space, numbers and time to maintain the space, talk to audience and research. In smaller venues (and therefore smaller rice piles and smaller cast) this all needs to be done but in concentrated periods of time. The world version also allowed more time for individual and pair research, time could be spent developing small and large sections, developing narratives. Yet, as there were multiple performers these narratives could also be removed daily, so there was no room for being precious or taking ownership.

The role of the performer is varied – we are ourselves, just a heightened version, more poised and controlled. We are factory workers, curators ... I see it as though we are all of these, creating and evolving with the piece.

... At the beginning we are the planners, we move on to being labourers, to scientists, to curators and invigilators. They switch back and forth throughout the run.[11]

In the main part of the factory, where the heavy industrial machinery would have been housed, piles of rice represented local, national and international statistics. The numbers of people born in the United Kingdom and living in Australia was set against the population of Australia and also compared with the population of Aboriginals and Torres Strait Islanders. A single grain of rice represented Dame Ellen MacArthur juxtaposed with the numbers of practising Satanists in Australia. I am reminded of meetings my parents attended for those attracted to the possibilities of emigration to New Zealand or Australia in a quest for new lives and a way out of the economic decline. Moving on, a modest pile of rice represented the population of the Falklands in 1992, set against the much larger pile of Argentinean forces occupying the Islands and the size of the UK Task Force sent to recapture. The smallest pile was the decreased size of the Argentinean army. Here, the simplicity of the rice and the lives and deaths represented in the grains moved spectators. Some sighed, some shook their heads and others contemplated with arms folded.

Throughout the installation national statistics and events were juxtaposed with local material. The diversity of religions in Birmingham isn't surprising, although Christians form the largest group. Muslims are in similar numbers to atheists and agnostics. Some of the juxtapositions create humour and irony:

> The numbers of professional storytellers in the UK are equivalent to people who filled in their tax returns on Christmas day, while the numbers at Woodstock in 1969 are equivalent to the number of people who missed the self-assessment tax return deadline. We learn that the number of people who auditioned for the *X Factor* series is more than double those who applied to train as teachers in the UK and this is set against the tiny pile representing the numbers training as Physics teachers. Piles of rice produce telling statistics on the social and cultural context in which the installation is situated and its relations to the rest of the world and to history. The deaths at Waterloo on 18 June 1815 are significantly higher than 9/11. The number of people who die today is smaller than those who will be born.

As my father's response indicates, the emotional connection was with the place of performance as well as with the physical and material features of the installation itself. Wherever the project is situated, local audiences respond from a particular perspective, bringing their lived experience of the histories of community and place to the performance event. This is embodied spectatorship, yet it is not 'immersive'. As in promenade performance we are within and outside of the performance, acutely aware of our relationship to the material (and our situation in relation to the statistics represented). It is a humbling experience to look at the gigantic mounds of

rice, representing India, China, the United States and the numbers of teenage smokers in China. Like de Certeau's rooftop spectator, we are conscious
of ourselves as ordinary practitioners, surveying something which is both
extraordinary and ordinary as a representation of everyday life. Unlike de
Certeau's spectator, we are not positioned as voyeurs, surveying the spectacle of everyday life from a position of authority as the owner of the gaze;
Yarker's piece places the spectator on the floor, in close proximity to the rice
structures and needing to walk through, in between and around the rice
as objects in an exhibition. There is a serenity created by the lighting and
colours, and a strange beauty (strange as we are perceiving rice differently)
which is derived not only from the colours, lighting and spatial organization but is part of our emotional engagement with the materials. We are
moved and keep moving. As Parry observes:

> There is a sense of the insignificance of the individual, an almost invisible
> single grain in a huge pile but also, significantly, they knew that each and
> every one was actually there. At least one teacher picked up on the poten-
> tial ethical educational force of this sense, commenting that 'it's quite
> good that they can see themselves represented in different piles and then
> look at another pile where children are going to die and see that they
> are very insignificant' (Maverick Television, 2004). *The students saw and
> reflected on how they were situated in relation to other people in the world.*
>
> (2010: 328; my emphasis)

A cognitive perspective might suggest that what is being described here
is how a mirroring mechanism establishes a connection to others which
facilitates an ethical and arguably empathic engagement. Whilst there is
considerable debate in neuroscience about the role of mirroring systems in
social cognition, theories of embodied cognition suggest that 'higher cognitive processes operate on perceptual symbols' (i.e. imagery and objects can
stimulate the embodiment of emotional states) while 'concept use involves
partial reactivations of the sensory motor states that occur during experience with the world' (Niedenthal et al., 2009). If we consider the rice as a
'perceptual symbol', the processes involved in producing our conceptual
responses to, and understanding of, the materials in the installation draw
upon the reproduction of embodied emotion.

For the students (and audience), seeing themselves represented physically and visually was a key to their learning, changing or deepening their
understanding of themselves in relation to others. Seeing statistics on a
page, it is implied, would not have been as *effective* as this would not *affect*
us in the same way. Using terminology which corresponds to educational
theory, Niedenthal distinguishes between 'deep' and 'shallow' modes of
cognitive engagement, arguing that 'bodily aspects of emotion concepts are
stimulated only when necessary; that is, in deep, but not shallow conceptual

tasks. A deep task requires recourse to meaning whereas a shallow task can only be accomplished by simple associative means' (2005: 40–1). The experience of the installation involves a level of participation which moves well beyond the associative, requiring us to create meaning through our interactions with the site and its contents, assimilate the statistical data and its visual representation and, as my father's response indicates, engage with place as well as space, the micro and the macro to perceive ourselves (as single grains of rice) in the contexts of the rice mountains of otherness. I suggest that in seeing ourselves as grains of rice and then visually and haptically experiencing how the grain of rice is situated in relation to others creates the perceptual shift described in Parry's account. Rice becomes what McConachie refers to as an 'emotion dependent cognitive object[s]' (McConachie, 2008: 112), its beauty and simplicity enhanced by lighting in some of the spaces, while its paucity, nudity and vulnerability is highlighted in others. We are simultaneously aware of the personal (through the grain of rice and our responses to the installation) and the abstract (the statistical data), the inner (our experience, embodied emotions and feelings) and the outer (the performativity of the event as demonstrated in the actions of the costumed performers).

'Affect', writes Sarah Whatmore, 'refers to the force of intensive relationality intensities that are felt but not personal; visceral but not confined to an individuated body. This shift of concern from what things mean to what they do has methodological consequences for how we train our apprehensions of "what subjects us, what affects and effects us" or "learn to be affected"' (Whatmore, 2006: 604). This bears an interesting relationship to discussions in cognitive science of the relations between emotion and feeling. For Antonio Damasio, feelings are emotions made conscious (1999, 2003). Emotions, as evident in Luc Ciompi's and Jaak Panksepp's paradigm (2005), can be categorized as a series of basic states or systems which are not confined to an individual experience but are universal.[12]

Of All the People In All The World and *Plague Nation*, I suggest, offer an embodied perceptual experience in which we are both critically and creatively engaged. Our affective understanding is created through embodied spectatorship (and, we might argue, critical empathy). In educational contexts, the processes involved in making these installations creates a dynamic learning environment that has informed other projects as the benefits of the relations between experimental art and education are realized. Although the work produced by Stan's Cafe resists categorization or branding, there is consistency in the methodologies used by the company. Learning and thinking are enactive and embodied through activities which physically engage participants in explorations of their environments. The project engages us intellectually, physically and experientially in meaning-making activity which is the foundation to perceiving, learning and thinking. Above all, we are engaged in the dynamics of site, space and place.

4.3   REMAKING MUSEUM SPACE: RECKLESS SLEEPERS' *CREATING THE PAST*

Royal Museum of Scotland, Edinburgh, March – September 2002

A grand instance of object performance, the museum stands in an inverse relationship to the theatre. In theatre, spectators are stationary and the spectacle moves. In the museum, spectators move and the spectacle is still (until recently). Exhibition is how museums stage knowledge. They do this by the way they arrange objects ... in space and by how they install the visitor.

(Kirshenblatt-Gimblett, 1998: 10)

In her introduction to *Reshaping Museum Space*, Suzanne Macleod outlines the changing state of museums as social, cultural and pedagogical spaces:

The space of the museum is increasingly recognized as an environment created through a complex of practices and systems of knowledge.

Figure 8   Reckless Sleepers' *Creating the Past*, Royal Museum of Scotland, Edinburgh, March–September 2002. Photograph by kind permission of Reckless Sleepers

Museum professionals are beginning to recognize the constitutive and transformative possibilities of museum space as well as the ability of museum users and museum professionals to reshape museum spaces through practices of appropriation. Museum space is now recognized as a space with a history of its own, a space active in the making of meaning and, most importantly, a space open to change ... common to all this is a repositioning of the museum as a flexible space, open to change, responsive to visitor needs and in touch with contemporary issues and agendas.

(Macleod, 2005: 1–3)

Access and inclusion agendas have been instrumental in driving these changes; cultural policy can be seen to be an ideological engine, fuelling the 'production of space' (Lefebvre, 1991). As Eilean Hooper-Greenhill has observed, the 'turn to culture' in the UK museum sector is linked to the separate policies emerging from Scotland and Wales post-devolution; this, she refers to as a 'remapping of culture', with the result that culture has come to be shaped as regional; 'in the case of museums this regionality operates within the centralized framework of government politics' (Hooper-Greenhill, 2004: 16).

The politics of national and cultural identity underpins many of the policy statements emerging from the various government bodies. The then UK's Department for Culture, Media and Sport issued this statement in 2004: 'As a Culture Department we still have to deliver the utilitarian agenda, and the measures of instrumentality that this implies, but we must acknowledge that in supporting that we are doing more than that, and in doing more than that we must find ways of expressing it.'[13] Hooper-Greenhill identifies similar trends in the United States and Australia with shifts to an 'instrumental approach to culture' through political and pedagogical agendas.[14] As a corollary of this functionalism, an impact agenda demands evidence of efficacy, requiring indicators for measuring social inclusion and learning (the subject of Hooper-Greenhill's study which proposes a paradigm for evaluative practice). As Hooper-Greenhill notes, 'museums were advised by their professional body, the Museums Association, that if the museum community were to secure increased central funding, then it had to prove to the Treasury that they're worth it' (Hooper Greenhill, 2007: 18).[15]

This utilitarian agenda, however, has also led to a shift in spatial practices (Macleod, 2005) as museums have become more open environments, seeking new ways of engaging audiences. Digital technologies and performance are two of the methods used to facilitate interaction and participation. The AHRC 'Performance, Learning and Heritage' project at the University of Manchester (2005–8) explored 'the use and impact of performance as a medium of learning and interpretation at museums and heritage sites' and the wide range of performance practices is evident in the essays collected in *Performing Heritage,* a publication arising from the conference associated with the project (Jackson and Kidd, 2010). As editors Anthony Jackson and Jenny Kidd observe: 'Visits to museums and heritage sites have in recent years become (not least in promotional rhetoric) less about the *object* and more about the *experience*: an "encounter" with a past that is "brought to life", peppered with "events" and advertised through a list of "What's On"' (2010: 1).

Whilst the turn from the object to experience via participation has led to charges of 'edutainment', as the heritage industry conspires with the utilitarian agenda to commodify learning through 'accessible' and often simulated means, this shift has a positive orientation, as evident in Jackson and Kidd's account, 'toward experimentation [and] playfulness'. Nevertheless, as Paul Johnson observes in *Performing Heritage*, the 'new museology' does not generally involve 'new' performance (with the exception of innovative companies such as Triangle):

> [T]hough there could be in theory a postdramatic museum theatre, which does not operate through dramatic representation but which subverts or substitutes the component parts of dramatic theatre (plot, character, dialogue), in practice this is not common in the field of performing heritage. Live art and performance art in gallery spaces seldom share similarities of either form or content with the mainstream of museum theatre. That is not to say that all museum theatre should operate as performance art, but rather that the possibility should be there for it to do so.
>
> (2010: 54)

In the case study which follows, I explore this possibility further through discussion of a performance art project by Reckless Sleepers, a collaboration with the National Museum of Scotland. In this project we see what happens when live art enters the museum experience.

The project arose in the context of devolution and the Scottish Parliament's commitment to reforming museums as sites for citizenship and education.

A paper entitled *Education for Citizenship in Scotland*, produced by Learning and Teaching Scotland, identified the following learning outcomes:

> Education for citizenship should aim to develop capability for thoughtful and responsible participation in political, economic, social and cultural life. This capability is rooted in *knowledge* and *understanding*, in a range of personal *qualities and dispositions*. It finds expression through *creative and enterprising* approaches to issues and problems. Capability for citizenship can be analysed in terms of four related aspects, each of which relates to a set of broad categories of learning and outcome. These aspects are: 'knowledge and understanding'; issues, skills and competencies; values and dispositions and creativity and enterprise.
>
> (in Hooper-Greenhill, 1994, 24–5)

It was in this context that *Creating the Past* was conceived as the National Museum of Scotland (NMS) collaborated with the performance art company Reckless Sleepers, in an endeavour to diversify its audiences and to make the museum more accessible and inclusive. The project was developed as part of the NMS's Social Justice Action Plan and aimed to:

> create new and diverse audiences for NMS by working collaboratively with; socially excluded groups, especially young people;
> increase understanding of and engagement with Scotlands [sic] past;
> use the museum environment as a resource for the development of life skills;
> create a legacy of new ways of working for NMS and other museums.
>
> (McLean, 2002: 2)

Much of this appears to be perpetuating the rhetoric of the New Museology, which, as Deirdre Stam summarizes, explores the 'relationships of the museum to its social, economic and political environment as part of the analysis of pertinence, relevance and meaning' (2005: 55). The New Museology questions and critiques the old for being too method based, too concerned with the preservation and display of objects as historical artefacts (perpetuating dominant ideologies in terms of value) and advocates a recon-ceptualization of museums in terms of *purpose*, arguing in favour of a more holistic, socially inclusive, participatory and pedagogical model in which museums consider the social significance and benefits of their organizations as purveyors of cultural values (Stam, 2005; Vergo, 1997).

Stam identifies five key areas questioned and challenged by New Museology's critique of traditional museum approaches: 'value, meaning, control, interpretation, authority and authenticity' (2005: 54). The tradi-tional museum apportions value to objects by virtue of their enshrinement in the museum. Meaning is socially, rather than materially determined (Taborsky, 1990; Bourdieu, 1984), dependent upon the context in which the objects are situated and, it is argued, can shift as objects are reinter-preted through strategies which involve meaning being socially rather than materially determined. Stam explains the concern with access in terms of Bourdieu's theorizations of cultural capital and taste: accessibility generally requires familiarity with the cultural code through which artefacts are inter-preted. Benjamin's discussions of authenticity in artistic production and the politics of authority are cited by Stam in conjunction with the statement of New Museologists Spencer R. Crew and James E. Sims: '[o]bjects have no authority: people do' (1992: 163). Thus the visitor's experience becomes associated with the 'product' of the museum. However, whilst the tradi-tional museum experience is considered to focus upon the individual and personal experience of the visitor, the New Museology, as Stam explains, emphasizes group identities (most frequently defined in terms of ethnicity or gender) and the 'social or collective behaviour' which might be 'bettered' through participation in the cultural activities museums can produce (2005: 61). This involves changes to organization and governance, a different pedagogical approach (whereby museums cease to function as custodians of tradition and convention through the representation of histories which are to be learned and consumed) and changes to display techniques and classification as a means of engaging visitors differently:

> Exhibits ought to further acknowledge that there are three sets of actors related to any exhibition: makers of objects, exhibitors of those objects and viewers. These players come into contact somewhere between the object and the label. The active relationships of these parties in an exhibition should be exploited, with the final integration left to the viewers.
>
> (Stam, 2005: 63)

Although the theoretical frameworks established by New Museology are potentially useful, Stam bemoans the lack of attention to practical strategies. In *Creating the Past*, however, we can see how many of the principles of New Museology can be utilized through a project which used visual and performance art as means to engage audiences as participants in the production of meaning through the museum experience. The project proposal for *Creating the Past* articulates its aims as an 'educational access' project, which 'will use alternative interpretative techniques not normally associated with object display, such as art and live theatre, to create an accessible, inviting and exciting environment for visitors to enjoy'.[16]

For Reckless Sleepers, the utilitarian agenda needed to be compatible with the company's aesthetic values and their commitment to the creation of high quality art. As the company's artistic director, Mole Wetherell explains: 'the museum's objectives were to engage participants from social inclusion zones but we were concerned not to ghettoize the project so built partnerships with a range of audiences through schools, youth groups and Dance Place. The focus for all participants was on quality with all the trappings; funding follows art.'[17] This project was distinctive and innovative for several reasons: its duration, including the pilot phase, was 18 months, an unusually extensive period of time for a performance company to be resident in a museum. Wetherell relocated to Glasgow for the duration of *Creating the Past*, thereby ensuring his immersion in the project and the environment in which it was being produced. As Reckless Sleepers are not based in Scotland, the local and institutional contexts for the work were unfamiliar, posing challenges for the company: 'a network of contacts within youth and community organizations is an essential part of what Reckless Sleepers do.'[18] As a company accustomed to working within community networks, Reckless Sleepers were confronted with a particularly difficult situation due to the dislocation of the social groups they sought to work with: 'From our point of view as outsiders it became apparent that organizations within Edinburgh seem reluctant to talk or work with each other. There is not a feeling of partnership and there is a disparate approach to developing projects within this city.'[19] One of the problems here was concerned with Reckless Sleepers as a company perceiving themselves as out of place geographically, culturally and artistically, whilst a further problem, compounding the situation was the absence of a connected communities infrastructure. Edinburgh is characterized here as 'citified/sitified' through the rhetoric associated with urban space: disconnected units, Casey's houses with gardens, de Certeau's 'separate islands', and the spatial fragments of isolated parts and interstitial zones which are part of the formal structures and order of the city. Wetherell's temporary relocation was an important gesture – a means of navigating this urban environment by inhabiting it, developing a lived experience of the social and material components which constitute Edinburgh and its National Museum as place. The performance activities of Reckless Sleepers within and beyond the museum were to become a means of creating connected communities, linking the various social groups together and creating a different set of relationships with the museum.

The working methods of the project were innovative and challenging for the museum. The devising processes which are fundamental to the work of Reckless Sleepers involve what they describe as 'an organic, developing environment, testing and trying out methods before rejecting or adapting them'. This iterative, flexible and responsive process, however, can be difficult to accommodate within the institutional context of a museum where staffing, room hire, opening hours, security arrangements are constraints which can be difficult to reconcile with a spontaneous model of working. For the National Museum of Scotland, the project was unprecedented in form, content and methodology: 'as a pilot project, working with performance artists and young people from Edinburgh SIP areas, *Creating the Past* inevitably challenged the way NMS operates.'[20]

The New Museology, however, as Johnson has written, has synergies with contemporary performance practice, and the status of the object is key to this: citing Stam, Johnson refers to the 'value of an object being "not an inherent property of the object, but rather an attribute bestowed upon objects by their inclusion in the museum (or the performance) ...[as meaning] is altered by museums through the recontextualization of objects in the museum setting' (Stam, 2005: 57). Summarizing Stam, Johnson explains that 'the meaning of objects in performance is altered through their being on stage, whether those objects are operating as props in a dramatic fiction or in some other way in some other type of performance' (Johnson, 2010: 54). Johnson's semiological reading here is developed in his framework for analysing the relations between performance, learning and heritage, which situates activities in terms of 'a series of binary oppositions: namely between history and fiction, between risk and safety, and between external and internal'. Johnson proposes that

> the binary history/fiction occupies the space between heritage and performance, as there are prior connections (and possible tensions) between heritage and history and fiction and performance. The binary risk/safety is suggested between performance and learning because of the perception of performance as a potentially unpredictable or unruly activity in comparison with the respectable act of learning. The internal/external binary is proposed as a link between learning and heritage, as learning can be thought of as operating on or internal to the individual in comparison with the shared, collective nature of heritage.
>
> (Johnson, 2010: 55)

I would suggest that a cognitive approach to these categories and relationships offers an alternative way of understanding how performance functions in the context of the museum. Conceptual blending, as discussed below, enables us to understand objects in performance as both historical and fictional. Learning is made active and embodied through the risk taking involved in improvisatory performance (which is unpredictable and dependent upon external stimulus from the audience) where audience and performers share the same space and process in the making of meaning. This is all evident in *Creating the Past* as a process of exploring environments and objects. In this project, I suggest, relations between objects and audiences were reconfigured; whilst audiences were engaged as participants and producers (rather than consumers) of meaning, the object was restored to the centre of the museum experience and a different kind of value bestowed upon it through strategies which actively engaged with issues of authenticity, origins, aesthetics and representation.

Creating the Past as post-dramatic museum theatre

In his reflection *On the Museum's Ruins*, Douglas Crimp offers the following analysis of the changing status of the object in the museum in the context of site specificity: 'The idealism of modernist art, in which the art object *in and of itself* was seen to have a fixed and transhistorical meaning, determined the object's placelessness, its belonging in no particular place, a no-place that was in reality the museum ... Site specificity opposed that idealism – and unveiled the material system it obscured – by its refusal of circulatory mobility, its belongingness to a *specific* site' (Crimp, 1993: 17). For Reckless Sleepers, the objects chosen for the project would meet a number of criteria. They would:

offer an insight into Scotland's past peoples;
have an obvious human dimension which visitors can easily identify with;

have a meaning which is open to interpretation;
be found in the Museum of Scotland;
offer contemporary parallels.

What is striking about the methods used by the company is the way in which the objects and the museum environment were defamiliarized for participants, enabling them to explore and experience from different perspectives, drawing upon sensual and cognitive faculties. This was in some ways a return to origins in terms of the objects featured and the means used to explore them. The company chose to work with Celtic and Pictish carved stones because they are 'probably the most difficult and abstract to interpret. Historians and academics have little recorded evidence or understanding of their meanings.'[21] The difficulty in articulating the objects appealed to Mole Wetherell who wanted to explore memory, interpretation and perception as key themes. In initial workshops, participants undertook a walk round the gallery and were asked to recount what they saw and to list objects they had encountered. An exercise in speed writing involved Wetherell reading out the list while participants produced drawing and symbols in response. The process is close to the automatic writing experiments popular with modernist writers and artists. Unlike modernist conceptions, however, the object was explored from a range of perspectives as aesthetic artefact, heritage asset in the context of the museum's material culture (and evidence of Scotland's past) and as a creative stimulus. Further exercises involved creating a narrative from the drawings, doing further exercises with different constraints (e.g., drawing without lifting the pen from the page and making a drawing without looking at the sheet). Other exercises involved participants being divided into groups and seeing objects in different parts of the museum and describing an object to others who drew in response to what they heard as well as participants having to locate objects from descriptions and drawing objects without looking at the sheet of Perspex (which was preferred to paper). Questions would be invited about the qualities of the object (texture, colour, etc.) and details recorded. In another speed writing exercise, five parts of the object were drawn. A further exercise involved a blindfolded participant touching the object and whispering their responses to another person who described it to others to draw. Finally, participants were asked to make speed drawing responses to descriptions from a larger group.

What is interesting about this process is the importance of perception and imagination in the ways the objects generate meaning. This is endorsed by comments from participants:

'made them look at objects/things differently by end of workshop'
'Communicated in a different language to normal – using visual/spatial language to communicate to someone else'

'Learnt to look at objects in a different way to a normal walk round the museum'[22]

As one of the participants recalls, 'two of us had one sheet of Perspex between us drawing what was being described by somebody else feeling it, not using their eyes, just touching it ...'[23] The drawings produced through this process have a distinctive curvaceous and non-linear quality; some were patterns and others were recognizable shapes and objects. The workshops were designed to develop skills of observation and communication but the methods used moved beyond this into a different perceptual arena, a space where participants were able to re-imagine and reconfigure the objects they worked with, using different parts of their brains to perceive differently. Recent neuroscience research, moreover, indicates that object recognition can be activated by touch alone.[24]

The drawings were produced through a form of play which involved participants responding instinctively to the objects as stimuli. Moving beyond the rational, the participants were engaging in a Bergsonian experience of 'entering into' objects through an effort of imagination. Bergson's pioneering philosophy engaged with a form of neuropsychology through his work on perception and his notion of virtual actions and motor diagrams. Indeed, his statements demonstrate a synergy between his thinking and subsequent work in cognitive neuroscience as he posits a sensorimotor theory of cognition:

> (Objects) send back, then, to my body, as would a mirror, their eventual influence; they take rank in an order corresponding to the growing or decreasing powers of my body. The objects which surround my body reflect its possible action upon them.
>
> (Bergson, [1912] 2004: 6–7)

A large number of subsequent findings suggest that the objects and events of the perceived world are mirrors of the biologic action capabilities of the body. For Bergson, action and cognition are inextricably related through forms of sensorimotor perception. As Trimingham has summarized in her discussion of Bergson's ideas in the context of Oscar Schlemmer and the Bauhaus, Bergson anticipates many aspects of postmodern performance in his conception of time, space, objects and motion: 'Bergson talks of our urge to quantify and analyse and logically categorize the material world and make "*symbols*" of it, instead of "entering into" the object to gain intuitive understanding of it and an "absolute" knowledge of it' (Trimingham, 2011: 125). In the traditional museum experience, knowledge of the object is acquired through external observation and intellectual engagement with information provided about the artefact. This equates to 'logical analysis', the first kind of knowledge Bergson describes. For Bergson, however, the relationship between subject and object is conceived in terms of time (which he understood not as sequences of moments, but akin to a musical melody where each note or state interpenetrates the next) whereby time/motion is indivisible: 'questions relating to subject and object, to their distinction and their union, must be put in terms of time rather than of space' (1896: 77). Bergson's temporal model has affinities with the concept of presence discussed in 2.1: 'This reality is mobility. There do not exist things made, but only things in the making, not states that remain fixed but only states in the process of change. Rest is never anything but apparent, or rather, relative' (Bergson, [1946] 1968: 222).

The devising process used by Reckless Sleepers, in common with many other contemporary performance companies is similarly process based: an iterative, non-linear, non-mimetic, spiral paradigm which corresponds, as Trimingham has noted, to developments in contemporary philosophy: 'an embodied approach to form acknowledges that meaning comes into being for each of us in our continual engagement with and therefore embodiment of the world: we are imbued with the world and it is imbued with us' (2010: 111). The exploration of objects in *Creating the Past* also builds on iterative, non-mimetic processes, using sensory information as well as temporal and spatial understandings to create meaning and re-create meaning. Husserl's concept of *epoche*, arising from phenomenological notions of intentionality, is invoked through this process; as Trimingham explains:

> Husserl identified a way of looking at phenomena that engaged with our consciousness alone, and not our *thinking about* the objects. This involved a state of non-thinking, a "bracketing off" of everything we know about the object and only being open to the phenomenon itself ... The phenomenological attitude attempts to look at the phenomenon shorn of any social, political, historical or cultural context, and to simply embed consciousness in physical reality.
>
> (2011: 40)

Here, the correspondence ends, however as although the workshop exercises used methods which 'bracketed off' the objects, divorcing them from other contexts, this was a temporary transportation to enable participants to perceptually explore the materiality of the artefacts; the objects were also investigated in historical and cultural contexts. Walking around the museum, following different routes to locate objects in the current space/time of the museum was juxtaposed with historical investigations of sources and origins. In the performance, this aspect of the past was conveyed through soundscapes, taken from the environments where the objects were first located (Wetherell recounts numerous site visits and encounters with Gaelic farmers, wind, fields and sheep). Thus the performance challenged the linear temporal frameworks in which objects are traditionally exhibited whereby hermetically sealed artefacts are located in history, fixed in the past and preserved for the present of the museum spectator. The soundscapes in the performance brought the historical origins of the objects into the present moment, while the objects themselves were available to be explored in workshops so that visitors to the exhibition could touch and feel the artefacts, experiencing some of the processes which had generated the exhibition. The textual frameworks in which museum objects are situated were also transformed through this process. Workshop participants were given the freedom to respond to, and engage with, objects through words or pictures and these responses formed part of the final exhibition.

Whilst the new paradigms for museums focus on experience and engagement rather than the object, this project returns the object to the centre of the museum experience but liberates it from the display cabinet. This was powerfully symbolized in the installation and performances. Four metallic glasshouse frames were constructed, a design concept which responded to the interior architecture of the Royal Museum main hall (influenced by Crystal Palace) with its glass and iron structure. The shape of the glasshouse was inspired by the Monymusk Reliquary, one of the museum's smallest and most treasured exhibits;[25] this house-shaped box, made of wood and covered in decorated bronze and silver plate is thought to have contained a relic from Saint Columba. The panels of the glasshouses were decorated with the Perspex sheets produced during the workshops (echoing the animal engravings on the original). A further layer of reference was created through white cardboard house-shaped cut-outs which were featured in the installation and performance, arranged in various configurations in the glasshouses. These white cubes were constructed by visitors to the exhibition who were invited to decorate the house boxes. During the central phase of the exhibition (19–31 August 2002),[26] improvised performances took place each hour, on the hour between 11.00 a.m. and 4.00 p.m. Costumed performers, dressed in elegant black and white Victorian attire (fitted jackets, lacey white shirts and trousers or long skirts/dresses) interacted with the glasshouses. At the launch event, the glasshouses were covered in vast lengths of black fabric, forming a huge train attached to the backs of four performers. The event opened with the slow and stately revelation of the glasshouses as the performers glided down the vast central hall. As the glasshouse emerged, the dark cloak continued to move down the aisle, a very striking, solemn and funereal image, evoking the ritual and grandeur of the Victorian funeral parade. Performers moved slowly with the neutral faces and bodies we associate with live art (and the death of character), whilst there was also a formality and gravity in their movements (akin to undertakers at funeral ceremonies). Images of death were also evoked in the improvisations; a young visitor commented on the body of one of the performers, lying flat on the floor of a glasshouse, being surrounded by boxes: 'Look, she's dead and he's placing the boxes around her to mark out her grave.'[27] The past of the museum as the container of dead artefacts is evoked in this ceremonial display, but there are other creative energies at work here, transporting the past into the present moment through the decorated white cubes and the white writing on Perspex which is the creativity of the present. The liveness of the improvisatory work was created through spontaneity and risk taking. Performers were required to respond in the moment to drawings produced by visitors to the exhibition: 'Each volunteer will be asked to produce a drawing or description of one of the objects, on to a piece of card. This card will then be deposited in a predetermined space on the display panel, and at regular intervals these interpretations will be reinterpreted by the theatre company.'[28]

This multi-textured, richly evocative performance, might be regarded as site responsive as its form and content is so clearly determined by its location. Indeed, it was presented to me as a site-specific piece by the company's artistic director. Yet, while the museum is an important context, there is very little here (other than the origins of the objects, the locally found stones) which is specific to the National (Scotland) or regional (Edinburgh) context. The piece is shaped by the architecture, history and identity of the building in which the work is situated, so in this sense it is site specific. But there is so much more at work in this project. As the title indicates, the past is being re-created in the present; the temporal and physical structures of the museum are challenged through the live art event and its celebration of the death of traditional museum culture with its nineteenth-century ideas about learning and education.

Hooper Greenhill proposes that 'the public museum was in part shaped by modernist educational ideas, three of which are of particular relevance to museum education: the project to produce single universal explanations of the world, the idea that the self is a fixed and stable entity and the concept that learning consists of absorbing and reproducing a fixed body of approved knowledge' (Hooper-Greenhill, 2007). The white cubes which populated the installation also invoked modern art and the gallery (cleverly blending the association with the historical Monymusk Reliquary and contemporary art). As Trimingham observes, Donald Judd's white-cube installations are regarded by Michael Fried as epitomizing the shift from product to process in the minimalism of the 1960s:

> objects which in their very blankness and apparent refusal of meaning draw attention to their context and the audience's own reception of them and moreover continue this process over time: the object has 'duration'. Fried identified this sort of object as 'theatrical', for him a pejorative term in relation to the art object since the object is no longer 'fixed', i.e., the artist no longer endeavours to fix meaning and contain meaning in the object ....
>
> (2011: 109)

So what are the implications here for history in the performance of heritage and the New Museology? In *Creating the Past* we see how performance is a means of creating and embodying knowledge. In *Performing Heritage* authenticity is redefined as a shifting, flexible concept, rather than an evaluative or value-laden measure in terms of history and fiction. As Johnson perceives: 'for a performance there is authenticity in the enactment, because that is the "real" before the onlooker ... Museum theatre can have the authenticity of history, but that may well clash with the authenticity of fiction, as the demands and consequence benefits, of these different authenticities may not always coexist' (Johnson, 2010: 59). I suggest that in *Creating the Past*, as in other forms of contemporary museum performance (e.g., Triangle's work) there is an authenticity of affect.

Perspectives on evaluation

Assessing the impact of learning in museum contexts has been an emerging theme in conjunction with the changing policies of the last decade. Hooper-Greenhill's work has established new paradigms:

> In September 2001, following a competitive tender, RCMG was charged by MLA, the Museums, Libraries and Archives Council, to develop a way of 'measuring learning' across museums, archives and libraries. The approach devised was grounded in the polydimensional theoretical model for exploring how museums and their visitors construct knowledge ... Museum-based learning which is grounded in active workshops is embodied and immersive, where learning experiences are multiple and kaleidoscopic.[29]

Reckless Sleepers used a range of methods to evaluate their work. Informal feedback sessions were conducted with participants, using a standard set of questions. Each participant was invited to write a comment in a book, handed around at the end of each session. Each participant was also interviewed and these were recorded and transcribed. Visitors to the exhibition also completed questionnaires. The company engaged in formative, ongoing and summative forms of evaluation at each stage of the project. It is evident from the final report as well as the evidence surviving from the project that *Creating the Past* achieved its objectives to create new ways of working in museum contexts and to create new audiences. Above all, however, the images from the project (which include the cover of this book) are evidence that the production values the company aspires to were achieved. Beauty and pleasure are part of the aesthetics of the piece.

In his speech at the launch of the performance, Mole Wetherell (wearing a kilt) referred to the company's struggle

> with our place within this building ... we and the fish have been the only live exhibits within this space ... and I suppose that's what we've

been trying to do, not just animate the space ... no we've been present-
ing something live within a space that is full of inanimate things, but
the processes that we have gone through have re-animated those objects
and things, brought some of them back to life. But then ... what really
animates this space (is the life) it is the people that come into the building and make the objects, animals and exhibits alive ... And what a
live presence does is create a space for dialogue ... to create a space for
interaction.[30]

As Mary Brennan writes in her review of the project:

Even before the performance begins, themes are emerging. What 'holds'
'the past'? How do we curate it? A subtle slippage between the words
'create' and 'curate' hints at intervention/imagination as a factor in how
we interpret objects, inscriptions, the past and the present. The performance sees two women moving in and around the glasshouses. Gathering
up and redeploying the tiny white models, they create settlements,
even turning the body into landscape with houses marching down a
woman's backbone. This introduces a slew of archaeological images. The
glasshouses move, creating sudden tunnels and labyrinths, echoes of
burial chambers even as they suggest our passion for nineteenth-century
conservatories. By the end, this piece is thrumming with questions and
concerns about how we relate to a past which, like ourselves, was flesh
and blood before it turned to dust.

(Brennan, 2002)

4.4 BEYOND SITE: ACCIDENTAL COLLECTIVE'S *PEBBLES TO THE PIER*

In *Creating the Past* site is a source and stimulus but this piece moves beyond the realm of site specificity. Site doesn't contain or constrain the piece; to some extent, we could be in any museum, anywhere in the world, while the working methods are also transportable and could be applied to other projects in museums and galleries. Indeed, this methodological and peda-gogical legacy was one of the project's objectives. The piece challenges the structural and metaphorical frameworks of museums as containers for his-tory, preserving the past in the 'presents' of its objects. In *Creating the Past* as the title indicates, the past becomes present through a process of becoming as the workshop practices and live performance change our perception of the objects. We engage in conceptual blending, understanding them within the context of the performance activity as both historical artefacts and aes-thetic objects. This is a non-representational theatre which can be concep-tualized in terms of Deleuze's discussion of affect. For Deleuze, 'affects are becomings' (Deleuze and Guattari, [1987] 2003: 256), they are 'experienced in a lived duration that involves the difference between two states' (Deleuze, [1970] 1988: 49). The objects in *Creating the Past* recreate meaning through a series of improvisatory acts, generating an affective atmosphere through the encounters between performers, objects and spectators.

My final case study in this chapter explores the role of affect in the prac-tice of place through the work of Accidental Collective, a company based in Kent. From its inception, Accidental Collective sought to bring a different kind of theatre to its audiences and did so by performing in streets, public squares, city halls and shop windows: *The Watching Game* (April 2007), for example, in Canterbury city centre, was a de Certeau-inspired exploration of practices of everyday life where shoppers, tourists and passers-by become creators and producers in their encounters with performers: 'Each individual encountered the project in a different way, depending on his or her own route through the city. Originally focused on surveillance, *The Watching Game* broadened its focus to include wider issues relating to watching and being watched: Inside and outside; private and public; observer and observed; the public becoming performers; performers becoming spectators' (Accidental Collective, 2007). *BIKINI State*, an intervention performed in Manchester's Exchange Square (scene of the 1996 IRA bombing) drew upon Guerrilla theatre through a provocative and playful blend of live art, com-edy and activism; the company aimed to 'puncture your experience of the everyday, challenge your assumptions and your deepest fears' (Accidental Collective, 2009). In *EveryONE's Looking for SomeONE* (2010), two perform-ers, dressed in exaggerated business attire (black bowler hats, black brief cases, white shirts, red ties), interacted with passers by in city streets:

> Two figures lost in the urban landscape trying to find one another. No
> phones, no maps, no compasses, no clue ... the two figures, along their

respective journeys, stop members of the unsuspecting public and have an unexpected exchange. This is the first audience. 'Have you seen this man? Yes, he is dressed like me. If you see him could you text this number? Can I please take a picture of you? I like to remember who I've talked to. Is there someone you are looking for? Everyone is looking for someone'.

(Accidental Collective, 2010)

The clues lead to a performance at a theatre venue, continuing the *Godot* echoes:

Recalling their respective journeys, the two figures trace their routes on a map to identify where they crossed one another's path, or walked along it, or had near misses. They also recount the individual encounters they had with members of the public, displaying their photographs, like proud butterfly collectors. Then, at a dramatic point, they unlock the box containing their mobile phones and share with the audience the text and voice messages they have received ... Unedited and certainly not pre-prepared, exactly who got involved and what they said, what they thought and experienced will be revealed ... or not.

In *Lost in Translation* (2008), a project initially developed for the streets of Canterbury as part of *Portrait of a Nation*, eight performers dressed in white, carried suitcases through the city of Canterbury and created a series of inter-active installations with the contents, each representing a different city. UK cities were mapped on to Canterbury in an event described by the company as 'psycho geography'. This piece was transported to Liverpool as part of the closing celebrations for the 2008 Capital of Culture. Seventeen 'lost' suit-cases in St George's Hall represented the 17 cities in *Portrait of a Nation*. The performers used tourist personas to interact with spectators, engaging them in discussion of their travels, collecting souvenirs and stories which were drawn or written on luggage tags and pinned on performers as 'interactive human installations'.

One of the defining features of Accidental Collective's work is the company's engagement with spectators which they define as audience-centred; another is the company's commitment to creating work which is socially engaged, using public spaces to explore and challenge performance in and through the practices of everyday life. Much of the practice of Accidental Collective contributes to the trend referred to by Gay McAuley to 'create site-based work' which functions to 'elicit memory, or anchor it, in rela-tion to place' (2006: 149). Further, she suggests that 'while performance provides a necessary trigger, the places themselves play an active and complex role in the memory process ... places function to "hold" events that occurred there and ... this holding process can continue over dec-ades.' McCauley cites Edward Casey: 'As much as body or brain, mind or language, place is a keeper of memories – one of the main ways by which the past comes to be secured in the present, held in things before us and around us' (Casey, 2000: 213). As McCauley indicates, 'the importance of this insight is to ensure that we are not just in a place but constitute our own place through our dynamic corporeal relations and practices' (2006: 213). These perceptions, alongside Cameron Duff's essay 'On the role of affect and practice in the production of place' (2010), a paper on design for youth development initiatives in urban settings, provide the context for my consideration of two community projects by Accidental Collective: the first, *Pebbles to the Pier* took place in the coastal town of Herne Bay (22–24 August 2007) while the second, *I Am Small THE WORLD IS BIG* (2011), was a five-month-long project culminating in the company taking over County Hall in Maidstone, home to Kent County Council (June 2011). In both projects we see the doing and making of place through performance activities, whilst it is also evident through the practices explored in each of these places (one coastal, one urban) that 'to experience place' is indeed 'to be *affected by place*' (Duff, 2010). Moreover, taking Duff's cue and drawing on Casey's terminology we can see how participants in these projects were involved in a transformation of 'thin or designated spaces into dynamic thick places' (Duff, 2010).

Mi Won Kwon's perception of site-specific art as an affirmation of self and community identity, protecting the viewer from 'social alienation, economic fragmentation, and political disenfranchisement' (2004) is evident in the cautious commissioning process for this project. Accidental Collective responded to a commission received from Canterbury City Council to create a 'new and original event for the Herne Bay Festival 2007'. The company's declared objective (in keeping with its mission statement) to bring live art to the coastal community of Herne Bay involved them building on the work they had successfully pioneered in the nearby Cathedral city of Canterbury (which, however, has a very different demographic). The company were perplexed that their initial proposal for interventions involving CCTV shop window displays and performance encounters designed to provoke a sense of 'watching me, watching you' which had been welcomed (and funded) by Kent County Council (and was well received by the Canterbury public) produced such a strongly negative response and a demand for the company to radically revise their proposal:

> I've read this through and am very unsure of the proposals you are making, they are not really what were [sic] thinking of. The brief if you recall was for something that could work within the context of the Tour de France, Whitstable Oyster Festival and Herne Bay Festival and I don't think these do.
>
> I think there are major issues around privacy, moderating content and suitability for the festival audiences ... I also think that the interventions

would encourage anti-social behaviour which as a Local Authority we cannot be party to ... I realize you have a current interest in surveillance but don't think this works in the context of the festivals, which are focused on family audiences and the positive atmosphere we are trying to promote. The work needs to be accessible and I think these proposals sound almost 'Big Brother' ... *I know the audience base for these events are not ready for something like this at present.*[31]

Accidental Collective were offered £400 for research and development. The company were presented with a major challenge as they later acknowledged; '*Pebbles to the Pier* took us outside our comfort zone, into an unfamiliar setting, to an unfamiliar audience' whilst they also needed to address the concerns of the City Council funders.[32] From its inception this was a piece designed to be site and community specific whilst it was also seeking to bring new forms of art and performance to east Kent. At this stage, Accidental Collective were a fledgling company, ambitious to challenge local audiences and to generate new ones. At the time of the project they described themselves as:

a creative think-tank focused on performance, live art, and media. We aim to confront lazy theatre, lazy performers and lazy audiences ... Using unorthodox approaches to performance we cater for audiences living in an age of microwave meals, internet and reality TV. By exploring the limits of 'theatre' and devising new modes for its presentation we seek to engage with these audiences in a provocative way.[33]

The project was promoted by the company as 'specifically created for Herne Bay, it took into account its physical environment, its history and community'.[34] The promotional material also referred to the project being 'a response to a commission by Canterbury City Council aimed at invigorating the more traditional programme of Herne Bay's summer festival'.[35] So from its outset this was a project with a transformational creative and cultural agenda. Herne Bay is in several respects similar to Margate as a coastal community in the early stages of regeneration. Its population is predominantly white and working class and its economy continues to be dependent upon tourism (hence seasonal employment patterns). Like similar towns, Herne Bay suffered severe post-war economic and social deprivation and has been a focus for regeneration initiatives. Throughout the project, there was a sensitivity to, and awareness of, the significance of place. Notes from one of the earliest company meetings refers to 'people that *make* the place' and asks 'How do we engage with these people? We're outsiders.'[36] A further note suggests an attitude towards the town which the project would later challenge: 'fed up with seafront/ can we reject it?'

In their initial proposal, the surveillance theme (which built on the company's previous work in public spaces) can be seen as a de Certeau-inspired resistance to the regulation of town space. De Certau refers to the 'dispersed, tactical and makeshift' procedures which involve individuals pursuing their own rules and routes (1984: xiv). Walking is a pedestrian speech act, a process of movement, improvisation and passage. Performance, however, can extend this through the kinds of activities Accidental Collective initiated in the first phase of their project at Herne Bay. A two-day durational event involved a series of staged encounters between performers and the public; these were carried out spontaneously and randomly, often involving objects (such as an umbrella) or singing 'Oh I do like to be beside the seaside'. Dressed in distinctive white dresses and suits and walking slowly down the high street in pouring rain and high winds, the performers attracted attention, producing a series of enunciations, to use de Certeau's terms which 'initiate, maintain or interrupt contact' (99). These interventions were a strategy to engage the public in interaction: 'the playful yet emotive nature of the interventions attracted attention yet never demanded it, causing our actions to be followed by curious stares which often led to questions about what we were doing. We would then use this opportunity to explain the project and encourage people to sit down and write a message to the pier.'[37] The company's use of the term emotive is significant here as this is where the work departs from de Certeau. During the research and development phase, the company devised various ways of interacting with Herne Bay's public (residents, shoppers, holidaymakers, day-trippers) and discovered the importance of the pier as central to the sense of community and heritage in the town. This is where the emotive responses to the performers were most clearly and strongly articulated as the company developed an understanding of community identity being dependent on material culture (as well as experience and memory) and a sense of place as being actively created as a constant process of becoming. As Ashworth and Graham have noted, identities are 'ascribed to places by people' they are 'user determined, polysemic and unstable through time' (2005: 3). The pier, it became evident, was iconic to the town's sense of identity. The dislocated pier head – is a haunting feature of the coastal landscape, the skeletal remains of its iron frame powerfully symbolize the history of Herne Bay as a thriving seaside resort and its faded grandeur as it sinks deeper into its watery grave. Landscapes, as Tilley perceives, are, like place, 'actively re-worked, interpreted and understood in relation to differing social and political agendas (and) forms of social memory' (2006: 8).

Bourdieu's notion of a working-class popular participatory aesthetic is relevant here as the company discovered local support for its activities and a high level of community engagement. The significance of the pier to the local community is evident throughout Herne Bay's history. Built in 1830, the Herne Bay Pier Company offered shares for the construction, which was subsequently referred to as 'the people's pier'. What is also evident in local parlance is the use of the female pronoun to refer to the pier, a personification which indicates a form of collective attachment and community identity. As with so many seafront piers, the history is one of decay, damage and destruction, mirroring the town's decline. Demolished in 1871 in a state of disrepair, it was rebuilt in iron (1890) and became a celebrated icon for the town during its period of popularity (1920s in particular). As the holiday crowds dwindled, the economy struggled and the town became something of a backwater, the pier suffered dereliction; damaged by fires and storms it became increasingly fragile; a serious fire in 1970 caused extensive damage and a vicious storm in 1978 decapitated the remains. All that survives is the head, cut off from its home town and stranded out at sea where it appears to be watching the sea front as a perpetual reminder of the town's faded fortunes. The poignancy of the pier's history, its tragic demise and its enduring absent presence by virtue of its location posed some problems for Accidental Collective, who were concerned about creating nostalgia or melancholia in their audiences, 'especially because this might have alienated younger people'. The white costumes emerged from this, inspired by (but not imitating) the pierrot troupes and popular forms of entertainment during the British seaside heyday; the costumes evoked the past positively whilst also indicating the playful aspect of the company's methods: 'we intended to reference the past, without copying it or recreating it.' Thus the costumes also evoked Englishness by referencing cricket outfits as well as having ghostly connotations.

The project was divided into three stages over two days: intervention (durational performance), exchange (participatory opportunities where the performers and the public engaged in dialogue) and 'celebration' (a final event on the sea front). During the interventions the company used a postcard of the pier as a stimulus, inviting passers-by to comment on the significance of the pier. Play was identified as an important part of their methodology and a means of engaging participants as they battled with umbrellas on windy beaches, played with beach balls on and off the sand, skipped and sang along the prom, wandered through the streets and up and down the sea front wearing flippers and goggles and observed passers by and scenery with binoculars. The activities played with incongruity, disrupting spatial and social orders which are the organizing principles of urban space. De Certeau refers to the 'leaps' and 'skips' of the pedestrian, travelling through insignificant spaces to places of meaning and purpose (1984: 101). In these performance interventions, the familiar was made strange and perception shifted; beach games in the high street drew attention to the ordered grid we are accustomed to and which constrains and regulates the practice of everyday life. Live art had arrived in Herne Bay, disrupting, challenging, transforming, creating, and making place.

In addressing the question posed by Hill and Paris, 'what is the place of this kind of work in this kind of place'? (Hill and Paris, 2006: 9), the company explored a range of locations for what they referred to as site visits: pubs, community centres, parks and the beach, all of which made them aware of the diverse and complex histories which constitute the particularities of place. A conversation with an ex-gangster provided a wealth of material; like many Herne Bay immigrants, he retired from London, attracted by the cheap housing, the coast and easy connections to the capital. He returned to his house to collect a book of poetry written about the town which he donated to the project.

In the exchange phase, the company took their cue from history and the centrality of the tea house. Setting up tables with lace table cloths, tea and biscuits and a huge windbreaker featuring a picture of the old pier head, they began to draw the community in. Children and teenagers were lured by the biscuits, others by the strange spectacle as evident in the recorded comments:

'Is it some kind of play?'
'It looks more like a Mad Hatter's tea party.'

The spectacle was also associated with itinerant fortune tellers, particularly in the context of the fairground features on the prom: trampolines, donkeys, various rides, amusement arcades, hot dogs, chips and candy floss. A wide range of clientele were engaged in these sessions: holidaymakers, day-trippers, a coach trip of ladies from Age Concern as well as locals. The company engaged participants in discussion of their experiences of Herne Bay, community identity, heritage and its relation to memory and the significance of the pier. What emerged in these conversations was a strong sense of place; there was a perception of Herne Bay as being inferior to its more fashionable neighbours, Whitstable and Canterbury. It was even suggested that Herne Bay, which used to have its own city council, had been 'raped' and abused by Canterbury, starved of resources and left to suffer as an area of deprivation. Council meeting agendas, the company were advised, reflected the priorities of those in power with issues specific to Herne Bay not as frequent or prominent as other localities. Herne Bay was persistently characterized as 'other' in relation to Whitstable and Canterbury.

Community participants wrote messages or drew pictures for the pier (which were later transcribed on to tissue paper and wrapped around pebbles for the final performance in which they were cast out to the old pier at the end of the celebratory event on the beach). Battling against the elements (in August), the performers changed the location of their windbreakers offering shelter as well as tea parties in public spaces. They also ventured into the cafes where the public sheltered and the British weather provided a further theme of community significance. The conversations in these contexts provided further material for the final performance and are recorded in the large photo album which beautifully documents the programme. Ninety-year-old Madge remembered the tea dances of her youth in the King's Hall, others remembered the pier before its decline, holidays in the seaside town's heyday and Herne Bay during the war. Not all the messages were written; some were drawings and some a combination of both:

> A large outline of the pier head. 'My mum used to play on the half penny machines.'

> They were wonderful. The dancers. Peggy Spencer and her formation team dancers in Streetham, 'Hold your head up when you dance.' But I taught myself dancing. One day my dear friend said to me, 'Where have you been, Madge?' He couldn't believe I went on my own. I used to just get up and go: Eastbourne, Bournemouth, Herne Bay. I was so much younger then, in my forties. Seen things get better, get worse, its all swings and roundabouts.

What emerges from the documentation, the event itself and the various lecture-performances about it subsequently (Manchester, 2008; Leeds, 2009) is the sense of place as lived experience and as relational. There is some nostalgia in the recollections and messages, but there is also a wealth of other emotions, the 'feeling states' or 'maelstroms of affect' (anger, shame, hope, fear, sorrow joy) Nigel Thrift refers to and which are cited by Duff in his account of being 'affected by place': 'Affects are, in this sense, not only indicative of the subjective mood of certain places; they also frame the array of activities and practices potentially enactable within that place' (Duff, 2010: 884). For Thrift, neglect of the 'affective register of cities' in urban literature is a serious oversight which needs to be redressed as affect plays an increasingly important role in the construction, perception and performance of urban life. Cities are required to demonstrate 'expressivity', Thrift argues and affect facilitates 'more sophisticated interventions', contributing to knowledges which are then deployed politically in the service of innovation, creativity and enterprise, the 'buzz' words associated with success and transformation (Thrift, 2004: 57–8). Duff also refers to Spinoza, arguing that affects 'also constitute *action-potential*'; an individual's motivation to 'act' is directly related to their affective capacities (Spinoza, [1631] 1989: 131). Affect, Duff argues, is experienced in the body, creating a dynamic interaction with place: 'just as bodies affect one another *in place*, bodies are inevitably affected *by place* such that place 'seems to be a vital element in the constitution of affect' (Duff, 2010: 885). These affects are subject to circumstance: 'Affect, therefore, describes both the distinctive set of feeling states realisable within a particular place as well as the store of action-potential, of expressions, capacities, and practices experienced in that space' (885). Above all, then, place is relational. This was evident in the final phase of the *Pebbles to the Pier* project, which was perceived and described by many as deeply moving:

> The idea was that the beach performance at dusk should unite the composite stages of the project, so it should tie together the intervention work we had done (our strangely surreal ghostly presence in the town) and the Exchange Point (the messages shared with us by holidaymakers and locals, adults and children). And last but not least, of course, it was important for the communities that contributed to have an opportunity to see their message as part of the performance. The casting out of the messages at dusk was a conscious decision to attempt to evoke [a] sense of vigil.[38]

There were over 100 individual messages and an audience of nearly 200 people for what the company referred to variously as the 'final ceremony' and 'celebration'. Above all, this was an event in a public space, attracting further attention from passers-by as well as the audience who had assembled to see the performance. In their documentation the company refer to the importance of the aesthetic, particularly in this aspect of the work; a contributory factor to the power of the performance element was the strength of the visual composition – the white costumes, choreographed movement, the fading light as the night drew in and the tea lights and torches became more visible (the audience were invited to bring a light). The coastal landscape at night provided an atmospheric backdrop as the pier head became less visible as darkness fell and the tide crept closer to the shore. Various texts provided a poetic counterpoint (extracts from Woolf's *To the Lighthouse* and e e Cummings's *maggie and milly and molly and may*) in conjunction with songs and shanties. This bricolage of elements was non-representational: 'the movement was never designed to illustrate the texts. The movement was expressly intended NOT to visually describe elements of the script. We were not interested in making that kind of work. Instead, we devised abstract actions, derived from the images conjured by the historical texts, and inferred in the poems.'[39]

The result was a rich blend of images and evocations drawing on the material generated through the previous stages of the project: themes included journeys, searching for something, memory, childhood, faded glamour, romance, loss and the passage of time. Umbrellas, binoculars and references to the bizarre happenings in the interventions created a sense of playfulness (as appropriate to the beach setting), while elements of popular performance (slapstick, stand-up, dance routines) punctuated the readings. The routines presented (like a series of acts) drew upon high and low culture as well as the material gathered from the public. The pebble-throwing ritual which concluded the event was particularly poignant. Audience members were invited to form a procession, take a pebble (which were handed out) which had been wrapped in tissue paper with one of the messages for the pier, and cast it out to sea. The company identified two factors which they had not

Figure 9   Pebbles to the Pier, Accidental Collective, 2007. Photograph by kind permission of Peter Fry (photography) and Accidental Collective

anticipated and which indicate the extent to which the participants actively and affectively engaged with the material. Firstly, people who had written a message wanted to cast their own pebble out to sea and secondly, they unwrapped the pebbles to see the messages on the tissue paper. This created a connection between themselves and the message writers they had never met. Finally, the four performers waded slowly into the water, until they disappeared from view. In their subsequence performance lecture, the company (standing in boxes of water) presented the audience with pebbles wrapped in tissue (taking the original messages and writing them out again on to tissue paper), provoking debates about authenticity when they revealed that these were reconstructions. The story is told of the 11-year-old girl who asked a performer, 'Where's my pebble? Who's got my pebble?', determined to cast her personal message out to the pier. As one couple were walking back to the beach they were overheard saying 'There's no way I'm chucking this in the sea, I'm taking it home and keeping it.' It is evident through this project that performance created a series of felt relationships with place: as Duff writes, 'Place ought never to be reduced to a determinate set of points on a map, a simple geographical expression. Rather, place always already conjures the lived, felt and relational experience of a thinking, feeling body/subject' (2010: 885). Whilst the project was not unsettling in terms of content, it clearly attracted new audiences, particularly teenagers who were drawn to the exchanges and returned for the final celebration. One of the most striking features of the evening performance was the mixed audience – passers-by, families, the elderly, groups of teenagers, university students (even in August), tourists (including day-trippers who had stayed on for the performance) and individuals who seemed to have some connection with the project. Above all, there was a sense of a community connected to the performance of place and the pebble-throwing ritual was deeply significant, symbolizing the relationship between community and heritage.

In his discussions of the politics of affect, performativity and place, Nigel Thrift is cautious about the term community: 'none of these approaches could be described as based on a notion of human individuals coming together in community' (2007: 175). Yet the affective approaches he outlines are pertinent to Accidental Collective's practices. Affect, Thrift explains, is 'embodied practice', the 'doing' of emotions. Expression of emotion is generally non-representational or physical (i.e., we talk 'about' emotions, which are physically manifest). Throughout this project, individual and personal engagement with place was explored – through one-to-one encounters, messages written on stones and even the final ceremony where each individual threw a stone with a different message (not their own). These messages articulated emotional engagement with the pier via memory and association: sorrow for the past the pier represents, anger at the demise of the town and its heritage, hope for the future, joy in the pleasures of the present and humour:

> Having moved to Herne Bay in October 1956 as a boy of 12, I remember many happy walks along the pier down to the landing stage, passing many enthusiastic fishermen along the way. It would be nice to see the old pier brought back so that I could do those walks once again.

> I would support funding a Herne Bay Pier as soon as possible.

> Used to come here loads as kids. Just had the most disgusting lunch. You don't get the service you used to. Now I'm nearly 90.

> [A big sun is shining on the paper] I made a friend. I am from Nottingham. Elliot aged 7

> As a holidaymaker from Zimbabwe I think the weather is rubbish, Love Rubin.

> This is Mike Almy aged 38: I used to fish on the pier, then later I ran boat trips detailing the history of the three piers, the cannon and the clock tower, which came from the end of pier one. I took 500 people out, then 2400 people the next year.

> Dear Pier,
> How do you feel stuck out there all alone?

Although the procession at the end involved a sense of coming together it was, to use Deleuze's terms, a formation as a social body ([1970] 1988). As an audience, we were a collection of individuals or groups with different relationships to the place and the event. Yet there was an affective force at work here as the audience was conjoined through social interaction; moving as one body composed of individuals as we processed to the water and cast our pebbles.

According to Edward Casey, affective engagement with place is the means by which 'thick' places can be differentiated from 'thin' places. Affective engagement transforms space (creating 'place'); there can be 'no place without self and no self without place' ('no place without self and no self without place' [Casey, 2001: 684]). Affect is produced through the interaction of places and bodies (Duff, 2010; Massumi, 2002; Thrift, 2007). For Casey, thin places are devoid of individuality or cultural specificity; associated with globalization, thin places, like Auge's concept of 'non-places', include airport lounges, shopping malls, chain stores and fast food outlets. Thick places, it is suggested emerge from affective engagement with place.

In *Pebbles to the Pier* we see the production of 'thick' place through performance processes which engage participants in felt and lived experiences and responses to place. This is not to suggest that Herne Bay typifies the 'thin' places Casey identifies. Indeed, much of the work on affect and place focuses on urban environments and this is also a focus of increasing interest in performance practice. Companies such as Blast Theory use performance and digital media as a means to engage with place. Blast Theory's work combines a range of multimedia technologies such as augmented reality, architectural mapping, digital projection, geotagging, social networking and virtual reality to enable participants as players to actively and playfully engage in place-making processes. Accidental Collective's subsequent work builds on their experience of working in both urban and coastal community contexts and offers an example of how performance engages in the politics of place making, providing a means of transforming thin places into thick as affect is embedded in place.

I am small THE WORLD IS BIG (2010–11) involved Accidental Collective working with a diversity of community groups in Kent and culminated in a whole day event at County Hall, headquarters of Kent County Council. This setting was important to the piece which was designed to involve occupation of sites associated with political power (especially a governing body) and legislation (the piece was developed from a pilot project set, for the most part, in the senate building at the University of Kent). Maidstone has none of the emotive or nostalgic connotations of Herne Bay, being a 1960s conurbation with a spatial lay out (high street, car parks etc.) that looks much like many other UK towns. As the title suggests, the project explored the relations between the local and the global, between 'our little patch and the wider world, and the interconnected nature of social-political, economic and environmental issues.' (Accidental Collective, 2011). These interconnections involved a range of contexts as the company worked with local community groups and used the internet to connect to the wider world, exploring relations and synergies, personal and global interests and experiences.

The project involved a series of workshops in a range of settings.[40] Participants were asked to create maps following a logic of their choosing (holidays, family, friends, wars, any aspects of personal or cultural history). At the centre of the project was a huge map (comprised of cut up atlases stitched together – a remapping of the world from a place-based perspective). The workshops used maps as a stimulus to explore memories of place. In these accounts, participants spoke about their personal engagement with places which have affected them. The Maidstone performance took the form of a huge installation, taking over the headquarters of KCC. Masking tape made the original signage both visible and invisible so that participants were aware of the usual routes around the building and the identity and function of the rooms, whilst also being aware of the changed routes and functions through makeshift cardboard signage. This created the sense of a takeover with permission to break rules and codes governing the use of the building. Visitors to the event were free to choose a route and to participate in a series of activities in the various spaces. The large central complex at the heart of the building was transformed into a marketplace environment with various stalls where visitors could design their own banner, choose a flag for a cupcake, join a tea party with world leaders (represented by puppet figures of your choice) and various one-to-one opportunities to engage in big issue discussions (e.g., how would you make the world a better place?). In the council chambers (replete with leather seats and individual microphones), a series of debates was held, initiated by participants and linked to the outside world via twitter. Topics included whether skateboarding should be allowed in public spaces, the school leaving age, capital punishment and CCTV. Finally, in a large room at the centre of the building, the map-making process took place.

This then was a project about place in which the site was appropriate to the content. There was an anarchic sense of playfulness throughout the day; the banners made by participants were taken to the council chambers for the finale (although several individuals asked to keep them or marched them around the building) and the huge map was paraded on to the public concourse at the end of the day to a rather bewildered and unsuspecting group of bystanders. What was remarkable about this event, however, was the way in which the public engaged, particularly groups of teenagers. The area surrounding County Hall, by virtue of its proximity to the town centre and the large open space which surrounds it, is frequented by teenagers, providing an ideal skateboarding area, while the shoe hanging from a lamp post indicates that this is also a spot where drugs can be obtained (indeed, a dealer is reported to have joined the audience). It is also in limbo, a nowhere zone, outside of the shopping area and close to the train station, an urban/spatial 'gap' which teenagers occupy. In his study of young people in Vancouver and the personal and social dimensions of place making, Duff observes that 'what emerged very forcefully was the sense that young people struggle to identify places of belonging and meaning. In almost every instance, participants described carving such places out of the order and routine of more formally designated places' (2010: 888). Indeed, in this instance, it was evident from the skateboarding discussion that one of the attractions of the space in front of the council offices was the fact that the setting was in view of the authorities, a space which was public but immediately adjacent to the very private confines of the corridors of legislative power; 'this art of cultivating private spaces from the interstices of the more public of designated sites was common to almost all triad members ... The identification of places for privacy and social interaction also involved the search for spaces to support specific activities or pastimes such as skateboarding, free running or breakdancing' (889). Spaces are chosen for 'privacy, interaction and spontaneity' but are also illicit and may well involve the risk of encounters with authority (security guards, etc.). As Duff observes, 'these are pedestrian speech acts in de Certeau's rhetorics of urban place; it is clear that participants experience privacy, social engagement, skateboarding and breakdancing as meaningful, significant and life affirming.' In the contributions from the teenagers in Maidstone, there was also a sense of the attraction of these spaces as potentially anarchic, risk-taking, intermediary spaces between private and public; this, I suggest, was part of the 'action potential' of these spaces. 'If these thick places are made in and of practice, they come to evoke a sense of belonging and meaning in affect' (Duff, 2010: 889). This project opened the doors to the teenagers to enter a previously prohibited space, one replete with significance as representative of the law, the symbolic order of law and authority. The opportunity to sit in the council chambers and give voice was clearly liberating; they phoned friends on mobiles telling them to come and get free tea and biscuits and talk: 'It's cool.' A nervous porter warned the company that some of the teenagers needed watching carefully as they were known to him, but they participated constructively and energetically, unconstrained. Duff's research explores how individuals negotiate the city in search of those sites which later become *places* in and of the practices they support. Thus he argues that 'affect – and not the asyndetic wanderings of practice – *is the principle mechanism threading urban places together* (891, my emphasis). What motivates and attracts these young people to place are the affective qualities of the environment and this is the most important criteria for selecting places to hang out, places which become personalized and associated with group identities:

> one is affected by the atmosphere, the *potential in place*, before one investigates its value as a space of and for practice. Skateboarders

encountering a courtyard outside an insurance firm, for example, are first affected by the quality of light, the expanse of flat concrete leading to a flight of stairs, and the privacy afforded by high walls on two sides.

(Duff, 2010: 891–2)

For Accidental Collective, the symbolic significance of site was a driver for this project which, they fantasized, might progress to the House of Commons and then to the European Commission. But, as the Maidstone example demonstrated, this is a project which, although it might be as portable as the Stan's Cafe model *Of All the People in All the World*, involves far more than site. Indeed, there are many thematic similarities with the Stan's Cafe project (globalization, environmentalism, internationalism, global and local, etc.) but what both projects also indicate, in common with the other examples in this chapter, is the importance of place in applying performance and the role of affect in the production of place.

This chapter, in foregrounding place, has deliberately featured several locations which have personal significance for me as the 'thick' places of my history. Stan's Cafe are based in Birmingham, close to the suburb in which I was brought up, while the two projects at the opening and close of the chapter are based in Kent where I have been based for the longest part of my working and adult life. In both examples we see how performance activities demonstrate and contribute to 'the significance of thick places and their production in diverse circuits of affect and practice, movement and sensation. Thick places punctuated participants' everyday experience of the city.' As Duff indicates, diverse experiences are documented in these thick places and performance contributes to the process of making place, establishing a sense of belonging and meaning. In the case of Accidental Collective's second project, moreover, participants were invited to play in a form of virtual environment, imagining how they might reshape and reimagine the world.

The next chapter explores the concept of the virtual further by considering how digital technologies transform and transport participants through performance activities, while in Part III, I discuss the work of the American practitioner, Martha Bowers and her site-responsive community participation performance with particular reference to *The Dream Life of Bricks*. This extends the discussion in this chapter, considering how applying performance provides a means and a space to respond to the changes that are taking place in the world and to reflect, rehearse and play with new visions of imagined futures. This draws upon what Barbara Kirshenblatt-Gimblett (2004) and Jill Dolan (2005) refer to as the utopian imagination. Performance can offer a Utopian Otherworld, challenging the constraints of existing structures, enabling us to imagine a better society and creating possibilities for transformation through the production of new knowledges.

Contemporary Performance, I suggest (and this is developed in my conclusion) is increasingly engaging in dialogue with, and seeking inspiration from, the affective practices of applied and social modes of theatre and performance, as a radical aesthetic begins to emerge from what might become a new avant-garde, one which is perhaps more concerned with individual than collective emancipation and one in which Isobel Armstrong's aesthetic principles are upheld of 'playing, dreaming, thinking and feeling' (2000).

5
Digital Transportations

Digital divides, digital natives and C&T

In *Technology and Social Inclusion*, Mark Warschauer describes a project in a slum area of New Delhi which sought to bridge the perceived digital divide between those with access to information and communication technologies and those without by providing computer and Internet access for the city's street children. The 'Hole-in the-Wall' experiment involved computers in booths with exposed monitors operated by joysticks and buttons in place of a keyboard and mouse. In accordance with a principle of 'minimally invasive education', no formal instruction was provided and the children were self-directed learners. Although considered a success by researchers and the Indian government due to the volume of users and the evidence of engagement in computer activity (children were reported to have mastered computer basics, using Microsoft Word and Paint and accessing the Internet), Warschauer articulates reservations, based on his fieldwork: 'the Internet access was of little use because it seldom functioned. No special educational programs had been made available, and no special content was provided in Hindi, the only language the children knew' (Warschauer, 2003). Some parents expressed concern about the new technology distracting the children from their education as they preferred to spend their time on computer games rather than homework (and the situation of the kiosks made them easily accessible en route between school and home). Warschauer offers a range of further examples to illustrate his central premise that technology requires the use of intermediaries:

> [it] does not exist as an external variable to be injected from the outside to bring about certain results. Rather, it is woven in a complex manner into social systems and processes ... the goal of using ICT with marginalized groups is not to overcome a digital divide but rather to further a process of social inclusion. To accomplish this, it is necessary to 'focus on the transformation, not the technology'.
>
> (Jarboe, 2001 cited in Warschauer, 2003: 8)

Digital technologies have an increasingly important role to play in everyday life as well as in theatre and the relations between the two is one of the most exciting areas of performance research and practice. Contemporary performance companies and practitioners such as the UK's Blast Theory and Stelarc, New York's 31Down and Johannes Birringer's AlienNation.Co produce cutting-edge work variously exploring the interface between the live and the virtual, the real and cyber performance whilst also exploring the potential of interactivity as a means of engaging spectators as players in the production of meaning (see Birringer, 2008; Broadhurst and Machon, 2007; Carver and Beardon, 2004; Causey, 2006; Dixon, 2007; Giannachi, 2004, 2007; Klich and Scheer, 2011). As performance practitioners and theorists fully understand, even in activities which are not orientated towards social inclusion, the importance of a physical element via the human interface is fundamental to generating meaningful interaction. Pedagogically, as Warschauer's study demonstrates, technology can operate only at a basic and superficial level if it is divorced from the social and interpersonal contexts which frame and shape our everyday realities. Warschauer challenges notions of the digital as a separate universe, arguing that information and communication technologies exist in conjunction with the other languages and forms we engage with in the production of meaning. In terms of learning, the technology needs to be embodied: 'what is most important about ICT is not so much the availability of the computing device or the Internet line, but rather people's ability to *make use* of that device ... to engage in *meaningful social practices*' (Warschauer, 2003: 38).

The ability to make use of technology is dependent on a range of factors – economic, social, educational and personal. Waschauer argues that 'community informatics' and 'communities of practice' are the most conducive to learning and the promotion of social capital. The emphasis here is on the importance of contextualizing learning (the situatedness of the learning environment) to promote individual and community engagement, making the learning meaningful. As Paolo Freire long ago demonstrated in relation to literacy, teaching needs to be sensitive to the social, cultural and economic contexts in which learners are situated (1971). Literacy is linked to economic posterity and computer literacy is similarly linked to wealth. In addition to physical capital (financial), social capital is also important for social and economic development. This is endorsed through social network theory and research which demonstrates the importance of connections between social and physical relations in conjunction with networked environments; as Warschauer concludes:

> strategies that take into account the social nature of access, recognize the interaction between face to face and online communications, and combine Internet use with a broad range of other new and old media provide the best opportunities for promoting social inclusion through ICT
>
> (2003: 197)

The potential of drama to facilitate access to digital technologies, promoting social engagement in a meaningful learning environment is evident in the work of the UK theatre company, C&T. Founded in 1988, C&T began work as a Theatre in Education Company: Collar and TIE. Committed to participatory theatre and process drama, the company worked in schools and community settings using the workshop-based approaches of Dorothy Heathcote and Gavin Bolton. The concept of the actor in role was fundamental to their methodology. Target audiences for the company were young people, people with disabilities, ethnic minorities, those in rural areas and the economically disadvantaged. In seeking to access these new audiences, the company became known for its pioneering use of new technology, including mass and popular media forms. One of the company's most successful early projects, for example, was *The Dark Theatre* (1994–6)) which involved various schools using drama to create a comic book. Another project *Cambat* (1999–2001) explored young people's perceptions of and anxieties about a surveillance society; through the use of live performance, video and a website, the project was designed to turn CCTV cameras back on the individuals operating them. One of the company's objectives was to cross-reference different forms of performance in its work, creating 'dramatic products that ... can continue to explore and develop through other dramatizing media.'[1] This led to the development of the concept of the 'dramatic property' as one of the defining characteristics of the company's work. This term is used to indicate the company's intention that the effects of the projects would have a life beyond the performance.

> DPs are grounded in the globalized culture young people are living in – therefore they often involve new technologies or other literacies with which young people are familiar. In other words, young people think DPs are cool and they attract people who might otherwise avoid the performing arts.[2]

As the company's work with new technologies developed, they found that many of the traditional forms of TIE employed in their projects were redefined in relation to postmodern performance strategies. The company continued to draw upon and to develop aspects of TIE practice (and continues to refer, for example, to Heathcote and Bolton in its training programmes), but changed its title to reflect its orientation towards a different model of applied theatre. The acronym C&T now encompasses a range of functions: Computers & Theatre, Community & Training, Creativity & Technology, Culture & Theory.

The terms of reference change in accordance with the rapidly changing contexts in which the company works:

> The dizzying pace of technological development and the endlessly creative ways technology is used and subverted means C&T has to ride the

wave of change. Whilst blogging, podcasting and texting are already widespread, machinima, wikis, blogs and a plethora of other developments are gaining momentum.[3]

At the heart of the company's work, however, are seven values they consider fundamental to theatre for young people in a globalized culture: collaboration, creativity, intelligence, learning, originality, quality and inclusivity. C&T's practice recognizes and responds to the need to engage young people in activities which are not only relevant to the social and cultural contexts in which they are situated, but which use the vocabularies and technologies they embody and practise as the 'digital natives' of the twenty-first century. Informed by Marc Prensky's pioneering work (2001a, 2001b, 2001c, 2005, 2010), C&T have developed a range of projects using methods appropriate for the new generation and their digital culture. As Prensky observes, the challenges for education are considerable as the pedagogies developed through the twentieth-century are not appropriate for the learners of the twenty-first century. The problems are fundamental as the brain's plasticity means that young people, immersed in digital technology are differently wired to their predecessors so perceive, think and learn in particular ways:

> Digital Natives are used to receiving information really fast. They like to parallel process and multi-task. They prefer their graphics *before* their text rather than the opposite. They prefer random access (like hypertext). They function best when networked. They thrive on instant gratification and frequent rewards. They prefer games to 'serious' work.
>
> (2001b)

Digital natives are predominantly non-linear, visual learners whose interaction with technology is embodied and socialized; as Warschauer concludes, with reference to Poster (1997), 'just as technology becomes part of the neural network of the mind, it also becomes part of the social network of humanity ... The Internet is not so much a tool as a new social space that restructures social relations' (Warschauer, 2003: 215).

Insights from neurobiology are informing education research as evident in Jonathan Barnes's study, *Cross-Curricular Learning 3–14*, where he suggests that the curriculum for adolescents should be responsive to new understandings of the developing brain and the influence of the environment and the individual's activities and practices on brain development:

> Neurologists tell us the mature brain is one where connections and inhibitors are widely distributed and collaborative, and less susceptible to impulse or purely emotional responses. To help 8–14 year olds' brains reorganize and refine in this direction, perhaps social collaboration and distributing intelligence between various members of a group should be more frequently

modelled within an educational setting ... If the thinking, predicting, reflecting parts of our brain come slowly to maturity and if through education we can make an impact upon which parts of the brain mature more quickly, then this would tend to affect the curricula we plan.

(2007: 81)

Thus Barnes advocates learning methods which emphasize the social, the physical and the sensual (rather than the abstract) and which cultivate emotional intelligence.

The changing environments in which digital natives are immersed are manifest in a range of ways, including language and cognition. As the performance vocabularies of postmodern youth have been constructed through the media, television, computer gaming and digital representations have, ironically, become the source to be copied. Thus, rather than art representing life, young people draw upon mediated versions of the real in their imaginative and creative acts. New techniques are needed to represent new realities. C&T have actively sought to appropriate media conventions in their creation of new models of participatory performance. Embracing Raymond Williams' notion of the 'dramatized society' (Williams, 1983), C&T appropriated digital technologies to create a performance vocabulary to work with the digital natives of the twenty-first century. As Rob Lines explains:

Digital immigrants are used to the post arriving once a day, low speed snail-mail, while natives expect their inbox to regularly update at the twitch of a mouse-click. Immigrants watch TV that tells them what happens next, but natives want to participate in the story and affect the outcome. Immigrants love a story with a beginning, middle and end, whilst natives want to custom-assemble their own narrative. Immigrants learn by passively listening – natives learn by actively collaborating.

(2007)

Thus C&T are committed to process-based methodologies and to projects which speak to and are produced by digital natives. In C&T's work, performance and media are involved in a dynamic dialogue of 'remediation', in terms of Hans Thies-Lehmann's analysis:

when film and then television first emerged they 'remediated' theatre, modelling themselves on theatre and on dramatic structures ... When contemporary experimental live performance now uses or references media, it is partially 'remediating' film and television but not in order insidiously to 'replicate' them to maintain its legitimacy ... but in order to probe their status and impact on us in a self-conscious manner – including their history of remediating theatre.

(2006: 13)

Prensky's advocation of games-based approaches and forms which draw upon the neural and social networks of digital natives is evident in C&T's methodologies. The Living Newspaper, for example, is a reinvention of the 1930s form of documentary theatre, using the Internet. There is a certain irony contained in the title if we pause to reflect upon the first part of the project's name. Why Living Newspaper? A newspaper that is 'living' (as, presumably, opposed to one that is dead') is one that is animated, participatory, immediate, intended to be truthful, and perhaps under popular and democratic ownership. The idea of a Living Newspaper, like that of the Living Theatre, seeks to relate the practice to a way of life beyond performance. This is both rhetorically and temperamentally affiliated to what Auslander has identified as a humane ethic of liveness which continues to be prized as the *raison d'être* of performance itself. In particular, Auslander notes, live performance is valued for 'its putative ability to create community (if not communion) among its participants, including performers and spectators' (Auslander, 1999: 4). In the context in which C&T's project was created, however, the notion of a performance community constituted through processes of presence and participation uncontaminated by the surveillance, recording, relaying and replaying technologies of a mediatized society is questionable. As Baz Kershaw notes:

> issues surrounding the idea of 'community' are intensified by the globalizing processes set in train by the late twentieth-century internationalization of capital and communication networks, brought about particularly by the spread of new digital technologies, such as the World Wide Web and the Internet.
>
> (1999: 193)

Community theatre traditionally aimed to specifically promote localized and immediate practices of participation, so that both process and performance were seen as actively creating and sustaining the networks of community in the here and now. Equally importantly, the subject matter frequently operated within a quasi-documentary form, with the resources of local memory and history providing material. One of the key considerations here is that the means and ends of performance were governed by negotiations between theatre professionals and local non-professionals, a process in which there were a range of theatre skills and vocabularies, and a variety of understandings of who and what this kind of theatre is for. The challenge for the Living Newspaper of the twenty-first century, however, has been not only that the terminology of community has been problematized, but the increasing marginalization of the discourses and practices of drama and theatre that were previously imagined to be a viable means of comprehending it. In what Auslander describes as 'a culture for which mediatization is a vehicle of the general code in a way that live performance is not (or is no longer)' (Auslander, 1999: 5), the personal camcorder is widely owned and it is digital media culture which provides a ubiquitous medium for non-professional self-documentation and self-dramatization. Such, then, are the grounds upon which C&T's twenty-first-century living newspaper.com began its work.

The dynamic relationship between process and product which character-izes the Living Newspaper form is different from traditional TIE practices as Paul Sutton, the project's director recognized. The project's attempt to mix two classic theatrical forms, 1930s Living Newspapers and 1960s Theatre-in-Education, invited contradiction from the outset. Living Newspapers, like TIE, were an inherently educational theatre form. Developed as a mode of documentary drama under the auspices of the Federal Theatre Project, Living Newspapers (influenced by Italian Futurists and Soviet Bolshevik artists) were a popular and accessible form of political theatre, designed to raise consciousness of social injustice and to provoke activism. However, whilst Living Newspapers taught through an audience's consumption of an essentially didactic theatre product, TIE taught through a predominantly child-centred approach to learning with an emphasis on process and par-ticipation. Sutton reconciles this apparent contradiction between different modes of performance by referring to Gavin Bolton, who recognized that the process and product is not a division but a continuum (see Davis, 2010).[4] What became clear was that for the project to embrace both genres' pedagogic approaches, the livingnewspaper.com needed to dramatize and encode the making of Living newspapers as well as the finished products themselves.[5]

Originally developed in 2001 as a 'digital drama experience' (Sutton, 2005: 127) C&T's Living Newspaper has involved a range of new technolo-gies, constantly evolving and adapting as technology has developed. Thus the current version of it has replaced the original CD-ROM with Twitter-style micro-blogging sites.[6] Its principles, however, are consistent as the company continue to find new ways of engaging digital natives in 'populist educational theatre that would engage young audiences with topical news content' (Sutton, 2005: 125). From the outset, the participants (generally school pupils) operated in a controlling authoring role; they decided on an issue they wanted to explore (examples have included the use of CCTV, climate change, the UK phone-hacking scandal and political protest) and used the resources supplied by the company to document their work and to share it with other audiences through the Internet. Teachers and young people worked alongside the company, learning a range of techniques for documentation and production. These initially included Real Player Video Streaming (e.g., for staged CCTV footage), Flash animation (for creating animated political cartoons) and chatrooms (for online improvisation of scripts). As technology has developed these have been replaced by YouTube and message boards. Participants create material by using a series of template tools (Still Image, Camera Voice, Video, etc.) which enables them to upload clips, photos and to add vocals and music. The website also contains a number of resources to facilitate these Living Newspaper Journalists, including a newswire, a library and a gallery.

The participants' autonomy is, however, illusory; what really controls the process and product is what the company refers to as a 'secret network'. When the project was initially devised and presented, Sutton developed an elaborate version of the actor in role. His idea proved to be very controversial with members of his company. What he proposed was a fictional newsroom whereby the actors would pretend to be characters, establishing Internet identities to create the illusion of a genuine media team and network. Members of C&T, however, expressed concern about this methodology; they felt it was ethically problematic because it involved deception. Sutton has explained the problem as follows: 'It was that the newsroom/secret network which young people were being invited to join, set itself up as being real (which it is, real kids in schools doing real drama about real issues), when in fact a key component of it (the six characters) were fictional. The concern was that we were lying to them about these characters.'[7] Here we have an example of the gap between digital immigrants as educators and digital natives as learners. For pupils accustomed to online gaming and rapid interaction between the live and the mediated, the willing suspension of disbelief becomes a sophisticated concept as the digital natives effortlessly assimilate fictional/mediated and lived reality. This is akin to the duality of perception observed by Matthew Reason in his study of children's perceptions of theatre, where children's drawings demonstrated their understanding of puppets as being both artificial objects, controlled by a puppeteer as well as representing a persona and affecting a felt experience (Reason, 2010).

Reason suggests that our abilities to read and respond to theatre are linked to Bourdieu's concept of cultural capital:

> A work of art has meaning and interest only for someone who possesses the cultural competence, that is, the code into which it is encoded ... A beholder who lacks the specific code feels lost in a chaos of sounds and rhythms, colours and lines, without rhyme or reason.
>
> (Bourdieu, 1984: 3)

In the case of the Living Newspaper, Sutton argued that the very fact of being in a drama lesson meant that pupils would be alert to 'things not being what they may seem'. He also argued that the construction of new identities on the Internet is an accepted convention and that this could be regarded as another form of being in role. This hypothesis not only endorses Bourdieu's conception of cultural capital and the production of knowledge but is also relevant to Prensky's neurological perspective on the cognitive abilities of digital natives. Children who are digitally literate, brought up in environments where access to computers, gaming, television and other forms of media are prevalent ' think differently from the rest of us. They develop hypertext minds. They leap around. It's as though their cognitive structures were parallel, not sequential' (Prensky, 2001b: 21). The concern about the Living Newspaper's fictional framework being lies is evidence of the logic, ethics and accent of the foreigner, whose understanding and perception is conceptually and cognitively different to the natives he encounters in the strange new world of globalized digital culture.

In the first instance, then, the livingnewspaper.com operated in the mode of dramatic playing, as what O'Toole would describe as a Fictional Context (2004: 64). Participants were invited to sign up to a covert network called thelivingnewspaper.com. This covert network comprised of a number of cells of documentary Drama Activists. This role of Drama Activists gave participants a frame through which to participate in the fictional context. Activists were first inducted into the network, its rules, regulations, membership structure, techniques and operations, through a membership pack which included historical materials on Living Newspapers, advice on techniques, and background information on the covert network itself. Once inducted, these cells (effectively a school) were charged with researching, investigating and dramatizing topical news stories. The command and control functions of the covert network were led by a small, anonymous and highly secretive team, who issued instructions and advice to participants through the website.

This was a complex and sophisticated dramatic frame. The actor/teacher pretended that the package had just arrived in the post, feigning curiosity about its contents. S/he asked the class if they wanted to see what was on it. At this juncture the actor/teacher had crossed the threshold into the familiar world of working in role and Heathcote's concept of the frame (1984). But the role was an uneasy one; when the *Livingnewspaper* first appeared on pupils' computer screens, an announcement framed the fiction in ways which invited participants to reflect on how their roles have been constructed.

Manifesto
The Living Newspaper does not exist.
The Living Newspaper.net does not exist.
The idea of a covert organisation committed to uncovering the truth behind the drama of world events is ridiculous.
To believe that the world's news media at best ignore young people, at worst twist and distort what they say, do, think and feel, is self delusion.
The notion that young people across the world could forge a network of Docu-Dramatist cells committed to challenging those distortions through theatre, is fantasy.

And that drama and the Internet could be the tools to challenge those
deceptions, lies and mistruths is plainly laughable.

And that this network, through its strength in creativity, might actually
change the world for the better is the biggest joke of all.

The idea is pure theatre.

Face facts.

(Sutton, 2005)

The manifesto was clearly designed to provoke young people to want to
challenge the text through participation in the theatre of the living newspaper. In so doing, they were conscious of themselves as journalists/theatre
makers. The CD-Rom provided a series of instructions for the class but it
also punctuated these activities with a regular series of bulletins which
flashed across the screen, interrupting the work in progress and functioning
as reminders that the pupils were operating within a mediatized context.
The frame was reinforced by an apparently authentic version of Google
which appeared on screen as an ordinary search engine. However, as Sutton
explains:

> It is in fact not Google at all but a secret mechanism for logging users into
> the covert messaging system of the living newspaper command and con-
> trol network ... This is the heart of the Drama. You have now triggered
> a sequence of pre-programmed messages to be launched in real-time on
> your computer screen ... They operate on two levels. Firstly, as dialogue
> between the fictional characters in our cover network – discussing issues,
> exchanging news, gossip and insults*/and as a device for issuing instruc-
> tions to participants ... as to how to develop their Living Newspaper
> drama live in the classroom. In effect it provides through the drama
> frame a kind of virtual Teacher-in Role.[8]

The actor/teacher followed the instructions on the CD-Rom and the pupils
discussed ideas for their version of a Living Newspaper. When the project
was piloted, however, the company discovered that the role play had been a
mutual exchange. At the end of the session, the director turned to the class
and confessed that the CD- Rom was not real, and that the characters were
the actors and the Living Newspaper newsroom was the company's invention. The pupils were nonplussed; they revealed that they had not been
fooled, but aware that they were playing a game from the start. The drama
operated within a complex self-reflexive framework: it was a meta-media
narrative. The actors were pretending to discover the contents of the CD-
Rom and created the fantasy of the Living Newspaper network. The fact that
it was a pretence was advertised in the opening announcement, but it was
made clear that the rules of the game were to contest this. In turn, the pupils
involved were aware of themselves as actors. Because they were familiar with

the concept of assumed identity through email, passwords and Internet personas, they were able to move in and out of the media framework easily and clearly. Thus the participants were often savvier than their teachers.

As well as the demonstration of the Brechtian concept of *Verfremdungseffekt*, Sutton acknowledged the influence of a popular culture model, the band Gorillaz. Formed by Blur's Damon Albarn, the band was originally launched anonymously, fronted by some cartoon gorilla characters, who appeared in the videos, on websites, posters and so on:

> even performing live through animated projections at the Brit Awards. No mention of Albarn, just mediated hype. But everyone knew they were Albarn's brainchild. You could recognize his voice on lead vocals. No public admittance, no public denial. However, fans were not duped or psychologically warped by this 'estrangement' from their 'real' pop heroes. They just got on with entering the fiction of Gorillaz and enjoying it for what it was: good music, jazzy graphics, and a new sense of identity and cultural validity for a slightly ageing pop star. What was important was the credibility and endorsement of the execution not the identity of the executioner under the mask. My thinking was if this can work in a popular music context, why not in a process drama?[9]

For many of us familiar with Theatre in Education and the methodologies of devised performance, the influence of other media forms can be problematic, leading to wooden, unimaginative naturalistic scenarios as participants draw upon the vocabulary of television and particularly soap opera to stage their representation of real life. In trying to simulate the real, these participants are doomed to failure as their performance can only ever be an inadequate imitation of the verisimilitude of film and television. C&T's work involves a different use of mediatized culture. As Sutton explains, 'if young people's dramatic vocabulary is so profoundly informed by the media texts of our dramatized society, then why should not theatre, the dramatic form from which all others derive, not appropriate the conventions, techniques and technologies of these media to construct new and original theatre texts designed to engage these media literate audiences?'[10] This is precisely what the *Living Newspaper* project aims to achieve as it continues to move forward alongside and in dialogue with 'the dizzying pace of technological development', to use Sutton's words. In its current form, the *Living Newspaper* is described as follows:

> Re-inventing documentary drama in the age of YouTube, C&T's own brand of Living Newspapers turn your students into Citizen Journalists researching, reflecting and articulating their responses to the changing world of which they are a part.
>
> (C&T, 2011)

Some of C&T's subsequent and recent work involves them using the gaming technology of the Nintendo Wii. This involves the performer/participant interacting with her/his mediated other on the screen in a dialogue between the virtual and the real. One of the C&T animateurs working in a special needs context invented a game called 'Copy Mii', in which the participants were required to copy a series of animated screen images depicting emotions. This game was a particularly pertinent one in this context as many of the young people involved (particularly those with autistic spectrum conditions) struggle to recognize, understand and respond to emotions in themselves and others. In the Wii game, however, we could see how the participants were able to physically interact with animated images which they appeared to embody through their facial expressions and actions. Drama's capacity to develop knowledge through kinaesthetic learning is a key feature here.

The Wii consoles were being used as part of a project called + *verb* in which participants were involved in the invention of a new word appropriate to young people's experience of the twenty-first century. The project aimed to use tools of the Internet age rather than word of mouth to get the word into common usage. Schools across the United Kingdom were using the Wii as stimuli to discover generic behaviours and using the Internet to share and exchange ideas. In this context, the signified becomes more important than the signifier and language is learned and experienced as a construct rather than a given. The participants in these activities were engaged in processes which, through the simulation of gaming technology, use mimesis and empathy as a means of learning. Sports-based games appeared to be the most frequently used on this project, particularly boxing. In a session I observed, however, the Wii stimulus was *Zelda* – a legend with a narrative base and a structure involving a series of quests. This was a rather more difficult and challenging stimulus than the sports-based activities, largely because its form and content were those of screen realism. The animateur running the session used a series of devices to facilitate active engagement with the stimulus: two or three students were positioned in front of the screen with iPods to create interior monologues, identifying what the screen characters and avatar were thinking and feeling. Rules were employed to control the action so, for example, the individual with the Wii wasn't allowed to do anything unless one of the voices 'thinks' it. Other students were asked to respond to the action physically. One student was positioned behind the monitor, so could not see the screen, and was asked to provide a commentary on the screen action based upon the physical responses of the student positioned in front of the screen. This produced something quite remarkable: firstly, the commentary was extremely accurate. Secondly, the student in front of the screen began to physically respond to the commentary in what was effectively a double mirroring. As the session continued, the animateur involved more and more students in physical activities which moved the action beyond the screen realism. Thus the activity progressed from a video game experience to the creation of a physical language.

Simon Shepherd considers how the development of audio and visual technologies in the modern world have been reflected in our bodily responses. Crucially, Shepherd writes:

> Listening, like speaking and seeing, happens in specific physical situations, happens as part of a whole bodily experience. But this bodily experience is thought about in different ways, and its physical techniques may alter, in different societies. There are cultures of listening and seeing. The suggestion, then, is that empathy is a response of the whole physical person. Where body and brain are interconnected, this would seem a logical inference.
>
> (2004: 8)

Mirror neuron theory explains this process. For theatre there are two factors here: firstly that mimesis is physically experiential and secondly what Shepherd refers to as the mimesis of the audience: 'In response to the show they are led into imitation by what they watch' (9).

What could also be observed during the Wii session was a shifting of the audience's interest from the screen to the physical activity in front of and behind it. This might lead us to conclude that mirror neurons are more likely to be engaged through the physical activity which constitutes performance. Shepherd's point about different cultures having different physical responses is also corroborated by mirror neuron theorists who argue that cultural stimuli influence neurobiological responses and behaviours. Moreover, there is evidence that the cultural and ethnic backgrounds of those conveying the messages is a variable and determining factor. Using transcranial magnetic stimulation (TMS) researchers found significant differences in neural activity in their subjects depending on whether the individual executing the action as actor/information provider shared the subject's cultural/ethnic background. 'Our data show that ethnicity and culture interact to influence activity in the brain, specifically within the mirror neuron network involved in social communication and interaction' (Molner-Szakacs, 2007).

This preliminary research has important implications for applied theatre and performance, particularly in terms of the debates surrounding the politics of cultural intervention. In this respect, Denzin's discussion of ethics and his model of a performative cultural politics is useful: Denzin advocates a 'participatory mode of knowing [which] privileges subjectivity, personal knowledge and the specialized knowledge of oppressed groups' (Denzin, 2003: 243). C&T's participatory performance methods, which respect, respond to and utilize the knowledges of digital natives, can be seen, albeit in a different context, as a model of such practice. The 'animateurs' (the title

C&T uses for their practitioners) are required to develop fluency in the languages and practices of the digital cultures which constitute their working environments. Their work engages with the physical and digital aspects of community, exploring interactions between real-world and online settings. The company's emerging social practices involve them in community workshops, creative use of technology and live/physical and virtual interactions. Thus they are practising and promoting what Waschauer describes in terms of social capital and community informatics:

> Promoting social capital is a key strategy of community informatics, but this is not seen as taking place principally through online communication. Rather, social capital is created and leveraged by building the strongest possible coalitions and networks in support of the community's goals, using technology as a focal point and organizing tool.
>
> (2003: 163)

This is akin to C&T's practice, as technology works in conjunction with participatory performance activities so that community is being built locally within peer groups (action learning) as well as through the online community of networks with schools in other parts of the world. The importance and value of digital technologies as a means of facilitating cultural inclusion has led to C&T's increasing involvement in projects in the developing world. As discussed in Chapter 1, the perception of the subject as 'other' in relation to theatre for development has been problematized by a number of critics and practitioners, where artists are deemed to 'parachute in' to stage cultural interventions which impose Western ideologies on developing nations. C&T's practice, however, is informed by Denzin's ethical approach to performance ethnography which addresses some of the concerns articulated by Hal Foster in his discussion of the 'artist as ethnographer' (1996). C&T's combination of participatory drama and digital media facilitates access to ICT, promoting social capital through peer interaction, social engagement and social networking.

Whilst computers are not readily available in developing cultures, smart phones have proved to be an accessible and versatile means of accessing the Internet. Computers, whether desktop or laptop, are counter-intuitive to process-based drama; the mobile phone is a pocket-sized computer with increasing capacities to communicate and connect across cultures (larger realities/aneroid operating system). In Malawi, for example, where C&T undertook a smart phone project, national broadband access has been abandoned in favour of a mobile phone infrastructure. Funded by the Arts Council's Digital Content Distribution scheme, C&T were able to develop mobile phone applications enabling children in Malawi to participate in online digital communities (linked to C&T's network schools framework), thereby creating a level playing field for collaboration and communication.

The project developed from field work undertaken in September 2010 when C&T made their first visit to the Polly School in Malawi. Working in mobile classrooms that had been adapted from huge cargo containers, the company encountered challenging conditions as they worked in an extremely hot environment without electricity, basic sanitation, limited supplies of food and water, and no prospect of broadband. However, many of the children had mobile phones, even though they were unfamiliar with other digital media: many had never seen or used a camcorder, for example. As an area of considerable deprivation, Malawi is a largely agricultural economy and is dependent on foreign aid. Mortality rates are high due to the prevalence of HIV and Aids, other diseases and natural disasters (to which the area is prone). C&T were struck by the comparatively small numbers of pupils in the senior part of the school which, it was confirmed, was due largely to the child mortality rates. Schooling is not compulsory but is available from the age of six. The curriculum is standard numeracy and literacy and the pupils have very little experience of drama. School is a refuge from the hardship the children encounter in their home environments, providing shelter and a daily helping of nsima, the staple dish of maize and water.

Back in the United Kingdom, the company developed a mobile phone application and returned to Malawi to test it in conjunction with their characteristic blend of process drama and digital technologies. One of the objectives of the project which was developed in collaboration with Oxfam and the United Nations Millennium Development Goals scheme was to enable UK schools to understand the UN goals and to persuade funders to support the campaign to achieve the millennium objectives. The goals are identified as follows:

To eradicate extreme poverty and hunger.
To achieve universal primary education.
To promote gender equality and empower women.
To reduce child mortality.
To improve maternal health.
To combat HIV/Aids, malaria and other diseases.
Ensure environmental sustainability.
Develop a global partnership for development.

C&T's work aimed to facilitate dialogue about these topics both through practical drama activities and its online network. Thus children in the developing world whose needs are represented through the millennium goals are able to take ownership of the material and communicate their experiences to their counterparts in the developed world. Children in New York and Birmingham undertake similar activities, responding to the stimulus and the three groups communicate with each other, exchanging their experiences and responses to the topics. The stark contrasts between the groups enabled them to gain understanding of the lived experience of the other. The Internet served as a space for dialogue and exchange, whilst the material generated emerged from practical engagement, facilitating embodied understanding of the concepts explored.

The children in Malawi were familiar with the Millennium goals, but when asked to identify them, the gender and inequality goal was the one most frequently omitted. C&T addressed this through the 'King of the Court' game, where the King gives permission (or not) for participants to join. When the African children were asked to play this game again, with a Queen, there was a shocked response, indicative of a cultural perception of gender and power relations. Participants were asked to devise scenes using each of the eight goals as a stimulus. The African children drew on their personal experiences, pretending to be a Doctor diagnosing malaria, for example, but their vignettes shared a political sensibility within a public or institutional framework: in the malaria diagnosis, for example, the Doctor states 'I see you have malaria but I have too many patients like you; the Government doesn't support me.'[11] The material was posted on the web and shared with partner schools and this initiated text message dialogues with children from partner schools in the United Kingdom. A key point here is the fact that the children from Malawi were generating material based on their own lives and experiences and this, in turn, meant the pupils at the networked schools in the United Kingdom were not responding to abstract information about conditions in the developing world but were engaging on a deeper, more personal and profound level. Sutton reflects that the work offers a different kind of authenticity.

A further project took the C&T team to Korogocho and the slums in north-eastern Nairobi.[12] Here, the conditions were particularly extreme, with open sewers in the streets, high crime rates and, as in Malawi, a hot climate and unsanitary conditions breeding disease. In Korogocho, Sutton refers to a sense of desperation as one of his first impressions of the urban environment. The Dandora landfill site is one of the many dumping grounds of Western society; each day scavengers look for items to retrieve and sell in the market place. It is even reported that airlines dumped surplus food from meals which is taken from the landfill to the villages and sold or eaten. Building on work undertaken in the company's *Everymap* project, digital mapping technologies link children in Africa with other participants in New York and Birmingham.[13] The network brings together different cultural experiences and the bigger the contrasts, the more exciting the learning opportunities, according to Sutton. He recalls taking his laptop outside to get a signal in order to Skype UK pupils at a school in Bradford to put them in touch with the children he was working with in Nairobi; he also recalls their excitement at being able to Skype children at a school in New York. Part of the excitement here is communicating in the moment; liveness is mediated through this technology, crossing time zones and creating a different kind of

Figure 10 C&T using mobile phones, Tendaba, The Gambia. Photograph by kind permission of Paul Sutton and Max Allsup, C&T

authenticity. The project in Korobocho involved participants creating maps which represented four same/different comparisons: pupils mapped things they liked to do, difficulties their community faces, histories and memories and important places.

The company worked with over 100 children on a piece of waste ground in sweltering temperatures. The drama work in these contexts needs to feel authentic and to have immediate relevance to the place in which it is situated, Sutton explains. Thus the C&T animateurs devise context specific games and activities; the dramatic property needs to be malleable so that it can be adapted and reshaped as appropriate to the players. In Malawi and Nairobi, C&T's animateurs were aware of and responsive to the high level of imaginative resources the participants brought to the work. Play in these contexts involved creativity with limited resources. One of the animateurs, for example, observed two teenage girls demonstrating ingenuity and skill in a game with stones. The stones were in a circle; one would be thrown into the air and before it hit the ground the other stones had to be moved to a different configuration. In another game, a ball on a string functioned like totem tennis. It was necessary to find a different tone to make the work happen here, Sutton reflects; optimism was needed to drive the work: 'you have to be up.'[14] The desperation they experienced on arrival needed to be transformed into hope.

According to Warschauer, the 'most effective method for leveraging community resources is to work through existing community organization or leaders to launch and manage community technology initiatives' (2003: 163). The example he cites of the hole in the wall computer kiosks in New Delhi was that 'no local community was involved in running them.' Indeed, he argues that 'mapping community resources is a critical component of launching a successful community technology initiative' where 'community mapping' is one of the participatory rapid appraisal (PRA) techniques. This involves different members of the community drawing maps from their own perspective in order to discover 'which locations, people and assets of the community are most valued' (165). This is close to C&T's method in the *Mappa Mundi*-inspired *Everymap*, a personalized mapping of place and perspective remediated through digital technologies as a twenty-first-century means of engaging participants in deeply meaningful play-based learning, thereby facilitating social inclusion, creating hope for the future and enabling cross-cultural exchange.

What is evident in C&T's work is the importance of the physical interplay between process drama and technology. This is not simply an interplay between the live and the mediated as the use of webcam and Skype facilitates live interaction through the web. As Johannes Birringer has indicated, the engagement and sense of community produced in multi-player digital gaming makes it an appropriate paradigm for experimental performance (and art), where audience interaction is generally not at the same level in terms of engagement or commitment (Birringer, 2008). The importance of the human element is also evident in Auslander's comment in his overview of the essays in *Performance and Technology*: 'technology cannot take the place of human presence at the heart of performance ... it is best used to extend the capabilities of human performers, to express humanistic themes more fully, and to allow performance to explore or evoke responses from realms of human physical and psychological experience or [make] directly accessible otherwise' (Auslander, 2006: 299). This alludes to forms of simulated experience, a further use of digital technologies in applied performance, facilitating empathic understanding of the felt experience of the other.

Embodying sonic technologies: Melanie Wilson's sound art

Sound is a technology that is often neglected in favour of the visual. Sound, however, is a transportative medium with the capacity to transform and remediate through the creation of interactive sonic environments in which participants can explore and experience other realities and perspectives. Melanie Wilson, a London-based sound artist, explores the interplay between live art and sonic worlds through studio-based performance pieces (*Simple Girl*, 2007; *Iris Brunette*, 2009).[15] Wilson uses sound sculpturally to create huge vistas, enabling her to 'combat the limited landscape of the material world' on a low budget.[16] Wilson developed an interest in manipulating sound through computers, initially using sound and music to shape narrative and to broker her relationship with audience. *Simple Girl*, for example, is a form of storytelling, taking its audience on a journey through a series of urban landscapes which we experience through listening and watching Wilson, speaking into a microphone and operating a sound board. We are aware of her powerful stage presence as well as her creation and control of the sonic environment and thus remain conscious of the interplay between the virtual and the real throughout the performance. Wilson describes her imaginary worlds as 'psychological predicaments', rather than considering them as alternative spaces. The experience of a Wilson performance is intimate and intense, requiring us to enter a cognitive space that is both individual and shared. Wilson describes her relationship with the audience as being like 'having a partner' while sound is envisaged as her co-performer. Thus, in *Simple Girl* she engages us in direct address (spoken through a microphone) whilst interacting with her own voice through voice over. In *Iris Brunette*, an intimate piece of café theatre for audiences of 20, the audience sit in small groups around coffee tables, sharing the space with Wilson who plays between them. Spectators find themselves vicariously participating in the construction of Wilson's mode of virtual reality:

> Together they embark upon a sortie into a curious cityscape of the future past, guided by Iris Brunette: part-time travelling refugee, part compassionate voyeur. As Iris delicately uncoils the events leading up to the destruction of the city, it becomes clear she is searching for a lost loved one. One by one, each audience member finds themselves cast in her journey through the city in time; sometimes passively, sometimes in hope of a response.[17]

The spectator assumes a persona, thereby participating from within as part of a collective creation with sound functioning, via Wilson, as the connecting discourse. Each of the audience's personas is a member of the city, although whether they are real or a figment of the imagination is deliberately unclear; we are uncertain whether the account is memory, fantasy or flashback. The personas are highly framed, rooted in space and identified through light as the loose narrative follows a man through a city. As in *Simple Girl*, sound is used to create physical and visual responses: we imagine the urban locations, vividly evoked through sound effects and music (pictures in our minds), whilst the piece also evokes emotive, felt responses as we engage in an act of collective imagining and experiencing, aware of the presence of others in the darkened space and interacting with them.

Wilson's work has increasingly involved her working in educational and social contexts. In schools, she has worked with children to explore how sound and location can be used as a means of young people looking at themselves and their relations to each other. School architecture is often regarded as oppressive, associated with authority and entrapment, but Wilson's work involves pupils exploring the school through a different lens, perceiving differently as they explore the sonic spaces of their learning environments. *In the footsteps of others* was an Arts Council-funded New Directions project at Queen Elizabeth's Girls School in London with Year 8 pupils in 2010. Wilson used sound to explore and re-imagine school environments and to unleash possibilities for narrative. Wilson wanted to make participants aware of how space affects them and how architecture impacts on their emotional lives. The pupils created a series of audio guides: imaginary creative worlds channelled into a practical marriage of creativity and critical editing. Two of the pieces took the spectator on a journey into secret or personal spaces within the school. These were both literal and metaphorical. The listeners were told to imagine themselves walking through corridors, opening and closing doors, climbing stairs and passing communal areas before arrival at their destination. In one piece, the journey involved a series of encounters with forbidden spaces – the sixth-form toilets requiring a PIN code, the locked doors to the swimming pool and the staff room. The listener arrived at a 'special place' under the stairs next to a locked wardrobe/cupboard containing something mysterious. In a further piece, 'scared' listeners were led through a series of scenes exploring the supernatural elements in the school (the sickly ghosts of the hospital which previously existed on the site) through the evocation of strange happenings when the building is empty. This was more clearly fantasy, using naturalistic sound effects, but the choice of form and content gave the pupils authorship and power as they explored what are clearly ambivalent relations with the site. In a final piece, a dream transported the listener to a school in Columbia – an escapist meditation where paella is being served rather then the plastic-smelling diet of the school canteen; before an imagined lunch could be enjoyed, however, the listener was wafted back to London and woken up from the reverie. In all these pieces, MP3 players, voiceovers and sound effects transport the listener into the psychological vistas Wilson creates through sound; here, the psychology is particularly interesting as the pupils in different ways explored narratives of desire, security, escape and release. In all four pieces, the private was sought in preference to the public and communal, while abstract work was shaped into concrete object. All the pieces used sound to explore the perspective of the teenage girls involved in the project, and this was something Wilson sought to investigate further through media technologies as a means to create what she describes as 'parallel worlds' that intersect and collide.[18]

Wilson's experience of working with children clearly informs her subsequent practice. Working with the theatre producer Ed Collier in a piece commissioned by Theatre Sandbox, *The Unicorn* experimented with responsive technologies to create environments which were open, non-prescriptive and participant centred. This project for 8 to 10-year-olds investigated what children see on the High Street through an interactive audio guide, building on Wilson's work in schools. The project took place in King's Mall and King Street in Hammersmith, London, and culminated in a resolution at the Lyric Theatre, thereby conjoining the everyday world of the high street and the theatre environment as well as bringing together the audio walk, emerging from performance art, and building-based theatre conventions. Children wore radio-receiving headphones, accompanied by an adult with a laptop in a bag (tuned to wi-fi, radio and video transmitters). The technology triggered receivers and projectors along the route as part of the audio sequence and in response to the movements of participants in the tour. Thus the laptop broadcast information to the projectors as the children approached, triggering the image of the unicorn who, the voice over told us, 'sees into your heart' when engaging in eye contact. The unicorn appeared and disappeared on a projection. Participants following the unicorn experienced the imaginary in the context of public spaces, creating a parallel world which the children navigate; their movements and senses triggered images to appear on shop windows and pavements. 'What do they see that we don't?' is one of the questions the project seeks to explore.

In a further piece exploring psychological worlds through headphone pieces as part of the BAC 1:1 festival, Wilson plays the role of a nurse/curator, tending to the blindfolded spectator whose headset explains that s/he has been blinded in an accident, transporting the participant into an imagined world outside the everyday, exploring the quotidian fragments of life through an interplay between live and simulated experience and the performance of being nursed. Here, the spectator submits to performer and action through a form of participatory performance which demands passivity on the part of the spectator. This form of imagined experience, created through sound and physical performance has considerable potential as an experiential and immersive learning environment. In these worlds, created through pervasive media technologies, we are aware of the illusion and participate in its construction, yet we are also developing an empathic understanding of an alternative perspective through this visceral form.

Wilson's work has also involved her exploring the psychological landscape of dementia in a Wellcome Trust-funded project, *Autobiographer* (2010, 2012). Wilson worked with the Clinical Director of the Croydon Memory Service to develop understanding of the condition, which she evoked through sound and performance. Four performers became the voices of a woman whose identity unravelled as the disease progressed. The piece explored the timeline between the older woman, her memories of being a young woman and the memories of her daughter. The depiction of the brain disintegrating through the sonic properties of language was graphic and moving, providing a felt sense of an encounter with the experience of the condition: the repetition of scenes, the survival of long-term memory and the retreat to the past when the present is overwhelming, the forgetfulness which makes everyday life impossible to manage, the confusion and disorientation when the familiar becomes strange, telephone numbers are forgotten, buses and bus routes are suddenly bewildering, and the sufferer finds themselves lost in a cognitive fog which occasionally clears in moments of clarity, only to descend again, thicker, obscuring even more of the landmarks the sufferer depends upon. The different voices of the sufferer and the physical presence of the performers prevented the audience from identifying with a single character, creating some sense of the fragmentation of memory and identity associated with the condition. Whilst it might be argued that this is not applied performance as it is not participatory or obviously transformational (it is a studio-based piece for an audience, rather than having a therapeutic objective for sufferers), I include it here as an example of how new forms of performance are emerging from, and are informed by, work in social and health contexts, generating new understandings and insights into conditions and situations which are alien to the audience's experience. This can be seen as another form of social inclusion through digital technologies (facilitating understanding of difference), but, in this example, performance creates an immersive sonic environment where an audience is transported into a different psychological plane and develops empathic understanding of a different perspective and experience. Digital technologies create a simulated experience, facilitating new knowledges and understanding of this medical condition.

The potential of digital technologies and participatory performance to create insight into the experience of disability is central to the practice and research of Petra Kuppers. Kuppers explores how 'visual technology and performance modes of audience address can merge and create a sensual space of engagement in which the other's body becomes tentatively experiential' (Kuppers, 2006: 169). Kinaesthetic empathy involves us developing forms of felt understanding of different experiences and perspectives through, for example, the simulation techniques of digital technology, whereby 'digital viewpoints often attempt to viscerally recreate the experience of a movement' (171). With reference to Olimpias' *Body Spaces* (Manchester, October 2000), Kuppers describes how in three site-specific installations (car park, theatre foyer and hospital) involving young disabled performers, the company used photography, sound and video in conjunction with mapping devices to explore normative and different spatial relations in shared architectural and environmental frameworks:[19] 'I was fascinated by the idea of re-colonizing different urban environments. Together, we created environments that choreograph the spectator's physical experience, that send him or her on a trajectory towards difference, and that distance their spatial/visual/tactile experience from the normative' (174). Thus objects were depicted from different perspectives such as the lowered level of the wheelchair user, while narratives associated with new arrangements of space involved spectators physically engaging in movements such as stooping down or stretching up to see/hear or experience the material in the installations. Here again, we see how technology is used in conjunction with the physically present bodies of performers and participants, playing in liminal spaces to develop new, embodied knowledges. What is also evident in the documentation and discussion of this piece are its aesthetic qualities as beauty was evoked through the choreography, the strange and haunting projections, photographs and narratives and traces of previous bodies and inhabitants in the three locations. In *Framing: Body Spaces: A Meta-Installation by the Olympias* for the fourth Digital Arts and Culture conference (Providence, Rhode Island, April 2001), Kuppers presented a meta-text about *Body Spaces*, engaging conceptually and practically with a series of questions and issues addressed in the work:

What is an accessible digital urban aesthetic?
What new insights emerge in these digital encounters with wheelchair-using young people, their perspectives and their stories?
What is social art?
How does 'Body Spaces' negotiate the issues of presence and absence, visuality and embodiment that haunt contemporary digital art practices?

(dac 2001)[20]

These questions are explored through the process of applying performance – using the forms and methodologies of contemporary digital and performance practices to create a series of encounters in which the spectators are both moved and moving, physically and cognitively. The questions Kuppers raises regarding an urban aesthetic, absence, the nature of social art, and the interplay between absence, presence and embodiment in digital art practices, are common to all of the case studies featured in this chapter. All the practitioners share a political commitment to finding new ways of accessing the experience of others, exploring difference and facilitating social inclusion whilst also being committed to creating high quality art.

Part III
Participation

6
Participatory (Syn)Aesthetics

This chapter explores a range of work whose practices draw upon the current vogue for what has been defined variously in the context of art and performance as 'collaborative', 'interactive', 'immersive' and 'participatory.' Although it might be argued that *all* applied theatre is participatory (and this is identified in Part I as a principle of applying performance), the focus on the participant's *experience* through the *form* of the work brings it into dialogue with Machon's '(syn)aesthetics', a '*re*defining' of 'visceral performance' (Machon, 2009). This body of work, Machon explains, is 'impossible to define as a genre, due to the fluidity of forms explored' but its style 'places emphasis on the human body' as well as the verbal as a 'visceral' act; it is 'sensate' and often 'transgressive' as 'its very form can produce a response in the individual audience member that goes beyond the discourse of critical analysis' its inarticulacy being 'due to the fact that the act of immediate perception is primarily located in the body' (2009: 2). This '(syn)aesthetic style she associates with productions such as Theatre de Complicite's *Street of Crocodiles* (1992), De la Guarda's form of 'shock' theatre in pieces such as *Villa! Villa!* (1998), Pina Bausch's *Bluebeard* (1984) and DV8's *Dead Dreams of Monochrome Men* (1990), as well as play texts such as Churchill's *The Skriker* (1994), Beckett's *Not I* (1972) and the corporeal writing of Sarah Kane. Machon identifies three 'performance strategies' as key features of the (syn)aesthetic performance style: the '(syn)aesthetic hybrid', which she defines in relation to Richard Wagner's *gesaamtkunstwerk* (or 'total artwork'); a 'pre dominance of the actual body as text in performance'; and an experimentation with 'writerly speech to establish a visceral-verbal *play*text' (4). Here, her emphasis is on the Kantian, ludic nature of play (discussed in Part I), in conjunction with a Steinian linguistic *jouissance* where sound and syntax create a nonsensical visceral form of orality. These three elements, however, are present in different combinations and emphases in (syn)aesthetic performance which may not always incorporate all three.

Machon's case studies are wide ranging, encompassing theatre, dance, live art, site-sympathetic work and 'technological performance practice' and includes the UK companies Punchdrunk, Shunt Theatre Collective, Graeae, Bodies in Flight and Curious. The '(syn)aesthetic style' can, however, also be applied to a range of work in international contexts, including many of the case studies in Di Benedetto's study of contemporary sensual theatre: the work of Robert Wilson, Robert Lepage, Societas Raffaello Sanzio and performance artists such as Franco B, Karen Finley and Marina Abramovic, to name but a few, all of whom produce work which is visceral and corporeal in form, content and response. As Machon's study acknowledges, '(syn)aesthetic work shifts between performance disciplines', and, as I discuss below, there are synergies with work produced by visual artists seeking to move beyond the gallery and to involve the viewer or attendant in experiential practice. Indeed, much of this work is situated in spaces between disciplines as it resists codification and 'explodes established forms and concepts' (Machon, 2009: 4). Perhaps the central feature conjoining this body of work is its simultaneous engagement with the turn to both spectatorship and to affect. Above all, the work seeks to produce what Machon describes as an 'innate' response, in 'performance and appreciation' creating what she refers to as a 'transcendent quality'. Her analysis (like Di Benedetto's study of a similar body of work) draws on neuroscientific research as a means to 'find a discourse for experiential performance events, which articulates both the *approach* to practice as well as the *methods* of appreciation that occur in the experience of that work, for practitioners and audience members alike' (3; my emphasis).

In using the term (syn)aesthesia, however (albeit with a playful parenthesis to distinguish her term from the condition, as such, and to emphasize the fusion between the 'aesthetics' of performance and 'the fused nature of visceral perception' (7)), Machon's vocabulary interacts with another and contradictory set of associations – the synthetic. Whilst the practices defined as 'visceral performance' by Machon and others (Fenemore, 2003) are often discussed in relation to concepts of authenticity or the 'real' of experiential modes of art, the turn to participation through, for example, 'immersive' environments is also subject to a critique as an artificial, manufactured, consumerist product, reducing art to a series of cheap (or expensive) simulated thrills. So, for practitioners who apply these modes of performance, there are risks; the integrity of the work can be seriously compromised, as is evident in the work featured below in section 6.2 ('theme park hells'). At the other end of the spectrum, however, there are significant rewards in the treasures of the practices featured in my final section ('a taste of heaven').

6.1 Unhappy relations: critiques of collaboration

I would like to argue that the best collaborative practices need to be thought of in terms other than their ameliorative consequences; they should also question the very terms of these ameliorative assumptions. My view is inevitably influenced by living in the U.K., where New Labour have for the last nine years instrumentalized art to fulfil policies of social inclusion – a cost-effective way of justifying public spending on the arts while diverting attention away from the structural causes of decreased social participation, which are political and economic (welfare, transport, education, healthcare, etc). In this context it is crucial for art practices to tread a careful line between social intervention and autonomy, since demonstrable outcomes are rapidly co-opted by the state. ... [This] requires intelligence and imagination and risk and pleasure and generosity, both from the artists and the participants.

(Bishop and Roche, 2006)

Claire Bishop's cautionary perspective on collaborative art can be set against (and enters into dialogue with) Baz Kershaw's vision of the potential of twenty-first-century performance practice, cited at the start of this book. For Kershaw, 'contemporary drama and theatre' in its form and content needs to embrace 'resistant' and 'transcendent' practices, creating work which empowers individuals as autonomous agents whilst also facilitating collective identities. Applying performance, as evident in the practices featured in this book, involves artists engaging with individuals and groups as participants in projects which seek, in various ways to challenge, intervene, liberate, change, transport or transform. This requires precisely the qualities Bishop identifies and I would argue that these are some of the defining features of the case studies featured here: intelligence, imagination, risk, pleasure and generosity from all involved. At best, the pleasures of being involved in events that are both effective and affective enable us to experience a form of 'utopia' in performance, to use Dolan's terms, engaging us cognitively, imaginatively, sensually and physically in new forms of embodied understanding which enable us to perceive differently. At worst, however, we find ourselves entering a purgatorial domain (and I will suggest that the vogue for 'immersive' performance moves in this direction). Bishop's book-length study of collaborative art draws on André Breton's account of the 1921 Dada season, borrowing his phrase for her title: *Artificial Hells: Participatory Art and the Politics of Spectatorship* (2012). For Bishop, and indeed for Breton, there is pain and pleasure in the artificial hell of participatory artistic practice. Breton's Dada essay uses similar terms to both Kershaw and Bishop, referring to 'resistance' and 'delight' in the creation of 'scandal' (Breton, 2003: 138); these events are described as 'more than entertainment' (140) and the evaluative criteria are defined thus: 'we ended up gauging appeal by the cries made against us' (138). 'Artificial hells' is deemed an appropriate term for the Dada events that function 'to wrest the human spirit from some of its fetters'. Thus it can be argued that both heaven and hell are associated with affect and with purposeful performance (and, as discussed below, Bishop advocates forms of socially engaged art which cause 'discomfort' or 'antagonism' rather than seeking to reinforce the social bond through harmonious interaction and exchange). For Bishop, however, 'the social turn' prioritizes artistic process, ethics and impact over the aesthetic, resulting in work that she describes as 'formulaic' and 'predictable' (Roche, 2006). She challenges the demise of artistic authority and autonomy which has been sacrificed at the altar of democracy: 'There can be no failed, unsuccessful, unresolved or boring works of collaborative art because all are equally essential to the task of strengthening the social bond', she writes (Bishop, 2006); while the enemy is perceived in Bourriaud's terms as 'the spread of the supplier-client relations to every level of human life' (Bourriaud, [1998] 2002: 83).

This section takes its cue from Bishop's work, drawing on both Bourriaud's and Rancière's discussions of spectatorship to explore the relations between ethics and aesthetics in participatory modes of performance and to consider the hells and heavens into which they transport us (willingly or unwillingly).

A variety of terms are associated with the turn to collaboration in contemporary art contexts: 'new genre public art', 'participatory', 'socially engaged', 'interventionist', 'dialogic', 'littoral', 'community/process/research based'. Much of this work has very clear synergies with the forms and methodologies of contemporary performance, while the cross-over with applied forms of theatre is evident in the work featured in Jackson's 2011 study, *Social Works: Performing Art, Supporting Publics*. The turn to collaboration is associated with the focus on spectatorship in contemporary forms of theatre through practices referred to variously as 'immersive', 'interactive' and 'participatory'. These terms are used in conjunction with new technologies, virtual realities and gaming, where the spectator becomes a player, a producer of meaning through the phenomenological relationship they develop with the performance environment. 'Immersive' increasingly refers to theatre and performance events that are all-encompassing, that submerge the spectator in an experiential environment where conventional boundaries between fiction and reality, performer and spectator are destabilized. In these forms of theatre, participation is associated with risk, imagination and pleasure. 'Immersion in digital culture', writes Bay-Cheng, 'refers to the sensory experience/perception of being submerged (being present) in an electronically mediated environment' (Bay-Cheng et al., 2010: 47).

In theatre criticism the term 'immersive' is used increasingly to refer to work which, according to Nick Curtis, is characterized by 'an ambition to get away from the traditional, passive process of experiencing theatre' (Curtis, 2009). In a review of three 2009 productions, Sound and Fury's *Kursk* (a promenade piece where the studio is transformed into the interior of a submarine), *Vagabond's Voyage* by Little Wonder (which he describes as a 'community-minded devised show involving a towpath walk and narrow-boat trip exploring the histories of those who have lived and worked on the London canal'), and Cardboard Citizens' *Mincemeat*, set in a semi-derelict house in Shoreditch, Curtis applauds the proximity between performers and audience and the sensory experiences evoked in these forms of 'immersive theatre'. Citing the work of Shunt and Punchdrunk as exemplars, he identifies pioneers of the form in Brith Goff's *Gododdin* (1988) and in Deborah Warner's 1999 Euston Tower project.

What critics refer to most frequently in writing about immersive, participatory, or intimate performance is the need to engage audiences differently in work which takes risks and which excites (or provokes) through affect. Whilst this might be seen as theatre's response to cinema and television, exploiting the physicality and immediacy of the live, theatre experience, cinema is not in an antithetical relationship to theatre's 'presentness' (as Auslander has argued in positing a continuum between the live and the mediated); cinematic experience offers the 'illusion of immediacy as an immersive non-liveness' (Chapple and Kattenbelt, 2006: 42). Moreover, contemporary performance makers harness digital media for the purposes of creating interactive, haptic and experiential modes of performance, mixing the virtual and the live, whilst engaging audiences in different capacities as players and spectators through live performance, the Internet and digital broadcasting (as in the cutting-edge work of Blast Theory, for example). Thus the vogue for immersive performance involves rather more than a challenge to theatre's fourth wall. Perhaps it reflects a desire for something more profound than 'reproduction' to use Walter Benjamin's oft-cited terms: 'Even the most perfect reproduction of a work of art is lacking in one element: its presence in time and space, its unique existence at the place where it happens to be' (Benjamin, 1968a: 214). Using terms which continue to have currency in contemporary discussions of aesthetics (and contrary to his predictions), Benjamin suggests, 'the presence of the original is the prerequisite to authenticity' (214). In immersive performance, the 'original' is the experience of the event, the here and now of the work of art ('its presence in time and space') equates to a form of authenticity which is unreproducible – even if we experience it again. Thus Benjamin's terms define the temporal and spatial qualities of contemporary performance; indeed, it can be argued that the ontology and ephemerality of the medium which I have discussed in the context of memory and trauma in Part II contribute to what Benjamin refers to as the 'aura'. In his 1939 essay, 'Some Motifs in Baudelaire', Benjamin describes the aura in terms which are particularly pertinent to cognitive perspectives on performance:

> looking at someone carries the implicit expectation that our look will be returned by the object of our gaze. Where this expectation is met …

there is an experience of the aura to the fullest extent. Experience of the aura [in objects] thus rests on the transposition of a response common in human relationships to the relationship between the inanimate or natural object and man. The person we look at, or who feels he is being looked at, looks at us in turn. To perceive the aura of an object we look at means to invest it with the ability to look at us in return.

(1968b: 188)

In this passage, Benjamin describes communicative and perceptual processes which cognitive science has conceptualized through the discovery of the neural networks involved in the transposition of the response. This process underpins the interactions between performer and audience (which Benjamin also refers to); thus Benjamin's description maps neatly on to Bruce McConachie's summary of the cognitive processes engaged in spectatorship: 'visuomotor representations ... provide spectators with the ability to "read the minds" of actors/characters, to intuit their beliefs, intentions, and emotions by watching their motor actions. This mode of engagement, also known as empathy, extends to our understanding of actors' use of props and even their gestures and spoken language' (McConachie, 2008: 66).

The 'auratic moment' is thus embodied in the object or artefact; we experience a recognition, an immediacy in which the artistic artefact is perceived and understood in its historical and contemporary contexts. Benjamin's grim prognosis on the future of aesthetics and his prediction that the aura of a work of art is 'that which withers in the age of mechanical reproduction' has not, however, come to pass. The terms he uses in relation to aura – 'authenticity', 'originality', 'history' and 'tradition' – are still valued. Benjamin, however, did anticipate many of the consequences of what we now refer to as mediatization and he certainly perceived something about the distinctive temporal and spatial nature of theatrical performance as distinct from cinema:

The aura which, on the stage, emanates from Macbeth, cannot be separated for the spectators from that of the actor. However, the singularity of the shot in the studio is that the camera is substituted for the public. Consequently, the aura that envelops the actor vanishes, and with it the aura of the figure he portrays.

(1968a: 223)

Cognitive scientists would agree, in that proximity is regarded as a factor in provoking empathic engagement. However, the 'recognition' evoked here is critical empathy; aura is dependent upon a distance from the art object which corresponds to Brecht's notion of *Verfremdungseffekt*, where the familiar is made strange. As previously indicated, however, with reference to McConachie, 'the ability to simulate another's state of mind is usually prior to the kind of judgment that induces sympathy or antipathy' and what Benjamin alludes to in his auratic 'transposition of a response' can be regarded as a cognitive mirroring mechanism. Moreover, as Robert Gordon has argued, drawing upon cognitive psychology, empathy can move spectators 'beyond the problematics of "othering" those who are looked at' (in McConachie and Hart, 2006: 5).

Benjamin is, however, writing about traditional forms of theatre, as evident in his comments on the differences between stage and screen acting:

> the stage actor identifies himself with the character of his role. The film actor very often is denied this opportunity. ... The feeling of strangeness that overcomes the actor before the camera, as Pirandello describes it, is basically of the same kind as the estrangement felt before one's own image in the mirror. But now the reflected image has become separable, transportable. And where is it transported? Before the public. Never for a moment does the screen actor cease to be conscious of this fact.
>
> (1968a: 223–4)

For the contemporary performance practitioner, self-reflexivity is part of the process of being present to an audience. Yet this mode of performance develops from Brecht. As Ivor Indyk has observed:

> One of the most remarkable aspects of [Benjamin's] work is the way he was able to transform the notion of aura, which had its roots in idealism and mysticism, into a political understanding of the distancing effect at work in Brecht's epic theatre. Brecht's habit of interrupting or punctuating the action gave his plays a gestural quality: in that moment, in which the gesture was held, what became apparent ... were the material conditions that gave the gesture its meaning. The proper reaction in the audience was one of astonishment, born of recognition.
>
> (Indyk, 2000)

In setting theatre against film as the live versus the reproduced, Benjamin did not anticipate the dialogue and blending which has ensued as digital technologies have interpenetrated live art and vice versa. But what is being sought through immersive performance, I speculate, is something akin to the auratic moment. In the current age of mediatization, the quest for authentic and intimate experience is pursued through various forms of live art and performance. The moment of embodied recognition where the spectator engages with the artefact corresponds to the felt experience of immersive performance and theatre of affect which moves or touches us. In contemporary performance, as Di Benedetto writes, 'we are simultaneously attendants and participants within the event because our senses are on a continuous state of alert' (2010: 21). This quest for a theatre of contact may also be a desire for a particular kind of communal experience in an informational age which has redefined notions of community and relationships. Individuals on Facebook can have thousands of friends they have never met as virtual communities redefine our understanding of the term. Communities are now networks and, as in cognitive science, the most significant feature is the means of connection, which in the twenty-first-century context is the Internet. Our engagement with the Internet, however, whilst it maybe interactive, is generally disembodied and often solitary.

In participatory and immersive forms of performance, what is being sought are embodied and shared experiences involving visceral as opposed to virtual forms of social contact. Thus touch becomes increasingly important to the experience of immersion, while the desire for intimacy and personal encounters involves an increasing proximity between performer and audience which is arguably at its most extreme in one-to-one performance. For some critics, these practices come with a health warning. Lyn Gardner has expressed concerns on various occasions about ethics, risks and anxiety in encounters between audience and performer in immersive and intimate performance:

> Theatre is changing so rapidly that many of the old conventions are going out the window. There may not be any seats. You may not know quite where to stand. There may not be any other spectators – or, indeed, any actors. You may discover that you are the show, which raises questions about exactly who is taking the risk and who should be paying ... Anxiety kills theatre ...
>
> The makers of immersive and interactive theatre experiences who are creating work that is exploring new ways of engaging with audiences are in completely new territory, both physically and mentally. They are going to have to find ways to create experiences for their audiences where risks can be taken without causing audience anxiety to rocket.
>
> (2009)

For Charlotte Higgins, the immersive experience has become formulaic and tired:

> When the actors ... blindfolded me and led me through into a disorientingly cold and inhospitable space, instead of feeling a frisson of 'What now?' I just thought, 'Oh, not blindfolded *again*.' ... At the same time, I also noted that one or two members of the audience, not as grotesquely jaded as I, seemed to be genuinely terrified – and I wondered whether that was entirely fair. The power relationship between the audience and the cast seemed to have tipped rather completely into the cast's favour ... As we left the theatre, I found myself saying to my friend: 'For God's sake, bring back the fourth wall. And seats.'
>
> (2009)

The trend for participatory, intimate and immersive performance has implications for both aesthetics and ethics as discussed by Bourriaud in his concept of relational aesthetics. Although his thesis has been criticized for its limited scope in terms of theorists and examples (Bishop, 2004; Freshwater 2009; Martin, 2007), his use of the term 'relational' remains useful as a means of challenging the binaries associated with ethics and aesthetics, or art and instrumentalism. Spontaneous social relations, he argues, are disappearing in the context of a globalized informational environment and artistic practice is responding by inventing 'models of sociability' focused on 'inter-human relations'. Drawing on Félix Guattari's aesthetics, he argues that 'social utopias and revolutionary hopes have given way to everyday micro-utopias and imitative strategies' (Bourriaud, 2002: 31). While his differentiation between 'total revolution' and 'micro-revolution' is not entirely clear, his central premise is that new relational interventions are being practised through art at a micro-political and interpersonal level. The spectator becomes a critically important component in relational aesthetics through art that concerns itself with creating encounters through non-scripted social interactions, while the author's importance is lessened 'in favour of that of the artist-cum operator' and in conjunction with 'the liberation of collective subjectivity'.

Bishop is one of numerous critics to takes issue with Bourriaud; her concerns and perceptions are particularly pertinent to the practices discussed here as work which seeks to be socially engaged, is produced in community, educational or social contexts and aspires to effect change – to 'transform' or 'transport' through participatory and immersive forms of performance. According to Bishop, collaborative artistic practices 'are less interested in a relational *aesthetic* than in the creative rewards of collaborative activity' (2006), a perspective which would appear (on the basis of the research undertaken for this book) to be challenged by the vast majority of practitioners involved in applying performance. Nevertheless, Bishop's work in conjunction with Bourriaud is of interest, importance and value as a means of interrogating applied performance practice and establishing criteria for evaluation.

In 'Antagonism and Relational Aesthetics', Bishop challenges the 'laboratory' paradigm of European art venues which promotes art as process: 'open-ended, interactive and resistant to closure' (2004: 52). Destabilizing the identity of the work of art, she argues, is 'a creative misreading of poststructuralist theory' and 'interpretations', rather than the art itself, is what is in flux. Her Lacanian influenced perspective challenges the 'ideal of subjectivity' in Bourriaud's relational aesthetics, whereby community is conceived as 'immanent togetherness' and 'micro-topian' practices produce 'a community whose members identify with each other, because they have something in common' (67). Relational aesthetics, she argues, 'requires a unified subject as a prerequisite for community-as-togetherness' (79). Whilst Bishop's questioning of the 'feel-good' positions adopted by some of the artists she identifies is legitimate, as is her critique of the idealistic concept of community in this work, the psychoanalytic paradigm she draws upon posits an oppositional relationship between self and other as the basis for the 'relational antagonism' she advocates, 'predicated not on social harmony, but on exposing that which is repressed is sustaining the semblance of this harmony' (79). Although the notion of 'relational antagonism' is useful and valid to many of the practices I discuss in the context of applied performance (some of which define themselves as 'interventions'), a cognitive perspective, as discussed in Part I redefines the binary relations of the psychoanalytic model.

Bourriaud's theoretical perspective is similarly predicated on psychoanalytic binaries: he refers to 'the realm of human interactions and its social context, rather than the assertion of an independent and *private* symbolic space' (2002: 14). The challenge to modernism is often couched in terms of the private versus public, but what needs to be questioned here is the basis of the opposition. Cognitive theory embraces a dynamic understanding of identity and subjectivity whereby bodily experience and social interactions shape the mind/brain and vice versa. Thus, as McConachie explains, 'the aptitudes, routines and body language of a social group, can be grounded in the mind/brain'(McConachie and Hart, 2006: 6). Contrary to Bishop's account, this means that cognitive materialism does not reduce agency to resisting dominant practices and ideologies: 'unlike many Marxists, cognitivists define agency as an image schema in the mind that allows a subject to intend and cause a material change in the world' (6). Indeed, he suggests that 'deploying an understanding of culture that includes human cognition, the theorist may redefine Raymond Williams' concept of a "dominant culture" as the material manifestations of the primary image schemas and their accompanying metaphors that legitimate the power of certain groups and classes' (7). In his concept of the 'emancipated spectator', Rancière's analysis appears to be in tune with cognitive perspectives, particularly in terms of his challenge to 'all those oppositions – looking/knowing, looking/acting, appearance/reality, activity/passivity' as 'allegories of inequality'. For Rancière, emancipation 'begins when we dismiss the opposition between looking and acting':

> It starts when we realize that looking also is an action which confirms or modifies that distribution , and that 'interpreting the world' is already a means of transforming it, of reconfiguring it. The spectator is active, as the student or the scientist: he observes, he selects , compares, interprets. He ties up what he observes with many other things that he has observed on other stages ...

> This is what emancipation means: the blurring of the opposition between they who look and they who act, they who are individuals and they who are members of a collective body.
>
> (2009a: 5)

For Rancière, however, participatory practices are called into question:

> the crossing of the borders and the confusion of the roles should not lead to some sort of 'hypertheatre' turning spectatorship into activity by turning representation to presence. On the contrary, it should question the theatrical privilege of living presence and bring the stage back to a level of equality with the telling of a story or the writing and the reading of a book.
>
> (2009a: 11)

Rancière has a point (and I will return later to his comments on representation and presence), but he raises a critical question (which he intends to be rhetorical) when he asks 'what does specifically happen between the spectators of a theatre which would not happen elsewhere? Is there something more interactive, more common to them than to the individuals who look at the same time at the same show on their TV?' (2009a: 8)

From a cognitive perspective, the response is affirmative. In terms of agency, the binary notions of the active versus passive in discussions of spectatorship (Brecht, Artaud, Debord, Bourriaud) are undermined by cognitive models. However, the cognitive position differs from Rancière in an important respect. In *Ways of Seeing* (2003), Pierre Jacob and Marc Jeannerod suggest the viewer/spectator has 'two-visual systems' and moves between them in accordance with their intentions: semantic processing is used for identifying inanimate visually presented objects, while pragmatic processing is involved in actions directed towards objects. This means that our cognitive processing of TV and cinema is perceptually different to the experience of live performance as the former involves semantic processing, while the latter engages us pragmatically in responding to animate live material. Moreover, our engagement through the contiguity of space/event/ action and the physicality of the 'visual visceral' is inextricably related to our agency as active spectators.

Bourriaud's conception of relational art producing rather than reflecting social relationships has implications for evaluation which, he argues, should consider the 'criteria of co-existence' through such questions as 'does this work permit me to enter into dialogue? Could I exist, and how, in the space it defines? (2002: 109). This is a further concern for Bishop, who raises pertinent questions:

> I am simply wondering how we decide what the 'structure' of a relational artwork comprises, and whether this is so detachable from the work's ostensible subject matter or permeable with its context. Bourriaud wants to equate aesthetic judgement with an ethicopolitical judgment of the relationships produced by a work of art. But how do we measure or compare these relationships? The *quality* of the relationships in relational

aesthetics are never examined ... what does 'democracy' really mean in this context? If relational art produces human relations, then the next logical question to ask is what *types* of relations are being produced, for whom, and why?

(2004: 67)

These are important questions for applied theatre scholarship. It is important to understand the ideological conditions of production – who is funding the work and for what purpose? For funders, moreover, demonstration of 'impact' is increasingly a feature of the criterion for commissioning a work as well as evaluating its efficacy. Indeed, in Kwon's discussion of new genre public art she raises a series of important questions about authority and agency as part of her problematizing of community and participatory practice:

[H]ow does a group of people become identified as a community in an exhibition program, as a potential partner in a collaborative art project? Who identifies them as such? And who decides what social issue will be addressed or represented by/through them: The artist? The community group? The curator? The sponsoring institution? The funding organization? Does the partner community pre-exist the art project, or is it produced by it? ... If new public art engages the audience as active participants in the production of an artwork, which to a degree, renders them subjects of the work too, then who is the audience for *this* production? What criteria of success and failure are posed now, especially to the artists, as this major reconfiguration of public art that moves aesthetic practice closer to social services?

(2004: 117)

These are also important and vexed questions for practitioners and scholars. The preoccupation with the relations between art and life (at its most extreme in 'reality TV'), the criterion of efficacy and impact which demand evidence of this relationship (strongly articulated by practitioners in the United States and the United Kingdom) in conjunction with a preoccupation for connecting communities (virtual and real) to demonstrate bonded social relations, has contributed to the turn to collaboration in the context of social engagement which, as Bishop cautions, can produce work which is consumerist and/or complicit in promoting the dominant ideologies of capitalism. For Bishop, relational aesthetics 'rest too comfortably within an ideal of subjectivity as whole and of community as immanent togetherness' (2004: 67). Bishop cites Kwon's interventionist notion of art which 'unworks' community in the context of her advocation of relational antagonism. Such work 'does not offer an experience of transcendent human empathy that smoothes over the awkward situation before us, but a pointed racial and economic non-identification: "this is not me"' (Bishop, 2004: 79). Again, however, we have a discourse of difference and oppositions based on notions of self and other as the basis of antagonist aesthetics. Bishop refers to the controversial work of Santiago Sierra as 'a mode of artistic experience more adequate to the divided and incomplete subject of today'.

Thus, although Bishop raises some crucial concerns and questions for practitioners working in social and community contexts to address, her concept of the fragmented subject is rehabilitated from a cognitive science perspective, rejecting the subject/object dichotomy in favour of a dynamic and integrated paradigm involving interaction between the organism and the environment. From the science perspective, the mind, according to Damasio, is 'a process, not a thing' (Damasio 1999: 183); he emphasizes that our ability to reason depends on how we feel 'the emotions and feelings we experience are integral to our intellectual processes' (159). Emotion is translated into feeling and leads to behaviour (which may or may not be linked to 'rational' thought). Bruce McConachie writes of 'emotional contagion' in theatre whereby 'people mirror and catch emotions from others through empathy'. Thus audiences are involved in group responses; '[they] will tend to laugh, cry, and even gasp simultaneously. The more spectators join together in one emotion, the more empathy shapes the emotional response of the rest' (97). These are the cognitive processes underpinning Dolan's 'utopia' and what McConachie refers to as 'communitas' (2008: 97).

McConachie's account, however, primarily refers to conventions associated with proscenium theatre. Contemporary forms of theatre challenge the fourth wall through anti-illusionist strategies which position the spectator differently, and this leads to kinaesthetic empathy. To be kinaesthetically connected, as Simon Shepherd has explained, we need to be close to performers and action: 'effects are produced in the spectator simply as a result of materially sharing the space with the performance. Many of these effects, bypassing the intellect, are felt in the body and work powerfully to shape a spectator's sense of the performance' (2006: 336–7). What Shepherd describes here is embodiment, the conjoining of mind and body, reason and emotion in 'kinesthetic empathy between the spectators; musculature and the performers' (46).

Bourriaud's perception, then, that 'art is the place that produces a specific sociability' because 'it tightens the space of relations, unlike TV' (2002: 16) finds endorsement in cognitive theories of performance. In the shared space of relational work, the conditions of production facilitate empathic engagement. Empathy, however, does not involve a surrender of reason to emotion; the experiences of spectatorship in contemporary forms of visual visceral performance involve encounters which have parallels with some forms of sport, as noted by McConachie: 'the empathic mirroring of physical movements, after all, is central to the enjoyment of prize fighting, a kind of spectatorship that Brecht held up as a model for theatrical engagement.' (2008: 76). Thus, although relational practices might be deemed to privilege 'intersubjective relations over detached opticality' (Bishop, 2004: 61), these dualisms can be reconciled through a cognitive approach.

Rancière's notion of 'emancipation' in spectatorship challenges the power relations between artists and audiences, performers and participants, as well as the privileging of one form of theatre over another. He expresses particular concern about the hierarchies and pedagogies he associates with contemporary practices:

> Those issues of crossing the borders and blurring the distribution of the roles come up with the actuality of the theatre and the actuality of contemporary art, where all artistic competences step out of their own field and exchange their places and powers with all others. We have ... installations and performances instead of 'plastic' works; video projections turned into cycles of frescoes; photographs turned into living pictures or history paintings; sculpture which becomes hypermediatic show.
>
> (2009b: 10)

This can lead, he suggests to 'the apotheosis of some strong artistic egos or the apotheosis of a kind of hyperactivist consumerism, if not both at the same time'. The validity of his concerns is evident in some of the examples discussed below. Rancière advocates a 'third way', 'which dismantles' the 'cause/effect' scheme and 'invalidates the opposition between activity and passivity' as well as the scheme of 'equal transmission'. He questions 'the theatrical privilege of living presence' and calls for

> the institution of a new stage of equality, where the different kinds of performances would be translated into one another ... linking what one knows with what one does not know, of being at the same time performers who display their competences and visitors or spectators who are looking for what those competences may produce in a new context, among unknown people.
>
> (2009b 11)

I will return to Rancière's model in my case study of Martha Bowers' *Dream Life of Bricks* and in my discussion of the pedagogies of participatory performance. Firstly, however, I want to take up two issues arising from Rancière's analysis in conjunction with Bourriaud's response to it. The first is the problematics of the role of the artist in relational and socially ameliorative collaborations, while the second and related concern is the criteria for evaluating work of this kind. Both issues return us to the debates surrounding ethics and aesthetics in applying performance.

Concerns about power relations, the exploitation of marginalized and vulnerable groups and ethical strategies to address this have been articulated in a range of writing about socially engaged art (Denzin, 2003; Kester, 2004; Lippard, 1998). Grant Kester has engaged in a series of debates with Claire Bishop about the problems, purposes and practices of participatory art. In *Conversation Pieces* his central premise is expressed in terms of a provocation which rejects interventionist art, advocating a 'dialogical aesthetics' as an alternative paradigm:

> Art's role is to shock us out of this perceptual complacency, to force us to see the world anew. This shock has borne many names over the years: the sublime, alienation effect, *L'Amour fou*, and so on. In each case the result is a kind of somatic epiphany that catapults the viewer outside of the familiar boundaries of a common language, existing modes of representation, and even their own sense of self. While the projects I'm discussing here do encourage their participants to question fixed identities, stereotypical images, and so on, they do so through a cumulative process of exchange and dialogue, rather than a single, instantaneous shock of insight, precipitated by an image or object. These projects require a paradigm shift in our understanding of the work of art; a definition of aesthetic experience that is durational rather than immediate.
>
> (Kester, 2004: 79)

Kester examines the work of artists who adopt 'a performative, process-based approach', describing them as 'context' rather than 'content' providers, who create a medium for 'exchanges [which] can catalyze surprisingly powerful transformations in the consciousness of their participants.' The relations between artists and participants are conceived by Kester as non-hierarchical and dialogical. Evaluation of this work, he suggests, 'is no longer centered on the physical object' and 'the new locus of judgment ... resides in the condition and character of dialogical exchange itself' (80). A dialogical aesthetics, Kester proposes, changes our understanding of the nature and function of art, moving away from what he refers to as 'the individual and somatic experience of liking' to embrace practices whereby 'subjectivity is formed *through* discourse and inter-subjective exchange itself.' For Bishop, such a position surrenders artistic autonomy and sacrifices aesthetics to the service of social amelioration:

> Kester's position adds up to a familiar summary of the intellectual trends inaugurated by identity politics: respect for the other, recognition of difference, protection of fundamental liberties, and an inflexible mode of political correctness. As such, it also constitutes a rejection of any art that might offend or trouble its audience.
>
> (2006: 178)

Thus the feuding between Kester and Bishop involves a familiar set of dualisms: art versus politics, aesthetics versus ethics, authorship versus spectatorship. In his defence of Rancière, Bourriaud makes similar points:

> It seems that the debates that have been raised by the 'relational' in art since the publication of the book essentially revolve around the respective positions of ethics, the political and aesthetics in the artistic practices that are described. These practices have been suspected of putting morals above form, generating a purely 'social' or even 'Christian' or 'compassionate' art; they have been accused of proposing an angelic ethical model, masking the existing conflicts in society.
>
> (2002: 2)

What is advocated by Rancière, Bourriauld, Kester and Bishop in their respective paradigms for collaborative art are, however, dynamic modes of practice and evaluative criteria which encompass ethical *and* aesthetic considerations. Critical to these conceptions is an interaction between two other (related) modes of engagement: the political and the empathic. Kester's dialogic aesthetics is indebted to Jürgen Habermas's concept of identity and subjectivity based on social and communicative interaction, but recognizes also the importance of both listening and what Mary Field Belenky identifies as 'connected knowing' (1989). In his discussion of empathy, Kester can be seen to develop a cognitive perspective on collaboration:

> a concept of empathetic insight is a necessary component of a dialogical aesthetic. Further, I would contend that precisely the pragmatic, physical process of collaborative production that occurs in the works I'm discussing (involving both verbal and bodily interaction) can help to generate this insight, while at the same time allowing for a discursive exchange that can acknowledge, rather than exile, the non-verbal.
>
> (2004: 83)

Bishop's discussions embrace a dialectic between ethical and aesthetic consideration. While she expresses concern about artists being 'increasingly judged by their working process' (in preference to artefacts) and critical 'accusations of mastery and egocentrism' for practitioners who are deemed to lead collaborative projects (rather than 'allowing it to emerge through consensual collaboration'), she clearly recognizes and values collaborative art in the context of contemporary practice and a 'socially ameliorative tradition'. The work she advocates endeavours 'to think the aesthetic and the social/political *together*, rather than subsuming both within the ethical' (2006). Bishop demonstrates an empathic understanding of the personal as political in her discussions, as well as raising critical questions about the relations between life and art. She is highly critical of Jeremy Deller's *The Battle of Orgreave*, a re-enactment of events from the 1984 English miners' strike as a form of celebratory community performance: 'The whole event could be understood as contemporary history painting that collapses representation and reality.' Her concerns here are ethical and aesthetic: Thus, for Bishop, 'the tasks facing us today are to analyze *how* contemporary art addresses the viewer and to assess the *quality* of the audience relations it produces.' In her view, 'the best collaborative practices of the past ten years address this contradictory pull between autonomy and social intervention, and reflect on this antinomy both in the structure of the work and in the conditions of its reception. It is to this art – however uncomfortable, exploitative, or confusing it may first appear – that we must turn for an alternative to the well-intentioned homilies that today pass for critical discourse on social collaboration (2006).

The debates between relational practice and aesthetics are pertinent to applied theatre which has explored similar concerns. In applied theatre, however, the artefact is performative: social amelioration or intervention involves a process of doing through particular forms of practice-based engagement (the 'action' which distinguishes and defines the work in the broad context of drama). Although I have argued this leads to embodied understanding, the quest for affective performance which moves its audience towards social change has generated work which uses immersive strategies to engage the spectator experientially. In the next section, I consider the nature and quality of audience relations produced by this work (responding to Kester and Bishop) questioning the ethics and aesthetics of the work discussed and the relations between art and the social.

6.2   THEME PARK HELLS: INCARCERATIONS

A new form of prison theatre has recently emerged in conjunction with the turn to participation in contemporary forms of artistic practice. This generally involves simulating the conditions of incarceration and immersing the audience in an experience which is socially and politically motivated, creating awareness of (and even sympathy for) the prisoners' perspective. Thus it could be argued that the form of the installation enables the practitioners making the work to generate an embodied and empathic understanding of a particular form of life through art. This trend for socially ameliorative immersive performance is part of a series of paradigmatic shifts in arts practices as discussed above. As Mi Won Kwon warns, however, this changing orientation in public art is potentially problematic in terms of the relations between means and ends:

> the slide of emphasis from aesthetic concerns to social issues, from the conception of an artwork primarily as an object to ephemeral processes or events, from the prevalence of permanent installations to temporary interventions, from the primacy of production as source of meaning to reception as site of interpretation, and from autonomy of authorship to its multiplicitous expansion in participatory collaborations. While these shifts represent a greater inclusivity and democratization of art for many artists, arts administrators, art institutions, and some of their audience members, there is also the danger of a premature and uncritical embrace of 'progressive' art as an equivalent of 'progressive politics'.
>
> (2001)

This is Camp X Ray

My first example is a performance installation, presented on the outskirts of Manchester, in Hulme from 10–18 October 2003. Jai Redman's *This is Camp X Ray* was presented as part of an exhibition entitled 'Don't Cross the Line'. Situated between a housing development and derelict wasteland, Redman positioned the piece as a strategy to move beyond the state-controlled and publicly funded art galleries; to 'expose the works to the gaze of the non-gallery-going public and the ethnically and experientially diverse population of Manchester' (Redman, 2003a). This gaze included Manchester commuters who could see the site from the train. The project was conceived as a 'fully operational, life-size replica" of the US internment camp in Guantanamo Bay (which in 2002 was replaced by Camp Delta). Although the Cuban camp has a high media profile, attracting international attention and considerable concern from Human Rights organizations for non-compliance with the Geneva Convention, Redman argues that art offers a more immediate forum for political engagement; progressive performance art is clearly allied with progressive politics in the conception of the project: 'What is the point of painting a picture of it or showing photographs or a video of it? People have seen those and are immune to them. I wanted to create a mirror image of the site and place it in the community which is the home of Ron Fiddler [known as Jaamal Udeen], one of the British prisoners in the camp, and see what local reaction would be' (Redman, 2003b).

The project recruited 14 volunteers; five guards and nine prisoners (representing the numbers of prisoners among the detainees) who were incarcerated as 'unlawful combatants' for nine days and nights. Surrounded by a razor-wire perimeter fence, this life-size reconstruction was carefully modelled on the original with watch towers, a guard's mess, prisoners' dormitories, parade ground, flood lights a sentry post and a 24-hour guard. The daily routine was based on the regime of a detainee with the national anthem played on loudspeakers every morning, regular prayers (commencing at 5a.m.), a sick call at 11a.m. and mail call in the afternoon. Locked in the interrogation centre after tea, the day ends at 9p.m. with lights out. The prisoners were subject to tied restraints, sensory deprivation and humiliation, with interrogations broadcast on radio. They were fed a standard diet of porridge, vegetable soup and beans and rice in accordance with Muslim Halal.

The 'action' (as depicted in documentary film footage) was durational, involving the performer/prisoners being subject to many aspects of the Guantanamo treatment, inflicted by the performer officers. For the participants, Redman's aim was to affect through the experience: 'I'm hoping that the nine prisoners and the guards who guard them will have a fundamental change happening in their lives' (2003a). The role of the participant performers was also conceived in relation to its legacy and impact. In addition to the film which accompanied the project, the participants functioned as a living archive, who, Redman hoped, would raise consciousness through dialogue: 'each of the individual prisoners and guards will have their own story to tell. That's the only way that political change can now be realized in this country, because voting and marching don't work' (2003a). The film also documented the experiences of the volunteer participants as well as the reactions from the local community.[1] Critical responses were mixed; for Andrew Rosindell, Conservative Member of Parliament for Romford, the project was 'an outrageous waste of public money'; the *Guardian* referred to the project as 'performance art with a mission to dump state terrorism on the doorsteps of the inner city'[2] and the *Observer* featured it as one of its performance theatre events of the year.[3] According to Redman, 'as art goes, this is pretty straightforward', and as politics it is also clearly and simply articulated: '*This is Camp X Ray* set out to challenge our apathy over the prisoners at the US Army's Guantanamo Bay Camp' (2003c).

However, the relations between art and politics in this piece are not as straightforward as Redman contends, particularly if we consider Bishop's concerns with *how* contemporary art addresses the viewer, and the *quality* of the audience relations it produces. The objectives of Redman's participatory methods are compatible with those articulated by Bishop when she writes of

> the desire to create an active subject, one who will be empowered by the experience of a physical or symbolic participation. The hope is that the newly-emancipated subjects of participation will find themselves able to determine their own social and political reality. An aesthetic of participation therefore derives legitimacy from a (desired) causal relationship between the experience of a work of art and individual/collective agency.
>
> (2006: 12)

However, while *This is Camp X-Ray* challenges the distinction between author and viewer, actor and spectator, production and reception through Artaudian physical and collaborative modes of performance, this particular 'theatre of cruelty' can also be seen to draw upon similar methods to those used in reality television and the simulated reality of theme parks. In reality TV, the viewer/voyeur observes the behaviour and interactions of participants in artificial living conditions (happening in real time but within a constructed context), whilst the immersive experience of the theme park remains a vicarious one as participants are plunged into sensory and visceral environments which, however, remain safe, as theatres of pretence. The invitation to participants read (albeit with self-reflexive irony) like an advert for a cheap thrills experience: 'your chance to be interned in your very own concentration camp for a week.' The repeated references in the critical responses to the project's authenticity clearly endorse its fake reality in connection with the quality of relations it produces, to use Bishop's criteria. Indeed, the *Guardian* refers admiringly to the piece as being 'chillingly authentic' (Redman, 2003b). This is followed by a contradictory revelation: '[The prisoners] are not forced to sleep in open cages (this is Manchester in October, remember) and are not tortured. But their stay will be otherwise authentic and far from comfortable.' Aside from the repeated use of the term authentic (which undermines the writing through neurotic reiteration), the acknowledgment of the comfortable pretence raises serious questions about the aesthetics and ethics at work in this piece and the response to it. 'Authenticity' is equated here with aesthetic value – the more 'real' it feels, it is implied, the better it is, but this is counterbalanced by ethical considerations which protect the participants from the extremes of discomfort suffered by those they are representing. According to Bishop, in the conclusion to her study of installation art 'the closer the ideal model to the literal viewer's experience, the more compelling the installation' (2005: 133). This is not the 'contradictory pull between autonomy and social intervention' Bishop refers to, but a different kind of contradictory conflict between the desire to affect the participants (so they become activated) and the need to do so without risk. Whilst the intention might also appear to be conducive to Kester's ideals and the concept of critical empathy (as participants experience what it might be like to be incarcerated), any pain or discomfort is numbed through the anaesthetizing effect of the fictive artistic framework. Those involved know they will be released at the end of the nine-day period and also have the assurance that this is not for real. Although the film documentation is designed to demonstrate impact, showing the effect of the project on participants and the community, its scope as a radical intervention to effect change is, I suggest, limited by the form this experience takes; it remains vicarious as the participants willingly engage with a fiction. Indeed, for the volunteer prisoners, part of the pleasure could be regarded as masochistic, while for the volunteer guards the appeal was arguably sadistic as the experience offered an opportunity to exercise extreme levels of control with permission to practice intimidating and aggressive behaviour over the enslaved and handcuffed victims of incarceration, as well as opportunities for self-righteousness.

This is not then straightforward as art, installation or performance, as the relations are complex and contradictory, raising questions about the aesthetics and ethics at work in the piece. In the conclusion to *Installation Art*, Bishops refers to the 'ambiguity at the heart of installation art: does the viewer's consciousness become the subject/object, or the subject matter?' (2005: 131) In this piece, the performance dimension complicates these relations; the physical presence of a viewer, which is one of the defining features of installation art, is absorbed into the installation as the viewer becomes a form of spect/actor (albeit within a work which is authored and wherein the spectator/participant is not at liberty to change the conditions of performance). There is, moreover, at the same time another viewer who is positioned as an audience for the installation, watching the action and behaviours performed within the environment, but not physically interacting with the materials. Thus the role of the viewer in installation art has been split and the contradiction Bishop refers to whereby the art claims to 'both *decentre* and *activate* the viewer' is addressed through the separation of the role into active participant (where the viewer's physical engagement becomes performance as part of the installation) and (the critical engagement of) the observer/viewer. The 'literal viewing subject' has entered the work as the object, becoming the watched who is observed by another viewer. In the quest for authenticity, the viewer is absorbed into the installation. According to Bishop, 'the degree of proximity between model subject and literal viewer may therefore provide a criterion of aesthetic judgement for installation art: the closer the ideal model to the literal viewer's experience, the more compelling the installation' (2005: 133). But whilst the installation may be compelling for those experiencing it as physical participants, the immersive experience as a state of 'not thinking' where 'meaning remains in principle postponed' (Lehmann, 2006: 87) may also negate or diminish the capacity for critical engagement through the blurring or confusion of the distinction between subject and object. As Adrian Heathfield has argued in relation to live art, the physical entry of the artist's body into performance unsettles distinctions between subject and object, life and art (Heathfield and Glendinning, 2004).

Here, it can be argued, there is no real sense of risk as participants are secure in the knowledge they are safe (and all has been carefully risk-assessed); the piece stems from an authored tradition which seeks to provoke participants rather than the collaborative de-authored lineage of collective and creative collaboration. Indeed, it can be argued that this piece, as a carefully controlled simulation of an experience, involves a relatively passive engagement rather than the activated spectatorship and activism that Redman intended. It is not necessarily the case that construction of a Debord 'situation' in which the viewer becomes the *viveur* produces new social relationships and realities, as Bishop suggests. Indeed, I suggest that it may risk having the opposite effect: 'a mode of passivity and subjugation that arrests thought and prevents determination of one's reality' (Bishop, 2007: 12–13). In this instance, nevertheless, the film documentation of the project provides testaments about the project's ethical efficacy in raising political and social consciousness of what Guantanamo Bay represents. I suggest, however, that its impact was due to the originality of the form and content of the piece rather than a radical aesthetics. It is also based on a complicit conception, reproducing the physical conditions (almost) and yet somehow implicating the political meaning.

State of Incarceration

My second example is also a socially engaged project exploring the conditions of incarceration, but involves a different form of participant experience, increasingly familiar to theatre audiences. *State of Incarceration* (2010–11) was a performance installation developed in the context of the LAPD (Los Angeles Poverty Department's Examination of the Personal and Social Costs of Incarceration in the United States). The performance was part of a range of activities within the LAPD's 'History of Incarceration' project which combined 'theatre, installation and public education to examine the personal and social costs of incarceration in the US' (LAPD, 2010). The project declares its aims as follows:

> One is that it will enable the public to visually and viscerally understand the conditions created by public policies that have led California to have the largest prison population in the US. The second is to create an opportunity for prisoners to share their lived expertise, about the prison experience, the state of incarceration and how to survive it. And the ultimate

goal of the project is to create a moment of exchange and reflection on how they and we, the people of California, as a state can recover from living in a state of incarceration.

(LAPD, 2010)

Thus, from its inception, the piece was ethically and politically motivated to explore social issues through the medium of public performance. California has the highest number of prisoners in the United States, the country with the highest rate of incarceration in the world. Skid Row in Los Angeles, where LAPD is based, houses one-third of released parolees, and many of those involved as performers in the project have custodial experiences. The devised piece, developed through workshops was structured as a narrative of incarceration, following a chronology 'from entry to release and re-integration'. The piece has been performed in a series of community locations and is generally described as a performance within an installation. As in *Camp X Ray*, a prison environment is reconstructed, but in *State of Incarceration* the action is confined to the interior of an enclosed space containing 30 bunk-beds on which the audience sits. The atmosphere is cramped with performers and audience in very close proximity. This is clearly designed to create authenticity, as the audience enter an environment which looks and feels like a large prison dormitory. Video monitors are installed on the beds, reminding the audience of the artificial and theatrical nature of the environment. The piece is described as being 'not character based but ... a litany of experiences suffered under similar conditions' (LAPD, 2010). However, in performance it is evident that actors are in role, performing a script. The devised basis for the dialogue is evident in the content and delivery; a performer walks between the beds, telling the audience over and over again: 'no TV, no books, nobody to talk to, just me and four walls. I sit, I look, I think. I walk, I sit, I think and I cry.' The monologues are punctuated with physical activity (including several fights) and narrative commentary delivered through a third-person form of address, as the actors switch from being in role to direct address. Thus, after falling to the ground, an actor explains from his position on the floor 'Damn, he knows I didn't go down in a pool of blood [looks to audience]. I gotta act like I don't know.'[4] Unlike *Camp X Ray*, however, the relations between audience and performer are very clearly delineated. The audience sits in cramped conditions within an intimate but claustrophobic atmosphere, while the performers are very obviously in role. The audience is aware of being within the safe confines of an artificial environment as well as being within the structure of a somewhat predictable script. There is no risk here, and certainly none of the anxiety Lyn Gardner referred to, as this piece does not involve an encounter with the unexpected. The audience may appear to be immersed in the environment of an installation, and are in close proximity to the performers but their engagement is not participatory or experiential. When the prisoners fight, it is spectacle; indeed, the whole experience feels somewhat voyeuristic as the devised script is confessional and somewhat uncomfortable to witness: 'I walk, I sit, I think, I cry, I cry', an actor repeats (somewhat unconvincingly as if he doesn't own the words), pacing around the audience in an endeavor to provoke our sympathy. The problem here is that the script creates closure; the work is not open to suggestion, in the way that Umberto Eco recommends: 'an artistic work that suggests is also one that can be performed with the full emotional and imaginative resources of the interpreter' (Eco, 1962: 27). This is linked by Eco to Merleau-Ponty's concept of consciousness and presence, whereby 'perceptive ambiguity' frees the observer to conceive openly and differently without recourse to 'habit and familiarity' (Eco, 1962: 33). Because the audience are configured here as observers, watching the events unfold in optical contemplation, their responses are inhibited and restrained. Thus while the performance may appear to be an installation, it is not participatory and the environment it creates is not affective. We remain unmoved and unmoving.

In both these pieces about incarceration, the aim has been explicitly identified as activating the spectator in a politically engaged response to conditions which are reconstructed through installations and which seek to create authenticity. Both are problematic due to the nature of the environment created and in spite of close proximity between performer and audience. These are indeed artificial hells, but not in the sense that Bishop conceives; contrary to Bishop, I suggest that 'immersion in a discrete space contiguous with the "real world" has been the tacit manifesto' (Bishop, 2006: 133) and limitation (rather than achievement) of these particular forms of installation art.

6.3 PARTICIPANT CENTRED PEDAGOGY AND THE AFFECTIVE LEARNING ENVIRONMENT: LIFT 2011

In my discussion above of the problems associated with the construction of authenticity through immersive environments, I conclude that we are 'unmoved', thereby implying that the shortcoming is a failure to affect the spectator. In both of these incarceration pieces, the closed formats in different ways prevented the creation of genuinely 'affective atmospheres', to use Ben Anderson's terms (2009). Anderson uses Marx's materialism in conjunction with the phenomenology of Dufrenne to explore the Deleuzian concept of affects as 'becomings' in relation to the liminality of 'affective atmospheres' which he associates with the production of subjectivity:

> It is the very ambiguity of affective atmospheres – between presence and absence, between subject and object/subject and between the definite and indefinite that enables us to reflect on affective experience as occurring beyond, around and alongside the formation of subjectivity.
>
> (Anderson, 2009: 77)

Anderson is interested in how writing about atmosphere unsettles the distinctions between affect and emotion that have emerged in discussions of 'how the social relates to the affective and emotive dimensions of life' (81). His discussion is relevant here for a number of reasons. Firstly, he considers how atmosphere is created by bodies but is not reducible to them: 'atmospheres are singular affective qualities that emanate from but exceed the assemblings of bodies' (81). Thus it is not merely the proximity between performers and spectators which produces atmosphere; there are other factors at work which Anderson identifies in terms of the environment's spatial and metaphysical qualities as open, indeterminate and provisional: 'atmospheres are unfinished because of their constitutive openness to being taken up in experience' (79). Thus the closure of the controlled and authored environment in *Camp X-Ray* and the scripted containment of *State of Incarceration* worked against the creation of affective atmosphere. In terms of participation, moreover, affective atmospheres require collective engagement of some form: whilst they belong to the perceiving subject, they emanate from 'the ensemble of elements that make up the aesthetic object'. Thus they also belong to the aesthetic object and are 'always in the process of emerging and transforming'. In applied theatre and performance, the nature, identity and status of the aesthetic object is a matter of debate, of course (although the emphasis on process and a state of flux is certainly pertinent to the practice of applying performance), but Anderson questions Dufrenne's emphasis on aesthetic objects and moves the conception of atmosphere beyond self-enclosed aesthetics: 'Epochs, societies, seasons, couples, places, buildings and much more can be said to be atmospheric in the sense that they are animated by singular affective qualities (and the resonances, interferences and tensions between different affective qualities)' (79). There is an important connection between Bishop's writing about participation and installation (as a mode of collaborative art) with Anderson's concept of affective atmospheres, and this 'relation of tension', to use Anderson's terms, is what holds the interplay between the opposites: 'presence and absence, materiality and ideality, definite and indefinite, singularity and generality' (81). This connects to Bishop's understanding of the split sense of the subject as 'both centred *and* decentred' through presence and absence in installation art:

> this conflict *is itself decentring* since it structures an irresolvable antagonism between the two. Installation art calls for a self-present viewing subject precisely in order to subject him/her to the process of fragmentation. When successful, this involves an overlap between the philosophical model of subjectivity presupposed by the work and the production of this model in the literal viewer who experiences it first-hand. By this means installation art aims not only to problematize the subject as decentred but also to produce it.
>
> (2006: 131–3)

Bishop's concluding suggestion is that 'on some occasions (and these may only be very rare), the ideal model of the subject overlaps with our literal experience and we genuinely do feel confused, disoriented and destabilized by our encounter with the work' (133). Whilst this might be connected to the anxiety Lyn Gardner attributes to some forms of immersive performance, I suggest that what is being described here is an affective atmosphere; this is destabilizing because it is in flux; the perceiving subject is in a state of becoming through the process of being transported in an affective and affecting event. In my concluding section I will return to this experience and consider it in terms of what Richard Schechner refers to as 'rasaesthetics' and the 'taste of heaven' which, I argue, can be experienced in and through affective applications of performance. Firstly, however, and by way of transition, I want to return to the liminal space identified by Anderson and Bishop in relation to presence and absence and the notion of the aesthetic object through a case study which explores how participant centred pedagogy creates an affective learning environment. The case study examines how school pupils worked with a theatre archive, transforming aesthetic objects through performance processes which explored (and challenged) relations between past, present and future.

Performing the Living Archive: *And the Winner is... London*

Since its inception in 1981, the biennial London International Festival for Theatre (LIFT) has been associated with highly innovative practice. The remarkable story of the development of LIFT, the creation of two university graduates Lucy Neal and Rose de Wend Fenton, is chronicled in *The Turning World: Stories from the London International Festival of Theatre* (2005). Invited to participate in an international festival of street theatre in Coimbra, they took a production of David Hare's 1975 play *Fanshen*, which they describe as 'totally cerebral, completely verbal', and in marked contrast to the diverse range of performance art featured in the festival: 'Everyone else had brought music, dance, mime. It was all visual. It was all such fun, And we thought "Why aren't we doing something like this?", so we did!' (Fenton, 1993).[5] From 1981 to 2001, LIFT presented work from 60 countries in a wide range of London venues, as well as performances in non-theatre spaces – in streets, parks, houses, industrial sites, rivers and canals. In 2001, the five-year LIFT Enquiry replaced the biennial format with a regular programme of events, and since 2006 the biennial festival has been accompanied by an ongoing programme of productions. A wide range of educational work emerged from the festival, often extending well beyond its relatively short season. In 1993, for example, the visit of the Hanoi Water Puppets inspired a six-month community project, *Sang Song – River Crossing*, a collaboration between the British Telecom LIFT Education Programme, Emergency Exit Arts and the Vietnam Refugee Project in Greenwich. This involved eight Greenwich schools and the Vietnamese Youth Arts Group, working with EEA artists to produce a devised piece using music, puppets and storytelling, to explore the culture and experiences of the Vietnamese community in Greenwich, The work was performed at the National Maritime Museum to audiences totalling 3500 over a two-day period. A teacher associated with the project described its impact:

> Some [pupils] denied their origins before, now they are proud to acknowledge their parents' lives and their connections with Vietnam. We had no idea what the scale of the performance would be. We were amazed and delighted. The group has grown 6 inches. We will use the Vietnam teaching pack again and again.[6]

Throughout its history, the work emerging from LIFT in educational and community contexts is aesthetically and ethically motivated with funding applications consistently emphasizing the importance of creating high quality participatory art of social significance. 'Out of Lift' was initiated in 1996 as an 'in-between season' involving collaborations between international artists and inner-city schoolchildren. It was launched in June 1996 with Christophe Berthonneau's *The Factory of Dreams* for an audience of 3000 people in Brockwell Park. Pyrotechnics, music, sculpture and the contributions of 120 thirteen to fourteen-year-olds were the raw material for the project. The initial proposal presented the project's objectives in terms which clearly indicate the aesthetic and social ambitions for the work:

> To commission the world's leading fire artist to create a spectacular open-air pyrotechnical theatre event for 5,000 people a night in Brockwell Park, in partnership with 5 London artists and 120 Brixton 13-year-olds.

And in so doing,

> To experiment with the form of large-scale open-air celebratory events within the context of an inner-city, multi-cultural community.

> To give creative expression to the dreams and visions of young Londoners by harnessing them to the energies and skills of artists of excellence.[7]

The year 2011 marked the thirtieth anniversary of LIFT. This was a year in-between festivals, and as part of the programme of celebratory activities a project in schools combined the history of LIFT with the immediate future in the form of the then forthcoming 2012 Olympic and Paralympic games. The growth and impact of LIFT's work in educational and social contexts is reflected in the organizational structures needed to support it. A Participation Producer, Erica Campayne, manages the programmes, liaising with schools, community groups and a wide range of practitioners to deliver the diverse range of projects. *And the winner is London...* (2011) involved a team of six artists led by Sue Mayo, creating seven pieces of work in seven London schools. The project formed part of a larger scheme, 'The Biggest Learning Opportunity on Earth', taking place in 150 schools across London as part of the activities surrounding the London Olympics. The LIFT 'Living Archive' was central to the conception of the project; the fusion of past and future through participatory performance is beautifully evoked in the project's opening caption: 'Would you like to look inside a special box which stores the memories of an amazing event?'

My discussion refers to my experience of seeing the process in three of the schools which generated very different outcomes in spite of the shared stimulus (the archive) and working methods. This is indicative of the extent to which the participants took ownership as authors of the work. Mayo works within flexible structures enabling her to facilitate and respond to the creative ideas of participants. Yet she is also very clear about the importance of appropriate guidance to ensure the artistic quality of the work produced. The process is an iterative one as ideas are generated, explored and reviewed with artists and pupils in constant dialogue and negotiation. Each of the projects commenced in the LIFT Living Archive, housed in the Special Collections at Goldsmiths University Library. In 2005, the LIFT founders wrote in their final newsletter of 'the longer term plan for an interactive website ... for users all over the world interested in how the "now" can be understood through the "then".'[8] The LIFT Living Archive was launched in June 2009.

As a living archive, this resource includes a particularly dynamic website as a digital online resource, as well as having physical and material artefacts stored in the library facility. In her 2009 report on the archive, Caoimhe McAvinchey discusses how the distinctiveness of the contents and the participatory practices developed facilitate access and interaction with the materials:

> The LIFT Living Archive is not a collection of video recordings of the pro-
> ductions that were staged during the LIFT festivals. Rather, it is a collec-
> tion of documents and objects which were made and left behind during
> the process of making a theatre festival. These include:
>
> Project proposals, descriptions and reports
> Correspondence including telegrams, faxes, emails, handwritten, typed
> and printed letters
> Budgets
> Contracts
> Production schedules
> Production notes
> Marketing materials: images of productions, programmes, posters
> Boxes of Objects – sometimes gifts from companies or things made/related
> to a specific show
>
> Twenty-five years of work – of negotiation, excitement, extraordinary
> spectacle, late-nights, imagination, memories, worry, audacity, detailed
> planning and optimism – generated by thousands of people from across
> the world have been gathered together and systematically re-viewed,
> labelled, recorded and filed in hundreds of archive boxes.
>
> (McAvinchey, 2009)

For the school pupils, familiar with digital media, the website was accepted as part of the standard diet of learning and entertainment and was not regarded as particularly unusual or exciting, whilst for theatre scholars of my generation (accustomed to recovering production histories in dusty stacks, boxes of photos, press cuttings, etc.) it offers a new dimension to archival research and the documentation of performance. For the school children, however, the hard material contained in the archives boxes engaged them differently, offering an exciting and unusual learning resource as their first experience of working with materials of this kind.

The materials and conventions associated with archive work were enthu-siastically embraced through, where appropriate, the use of plastic gloves, pencils and book supports to protect the artefacts. Like forensic investiga-tors, the pupils were cast in the role of detectives, uncovering clues and evidence through their examination of the historical remains of theatre productions. Mayo refers to project participants as co-explorers, and has developed a model for articulating the different ways of engaging with his-torical material and archival evidence:

> Plunging in means delving deeply into the archive, learning all the infor-mation that you can glean about a particular moment or show from the many sources available there.
> Bouncing off means using an encounter with one image, piece of text, or idea to inspire a new and original piece of creative work
> Exploring means setting off with your own question of theme, and mak-ing your own trail through the archive in order to answer this
> Dialogue means entering into a discussion, whereby what you have to say is shedding light on what you discover in the archive, and what is in the archive is illuminating your own experience.
>
> (Mayo, 2010)

As Mayo perceives, this process of action research 'challenged any sense of the archive as monologue'. Central to the conception of the work I observed is the relationship between the histories of the aesthetic objects contained in the archive, the personal histories of the participants and the presentness of the aesthetic objects created through the performance process. This worked on a number of levels, but the process can be seen to respond to Bourriaud's concerns about the value of endurance in aesthetics: 'endurance, whether it concerns objects or relations, has become a rare thing' (2009: 23). In this project, objects and relations were brought into dialogue. The association and fascination with the archive as a dead, rather than living resource was evident in the response of a pupil to a letter from a production manager when he realized that the name corresponded to someone who was still listed on the LIFT website. He expressed considerable surprise that the indi-vidual concerned was still alive as he had assumed that as he had a letter in the archive, this must mean he was dead.

The tasks and items were carefully selected to create connections between the histories and experiences of the pupils and the historical and cultural contexts in which the productions had been created. As Mayo explains, 'while wanting to allow a sense of exploration it always seemed important to mediate the experience of the archive by making some presentation. We looked for material that would intrigue, for themes that would reward, and for shows that made their presence felt through the archive.' Two of the schools I observed worked with materials from the 2001 production of

Figure 11 LIFT archive. Photograph by kind permission of Tim Mitchell

Buchettino by Societas Raffaelo Sanzio. I offer a brief summary of the original performance as a context for my discussion of the complex relationship between the original artefact (the performance and its remains) and the reinterpretations the pupils produced from the historical sources.

Buchettino offers us a further example of an immersive bunk-bed performance. In this piece, however, the audience were on individual bunk-beds, and were encouraged to lie down under the blankets provided to experience the performance as a bedtime story. The tale of Thumbkin was narrated by a single performer: 'there is nothing to see', the audience were told; they should lie back, 'open your ears', and experience the narrative and soundscape which transports them into an imaginary realm. Unlike *State of Incarceration* there was no visual spectacle; the piece was entirely dependent upon storytelling, sound, smell and the imagination of the audience for the generation of meaning. Affective engagement in this context, as cognitive theorists writing about fiction have discussed, involves the creation of worlds and spaces which are not wholly narrative and character driven. Physically, the audience is embedded (literally) in darkness and emptiness and in this particular theatre space they were required to explore an environment which was only partially conjured through sound and narrative. Pine shavings on the floor transported the audience to the forest, but may also have had other associations for listeners whose minds wander associatively through the woods of individual memory. Within the beds, the audience felt the vibrations of the ogre's stamping transmitted through the wooden pillars. Thus the space became a resonance chamber, a perceptual environment characteristic of the work of Societas Raffaello Sanzio. This piece was originally conceived as a piece of experimental and participatory children's theatre:

> The pre-linguistic and sounds play an important role in the artistic work of Socíetas Raffaello Sanzio. The childhood (Infantia) means 'before language'. 'What kind of knowledge is it that the child acquires through its senses?' The voice is first of all sound. That is important in *Buchettino*. The voice is the material. The child must use the sound of the voice to create, sculpture and form a dramaturgy. In *Buchettino* the child will experience a dynamic exchange between its inner noise and the external noise. The child will, so to speak, learn to see with its voice.[9]

In the archive, the identity of the production was gradually revealed through the process of gathering evidence from the traces of performance history. The children worked with different artefacts in groups and then reported on their findings. They were encouraged to distinguish between fact and guess work as they worked like amateur sleuths on the contents of their boxes. These included photos from the production (showing the story being read with glimpses of the beds), props lists containing reference to sheets and blankets and children's pictures made with rice and seeds, emerging from some of the educational activity emerging from the production. A timeline was created as a means of personalizing cultural history. Most of the children were born in 2001, the year of the production. They constructed a history commencing in 1981, the birth of LIFT, identifying important dates and events they were aware of (from formal and informal accounts of history) but had not directly experienced. Thus they were engaging with the narrative construction of history and issues of representation as it became evident that their cultural and family backgrounds contributed to the different versions of history they brought to the project. History is revealed though this process as fluid and polyvalent, rather than a series of facts. As Ricoeur has written: 'we have nothing better than testimony and the critique of testimony to give credibility to the historian's representation of the past' (2004: 278).

A Polish boy was particularly knowledgeable about the fall of the Berlin Wall in 1990 and the collapse of communism in Poland. The 9/11 attacks on the World Trade Center had made a significant mark as one of Ricoeur's 'collective memories' (whereby a social or familial group is familiar with an event or experience though the testimonies of others, creating a shared cultural history). The historical accounts produced by the pupils connect with Marianne Hirsch's (2008) concept of post-memory, a form of secondary memory constituted through accounts of trauma and which is constructed by the second generation rather than primary witnesses. These accounts become embodied as post-memory. Thus a broad historical framework was created though a process of personal engagement with history. Various exercises helped the children to embody the learning approaches used. They were asked to play a detective game, using each other as mystery objects whereby the physical appearance of the person and the clues obtained from the limited questions permitted (with only yes or no answers allowed) were used as evidence to build a profile of the identity of the subject they were working with. This process of creative mirroring was also used as a means of engaging with the production methodologies. Thus the children were asked to create a story using only sounds made with newspaper. These were presented to each other with the audience for each group lying on the floor with their eyes closed, reflecting the conditions (albeit without beds and blankets) of the performance. Having listened to each other's sound stories, the audience members were asked to describe what they had imagined through the sequence and discussed the relations between this and what was intended and the individual differences in their perceptions of and responses to the same stimuli. In this way, the differences between individual audience experiences were evident as well as the gap between the intentions of creative producers and the experience of spectators.

Throughout the process, the material produced by the children was collected as a new archive for the productions they would create. In subsequent practical workshops the pupils were encouraged to engage differently with the familiar environment of their school, using some of the approaches developed in the archive. Having heard the story of Tom Thumb, they identified the feelings from the story and mapped this emotional structure on to the fabric of the school buildings. The bus shelter was identified as a place to go when you felt sad or alone as the pupils were encouraged to look out for anyone seeking refuge in this space. The Headmistress's office was identified as the place associated with being in trouble. The history of the school was also investigated through the school archive, containing photos, a ledger and a punishment book offering a wealth of insight into the changing face of schooling during the twentieth century. Interviews with teachers and readings from the archive were recorded and used in the performance. Thus the pupils worked with a variety of historical documents which referred to a past and a production they did not experience. They engaged with Ricoeur's perception that 'the past is something which is no longer there, but which has been there, which was once there ... it is no longer and yet it has been' (Kearney, 2004: 154). Ricoeur speaks of the borderline between imagination and memory; in this work, the participants were situated in a liminal space and a liminal temporality, exploring the relationship between a *re*-membered past and the imagined future of the artefact they were creating for performance. The school became a form of living archive for the performance, as storytellers escaped from hidden cupboards (housing the boxes they had created as personal archives and playing the sound track as a series of installations) to perform in every classroom, engaging an audience of teachers, parents and elders. The large glass-fronted cupboards had inspired the production team on their initial site visit as potential containers for performers and archive materials, boxes within boxes revealing memories, objects and historical artefacts which were interwoven in the stories the pupils created.

In this project, then, the pedagogic practice involved an encounter with performance mediated through documentation. Peggy Phelan refers to the 'conditions of witnessing what we did not (and perhaps cannot) see' (2004: 569). In working with the archival traces of performance, the participants in this project developed an embodied engagement with performance material they had not seen and which they transformed into new aesthetic artefacts – a re-imagining through performance (rather than a re-presentation). The LIFT Living Archive projects do not seek to represent the work in

Figure 12   And the Winner is… London. St Mary's Catholic Primary School, Punishment Book from School Archive. Photograph by kind permission of Erica Campayne and LIFT

the manner of a reconstruction (or in the form of the reworkings of iconic past performances, such as those featured in the Live Weekends Futures and Pasts at the Institute of Contemporary Arts, 21–23 May 2010), but there are some synergies with these practices as creative re-imaginings which return to production histories and transform them into something which is both familiar and strange. Foster's (1996) return of the referential is also pertinent to this particular performative turn as is Auslander's paradox of immediacy produced through mediation (1999). In all these accounts, the concept discussed is situated in a place that is nowhere: the now and the here of performance. Heike Roms' research on Performance Art in Wales (Roms, Pearson and Daniels, 2010a), draws on related methods, using embodied memory to create documentation. She refers to 'sited interviews' in her work with Mike Pearson, where the site becomes a prompt for memory as practitioners and audiences engage creatively in a 'return' to the original conditions of performance. A series of re-enactments create a relationship between theatre history and the remembered present of the current performance and these, in turn, trigger memories from participants who experienced the original events. In seeking to move beyond audio-visual representations of performance, Roms' work also foregrounds agency in the roles of both the documenter and the audience as creative authors of re-imaginings. The pedagogical potential of these methods as a means of embodied cognition through immersive approaches to documentation is evident in the LIFT Living Archive project. The documentation is more than a stimulus. The practical methodologies enable participants to engage with performance histories through visceral means. In the play between a past production the pupils didn't see and the performance they are creating, there is absence and presence as the participants create an alternative experience with a different value.

Pupils at Winchmore School also worked with the *Buchettino* archive, but responded very differently to its contents. Intrigued by Thumbkin, they invented a non-human character, neither male nor female, who has no language and can only speak through found sound. The workshops with sound artist Dan Scott developed these ideas as the pupils created a series of scenes through atmospheric soundscapes. The androgynous protagonist, Unknown, embarked on a journey though a range of places, each of which was evoked through sound. The form of radio drama also engaged pupils in new relationships with digital technology. In one of the sessions, they were shown the work of the Foley artists and asked to create sound effects to a silent Buster Keaton movie. One of the pupils asked about the people behind the cinema screen, genuinely believing that this was how sound effects were created in the 'olden days'.

The connection between the children's practical responses to this material and the original concepts informing the work of Societas Raffaello Sanzio, particularly their interest in the pre-verbal and language development is striking and profound. Creative processes facilitated an engagement with the original performance which moves deep beneath the surface of photos, prompt books and memorabilia, penetrating to the heart of the production and the ideas which generated the performance.

Through the round window

For Year 8 pupils at Compton Secondary school a different stimulus was used. *The Urban Dream Capsule*, a performance art installation which has been presented around the world was featured in the LIFT programme for 1999. Four men occupied the Arding and Hobbs shop window in Clapham Junction from 18–30 June 1999, living their daily lives in full view of the public gaze. The capsule was conceived as 'a space to dream inside a city', but for the pupils working with the documentation, 12 years later, the stimulus generated a very different event. Thematically, the notion of urban dreams in the London of 2011 creates a clear connection to what is often referred to as the 'Olympic dream' and one of the activities involved students interviewing staff and pupils about their dreams of participation, identifying which sport or event they would like to imagine themselves participating in. However, the announcement of London's Olympic success on 6 July 2005 was followed by the terrorist attacks on London's transport network the following day. When interviewees were asked to describe their responses to the Olympic announcement and their expectations of the London Games, many referred to the terrorist attacks the next day (7/7), and the poignancy of the timing as 'joy turned to sorrow', to quote one of the pupils. This is the story that Compton school chose to tell, inspired by the moving account of the school caretaker for whom the events of 7/7 were a 'miracle', due to the survival of his wife who was uncharacteristically five minutes late at Baker Street Station for her regular train, one of those which failed to arrive. This group of 12 to 13-year-olds were seven years old when these events took place and they remembered them as formative experiences of their London childhood. The 'urban dreams' of 1999 were imagined in a very different context to 2011; the city's landscape was not physically damaged by the terrorist attacks (unlike New York's on 9/11), but the emotional landscape was affected as the children of the millennium experienced trauma. The piece produced by the Compton pupils involved a different encounter with the past as they worked with living memories of the events of 7/7 when they themselves were seven. Aside from the uncanny coincidence of the correspondences between ages and dates, seven-year-olds in the United Kingdom often remember this year as one of change, transformation and occasionally trauma as they move from infant to junior schooling – even if it is within the same school. Seven was considered the age of reason, but for this generation entry into the seventh year of age is marked by a shift from Key Stage 1 to Key Stage 2, a transition which is generally effected through a formal rite of passage through the compulsory assessments known as SATS (statutory academic tests). In short, the age of seven is one that will be remembered for a pedagogical shift from the play-based learning associated with KS1 to the more formal methods of KS2. Writing this, I am conscious of my own memories of this uncomfortable transition, but the image which haunts me of the 1999 production of 'Urban Dreams' seems peculiarly and uncannily appropriate to the experience of being seven.

Whilst the site responsive and durational nature of the work produced by the Compton pupils may well have been attributable to their encounter with the documentation from the *Urban Dream Capsule* production ('What better starting point for challenging the pupils' traditional ideas about theatre and thinking about how they might use their school's more surprising places as a performance space?'[10] I suggest that there is a much deeper level of engagement at work here. The image below, taken from day one of the 1999 London production, will remind some readers (of my generation) of the three windows (round, square or triangle) of the BBC Television (preschool) children's series *Play School*, through which we glimpsed the realities of the life we were about to enter. But for the teenagers at Compton, the submarine-like portholes through which an innocent child peers might well be

Figure 13   *Urban Dream Capsule*, 1999. Photograph by Michael J. O'Brien

associated with an underground transport experience which haunts them, whether or not they were there. In trauma theory this is the unbearable act of remembering an event that cannot be remembered.

A bag was the central aesthetic object for this performance, while the journey motif defined its form and structure. Described as a promenade and audio piece, the audience was led on a trail around different locations in the school, searching for the owner of a lost bag. The process involved the audience as investigators, using similar methods to those the pupils had used as co-explorers in the archive, using clues and evidence to create a hypothesis. The process of plotting the routes, moreover, involved complex organization to ensure that the audience groups did not encounter each other, as well as avoiding particular parts of the school so that the action was not disruptive to the working environment. Such considerations were analogous to the plotting executed by the London bombers as they designed their different paths to destruction through the London transport system.

This was, however a piece exploring the different experiences and responses of Londoners to the two events which framed the performance and a cross-section of the community were represented. A range of bags were carefully chosen to represent the different identities and perspectives of the personas featured. A workshop exercise explored the significance of the bag as an object associated with identity, its contents revealing much about the gender, occupation, age, ethnicity, personality and habits of its owner. A briefcase was associated with a politician, a sports bag with an athlete training for 2012, a Paul's Boutique bag with a teenager and a black fashion bag with a young mother. Audience members were divided into groups and given a bag. Led by a performer, each group set off on a different route, looking for the various individuals in white gloves who acted as 'givers' of objects providing clues for the bags. At the end of the journeys, the groups arrived at a central area where various scenes were performed as well as the audio piece, demonstrating the identities of the personas and their experiences of, and responses to, the consecutive events of the Olympic announcement and the London Bombings the next day. Finally, the owners were movingly reunited with their bags.

My experience of the processes involved in working with the relics of contemporary performance, deposited in a living archive, bears an interesting relationship to recent scholarship challenging the ephemerality of performance as anti-archive (Schneider 2011; Taylor, 2003). As Schneider asks in a 2001 essay: 'in privileging an understanding of performance as a refusal to remain, do we ignore other ways of knowing, other modes of remembering, that might be situated precisely in the ways in which performance remains, but remains differently?' (Schneider, 2001: 101). In her 2011 study, *Performing Remains*, Schneider develops her argument that 'performance can be engaged as what remains, rather than what disappears' and returns to her earlier work to 'reperform' her 2001 essay, thereby challenging 'several basic tenets of performance studies: first, that performance disappears and text remains; second, that live performance is not recording; and third, that the live takes place in a "now" understood as singular, immediate and vanishing' (2011: 87). Drawing on Gertrude Stein's discussions of temporality in theatre, Schneider challenges the privileging of ephemerality in performance studies scholarship (Schechner's claim that theatre can have 'no originals', Blau's notion of performance being 'always at a vanishing point') and suggests that to conceive of performance as 'that which refuses to remain' is to be constrained by the 'logic of the archive' which, as Derrida observes in *Archive Fever*, is associated with the Greek term *archon*, meaning Ruler or Lord (the masculine present participle of the verb meaning to rule), while the archive is the *archon's* house. Thus the archive is a powerhouse, associated with patriarchal law. The image schema of the container comes into play here, housing that which is legitimated as performance history while other forms of memory are dismissed as that which has disappeared (as archive logic presumes that 'oral storytelling, live recitation, repeated gesture and ritual re-enactment are not practices of telling or writing history' (Schneider, 2011: 98). Thus the dominant culture privileges and perpetuates particular forms of social memory, causing Schneider to ask '*Is it not the case that it is precisely the logic of the archive that approaches performance as of disappearance?*' (99) and suggests that performance might 'interrogate archival thinking', which is monologic and negative in its preoccupation with decomposition, disappearance, loss and the quest to preserve the fragile, decaying and singular 'original'. The turn to affect is welcomed by Schneider as a means of re-evaluating and reconceptualizing what remains of performance, moving discussion beyond the monologic of the archive to embrace other kinds of remnants and traces of performance:

> To be touched and to be moved indicates a level of libidinality in affective engagements in the social, suggestive of shift and slip. ... To unsettle the rootedness of identity, to gesture not only to mobility but also to the always already *crossingness,* or *inbetweenness,* or *relationality* of the sets of associations that make up something resembling identity.
>
> (2011: 36–7)

The participatory performance work in the LIFT archive can be seen as a means of responding to Schneider's call for 'different ways of accessing history' (102). The Post-It notes which formed the multiple timelines between official and unofficial histories, personal memories and recorded or reported events, as well as the production history of the LIFT festival, demonstrated the crossingness, betweeness and relationality Schneider refers to.[11] Schneider talks evocatively of the archive as the flesh removed from the bones. 'According to archive logic, flesh can house no memory of bone. In the archive, only bone speaks memory of flesh' (100). Yet muscle memory remains (and can do so after the loss of a limb), while the body can also remember long after the mind has forgotten. Moreover, the instability of memory also works against the logic of the archive.

Performance troubles the distinction between then and now, as this project demonstrates; it goes not only back but forwards and sideways as participants engaged with the projected future of performance and the various histories contributing to the devising process (indeed, my experience was a rehearsed run rather than the final event). Schneider refers to 'a negotiated future that is never simply *in front of us* (like a past that is never simply behind is) but in a kind of vicious, affective surround' (2011: 37). The oral history accounts, heard on the soundtrack at the culmination of the piece, constitute other forms of memory which are materialized through the performance; as the voice of an interviewee breaks in her account of her memories of 7 July (when she was six months pregnant and working next to one of the largest tower blocks in London), she pauses and there is a gap in the recording which registers her pain, before she continues: 'I will never forget sitting on the bus going home [*pause, cough*] sorry; it actually makes me feel quite emotional, even now.'[12]

If the archive is conceived as a space of performance, and in this case as a stimulus for performance, new methodologies and new knowledges can emerge. Schneider refers to the flesh and the bones of archival remains. But the process of decay involves transformation as the remains transmute into something else. All flesh is grass, we are taught in biology, and the archive can be seen as a creative and living resource, fuelling and informing new ways of mediating between the past, present and future. The LIFT Living Archive and the participatory performance practice emerging from the resource, illustrates and embodies Schneider's thesis that 'performance remains, but remains differently.'

In my final section I consider the affective potential of visceral participatory performance as a means of effecting transformation in audiences as well as participants. In the projects featured, the relations between performer and audience involve a radically different aesthetics of engagement, defined by Machon.

6.4 A TASTE OF HEAVEN: (SYN)AESTHETICS AND PARTICIPATORY VISCERAL PERFORMANCE

This section discusses the work of three companies whose immersive and visceral practice, in various ways, connects to the work discussed by Machon and referred to at the start of this chapter. In conceptualizing the practices Machon defines as (syn) aesthetic, she emphasizes 'the central features within interpretation of 'corporeal memory' and 'embodied knowledge' (2009: 5). As Machon explains:

> What I intend by 'corporeal memory' is that the sensate external body both produces and appreciates its own 'language' in performance. The 'language' of the performing body alongside the visceral impact of any other sensual element of the performance work is experienced by the audience through the traces of this language in our own flesh; both the external tactile flesh and the internal viscera. This 'internal' encompasses the emotional *and* the physiological or sensational capabilities of the physical body. Work invested with such a quality has the potential to appeal to an equivalent chthonic sensibility within audience reception that allows for the slippage between the human faculties of *intellectual* and *instinctual* perception.
>
> (6)

These affective qualities are at the heart of the work featured in this section and the next. The case studies are a site specific community piece at the Massachusetts Museum of Contemporary Arts: *The Dream Life of Bricks* directed by Martha Bowers (June 2002) and in the following section, two companies who specialize in producing participatory theatre for children with autism: Chicago Children's Theatre and their *Red Kite* project; and the UK's Oily Cart.

Martha Bowers: *The Dream Life of Bricks*

Martha Bowers describes this 2002 site-specific community project as 'a journey from the past to the present, a slow awakening of a land of sleepers from a gritty industrial past to an uncertain present on the extreme edges of aesthetic experimentation' (Bowers, 2002). In many respects the context for this piece might appear to be a familiar narrative of globalization, progressing like a freak weather system on a course which transforms the landscape as it sweeps through urban and rural environments, enveloping everything in its path. The changing relations between corporations and the communities in which they are situated and the physical and human consequences of regeneration are part of the history of this piece, contained in the old, brick mill buildings of the Marshall Street Industrial Complex (North Adams,

Figure 14   Martha Bowers *Dream Life of Bricks*. Photograph by kind permission of
Kevin Kennefick

Massachusetts), a vast site 26 buildings on 12 acres which, in 1999, became
the Massachusetts Museum of Contemporary Arts (MASS MoCA). In 2001,
Bowers (a director and choreographer with a reputation for site-responsive
work in public space with community participants) was commissioned by
the Museum's Performing Arts Director, who was looking for ways of integrating the local community through dialogue about the changes to the site
as its identity and role shifted from an electronics manufacture (Sprague
Electronics) to a cultural factory, moving from the manufacturing industry
to cultural tourism. Thus there are some synergies here with the work of
Stan's Cafe at the A. E. Harris factory in Birmingham, while the dramaturgy
and design bears some striking relations to the Reckless Sleepers project
in the National Museum of Scotland (including the presence of oversized
funereal or ancestral figures with long black trains, signifying, perhaps the
death of the factory and birth of the museum). This was, Bowers explains, a
particularly complicated and sensitive context as the development plan was
not embraced by the whole community.[13] Gender divisions in the production reflected the site's troubled gender history, as I discuss below.

Whilst the funders had an ideological agenda, seeking to persuade the public of the legitimacy of the conversion and to make the museum responsive
to the local community, the fact remained that it had damaged lives and the
scars continued to be keenly felt. Sprague Electrics, a family-owned business,

made 7000 employees redundant when they shut the plant down. The closure incited anger and guilt as the divisions of labour which had divided men and women, as well as blue-collar and white-collar workers, split the community into factions. In its 1960s prime, Sprague Electrics employed physicists, chemists, electrical engineers and skilled laborers who worked alongside unskilled workers on the production line, designing and manufacturing high-tech weapons, including components for the first atomic bomb. At the cutting edge in terms of research and equipment, the company went on to produce parts for the Gemini Space Programme before moving into the rapidly developing field of consumer electronics. Like similar companies in the United States and the United Kingdom, the industry declined in the face of fierce international competition, particularly from the East. When Sprague closed its Marshall Street operations in 1985, the victims of its tragic decline were the male blue-collar workers who found it difficult to secure alternative employment. Skilled workers relocated, while the female workforce adapted more readily to the new kinds of work available through MASS MoCA as clerical assistants and office staff, retail workers, ushers, domestic and catering staff. History repeated itself as this generation of women, liberated into the public workforce during the war, demonstrated their abilities to adapt to the changing times. These were the women who Bowers worked with, the 'Sprague Ladies', who she described as the 'heart blood' of the project.[14] Thus Bowers sought to build a community around the piece, investigating the psychological histories emerging from the site through the devising process. The work was situated in a fractured, emotionally complex space, while some of its aesthetic features can be associated with Broadhurst's notion of 'liminal' performance, producing a consciousness through emotive experience whereby the spectator finds meanings in the 'free association of themes rather than a linear narrative' and turning to 'his or her own life experiences' (Broadhurst, 1999: 77). The physical geography of the site itself, as well as the participation of several community groups contributed to the complexity of its aesthetic composition:

> listed in the National Historic Register, the site's 26 buildings form an elaborate system of interlocking courtyards and passageways rich with historical association. Bridges, viaducts, elevated walkways, and red brick facades lend a distinct architectural ambiance to the complex, which throughout its history has been a place for innovation and fabrication using the most advanced knowledge and technology of the day.
>
> (Massmoca, 2011)

Bowers chose to work in areas of the complex not yet open to the public, conceiving of the whole piece as a walk through the closed spaces of a site that was sleeping and buildings that were beginning the process of waking up. The set designer, Ed King, worked with found materials, using the site as stimulus and source for the visual and physical fabric of the piece. As the site was built on the confluence of two rivers, this involved finding ways to float words and objects under a bridge; in 'A youth perspective on *The Dream Life of Bricks*', an audience member describes their journey:

> The path through the buildings was lined with sleeping actors in windowsills, on equipment and on the ground. Quotes and dreams from area residents were spelled out with stones and sticks. One quote was even illuminated under a bridge.[15]

Although the piece was structured as a journey which spectators experienced as a group (and Bowers walked with them to watch their discoveries and responses), the composition was non-linear, using repetition with some repeated scenic components reappearing in different formats. In 'kitchen variations', for example, a family's daily breakfast conversations were performed in different ways using various forms of modern art as an improvisatory stimulus, described by Bowers as 'a metaphoric reflection on how events at this site seeped into both work-a-day and private lives.'[16] The promenade performance blended a number of styles and forms, and included installations, dance, choral music performed by a community choir (leading the audience to particular locations), as well as scenes and skits. The piece concluded by returning the audience to the main courtyard of the complex to view the finale, a slow dance in which each member of the cast participated.

The piece needed to be sufficiently flexible to reflect the multiple perspectives of the participants, honouring the imagination of 10 to 12-year-olds as well as the Sprague Ladies, ranging in age from 50 to 83. Bowers describes the 'wildly creative' imaginations of participants from the Greylock Theatre project, a scheme for children from low-income families on a North Adams subsidized housing estate. One boy produced an evocative piece of writing involving him emerging from a coffin to deliver his story of the site. In another example, a participant imagined bricks from the World Trade Center had been transported to the site and told the story from the perspective of the brick. This triggered the primary visual metaphor of each brick being a dream. At the outset of the project, Bowers asked all participants the question which provided the frame for the project: 'if a building could dream, what would these dreams looks like?' She felt dreams were pertinent, she explains, as a blend of fantasy and real-life experience. Thus the dream structure provided a means whereby site interpenetrated the creative process and vice versa. Dreams offered an entry point and an aesthetic strategy as a metaphor for the building as a repository of peoples' dreams, a place in which lives had been lived, and dreams realized or not. *The Dream Life of Bricks* can be seen as an example of the shift Kwon describes from site specific to community specific in new genre public art, whose proponents 'favor temporary rather than permanent projects that engage their audience, particularly groups considered marginalized, as active participants in the conceptualization and production of process-oriented, politically conscious community events or programs' (Kwon, 2004: 6). The construction and conception of community in work of this kind is, however, problematized by Kwon (as discussed in section 4.1 on place). She argues against 'the common notion of the community as a coherent and unified social formation' and proposes an alternative notion of community as unstable: 'an "inoperative" specter in order to think beyond formulaic prescriptions ... to open onto an altogether different model of collectivity and belonging'. Hence her provocation to imagine 'collective artistic praxis' as opposed to 'community based art' (2004: 7). Although Bowers describes the process as 'deep work within the community', her understanding of community embraces difference, instability and contradiction and this is evident in the form and content of the piece. She admits that some of the 'ethical complexities were not entirely resolved', referring to her political consciousness of the significance of the patriarchal histories represented by the Sprague Ladies: 'when the women spoke about their memories', she explains, 'they were speaking about a different time. They broke the mould for many women after the war and I wanted to reflect this labour history in the piece' (Bowers, 2002).

In the six months of research and development which informed the content of the piece, Bowers worked closely with the Sprague Ladies, whose memories guided much of the content of the project. Many were teenagers when they started working at the site and Bowers was struck by the differences between their aspirations and those of twenty-first-century teenagers who also featured in the project. Many of the women were volunteering as ushers, indicating their desire to sustain a continuing engagement with the site and to participate in its changing identity. Workshops took place in the dance studio at Mass MoCA and were initially a rather polite affair: 'Tea was served and they sat with cups on their laps. Eventually I asked them to put down their cups and then to produce an individual sigh, expressing everything about themselves, their history, their lives.' The result, she describes as 'astounding' in terms of the different interpretations and variations: 'some were sexual, some funny, some very long and cathartic'. So, for Bowers, breath was a starting point – a bodily, non-verbal expression (equated with the concept of Rasa): 'I had to get beyond the verbal with them; then we had some basis to start talking.' In one of the sessions Bowers asked the group to recount a typical day of working at the factory. This became 'The Book of Days':

> Our set designer, Ed King, built eight brick beds, each with its own glowing white satin pillow. The women rose and reclined on these beds as they described the work and home worlds they traversed in their younger

years. They also spoke lines about the community's reactions to the closing of Sprague and the advent of MASS MoCA.

(Bowers, 2002)

Throughout the process, Bowers explains, she 'struggled not to impose [her] own judgments about women's rights, labor relations and entitlement on the choices made by the residents of North Adams.' In her conversation with me she also stressed the difficulties she experienced with the gender politics underpinning the lives of these women as factory workers. She asked the group to describe one of the best moments of their lives and recounts how one of the women told the story of attending the opening gala for MASS MoCA, drinking champagne and dancing in the ball: 'I felt like Cinderella' was Bowers' favourite line in the performance:

> [It] captured a whole realm of issues. MASS MoCA redefined the community's relationship to this site. For one night, Rose Marie felt transformed. She traded in her work clothes and position as a powerless employee in a paternalistic corporation for a place at the ball as an honored guest.
>
> (Bowers, 2002)

This is also evidence of Bowers participating in Kwon's notion of a collective artistic praxis that accommodates contradictions and difference. In her approach to collaborative practice, Bowers acknowledges the influence of her long association with the Irish community arts movement. She describes this as a liberating environment in which she was free to play, away from the 'highly visible and critical environment of New York'.[17] Having encountered the environment of patriarchal curating and the gate-keeping of downtown venues associated with proscenium work in New York, she decided to self-produce. Bowers recognizes the differences between her dreams and the aspirations and experiences of the Sprague Ladies:

> During our rehearsals in Building 6, I walked with the Sprague Ladies through dank, dark hallways into the enormous space we had chosen as our indoor site. This 40,000 sq-ft. floor was empty now, save for the forest of pillars that support it. It had once been teeming with women seated at tables assembling intricate electronic components. Their handbuilt products that steered submarines, were used in space exploration, and even triggered nuclear weapons. Rose Marie had worked in this building for 40 years. I couldn't imagine what it must have been like for her to hear live music replace the whine of machinery, see dancers rehearsing in the clothes she had worn to work every day and theatrical lights replacing the overhead fluorescents.
>
> (2002)

Rose Marie's Cinderella story, Bowers reflects, says so much about this woman's sense of self in relation to class and gender struggle. This memory was also evoked in the dancing that closed the show as performers and audience moved outside for the final musical sequences. The oldest and smallest member of the Sprague Ladies group waltzed with every member of the cast to 'Save the Last Dance for Me', ending with the tallest performer, a dancer elevated in her large gown, a giant representation of the mill-working women. This character was Ms Mass Moca, who appeared throughout the event as a symbol of the museum and its high art aspirations. Thus the final dance was a ritual conjoining the past with the present.

Bowers does not speak of the work in terms of community celebration, but acknowledges its complexities and tensions. She described MASS MoCA as 'an improbable savior. The verdict is still out on whether this institution will provide the needed boost to the town's economy.' However, she is very clear about her role as artist and the participants as collaborators:

> As I saw it, the project's purpose was to provide an art-based dialogue for the community to voice their opinions about the role this institution would play in their future and reflect on how this site had affected their past. It also gave participating community members a sense of ownership. It was their show, not something MASS MoCA brought in to boost ticket ales. Whether this was a temporary show of collaborative spirit, another Cinderella's ball, remains to be seen.
>
> (Bowers, 2002)

There was, however something else at work here in terms of the (syn)aesthetic vocabularies Bowers was using and the affect of the performance on those who experienced it. The dream environment was visual, visceral and vocal. The 'walking tour' involved the 'Mysterious Dream Life Choir' summoning the audience towards its sound, while the audience passed 'dancers in nightgowns' who 'walked solemnly holding out pillows with bricks laid on top of them'.[18] The youth perspective refers to 'a hallway lined with women telling stories of the past, eyes closed as if they were speaking in their sleep.' Bowers referred in her interview to the high level of production values and the role of technology, with 'state of the art lighting' contributing to visual and physical choreographic compositions epitomized by the poignancy and strange beauty of the two elevated dancers, decked in large gowns as the giant mill ancestors. The influence of contemporary dance pioneers is strongly felt in this work: Martha Graham's student, Bessie Schonber, was a mentor for Bowers, while the vocal soundscapes and oral composition have affinities with Meredith Monk, an artist whose work deeply impacted upon Bowers. The poignancy of the ending was the culmination of the production's visceral and experiential qualities. The tallest dancer, Bowers explains, had developed a relationship with the oldest and smallest lady in the cast and their dancing together was a fusion of past and present as well as a comment on how we touch each others' lives. The beauty of the piece as an aesthetic object connects to Benjamin's notion of the auratic moment: 'The communication that takes place in the auratic moment is one between the present and the past as embodied in the object, but this past is itself dynamic, an accumulation of present moments, including the present in which the object is now observed' (Indyk, 2000). And it is here, in the liminal space between past, present and future and in the gap between public art and performance and in the fusion of the visual, aural and visceral as well as the unsettling elements of the collaboration that we have a taste of heaven.

6.5 'SOMETHING MOVES': (SYN)AESTHETICS, RASAESTHETICS AND THE PERFORMANCE OF AUTISM

In my final case studies I move into the neuro-divergent realm of the autistic imagination to consider how contemporary performance and the (syn)aesthetic practices of two companies (Oily Cart and Chicago Children's Theatre) provide a means of engaging with this complex, increasingly prevalent and often controversial condition. The section heading takes its cue from Petra Kuppers' essay, 'Dancing Autism' (2008). Kuppers explores 'the performance potential of autism' through her analysis of *Bedlam*, a dance/film piece by the dance company FrenetiCore (Houston, Texas, June 2006). Kuppers brings an embodied experience of disability and contemporary performance to her critique of stereotypical representations of difference, the 'alienated lens' through which autism is most frequently viewed (2008: 193). Mark Haddon's popular novel about the experience of Asperger's Syndrome, (*The Curious Incident of the Dog in the Night Time*), which constructs a neuro-divergent perspective through his central character, Christopher, is, Kuppers suggests, a somewhat distorted (albeit compelling) representation of difference. She uses Eric Chen's exercises in rewriting Haddon's prose to demonstrate the mismatch between writing which feigns autism (Haddon's) and writing which *is* autism (by Chen, a diagnosed author). This is not to suggest that Kuppers is making a case for autistic 'authenticity', however. Her interest is in representations of autism and how 'the question autism poses to the non-disabled world' might be addressed through art. The performance of autism has taken a variety of forms as the condition finds expression through the visual, kinaesthetic and oral vocabularies of theatre and dance. At its worst, Kuppers remarks, 'autism on the stage becomes an opportunity for angel beings to move among us: and projections of innocence and savants can become a disrespectful and annoying representation of disability' (196), but in the production of *Bedlam* the potential of contemporary performance as a means to engage audiences imaginatively and differently is evident in Kuppers description (196). What Kuppers describes is sensuous, transgressive, physical, visceral, beautiful and disturbing:

> In *Bedlam*, autism emerges as a category within visions of the asylum: a place apart, in metaphor, sitedness and emotional connect. The asylum offers asylum and separation, and, witnessing the show from a crip perspective, I find the disconnects across spectacle and audience so much more intriguing than any acted-out disconnects between performers or actors. What do audiences come to feel in the presence of strange pointe work, those moving spiders, these uncomfortable alienated lifts, these familiar film narratives broken by the joy of live movement, this theatre space in an empty building, the debris of Houston's industrial heritage? If *Incident* presents the chaos of our world by using a disabled character's

perspective and ability to make sense strangely, then *Bedlam* presents a vision on the edge of sensorial overload and calls upon its audiences to engage and find pathways through the discordant but never harsh imagery, sounds and kinaesthetic information.

Making up your mind: how much can you open your imagination to autism, without wishing for secure knowledge? Can art destabilize what we know in ways that are productive, and generate a more accessible world?

(2008: 204)

I will return to Kupper's closing questions in my final case studies, which, I will argue, respond positively to her challenge through practices which have the potential to change the way we engage with and understand autism (and difference), but which also offer a medium through which autistic participants can communicate, interact, imagine and play. This is, in my experience, where applying performance is at its most profound. I suggest, moreover, that the reason why autism and contemporary performance engage in dialogue is the connection between them, as I have discussed in relation to a practice-based research project at the University of Kent, involving a series of immersive, multi-sensory and intermedial environments, using puppetry, objects and digital media as an exploratory playground:

In the course of our work we discovered a synergy between the autistic consciousness and contemporary performance paradigms: the highly visual, kinesthetic and aural qualities of the autistic imagination shifts perception from sense to sensuality.

(Shaughnessy, 2012: 44)

'Making up your mind': engaging with autism

Kuppers' evocative account of the *Bedlam* production can be seen to correspond to Machon's concept of a '(syn)aesthetically styled performance, as 'work [which] shifts between performance disciplines, just as it shifts between the sensual and intellectual, the somatic ("affecting the body" or "absorbed through the body") and the semantic (the 'mental reading' of signs)' (2008: 4). Although we might question her distinction between the somatic (body) and semantic (mind), Machon refers also to the 'fused somatic/semantic manner' of both 'performance style' and 'audience response' as one of the defining characteristics of (syn)aesthetics. The relations and tensions between these dualisms in Machon's writing, in conjunction with the 'disconnections' Kuppers perceives, goes to the heart of the autistic condition (as far as we 'know' it) where difference is generally defined (and diagnosed) in relation to somatic and semantic features and divergent interactions between mind and body. Difficulties in developing an embodied understanding of language (as opposed to echolalia and rote learning), problems engaging in meaningful social interaction (verbal and physical), and restricted imaginative play are the diagnostic criteria for autism, often referred to as the 'triad of impairments'. Although writing on autism increasingly explores difference rather than focusing on deficit, current research suggests that the autistic brain and body process the world in a particular way (Baron-Cohen, 1995, 2009; Frith, 2003; Mills, 2008) and this creates a different engagement with the physical and social environment (Berthoz, 2002; Gallagher, 2005). As Allain Berthoz has speculated: 'How is it possible to imagine that children can coherently evaluate the people they see if they cannot evaluate relationships between their own bodies and the environment?' (2002: 96). Whilst there are a range of complex and competing theories surrounding the aetiology of autism, it is most generally understood as a condition which 'affects how a person communicates with, and relates to, other people. It also affects how they make sense of the world around them' (NAS, 2011).

'Theory of Mind' accounts focus on the difficulties autistic individuals have in understanding and interpreting the intentions of others as well as noting 'impairments' in pretend play and 'metaprepresentation' (Baron-Cohen, 1995). As Baron-Cohen suggests, 'having a theory of mind is to be able to reflect on the contents of one's own and other's minds [beliefs, desires, intentions, imagination, emotions, etc.]. Difficulty in understanding other minds is a core cognitive feature of autism spectrum conditions (Baron Cohen, 2001). Theory of Mind's critics, however, argue that this approach focuses on the social aspects of autism and doesn't explain other features which are also characteristic (although they may not always be present and to varying degrees): need for sameness, preference for routine and difficulty coping with change, restricted range of interests, preoccupation with objects or parts of objects, high cognitive ability for rote memory, echolalia, and various sensory and motor behaviours which are repetitious and self stimulatory (see Happé, 1995). The 'central coherence' theory developed by Uta Frith (1989) suggests that autistic individuals perceive differently, particularly in terms of 'Gestalt Perception'. This explains some of the higher functioning capabilities of autistic spectrum conditions through a focus on non-contextualized detail (e.g., rote memory of unrelated items, calendar calculation, etc.). As Olga Bogdashina notes:

> the inability to filter foreground and background information can account for both strengths and weaknesses of autistic perception. On the one hand, they seem to perceive more accurate information and a larger amount of it. On the other hand, this amount of unselected information cannot be processed simultaneously ... They may be aware of the information others miss, but the processing of 'holistic situations' can be overwhelming.
>
> (2003: 48)

Although central coherence theory, like theory of mind has been challenged as not being appropriate to *all* individuals with autism (Frith, 2008), it is clearly relevant to a large subgroup (and the concept of the spectrum has facilitated understanding of autism as a complex condition with many variables and interventions needing to cater for individual manifestations of the symptomologies). Most importantly for our purposes, it is helpful to understanding how the world might be seen differently from an autistic individual's perspective. As Uta Frith indicates:

> A detail-focused processing style not only applies to vision. It also applies to hearing and language. What about other senses – touch, for example? Here an intriguing phenomenon is that many people with autism are reported to be hypersensitive to touch. Possibly, having hyper-acute touch might be like having absolute pitch.
>
> (2008: 93)

Whilst there is continuing debate about causes and therapeutic strategies, research in the areas of neuroscience, phenomenology and psychology has led to increased understanding of the sensual, perceptual and cognitive processes in autism and recognition of the importance of an embodied approach to interventions (Bogdashina, 2003; Frith, 2008; Gallagher, 2005). As Gallagher speculates:

> If ... we consider the effects that both sensory-motor problems and problems of central coherence may have on primary and secondary intersubjectivity, as well as their connections to the non-social symptoms, we could develop a fuller theory ... We may also ask whether there is any connection between sensory-motor problems and the problems with central coherence ... there are good reasons to think that body-schematic processes are closely related to perceptual and cognitive abilities.
>
> (2005: 235)

Thus, strategies are needed which use physical and sensual stimuli to integrate mind and body. Contemporary performance is a particularly appropriate medium for engaging with autism offering a range of vocabularies (physical, visceral visual, aural, spatial, tactile and kinaesthetic) which can be adapted, as appropriate, to the needs and abilities of the individual. Lorna Wing changed the landscape of autism when she introduced the concept of a spectrum, recognizing the wide range of features and variables associated with the condition (Wing, 1996). Likewise, the individual child can be considered as a spectrum with a unique profile of needs, interests and abilities, as well as the difficulties which determine the diagnosis. Contemporary performance, as discussed in the case studies which follow, creates opportunities for an encounter with the autistic child through active participation in events which are experiential and sensory.

Through the looking glass: the autistic consciousness and post-dramatic theatre: Jacqui Russell and Red Kite (Chicago Children's Theatre)

Drama has a long history as a therapeutic medium and its mimetic aspect is the basis of many of these practices. The fictional world in which participants can perform roles as others offers a safe space to explore, rehearse and to play with identities and experiences. Mimesis, however, as Shepherd and Wallis remind us, 'is not simply a faculty of imitation' but is a means of learning: a way of knowing through the understanding of otherness (2004: 216), and they cite Michael Taussig's description of mimesis as 'deployment of that faculty in sensuous knowing, sensuous othering.' (1993: 68). 'Imitation', however, is a term featuring prominently in autism research and is generally identified as a 'skills deficit', as the autistic child does not copy the behaviours of others in the same way as a typically developing child. Lack of pretend play is one of the most frequently cited manifestations of autism in the pre-school child and is thought to contribute to difficulties in empathizing as the child struggles to engage in understanding the perspective of another. Developmental psychology uses analogies from theatre to describe 'mutual self and other understanding'. Evan Thompson draws upon Tomasello's account: *The Origins of Human Cognition*:

> Once the infant understands other individuals as intentional beings and herself as one participant among others in a social interaction, then whole new cognitive dimensions arise. The child comes to be able to participate in joint attentional scenes – social interactions in which the child and the adult jointly attend to some third thing, for an extended period of time, and in which the child can conceptualize her own role from the same 'outside' perspective as the other person. Joint attentional scenes in turn provide the framework for the acquisition of language, symbolic representation, and communicative conventions.
>
> (Thompson, 2010: 399)

Whilst this is clearly an area of considerable difficulty for the autistic child, drama can offer ways of facilitating the development of empathetic engagement and understanding by offering a space in which to rehearse social interaction and to play with real-life scenarios. Thus role-play through drama is frequently used as an intervention.[19] This is how Jacqueline Russell, artistic director of Chicago Children's Theatre first encountered autism through her work at Agassiz Elementary School in Chicago, where she taught in two autism specific classrooms. Agassiz is a public school with two mixed-age autism classes, a common model of special needs integration in the United States. Beginning (in 1997) with weekly workshops designed to develop what she describes as a 'vocabulary of emotions, Russell's work developed into a more intensive programme as teachers and pupils realized the benefits of what was referred to as 'drama time'. Teachers reported significant progress in communication skills, behavioural improvements and observed pupils engaging more deeply in interpersonal relationships. Russell became artist in residence, funded through Chicago Partnerships in Education (CAPE) and over a 13-year period (and in collaboration with teachers at Agassiz) developed a comprehensive theatre curriculum and approach for working with autistic children.[20] Russell's work moves beyond the simulation methods associated with behavioural interventions where children are taught social scripts as a means of facilitating basic communication skills and socially appropriate behaviour. Whilst these techniques build on the autistic child's ability to imitate, they can lead to an artificial and stilted way of speaking and behaving. The autistic child's performance here is not embodied as s/he is copying responses which are not felt. Neurological research suggests that although an autistic child can imitate speech and actions, their copying uses a different part of the brain to neuro-typicals (Dalpretto et al., 2006; Pineda, 2009); this might explain why imitation in autism appears to be detached from the emotional engagement we associate with empathy. According to Gallagher:

> the evidence that a subject's understanding of another person's actions and intentions depends to some extent on a mirrored reverberation in the subject's own motor system is relevant ... it is possible that developmental problems involving sensory motor processes may have an effect on the capabilities that make up primary intersubjectivity, and therefore the autistic child's ability to understand the actions and intentions of others.

> (2005: 232)

In the midst of debates about mirror neurons, simulation theory and autism, it is clear that social and emotional disengagement is central to the autistic experience; thus kinaesthetic strategies are needed, using physical and sensual stimuli to connect body and mind. Russell's drama workshops are designed to facilitate embodied understanding of emotion through strategies which integrate the somatic and semantic. 'Which season are you?', she asks a 13-year-old autistic boy; 'Summer', the boy responds before preparing his cartwheel. 'Show me the move for Fall', Russell requests, and the boy pauses before leaning back and raising his arms: 'Throwing leaves up high', he exclaims. Winter follows as he pretends to throw snowballs. 'What's your favourite season?', asks Russell, and the boy responds, 'Spring.' 'Show me the move again', Russell requests, as the school bell interrupts.

'I'm late, I have to go', the boy responds, and the session ends. What is striking about this session is the autistic boy's ease in his verbal and physical expression as he translates conceptual material into actions. We can even see some rudimentary Meyerholdian biomechanics at work here in teaching the body to 'think'. In group sessions, the body is a focus as the students learn kinaesthetic, spatial and relational awareness through a series of drama games and exercises. A teacher talks about the 'flat aspect' in the face of the autistic child, which changes through Russell's work as an embodied understanding of emotions begins to develop. In Russell's class, the request to 'Show me happy' produces a physical and spontaneous response (jumping up and down, smiling and cheering) in stark contrast to flashcard teaching where children are encouraged to identify and then imitate emotions, producing exaggerated facial responses which copy but fail to embody the feeling associated with the emotion. 'Show me', Russell encourages repeatedly, 'Show me with your head.' We see children being taught to shake their heads as they say 'No thank you', and nodding to 'Yes please.' Whilst this is clearly a repeated drill, it does not lead to contrived responses. Smiles swiftly accompany this movement, without instruction, as the children respond spontaneously, associating the 'yes' with a desire. In teaching the 'emotional alphabet' through techniques which involve physically modelling behaviour, Russell emphasizes the importance of repetition. She estimates that 80 per cent of a drama-time session will involve repetition of familiar exercises. This is because repetition is one of the means through which autistic individuals embody learning as the 'systemizing brain' responds to logical structure, predictable sequences and routine.[21] Repetition, moreover, produces pleasure through the delight of recognition as the autistic child (who so often struggles to engage with the language and systems of a neurotypical world) enjoys working within familiar structures (and often responds well to simple narrative and repetition). Russell's work values and respects neuro-diversity. The autistic child, she explains may not understand that we hear with our ears and see with our eyes as so many of them experience synaesthesia in conjunction with autism. She describes an early experience of using flashcards to match senses to body parts and objects. When a young boy placed a picture of a tongue on top of a picture of a dog, his response to the question 'What sense is that?' was 'sense of humour', an anecdote she cites to illustrate the sophistication, unpredictability and surprises which are so frequently encountered in working (and playing) with individuals on the spectrum.

As well as facilitating social interaction and communication, Russell's workshops engage participants imaginatively. A favourite is 'Stinky Pig', a toy who 'smells bad' but is then transformed into a sleeping baby pig. The facilitator models the behaviour, letting the children continue, using a minimum level of language. The game teaches an empathic response as the children move from treating the object with comic disgust to gently handling and stroking it. In Russell's experience, every child can play this simple game which she transfers into the object theatre I discuss below. In workshop exercises, imaginary objects are transformed as they pass from one pupil to another, often with virtuosity and ingenuity. It is not the case that autistic children lack imagination, but they imagine differently and the (syn)aesthetic medium of contemporary performance is a particularly (perhaps peculiarly) appropriate medium to explore this.

Russell's experience of autism has informed her work as a theatre maker. Throughout her career she has continued to pursue her pedagogic practice in conjunction with her work as a curator, director and writer. Having worked as artistic director of Lookingglass Theatre Company, Russell founded Chicago Children's Theatre in 2005 and in 2006 developed the Red Kite Theatre project, an initiative which brought together Russell's educational and theatre work through a performance programme specifically designed for children with autism and their families. Following a seven-month collaboration with the UK's Oily Cart Theatre Company, the immersive installation *Red Kite/Blue Moon* was produced in Spring 2008 at the Chicago Children's Museum. As well as being conceived as a participant-centred performance experience (one of the defining features of Oily Cart's work), the autistic consciousness was central to the devising process which started in the classroom at Agassiz. Practitioners from Oily Cart joined Russell and her company colleagues as well as autism experts from the University of Illinois (a centre of excellence for autism research) working alongside the children in developing a performance which they describe as being 'based on the thinking and feeling' of the autistic participants. Wind, kites and the seasons emerged as central themes from the earliest sessions. The extensive experience brought to the project through the various collaborators facilitated a depth of engagement and intuitive understanding of the community for whom the project was created. The concept of the spectrum was fully embraced as well as an understanding of autism as difference, rather than deficit:

> we like to refer to it as a culture of autism ... They call us neurotypicals. Really, we think of ourselves as cross-cultural interpreters. We interpret what they do. They interpret what we do.
>
> (Elizabeth Daley, Impact coordinator for Autism Program UIC)

> There's quite a lively political debate going on about whether we should just let people be autistic ... Being an autistic person is a perfectly valid way to live on this planet. It's just that society was designed by the rest of us.
>
> (Tim Webb, Oily Cart)[22]

Whilst the experience of autism was central to the project, this was a piece not about, but for children on the spectrum; in keeping with Oily Cart's values, the primary objective was to create a high quality performance event facilitating participation in theatre and providing 'gratuitous pleasure' for a particular audience, rather than delivering therapy.[23]

In Oily Cart's performances, the 'theatre/therapy' debate is challenged through work which is praised by theatre critics for its production values (Gardner and Billington),[24] whilst its engagement of individual audience members with profound and multiple learning difficulties is clearly enabling and beneficial for those involved. As Helen Nicholson has written of Oily Cart, 'their work is artistically and aesthetically groundbreaking, and leads the way in making playful theatre in which learning and participation are embedded in the art form itself, blurring the lines between audience and spectator, artist and learner' (Nicholson, 2011: 205–6).

This is also evident in the Red Kite project, in performance activities which stimulated communication (manifest in increased eye contact and gesturing as well as verbal expression), social interaction (whereby audience members engage with performers) and imagination (through the process of generating the material and in their responses to material within the performance):

> The pilot project at the end of the workshop process involved the children (seven at a time) sitting in lounge-style chairs which could be gently rocked. Four performers represented the four winds, one for each season. The wind personas met the children outside the environment and ushered their guests into a cool little canopy on the second floor. And so the performance began:
>
> > Video images of clouds floated on a big screen. Musicians played an original score.
> >
> > A young theatergoer could sit or stand, talk loudly or remain silent, dance wildly around the circle or curl up silently in a chair. The winds were ready for anything.
> >
> > If you were into verbosity, Tim Webb's Captain of the Winds was ready to chat with you. If you were into movement, you could dance with the summer wind. If you were into music, Max Reinhardt's cool tunes were ready. If you were just into being touched, bubbles would brush against your face as snowflakes fell. ...
> >
> > So which wind was best for flying kites?
> >
> > (Chicago Children's Theatre, 2007)

As in Oily Cart's work, a range of multi-sensory stimuli were available for participants to experience and they had autonomy in being able to express their sensory preferences, as appropriate to individuals on the spectrum. Thus the children were involved in shaping and creating the performance experience, choosing whether they wanted to be fanned, or to dance or engage in music making. Whilst the performers were clearly in tune with the special needs and interests of their individual audience members, the children were also open to theatre in ways that neuro-typicals are sometimes not. In Oily Cart's experience, autistic children are 'better able to live in the moment, more flexible, more imaginative and less troubled by blocks, uncertainties and insecurities' (Chicago Children's Theatre, 2007). As Max Reinhardt, one of Oily Cart's founder members, observes, working with special needs 'has freed us from the constraints and the usual conventions of the arts in general and children's theater in particular. Autistic kids aren't much interested in fakery. They're more inclined to demand the truth.' This perception is crucial and goes to the heart of a 'neuro-divergent' aesthetic, where the emphasis is on 'the sensuous and experiential dimensions of the event, rather than upon mimesis or narrative' (Shaughnessy, 2005: 211). Whilst Oily Cart's work generally involves loose narrative structures, the focus is on being in the moment, within a temporal framework in which the autistic individual foregrounds the present experience and relates to the immediacy of the encounters within the environment s/he inhabits. These qualities are at the heart of post-dramatic contemporary theatre as defined by Lehmann in terms of Text/Space/Time/Body/Media (2006) and this paradigm has some synergies with the (syn)aesthetics of these specially created immersive environments for a neuro-divergent audience. This is not Forced Entertainment, Gob Squad, Angelus Novus or Robert Wilson, but the influences and performance vocabularies draw upon live art, shared space, playing with presence, bodies, objects, sound, light and digital media to create work for partakers who maybe non-verbal and who perceive differently.

Red Kite/Blue Moon grew out of the preview performance as a participatory, multi-sensory multimedia performance installation, presented in 2008 to coincide with national autism awareness month. A journey motif served as a structuring device as children were invited on to the pretend red kite ship for an imaginary adventure to the moon. The mixing of nautical and lunar references created an incongruous blend of elements which moved beyond a pretence framework into self-reflexive impossibility. Part of the pleasure is the knowledge that this is not real, and a series of strategies ensured that children were aware of the structures of the piece and were in control of their experience, choosing how and when to participate. A social story accompanying the production emphasized the fictive elements and prepared children for the experiences they were going to encounter. As in the preview, children were assigned to an individual performer but could identify their preferences in a 'lunar passport', which built on the idea of communication passports as used in special needs contexts (offering information about a child's individual needs). Children were able to complete the passport themselves, indicating who they wanted to meet on their lunar adventure and which activities they preferred. Prior to the performance, parents were interviewed to provide information for the performers, facilitating the one-to-one interactions which were part of the event. Seven personas created the action through storytelling and interaction with the audience using a range of sensory stimuli and strategies. The children could choose to stand or sit in the blue rocking chairs as they embarked on the journey. Those who liked air on their faces could be wafted by huge fans as they flew through the sky; umbrellas were provided for shelter from 'real' rain, moon rocks pelted down to squeals of delight and were pelted back by the children and the 'baby stars' (white, doll-shaped bundles of blanket which blinked fairy lights) were tenderly held and rocked. Not only was this beautiful object theatre, it is also hugely significant for autistic children to engage in pretend play of this kind, a mode of cognitive blending as they move in and out of the pretence framework in their interaction with objects and performers.

Lehmann refers to a 'perceptual conflict between text and scene' in his concept of post-dramatic theatre. There is something of this at work in the delightful impossibility of these environments. The children embraced incongruity as objects were transformed into something strangely familiar, a baby represented by blankets which is, however, alien, while familiar narratives were also made strange through the fantasy landscape created, as a ship complete with a captain (a combination of pirate and pilot) and sailors 'flies' to the moon; on board are characters associated with space, but all are strange blends as if several stories have been mixed together: the silver robot 'isailor' combined the nautical and lunar, while the mechanical 'HG', 'inventor of the ship', had a costume like a miner's with flashing subterranean head gear. This is not a 'normal' world of make-believe and the invitation is not to 'pretend' but to be in the room, to be present and engaged in the moment of performance making. This need not involve joining in the action (although the invitation is there to do so), as engagement can be registered through shared eye contact, pointing, bodily responses as children rock their chairs in excitement, physically responding to the rhythms and energies of the performers around them.

The language of Lehman's 'new' theatre has synergies with the language of autism: Lehman refers to 'the deconstruction of a discourse oriented towards meaning and the invention of a space that eludes the laws of telos and unity'. He cites Corsetti's thesis that theatre needs the *text as a foreign body*. To some extent, the autistic child's relationship to language corresponds to this; language is an artificial structure which the autistic child experiences from the outside and struggles to embody. Yet those with verbal abilities will often enjoy word play, nonsense, rhymes, puns and Dr Seuss. 'Instead of a linguistic *re*-presentation of facts', Lehmann writes of post-dramatic theatre, there is a 'position of tones, words, sentences, sounds that are hardly controlled by a "meaning" but instead by the scenic composition, by a visual not text orientated dramaturgy' (2006: 146). Polyglossia is evident in autistic speech as children play with the sounds of words, experimenting with noises, utterances and enjoying echolalia. In describing multi-lingual theatre texts, Lehmannn states 'these verses were being sung more than recited, the language perpetually tipping over from beautiful perfection into broken stuttering and noise' (147). This could equally be a description of an autistic child's language. A nursery rhyme is suddenly recited out of context, a phrase or command is used which bears no apparent relation to the current situation, but has clearly been triggered by something within the environment. Autistic children often exhibit odd intonation and prosody which corresponds to what Lehmann describes: 'Frequently we are made aware of the physical, motoric act of speaking or reading of text itself as an *unnatural, not self-evident* process' (147). Indeed, the video version of the social story accompanying *Red Kite/Blue Moon* has a monotone voiceover which corresponds both to Lehmann's description and the vocal qualities often associated with autism or the earlier stages of 'second' language acquisition.

Lehman's second distinguishing feature is space:

> the blurring of the borderline between real and fictive experience to such an extent has far reaching consequences for the understanding of theatre space: it turns from a metaphorical, symbolic space into a metonymic space ... In this sense of a relationship of metonymy or contiguity, we can call a scenic space metonymic if it is not defined primarily as standing in for another fictive world but is instead highlighted as a part and continuation of the real theatre space.
>
> (2006: 151)

In keeping with the perception of autistic children not being interested in 'fakery', there is no fourth wall in these immersive environments: the whole space is both real and fictive. The design concept for *Red Kite/Blue Moon* was self-reflexive, enhanced by the strange mixture of elements which bordered on the surreal; the voyage to the moon in a space ship involved encounters with fish, darting lights which the children tried to catch as well as stars, swimming together in a sea sky; images of the audience were projected on to screens in a live feed, making them conscious of themselves as participants in this fantasy world of sea and space. Oily Cart uses similar mirroring strategies. In *Conference of the Birds*, for example, each child is filmed and has their still image projected on to a screen as the cast of birds sing a song using each child's name as the focus of the improvised lyric. These are particularly emotive moments, a form of direct address to an audience who are not anonymous or silent witnesses, but are part of a personal and intimate encounter.

The third element Lehmann identifies is the postdramatic aesthetic of time. As Adrian Kear has argued, 'the time of the present replaces representational time as the currency of performance; performance becomes less an art of narrative presentation than an art of being *in* the present' (1999: 49). The autistic sensibility is one in which the immediacy of the current moment is foregrounded. Many autistic individuals struggle to conceptualize future concepts and are often anxious about changes to their current environment. The continuous present which characterizes immersive contemporary performance is important for other reasons, however. Husserl's concept of the living present of time consciousness as a tripartite structure, and his example of a melody to explain the temporal structuring of the primal impression in conjunction with retention and protention, involves a logical and emotive structure appropriate to the autistic systemizing brain which may help to explain why the autistic sensibility often responds positively to music (Husserl, 1999). Live music is a feature of the Red Kite performance, with the guitar-playing 'whistle' communicating predominantly through sound. It is similarly part of Oily Cart's vocabulary and will often involve improvised sequences sustaining and responding to an individual child's engagement through music-based interaction.

The fourth aspect of post-dramatic performance defined by Lehmann is the body: 'Theatre represents bodies and at the same time uses bodies as its main signifying material' (2006: 163). Post-dramatic theatre has 'overcome' the semantic body and, as Lehmann puts it, 'sensuality undermines sense'. Lehmann stresses the importance of new energies and gesture. The body 'becomes its own message and at the same time is exposed as the most profound *stranger of the self* ... impulsive gesticulations ... autistic disintegrations of form' (163).

The 'strange spiders' Kuppers refers to in the pointe work of *Bedlam* spring to mind here. Physicality is a defining characteristic of both Oily Cart's work and the Red Kite performances. In *Red Kite/Blue Moon*, physical exercises on the seasons undertaken in the workshops were developed through the production. Inspired by Temple Grandin's *Thinking in Pictures*, Russell played a game with the children 'getting them to sit down on the floor, just as a kite would fall to the ground' while 'actors remembered the kids interest in moving the body through space'; this informed movement and music in the performance. The body, in this work, is both an expressive instrument and a perceiving medium. The aesthetic experience does not involve reading or interpreting the *mise-en-scène*, but experiencing the visceral qualities of the performance as rain falls to wet bodies, fans blow on faces, and children rock in excitement in their chairs. Dance is also a component for those who want to participate in 'moon walking'.

The final aspect defined by Lehmann as a feature of post-dramatic theatre is the use of media; the fusion of the live and the mediated through the use of projection and live feed creates an intermedial environment, a space in-between realities for performers to meet and play with the autistic imagination, using sensual, sensory media.

These aesthetic qualities are developed in Red Kite's subsequent work. *Red Kite Round Up* involves a similar aesthetic blend to appeal to the autistic

Figure 15 Red Kite Theatre Company in *Red Kite Blue Moon*. Photograph by kind permission of Jacqui Russell, Margaret Strickland and Chicago Children's Theatre

imagination. Described as a 'digitally simulated camping trip' where autistic children aged from 5 to 13 'can hike, chase fireflies and star-gaze', this journey featured a vehicle (a rubber dinghy) and a range of personas associated with sensual stimuli. Participants could look at the oversized and vividly coloured puppet bugs through a magnifying glass and capture magic fireflies, while furry baby chicks are the focus of playing with objects (indeed, the piece has worked well with visually impaired children where the tactile stimuli were foregrounded). A wooden bench replaces the blue chairs, while a slow-motion nature hike and square dancing offer physical opportunities for participation. Sound and music play a central role with camping songs and improvised moments, punctuating the action. When a 13-year-old joked, 'Alligators are going to eat me!', during the mock raft sequence, 'The staff made up a song about him.' Like its predecessors, *Red Kite Round Up* involves playing with presence, the body and the mediated through conceptual blending of the fictional within a self-reflexive framework.

Red Kite's theatre performances operate on a different level to the workshops in schools, according to Russell. Something happens in the shared space in these environments, which she described as 'charged', 'immediate' and 'profound'. At the end of *Red Kite Round Up*, shooting stars are projected and the children are invited to lie down together and whisper their wishes. The moment when the child leaves the parent's lap is highly significant as they

Figure 16   Red Kite Theatre Company in *Red Kite Round Up*. Photograph by kind permission of Jacqui Russell and Chicago Children's Theatre

move into the performance, feeling the need to engage with performers and objects because they want to participate. Parents have described how these possibilities are taken away and further explored through shared playtimes when they return home and want the experience repeated. All Red Kite shows develop material in workshops, deepening the engagement and significance through performance. Thus the stinky pig exercise is transformed into the cradling of baby stars or baby birds which the children often want to take back to their mothers as they enact and embody caring for another.

Thus Oily Cart, Red Kite and companies such as the UK's Horse and Bamboo (whose guided imagery for participants with learning difficulties also involves immersive installations) create new and exciting ways of engaging audiences and performers, drawing upon contemporary forms of performance making and in so doing, produce work which does not pretend to be something it isn't. These experiential and sensory journeys do not involve 'fakery', but use performance vocabularies which, according to Horse and Bamboo, 'achieve great emotional impact' by 'reaching depths of experience for which words cannot easily be found'.[25] This is encapsulated in Russell's account of a male adult with autism who, having participated in *Red Kite Round Up*, was asked 'how was your day' on the drive home, and responded 'today, memories were made.'[26]

There is an affective and emotive engagement here that connects to Richard Schechner's concept of 'Rasaesthetics'. Although the performers are not using Eastern training methods to communicate *Rasa*, the performance connects to its audiences through cognitive and perceptual means associated with autism. In his discussion of the 'gut reaction' and the 'brain in the belly' connecting body to mind, Schechner cites his correspondence with the neurobiologist, Michael D. Gershon, whose *The Second Brain* (1998) discusses the role of the 'enteric nervous system' (ENS), a vast and complex structure of 100 million neurons (more than the spine) discovered in the linings of the esophagus, stomach, small intestine and colon. 'What this means', Schechner summarizes, 'is that the gut ... has its own nervous system. This system does not replace or preempt the brain. Rather it operates alongside the brain, or – evolutionarily speaking – "before" or "underneath" the brain' (2001: 37). Schechner wrote to Gershon, asking him about the implications for 'emotional feelings' in relation to his concept of Rasaesthetics, and cites his response:

You touch a bit of raw nerve. You are certainly correct in that we in the West who consider ourselves 'hard' scientists have not taken Eastern thought very seriously. The problem with a great deal of Eastern thought is that it is not based on documentable observation. You cannot quantify ideas about strong feelings or deep power. We, therefore, either ignore Eastern ideas about the navel, or take them as metaphors, which are not very different from our own metaphors about 'gut feelings'. On the other hand, I have recently become aware of quantifiable research that establishes, without question, that vagus nerve stimulation can be used to treat epilepsy and depression. Vagus nerve stimulation also improves learning and memory. Vagus nerve stimulation is something physicians do and is not natural, but 90% of the vagus carries ascending information from the gut to the brain. It is thus possible that vagus nerve stimulation mimics natural stimulation of the vagus nerve by the 'second brain'. This relationship is particularly important in relation to the human condition of autism. Autism affects the gut as well as the brain. It is thus conceivable that autism could be the result in whole or in part of a disturbed communication between the two brains. In short, I now take the possibility that the gut affects emotions very seriously. This seems much more likely to me now than it did when I wrote my book.

(Schechner, 2001: 37)

Whilst Schechner refers to 'autistics' as exhibiting 'lack of affect or lack of range of affect', the visceral and tactile forms of performance practised by Oily Cart and Red Kite clearly produce an affect response in the partakers of this experience. Thus it could be argued that for the neuro-divergent consciousness there is a different configuration between the two brains whereby the second brain engages in perception, seeking and responding to features which work on the ENS. Thus the 'emphasis upon the sensuous and experiential dimensions of the event, rather than upon mimesis or narrative' which I have observed in work created for and with autistics corresponds to Schechner's notion of rasaesthetics as performance which is gut-brain rather than head-brain centered.

In *Different Sensory Experiences, Different Perceptual Worlds*, Olga Bogdashina urges researchers to:

understand the underlying causes of the behaviours and try to develop an approach not based on symptoms but on prevention. Challenging behaviours are caused by problems of communication, social understanding, by different imagination, by sensory problems ... Therefore try to understand autism 'from within ... it requires an enormous effort of imagination.

(2003: 183)

I suggest that the embodied, intermedial and live qualities of contemporary performance, as evident in the work of Oily Cart and Red Kite, create an opening into the autistic child's world. It is through this door that we may enter their world and they may vicariously enter ours.

Conclusion: Affective Practice

My final example returns us to the issues of aesthetics, ethics, affect and evaluation, as well as to the principles of applying performance, and draws on my own experience. During 2005 I was involved in an intergenerational project, a collaboration between Canterbury Museum, Year 6 primary school pupils from four local schools, and the Departments of Drama and Theatre Studies and Electronics at the University of Kent. This was a C&T-style Living Newspaper project (the company trained the university students during a residency), focusing on the 1942 Canterbury Blitz.

The project involved a range of elements whereby the final performance (which took the form of an interactive installation) was only one component of what was effectively a huge living archive. Four groups of participants were involved in the performance-making process: final-year students on the Masters Level Applied Performance specialism at Kent, final-year students on the Digital Media programme at Kent, final-year primary school pupils and, most crucially, a group of 79-year-old men and women, many of whom were children during the Second World War, who contributed their memories of the Canterbury Blitz. The university students worked with the primary school pupils to conduct interviews, undertake archive research and assemble a range of materials for an interactive website, the performance event and a DVD. A series of workshops involved all the participants working together to devise material, some of which also featured on the project website.

One story in particular was central to the project. Below is an extract from Jack Waller's story which was featured in the performance as a soundtrack, spoken by the 80-year old author, interspersed with a narrative commentary.

Monday 1 June
Narrator: Jack Waller, a bus driver, returned to wife and young son after his late shift as the sirens began to wail.
JW: Anyway we never used to worry until the tugboat started; well, as I was undressing the tugboat went. You see, it was bright

moonlight and I think that's why I went in the back bedroom to get undressed coz there was more light comin' in there than the front and it saved switchin' on the light. Anyway, the sky lit up, you could hear this plane and the sky, you know, cor, it was absolutely brilliant, bright as anything.

Narrator: [The family took shelter in the bake-house close by.] Seeing his family safely inside, Jack decided to return home to collect some clothes. He had no idea the danger this would put him in.

JW: Went through the front room and as I was going into the kitchen a bomb dropped, or may 'ave have been a gas mains went up, ooh, shook the house, like that.

Narrator: The blast brought the kitchen dresser crashing down, noticing an incendiary bomb burning in the back yard, Jack rushed to extinguish it with a sandbag. However, out in the yard he was to look up and receive another shock. His entire roof was ablaze. Realizing his house was lost and he had precious little time, Jack rushed upstairs to save what he could.

JW: I dashed upstairs, opened the wardrobe, took 'em off the hangers, altogether, threw 'em out the winder, I thought, I'll pick them up later on. As I come downstairs, I thought, ooh, I'm not gonna leave our holiday money behind, well that was on the stairs, half-way up the stairs on a little shelf in an Oxo tin. It was almost full! We were saving that for our holiday and, er [laughs], I grabbed that.

Narrator: Wondering what to save next, Jack paused, when a blast from an exploding bomb blew down the front door and sent rubble crashing about him.

JW: I thought crikey, I've gotta save meself, so I [laughs] rushed out the door and I must 'ave caught the tin on the side o the door and all the money, it went out in the lane! [laughs]

Narrator: Having gathered his family savings from his doorstep in Canterbury Lane, Jack Waller returned to the bake-house next door where his wife and son and a small group of neighbours were sheltering. However, there was to be no respite.

JW: Well anyway, when I went back in the bake-house, Mrs Barwick's sister, she said, 'Ooh, I've left me false teeth in the kitchen', she said, 'could you go and get 'em for me?'

Narrator: Once again, braving the falling bomb barrage and flaming buildings, Jack tried his neighbour's door and found it was locked

JW: I could see everything was going to be finished so I thought I'll bash the door down [laughs], I took a running leap and, er, I'd still got plenty of momentum and the blessed door went easier than I thought and I went in on all fours. [laughs]

Narrator: Rushing to the kitchen door, he was totally unprepared for what lay within.

JW: I opened the kitchen door and, wooh, a loada flames came out! Phew! – I shut the door again and thought cor, you've 'ad your teeth, missus![1]

Although the project was celebrated as hugely successful, in considering how we evaluated the project, and the impact of Jack's story, I have been conscious of a missing dimension. From the museum's perspective, the project attracted new audiences – young and old to see the performance and to participate in the installation. It also facilitated different modes of engagement with the materials and exhibits through the use of performance and live art.

From the perspective of the schools involved, the project engaged and excited pupils, bringing history to life and facilitating a dialogue between themselves and those with experience of the historical period and events they were studying. The DVD was one of the legacies of the project and continues to be used in schools in conjunction with similar performance strategies for teaching this aspect of history. In 2008, my 9-year-old son was asked to dress up as an evacuee for a journey on a steam train, while the DVD was used in the classroom as a stimulus for writing diary accounts of imagined wartime experiences. For the third generation (the term the museum used), evaluations of the event (written and verbal) were extremely positive; benefits identified by these participants included feeling valued, enjoying access to new technology, enjoying the collaboration with different age groups and the benefits we associate with reminiscence theatre in terms of access to long-term memory, benefits of socialization with peers, and contributing to a sense of well being. Thus several of the principles of applying performance can be seen to have featured strongly in this project in terms of its pedagogical objectives, participatory methods and play-based learning.

These are all functional benefits which might contribute to a project being considered effective. For the audience, however, there was also an affect which contributed to the project's impact and this is particularly evident in Jack's story. In listening to the detail of the courageous rescue of the family's holiday savings in the Oxo tin and the failed endeavour to recover a neighbour's false teeth from the burning home, we are moved by its honesty, humour and poignancy; it is this empathic dimension which contributed to the pleasure and power of the event as a whole and it survives on the DVD, where Jack's story is beautifully illustrated with animated drawings accompanying his voiceover. Jack's Kent-accented, ageing voice, the pauses, laughter and occasional faltering, contribute integrity and a sense of truth to this particular representation of experience. Empathy, I would argue, is fundamental to the aesthetic values of applied theatre and the pleasures it can provoke. This book has used cognitive neuroscience to consider how and why we are moved in our responses as well as considering how this contributes to our development of knowledge and understanding.

By way of conclusion, I want to return to the dichotomies Jackson and Thompson challenge in their subtitle and title respectively (*Art or Instrument*, *Performance Affects: Applied Theatre and the End of Effect*) and to Isobel Armstrong's call for a 'radical aesthetic'. Armstrong's project 'arises from the impasse of both conservative and left-leaning thinking about the aesthetic' (2000: 5). Drawing on Gillian Rose's work, she argues that 'the broken middle is the constitutive moment of the aesthetic' (Armstrong, 2000: 17). This broken middle is a fertile space for the radical and the creative. Indeterminacy is also critical to Jackson's argument: 'At the heart of all effective educational theatre practice, and more critical even than the active participation of the audience, is the existence in whatever form, of that aesthetic space, those "creative gaps" within which audiences and participants can forge, negotiate and own, meaning' (Jackson, 2007: 271). For Thompson, an affective realm contains the effective; citing Gumbrecht, he states that 'while the demand for "oscillation" or "negotiation" is entirely legitimate, the polemical nature of [his] book has sought to emphasize *affect* against *effect* ... being cerebral must also be an embodied response to the world (2009: 181).

For Rebecca Schneider, affect is also situated in a liminal space and challenges dualities, 'when we choose to invest in the betweenness or given relational aspects of affect. The *stickiness* of emotion is evident in the residue of generational time, reminding us that histories of events and historical effects of identity fixing, *stick* to any mobility, *dragging* ... the temporal past into the sticky substance of any present' (2011: 36). Thompson echoes the point: 'by working solely in the realm of effect, where performance communicates messages or concentrates on identifiable social or educational impact, the practice becomes restricted or weakened. By failing to recognize affect – bodily responses, sensations and aesthetic pleasure – much of the power of performance can be missed' (2009: 7). For Jackson, 'any theatre project that aims to educate will do so effectively only *if* it is also conceived as an artistic entity' (2007: 4).

Armstrong's concept of a radical aesthetic has significance and resonance for our work in applied and social theatre and performance: 'to give a new content to the concept of the aesthetic means broadening the scope of what we think of as art', she writes, 'the project that arises from questions about democratic access to art is actually that of changing the category itself, or re-describing it, so that what we know looks different and what we exclude from traditional categories of art also looks different' (2000: 2, 16).

Cognitive Science has been criticized for 'neglecting emotion, affect, and motivation (LeDoux, 2002: 24). Research on autism and interventions has similarly been criticized for its systemizing orientation; indeed, I have suggested that even Baron-Cohen's account of the systemizing/empathizing theory of autism, prioritizes the former and neglects the latter (Shaughnessy, 2009). What is important throughout applied theatre research is an approach which is empathetic; to *effect* change through *affect*. For Erika Fischer-Lichte, the 'transformative' potential of performance lies in its capacity to trigger liminal and embodied experiences: 'Essential to this project and to the shift from art object to art event, is the collapsing of binaries, headed by that of subject and object, or in the case of performance, spectator and actor' (2008: 8).

Whilst endorsing Fischer-Lichte's study of theatre as event rather than an autonomous work of art, a process of embodied action and transformed understanding, the new aesthetics she articulates can and does embrace the work discussed here. Poiesis and praxis engage in dialogue throughout the case studies discussed, process can become performance, play is emotion and emotive, participation engages audiences differently and cognitively through embodied encounters that can also become performance, as audiences become collaborators the publics become the art, while the continuous present, the physicality of 'being in the room' and in the moment of performance as event is fundamental to the pleasures generated through both shared and individual experiences, all of which can be profoundly affecting. What is needed, as various theorists have suggested (see Gaut, 2006; Hagberg, 2010; Kieran, 2006; Levinson, 2001; Wolff, 2008), is a shift in our understanding of aesthetics. Armstrong's call for a re-evaluation of the aesthetic develops ways of describing the aesthetic cognitively and affectively. Anti-aesthetic challenges, she argues, continue to be predicated on idealistic Kantian/Hegelian notions of aesthetics, which are simply not appropriate to contemporary culture. As ever, new models are needed for new forms. Most crucially for our purposes, she suggests that explorations concerning the politics of beauty, the functions of affect, and emotionality need to be rehabilitated as a means of establishing a democratic aesthetic of commonality: 'to neglect the concept of beauty as bourgeois, elitist and associated with cultural hegemony is to fail to address the democratic and radical potential of aesthetic discourse' and 'to give a new content to the concept of the aesthetic means broadening the scope of what we think of as art' (Armstrong, 2000: 2). Moreover, she argues that the challenge arising 'from questions about democratic access to art is actually that of changing the category itself, or re-describing it, so that what we know looks different and what we exclude from traditional categories of art also looks different'. Berys Gaut's work is also highly significant, making an important contribution to debates on the relations between aesthetics and ethics (through his conceptualizations of 'ethicism' and aesthetic cognitivism), whilst highlighting the importance of emotion and cognition to aesthetic criteria and values (2006, 2009). For Gaut, moral goodness can be considered as a form of beauty, as ethics and aesthetics are inextricably related in Gaut's moralism:

> Ethicism holds that a work is aesthetically flawed in so far as it possesses an aesthetically relevant ethical flaw and aesthetically meritorious in so

far as it possesses an aesthetically relevant ethical merit. The ethical flaws referred to are intrinsic ethical flaws, not the ethically bad effects that works may have on actual audiences. Intrinsic ethical flaws are ethical flaws in the attitudes that works manifest toward their subjects.

(2009: 229)

Gaut's thesis is supported by arguments about moral beauty, the importance of cognitivism (i.e., that aesthetic merit can be judged on the capacity of art to teach us) and what he refers to as the merited response argument which foregrounds the role of the viewer/partaker and the importance of their response to, and engagement with, the artwork they encounter as a determinant of aesthetic success. Janet Wolff similarly draws attention to the engagement of the reader/viewer in her conclusion to *The Aesthetics of Uncertainty*: 'The work of art ... always meets its viewer, even at its most non-representational, in the context of a specific social and historical moment in which the aesthetic, the ethical, and the political, as we now know, are never quite separable' (2008: 141).

There is, moreover, evidence of a different kind of engagement and a new aesthetics emerging in contemporary performance practice as the influence of applied theatre and socially engaged art contribute to an ethical turn through work which is process orientated, produced in social contexts, and which foregrounds the role of audience as partakers whose experiences and responses are valued as aesthetic criteria for success. Examples include Fevered Sleep's 2010 production *On Ageing* (performed by seven children aged 7 to 13, involving collaboration with groups of elders and gerontologists); Lone Twin's work in community contexts (*The Boat Project*, 2012, a living archive of people's stories and donated wooden items, featuring community participants), as well as the participatory work of Improbable and Third Angel, to name but a few. As Lyn Gardner has observed, 'The future may look like this – Theatre with rather than Theatre for' (July 2011).[2]

Conceptualizing, experiencing and responding to the range of artefacts we encounter in and through applied performance involves the different approaches Armstrong and Gaut advocate. Applying performance enables us to perceive differently and this demands different kinds of critical vocabularies, theoretical perspectives and methodologies to discuss, analyse and evaluate so that impact might be understood as being evident in the words of the autistic partaker: 'Today, memories were made.'

Notes

Preface

1. Definitions are from the *Oxford English Dictionary*, 2012 (see www.oup.com/uk).
2. For Rancière, 'the aesthetic regime abolishes the hierarchical distribution of the sensible characteristic of the representative regime of art ... the aesthetic regime destroys the system of genres and isolates "art" in the singular, which it identifies with the paradoxical unity of opposing *logos* and pathos. However, the singularity of art enters into an interminable contradiction due to the fact that the aesthetic regime also calls into question the very distinction between art and other activities' (2006: 81).
3. Rancière distinguishes 'between a type of art that makes politics by eliminating itself as art and a type of art that is political on the proviso that it retains its purity, avoiding all forms of political involvement' (Rancière, 2009a). Yet these are not conceived as oppositional or incompatible but as fragments of an 'originating configuration', which are two complementary modes of a political aesthetics.
4. Storer, programme note to *The Fat Girl Gets a Haircut and Other Stories*, Roundhouse, April 2011.
5. 'Partaker' is a term used by Schechner to refer to the experience of audience members in Asian modes of participant theatre: 'Like postmodern performance in Europe and America, the Indian system is a braid of several strands of activities; these require that performer and partaker attend together to the here and now of the ever-changing relations among the strands.' (2001). The terminology is used in conjunction with Schechner's discussion of *rasa* (the taste or essence of performance – a concept explored in Chapters 2 and 5). In another essay, he refers to the rasic performer as a partaker as well as the spectators responding: 'In rasic theater, the partakers empathise with the experience of the performers playing. ... The partakers do not want to "see what happens next" but to "experience how the performer performs what is happening"' (1983, 2003: 356).

Part I

Chapter 1   Setting the Scene: Critical and Theoretical Contexts

1. See Sally Mackey's work, in particular her AHRC-funded research project, 'Challenging Concepts of "Liquid" Place', which uses place responsive performance practice to explore, for example, dislocation. Can applied performance change our perception of, and relationship to, place? Margaret Ames and Mike Pearson are co-investigators in this research.
2. Interview with the author 17/04/2011.
3. See Nicholson (2006) 'Applied Theatre/Drama: An e-debate in 2004', Viewpoints. *RIDE: Research in Drama and Education* 1.1: 96–8.
4. See Prentki's review of Philip Taylor's *Applied Theatre* in *RIDE* 11.1 (2006): 111
5. John Fox, cited by Kershaw in a keynote speech for the 2005 IFTR conference: 'Citizen Artists in the Twenty-First Century'.

Chapter 2   Pasts, Pioneers, Politics

1. See, for example, FEAST (London International Festival of Theatre, 2009); the work of Clare Patey and Cathy Wren (e.g., 'Eat on the Bridge') and Anna Ledgard's *EastFeast*.
2. See G. Sturrock (2003), 'The Ludic Third', British Institute of Therapeutic Playwork, http://www.playworklondon.org.uk/upload/files/events/report/15_Psycholudics.pdf (accessed 20/09/2011). I am also indebted to Helena Bryant (MA PaR, Kent, 2008) whose conceptualization of play theory and live art practice informs my discussion.
3. 'Performing Presence: From the Live to the Simulated' was a collaboration between Nick Kaye and Gabriella Giannaci (University of Exeter), Mel Slater (University College London) and Michael Shanks, Stanford, USA. The project ran between 2004–8. See http://presence.stanford.edu/

Part II   Practices

Chapter 3   Performing Lives

1. Mierle Laderman Ukeles (2008), *Participate*, see http://www.thecjm.org.
2. For further discussion of psychoanalytic theory in relation to cognitive approaches, see B. McConachie and E. F. Hart, eds (2006), *Performance and Cognition: Theatre Studies and the Cognitive Turn*; and B. McConachie (2008) *Engaging Audiences*.
3. See P. Auslander (1999) *in Liveness: Performance in Mediatized Culture*.
4. I draw here upon Bruce McConachie's (2008) discussion of memory in his chapter on 'General Cognition for Theatre Audiences' which provides a useful summary and frame of reference on memory theory.
5. See Ciompi and Panseek (2005).
6. See, for example, Hauser (2006), whose study of morality makes the observation that 'proximity was undoubtedly a factor in the expression of empathy.' The use of particular kinds of technology in military contexts, it has been argued, is designed to desensitize and circumvent empathy in soldiers by distancing them from human targets (Carlisle, 2007).
7. See, for example, K. Malpede (1996) 'Teaching Witnessing: A Class Wakes to Genocide', *Theatre Topics* 6: 167–79. See also Bennett (2005).
8. I refer here to Katherina Pewny's research presented as a shift for the 2011 PSi conference at Utrecht ('Caring, not Curing: I feel your pain', Shift presentation with Nicola Shaughnessy, Melissa Trimingham and Cristel Staelwart.
9. This is Bennett's term and is used in a non-clinical sense.
10. Vayu Naidu is a performance storyteller originating from Delhi. Having studied in India and the United States, she came to the United Kingdom in 1988 to study for her PhD at Leeds University on Indian Performance Oral Traditions. She founded the Brumhalata Intercultural Storytelling company and is currently founder and artistic director of the Vayu Naidu Company in London.
11. Citations from Aston and Harris (2008) use the first name, as in the original.
12. I draw here on my experience of working with Naidu from 2003 to 2008 at the University of Kent and as the education representative on her Board of Directors, prior to the company's relocation to London. As such, I experienced her work in rehearsal and performance and in a range of educational and theatre contexts.
13. Schechner used rasaboxes as part of the rehearsal process for his production *Imagining O* at the University of Kent in June 2011.

14. Brown's discussion of practical exercises exploring *Rasa* (and his references to Stanislavski) are also relevant to the cognitive approaches to acting discussed by, for example, Rhonda Blair (2008)and John Lutterbie (2011).
15. Interview with the author, 19 June 2008.
16. The phrase first appears in 1929 in 'Saving the sentence' where Stein writes, 'what is a sentence for if I am I then my little dog knows me.' See Stein ([1931] 1975). In 1936 in *The Geographical History of America,* the phrase has become a repeated refrain in a sketch (developed for a puppeteer) and entitled 'The question of identity: A play', and it is here the meditation on identity begins 'I am I because my little dog knows me', although she eventually concludes 'That does not prove anything about you it only proves something about the dog ([1936] 1995: 103).
17. Arti Prashar, interview with the author, 8 June 2011.
18. The Lothian Birth Cohort study involved every child born in the region in 1936 taking an intelligence test (aged 11). At the age of 70, 1000 participants were tested again. Spare Tyre's production explores the stories of participants and scientists.
19. Prashar, interview with author 8 June 2011.
20. Prashar, interview.
21. Prashar, interview.
22. See, for example, Magic Me's *Cocktails in Care Homes* (2010/11), an intervention in the infantilizing schedule which so frequently involves imposing an early evening bedtime on residents, often as a consequence of staffing shift patterns.
23. *Blackbirds* was first performed at Dilston Grove, London, during May 2011.
24. Marigold Hughes, interview with the author, March 2011.
25. Jonathan Petherbridge, post-show discussion.
26. Moving Lives Project Report, Mayo, 2011. A summary can be found at http://www.magicme.co.uk/index.php.
27. One of the aims identified in the project was 'to build strong relationships between people who would not otherwise meet, helping to break down assumptions about groups and individuals' (Magic Me, 2011).
28. Mulberry School for Girls is a Community School in East London, with a roll of over 1350 students, 98 per cent of whom are of Bangladeshi origin. The School has Specialist Performing Arts Status.
29. Mayo, interview with author, June 2011.
30. I use the term 'connection' in conjunction with neurological research which, as Rhonda Blair (2008) summarizes, has significance for performance methodologies. etc.
31. Mayo, interview with author, June 2011.
32. Storer, *The Fat Girl Gets a Haircut and Other Stories,* programme note.
33. *My Home,* programme note.
34. *My Home,* programme note.

Chapter 4   Placing Performance

1. I am drawing here on Katherina Pewny's discussion of contemporary performance in a shift presentation for PSi, 27/05/2011: 'Lévinas' Ethics of Encounter & Posttraumatic Theatre'.
2. South East Coastal Report authored by David Powell (David Powell Associates) with Professor Fred Gray (University of Sussex), November 2009, *South East*

Coastal Towns: Economic Challenges and Cultural Regeneration. Report funded by SEEDA and commissioned through the Creative Foundation on behalf of Arun District Council, Creative Foundation, Margate Renewal Partnership, Portsmouth City Council, Shepway District Council, SEEDA, University of Chichester and the University of Portsmouth. London: David Powell Associates, citation, p. 9.

3. Tracey Emin, *The Sun*, 30 April 2010.
4. Kerrie Reading, e-mail to author.
5. James Yarker, e-mail to author.
6. Kerrie Reading, e-mail to author.
7. *Plague Nation* (2004) was funded by the Wellcome Trust's Pulse Initiative. It involved 989 kg of rice in school halls and gyms around the country, 1 grain for every person in the United Kingdom. Over a period of one or two days in each of the schools, we created with students a performance installation in which this rice was weighed out to represent a range of human statistics with a focus on infectious disease and vaccination. In each of the schools Stan's Cafe worked with small groups of students, talking about the history of epidemics, the development of vaccinations and the science involved. They also learnt the maths needed to translate the number of people into a weight of rice.
8. Stan's Cafe staged *Of All the People In All The World* in a vacated section of A. E. Harris, a metal producing factory in Birmingham, United Kingdom. This industrial site consists of shop floors, tool rooms and offices. Subsequently, the company have continued to be resident in the space, developing its use as an arts venue. Arts Council funding was secured in 2010 to continue this work. See http://www.aeharrisvenue.co.uk.
9. BSR; see Cox, 1997. This edition also includes 'When All the World was Young: the life and achievements of Dr Daniel McDonald' (McDonald founded Birmingham Sound Reproducers in 1932).
10. I use the term 'embodiment' in relation to Paula M. Niedenthal and colleagues' 2005 study.
11. E-mail to the author.
12. The six emotional states identified by Ciompi and Panksepp are: FEAR, RAGE, PANIC, CARE, PLAY and SEEKING . See Ellis and Newton (2005). This scheme is used by McConachie (2008) to analyse the emotional content of a range of texts.
13. Tessa Jowell (2004) DCMS publication *Government and the Value of Culture*, cited in Hooper-Greenhill, 2004: 19.
14. See, for example, Ansbacher (2002); and Motylewski (2001), www.imls.gov.
15. Hooper-Greenhill cites Wilkinson (2003).
16. Mole Wetherell, 'Creating the Past Project Proposal', National Museum of Scotland (2002).
17. Mole Wetherell, Interview with author, October 2010.
18. McLean (2002): 20.
19. Wetherell, interview with author.
20. McLean (2002): 12.
21. McLean (2002): 15.
22. McLean (2002): 19.
23. McLean (2002): 8.
24. See, for example, H. A. Allen and G. W. Humphreys (2009) 'Direct Tactile Stimulation of Dorsal Occipito-Temporal Cortex in a Visual Agnosic'. *Current Biology*, DOI: 10.1016/j.cub.2009.04.057.

25. See NMS website, http://www.nms.ac.uk/our_museums/national_museum.aspx.
26. The exhibition opened on 12 August 2002; performances were presented from 19–31 August and the exhibition closed on 14 September 2002.
27. McLean (2002).
28. *Creating the Past* proposal: 24 April 2001.
29. See http://www.le.ac.uk/ms/contactus/eileanhoopergreenhill.
30. Wetherell, script for speech at launch event, 12 August 2002.
31. Email correspondence with Arts Development Officer dated 1 February 2007, Accidental Collective Archive; my emphasis.
32. Interview with author, September 2008.
33. Original website, 2007, www.accidentalcollective.co.uk.
34. Evaluation document, *Pebbles to the Pier* (2007), Accidental Collective Archive.
35. Promotional material, Accidental Collective Archive.
36. Accidental Collective Archive, note dated 5/3/2007.
37. Accidental Collective Archive, notes for presentation at *Performing, Learning and Heritage* conference, Manchester, 2008.
38. Evaluation report.
39. Script for performance lecture, Leeds, 2009.
40. Participating community groups were:

    UCMat group, Connexions, Folkstone
    ME4 Writers, Medway
    Franciscans, Canterbury
    Age UK, Hollybush Day
    Care Centre, Sevenoaks
    Transition Town, Faversham
    2M Class, Cliftonville Primary School

Chapter 5   Digital Transportations

1. C&T Business Plan, April 1988 – March 2001: 1.
2. See http://www.candt.org/index.php/about/what-is-a-dramatic-property. See also Sutton's unpublished PhD thesis, *The Dramatic Property: A New Paradigm of Applied Theatre Practice for a Globalised Media Culture*, downloadable from the C&T website.
3. http://www.candt.org/index.php/about/what-does-ct-stand-for/.
4. Paul Sutton, interview with the author, December 2003.
5. My argument draws upon a paper jointly authored and presented between myself and Paul Sutton for the 2002 International Federation of Theatre Research (Amsterdam), 'Tomorrow's Front Pages, Yesterday's News: The Living Newspaper.com'
6. For current version see http://www.candt.org/index.php/projects/entry/the-living-newspaper/ and http://www.livingnewspaper.net.
7. Interview with author, February 2002; this material was included in the jointly presented conference paper.
8. Sutton, interview with the author, December 2003.
9. Sutton, interview with the author, December 2003.
10. Sutton, interview with the author, December 2003.
11. Sutton, interview with the author, April, 2011.
12. Child Peace Africa invited C&T to Korogocho in north-eastern Nairobi, close to the Dandora rubbish dump. Director, Dr Paul Sutton and Assistant Director, Max Allsup visitied Korogocho in March 2011, meeting development workers and engaging over 100 young people in participatory drama activities.

13. The *Everymap* project is inspired by Hereford's *Mappa Mundi* (1300), the largest surviving medieval map and a compendium of religion and mythology with inscriptions, beautifully painted scenes and symbols. It provides an insight into medieval beliefs and perceptions of lived reality and the imagined world beyond. Christ, at the apex watches the world (with Jerusalem at the centre).
14. Sutton, interview with author, April, 2011.
15. See http://www.melaniewilson.org.uk.
16. Wilson, interview with the author, June 2010.
17. See http://www.melaniewilson.org.uk.
18. The audio guides can be located on the school website: http://www.qegschool. org.uk/page_viewer.asp?page=Media+Activity+Days+&pid=276.
19. *Body Spaces* was an Olimpias production created by director/choreographer Petra Kuppers, video artist Sara Domville and sound artists Sarah Frances and Sam Richards as part of Digital Summer, Manchester Metropolitan University, in October 2000.
20. See http://www.stg.brown.edu/conferences/DAC/abstracts/kuppers.html.

Part III Participation

Chapter 6 Participatory (Syn)Aesthetics

1. See *This is Camp X –Ray, A Documentary by Damien Mahoney*, www.cultureshop.org.
2. See *Guardian Newspaper*, 11 October 2003.
3. See *Observer Newspaper*, 12 October 2003
4. Performance footage can be viewed on the website, http://lapovertydept.org/state-of-incarceration/index.php.
5. Fenton cited in *The Times Educational Supplement*, June 11 1993.
6. Report on Presentation of Hanoi Water puppets and SANG SONG to LAB's London Collaborations Fund and the Arts Council's International Initiatives fund), in LIFT archive.
7. See the LIFT Living Archive, www.liftfestival.com/living-archive.
8. See the LIFT Living Archive, www.liftfestival.com/living-archive.
9. See http://hjemstavn.com/english/box_4/societas-raffaello-sanzio-buchettino/2/.
10. Sue Mayo, LIFT 2011. See http://www.anewdirection.org.uk/content/320/LIFT
11. To see how events are recorded in the timeline exercise, see Caoimhe McAvinchey's report which can be downloaded from www.liftefest.com/living-archive/making-an-invitation.
12. The soundtrack can be heard at http://soundcloud.com/lift-living-archive/comptons-school-eight-million.
13. Private correspondence and telephone interview with author on 23/08/2011.
14. Interview with Martha Bowers, 23/08/2011.
15. See http://www.iberkshires.com/story/6718/A-Youth-Perspective-The-Dream-Life-of-Bricks-.html.
16. Bowers, interview with author.
17. Bowers, interview with author.
18. Youth Perspective.
19. See http://www.autismtheatre.org.
20. In particular, Russell worked with David Rench, a teacher at Agassiz to develop the Emotional Alphabet. Russell would bring the drama work into the classroom and Rench would integrate it into the rest of the curriculum.

21. See Baron-Cohen (2009).
22. See http://www.chicagochildrenstheatre.org/chicago-tribune-october-14-2007. htm.
23. Webb, interview with the author, November 2003.
24. See, for example Billington (2004) July 7, *Guardian*) and Gardner (2008), (http:// www.guardian.co.uk/stage/theatreblog/2008/jul/14/oilycartstheatremakesasplah) who writes that 'Regular readers will know of my devotion to Oily Cart, and admiration for a company whose work has always been theatrically way ahead of many of our most internationally celebrated companies, despite the fact that it works in a sector which is under-funded, under-celebrated and woefully under-valued.'
25. See Horse and Bamboo publicity www.horseand bamboo.org.
26. Russell, interview with author.

Conclusion: Affective Practice

1. The transcript of the taped extract of Jack Waller is reproduced by permission of Canterbury City Council Museums and is taken from *Canterbury '42: Experience Life on the Home Front*, Directed by John Batchelor (2006), University of Kent Multimedia.
2. Lyn Gardner commenting in a tweet on Punchdrunk's enrichment project: 11 July 2011, https://twitter.com/#!/lyngardner/status/90334699964215296.

Bibliography

Accidental Collective (2007) http://www.accidentalcollective.co.uk/ap11.html.
—— (2008) http://www.accidentalcollective.co.uk/ap5.html.
—— (2009) http://www.accidentalcollective.co.uk/ap4.html.
—— (2010) http://www.accidentalcollective.co.uk/fp23.html.
—— (2011) http://www.accidentalcollective.co.uk/fp1.html.
Agnew, J. (1987) *Place and Politics: The Geographical Mediation of State and Society.* Boston, MA, and London: Allen & Unwin.
Ahmed, S. J. (2002) 'Wishing for a world without "Theatre for Development": Demistifying the case of the Bangladesh'. *Research In Drama Education* 7.2: 207–19.
—— (2004) 'When theatre practitioners attempt changing an ever-changing world: Response to Tim Prentki's "save the children? – save the world"'. *Research in Drama Education* 8.1; *Research in Drama Education* 9.1: 96–100.
Ahmed, S. (2010) 'Happy Objects', in M. Gregg and G. Selgworth (eds), *Affect Theory Reader.* Durham, NC, and London: Duke University Press: 29–52.
Alreik, T. J., and A. Baerheim (2005) 'Elements from theatre art as learning tools in medical education'. *Research in Drama Education* 10.1: 5–14.
Anderson, B. (2009) 'Affective Atmospheres'. *Emotion, Space and Society* 2: 77–81.
Ansbacher, T. (2002) 'On Making Exhibits Engaging and Interesting'. *Curator: The Museum Journal* 45: 167–73.
Arbib, M. A. (2006) *From Action to Language via the Mirror System.* Cambridge: Cambridge University Press.
Arendt, H. [1958] (1998) *The Human Condition.* Chicago, IL: University of Chicago Press.
Armstrong, I. (2000) *The Radical Aesthetic.* Oxford: Blackwell.
Ashworth, G. J. and B. Graham (2005) 'Senses of place, senses of time and heritage', in G. J. Ashworth and B. Graham (eds), *Senses of Place, Senses of Time.* Aldershot: Ashgate: 3–12.
Aston, E., and G. Harris (2008) *Performance Practice and Process.* Basingstoke: Palgrave Macmillan.
Auslander, P. (1999) *Liveness: Performance in a Mediatised Culture.* London and New York: Routledge.
—— (2006) 'An Afterword: Is There Life after Liveness?', in S. Broadhurst and J. Machon (eds), *Performance and Technology: Practices of Virtual Embodiment and Interactivity.* Basingstoke: Palgrave Macmillan: 292–9.
Avery, C (2007) *Walking and Autobiography: Performance Writing.* Bristol: Intellect.
Barba, E. (1995) *The Paper Canoe: A Guide to Theatre Anthropology*, trans R. Fowler. London and New York: Routledge.
Barnes, J. (2007) *Cross-Curricular Learning 8–14.* London: Sage.
Baron-Cohen, S. (1995) *Mindblindness: An Essay on Autism and Theory of Mind.* Cambridge, MA: MIT Press.
—— (2001) 'Theory of Mind in Normal Development and Autism'. *Prisme* 34: 174–83.
—— (2009) 'The empathising/systemising theory of autism: Implications for education'. *Tizard Learning Disability Review* 14.3: 4–13.
Barthes, R. ([1968] 1977) 'The Death of the Author', ed. and trans. S. Heath, *Image, Music, Text.* Glasgow: Fontana: 142–8.

—— (1975) *The Pleasure of the Text*, trans R Miller. London: Jonathan Cape.

Bay-Cheng, S., C. Kattenbelt, A. Lavender and R. Nelson (eds) (2010) *Mapping Intermediality in Performance*. Amsterdam: Amsterdam University Press.

Bell, J. (1998), 'Beyond the Cold War: Bread and Puppet Theater and the New World Order', in J. Colleran and J. Spencer (eds), *Staging Resistance: Essays on Political Theatre*. Ann Arbor, MI: University of Michigan Press: 31–53.

—— (1999) 'The End of Our Domestic Resurrection Circus'. *TDR: The Drama Review* 43: 62–80.

Benedetto, di, S. (2010) *The Provocation of the Senses in Contemporary Theatre*. Abingdon and New York: Routledge.

Benjamin, W. ([1936] 1968a) 'The Work of Art in the Mechanical Age of Reproduction', in *Illuminations*, trans. H. Zohn, ed. H. Arendt. New York: Schochen: 217–52.

—— ([1939] 1968b) 'Some Motifs in Baudelaire', in *Illuminations*: 155–201.

—— (1970) 'The Author as Producer', trans. John Heckman. *New Left Review* 62: 135–44.

Bennett, J. (2005) *Empathic Vision: Affect, Trauma and Contemporary Art*. Stanford, CA: Stanford University Press.

Bergson, H. ([1912] 2004) *Matter and Memory*, trans. N. M. Paul and W. S. Palmer. New York: Dover.

—— ([1946] 1968) *The Creative Mind: An Introduction to Metaphysics*. New York: Dover Publications.

Berrol, C. F. (2006) 'Neuroscience meets dance/movement therapy: Mirror neurons, the therapeutic process and empathy'. *The Arts in Psychotherapy* 33: 302–15.

Berthoz, A. (2002) *Mind and Motion: The Brain's Sense of Movement*. Cambridge, MA: Harvard University Press.

Bigsby, C. W. E. (1985) *A Critical Introduction to Twentieth-Century American Drama*, Vol. 3: *Beyond Broadway*. Cambridge: Cambridge University Press.

Birringer, J. (1991) *Theatre, Theory, Postmodernism*. Bloomington, IN: Indiana University Press.

—— (2008) *Performance, Technology and Science*. New York: PAJ Publications.

Bishop, C. (2004) 'Antagonism and Relational Aesthetics'. *October* 110: 51–79.

—— (2005) *Installation Art*. London and New York: Routledge.

—— (2006) 'The Social Turn: Collaboration and its Discontents'. *Art Forum* (February): 178–83.

—— (2007) *Participation*. Cambridge, MA: MIT Press.

—— (2011) *Artificial Hells: Participatory Art and the Politics of Spectatorship*. London: Verso.

Bishop, C. and J. Roche (2006). 'Socially Engaged Art, Critics and Discontents: An Interview with Claire Bishop'. *Community Arts Network*, http://www.communityarts.net/readingroom/archivefiles/2006/07 (accessed 08/11/10).

Blair, R. (2008) *The Actor, Image and Action: Acting and Cognitive Neuroscience*. London and New York: Routledge.

Boal, A. (1985) *Theatre of the Oppressed*. New York: Theatre Communications Group.

—— (1995) *The Rainbow of Desire*, trans. Adrian Jackson. London: Routledge.

Bogdashina, O. (2003) *Sensory, Perceptual Issues in Autism and Asperger Syndrome: Different Sensory Experiences, Different Perceptual Worlds*. London: Jessica Kingsley.

Bolter, J., and R. Grusin (2000) *Remediation*. Cambridge, MA: MIT Press.

Bourdieu, P. (1984) *Distinction: A Social Critique of the Judgment of Taste*, trans. R. Nice. Harvard, MA: Harvard University Press.

Bourriaud, N. ([1998] 2002) *Relational Aesthetics*, trans. S. Pleasance, F. Woods and M. Copeland. Dijon: Les Presses du réel.

—— (2009) 'Precarious Constructions: Answer to Jacques Rancière on Art and Politics', in J. Seijdel and L. Melis (eds), *Open 17: A Precarious Existence*. Rotterdam: NAi Publishers: 20–37.

Bowers, M. (2002) *Letter from an Artist: The Dream Life of Bricks*, www.communityarts. net/readingroom/archivefiles/2002/12/letter from an 2.php (accessed 12/09/2007).

Brecht B. (1964) *Brecht on Theatre*, ed. and trans. John Willett. London: Methuen.

Brennan, M. (2002) 'Review of *Creating the Past*', *Glasgow Herald* (29 August).

Breton, A. ([1988] 2003) 'Artificial Hells. Inauguration of the 1921 Dada Season', trans. M. S. Witkowsky. *October* 105: 134–44.

Broadhurst, S. (1999) *Liminal Acts: A Critical Overview of Contemporary Performance and Theory*. New York: Continuum.

Broadhurst, S., and J. Machon (eds) (2007) *Performance and Technology: Practices of Virtual Embodiment and Interactivity*. Basingstoke: Palgrave Macmillan.

Brodzinsky, E. (2010) *Theatre in Health and Care*. Basingtoke: Palgrave Macmillan.

Brook, P. (2005) lecture for Tel Aviv University, in video archives, Faculty of Arts; cited in Linda Ben Zvi, 'Staging the Other Israel: The Documentary Theatre of Nola Chilton', *The Drama Review* 50.3 (T191) (Fall 2006).

Brown, C., and M. Cole (2000) 'Socially Shared Cognition: System Design and the Organization of Collaborative Research', in D. H. Jonasen, and S. Land (eds), *Theoretical Foundations of Learning Environments*. Mahwah, NJ: Laurence Erlbaum: 197–214.

Brown, J. R. (2005) 'Shakespeare, the *Natyasastra*, and Discovering *Rasa* for Performance'. *New Theatre Quarterly* 21: 3–12.

Burger, P. (1984) *Theory of the Avant-Garde*, trans. M. Shaw. Minneapolis, MN: University of Minnesota Press.

Butler, J. (1993) *Bodies that Matter: On the Discursive Limits of 'Sex'*. London and New York: Routledge.

CandT (2011) 'The living newspaper', http://candt.org/index.php/projects/entry/the-living-newspaper (accessed 09/09/2010).

Callois, R [1958] (2001) *Man, Play and Games*, trans. M. Barash. Champaign, IL: University of Illinois Press.

Carlisle, J. (2007) 'Empathy, mirror neurons, technology and war', www.assocatedcon-tent.com/article/474799/empathy mirrorneuronstechnology-and.html (accessed 26/04/08).

Caroll, J. (2006) *Real Players? Drama, Technology and Education*. Stoke-on-Trent: Trentham Books.

Caruth, C. (ed.) (1995) *Trauma: Explorations in Memory*. Baltimore, MD: Johns Hopkins University Press.

—— (1996) *Unclaimed Experience: Trauma, Narrative and History*. Baltimore, MD: Johns Hopkins University Press.

Caruth C. L., and J. Panseek (2005) 'Energetic Effects of Emotions on Cognitions: Complementary Psychobiological and Psychosocial Findings', in R. D. Ellis and N. Newton (eds), *Consciousness and Emotion: Agency, Conscious Choice, and Selective Perception*. Amsterdam: John Benjamins Publishing: 23–56.

Carver, G. and C. Beardon (eds) (2004) *New Visions in Performance: The Impact of Digital Technologies*. London and New York: Routledge.

Casey, E. S. (1987*) Remembering: A Phenomenological Study*. Bloomington, IN: Indian University Press.

—— (1993) *Getting Back into Place: Toward a Renewed Understanding of the Place-World*. Bloomington and Indianapolis, IN: Indiana University Press.

—— (2000) *Imagining: A Phenomenonological Study*, 2nd edn. Bloomington and Indianapolis, IN: Indiana University Press.

—— (2001) 'Between Geography and Philosophy: What does it mean to be in the place-world?' *Annals of the Association of American Geographer* 91.4: 683–93.

Catmur, C., and Heyes, C., (2007) 'Sensorimotor Learning Configures the Human Mirror System'. *Current Biology* 17: 1527–31.

Causey, M ([2006] 2009) *Theatre and Performance in Digital Culture*. London and New York: Routledge.

Certeau, de, M. (1984) *The Practice of Everyday Life*, trans. S. Rendall. Berkeley, CA: University of California Press.

Chaikin, J. (1972) *The Presence of the Actor*. New York: Atheneum.

Chapple F., and C. Kattenbelt (2006) *Intermediality in Theatre and Performance*. Amsterdam and New York: Rodopi.

Chicago Children's Theatre (2007) http://www.chicagochildrenstheatre.org/chicago-tribune-october-21-2007.html (accessed 01/07/2011).

Chin, D. (1989) 'Interculturalism, postmodernism, pluralism'. *Performing Arts Journal* 11: 163–75.

Ciompi, L. and J. Panksepp (2005) 'Energetic Effects of Emotions on Cognitions: Complementary Psychobiological and Psychosocial Findings', in R. D. Ellis and N. Newton (eds), *Consciousness and Emotion: Agency, Conscious Choice and Selective Perception*. Amsterdam: John Benjamins Publishing.

Cixous, H. (1976) 'The Laugh of the Medusa', trans. K. Cohen and P. Cohen. *Signs* 1: 875–93.

—— (2005) *Stigmata: Escaping Texts*. London: Routledge.

CLG (2008) *Transforming Places: Changing Lives: A Framework for Regeneration*. London: Department of Communities and Local Government.

Clough, P. and J. Halley (eds) (2007) *The Affective Turn: Theorizing the Social*. Durham NC: Duke University Press.

Cohen-Cruz, J. (2002) 'The Motion of the Ocean: The Shifting Face of US Theater for Social Change since the 1960s'. *Theater* 31: 95–107.

—— (2005) *Local Acts: Community Based Performance in the United States*. New Brunswick, NJ: Rutgers University Press.

Colleran J., and J. S. Spencer (1998) *Staging Resistance: Essays on Political Theatre*. Ann Arbor, MI: University of Michigan Press.

Conquergood, D. (1985) 'Performing as a Moral Act: Ethical Dimensions of the Ethnography of Performance'. *Literature in Performance* 5:1–13.

—— (1998) 'Beyond the Text: Toward a Performative Cultural Politics', in S. J. Dailey (ed.), *The Future of Performance Studies: Visions and Revision*. Washington, DC: National Communication Association: 25–36.

Coult, T., and B. Kershaw (eds) (1983) *Engineers of the Imagination: The Welfare State Handbook*. London: Methuen.

Cox, A. R (1997) *Just fort he Record: The Story of BSR and its Employees*. Tipton: Black Country Publications.

Cresswell, T. (2004) *Place: A Short Introduction*. Oxford: Blackwell.

Crew, S. R., and J. Sims (1992) 'Locating authenticity: Fragments of a dialogue', in I. Karp and S. D. Lavine (eds), *Exhibiting Cultures: The Poetics and Politics of Museum Display*. Washington, DC, and London: Smithsonian Institution: 159–75.

Crimp, D. (1993) *On the Museum's Ruins*. Cambridge, MA: MIT Press.

Curtis, N. (2009) 'It's all going on off stage', *Evening Standard* (16 June), http://www. thisislondon.co.uk/theatre/article-23708160-its-all-going-on-off-stage.do (accessed 21/01/2010).

Dalpretto, M., M. S. Davies, J. H. Pfeifer, A. Scott, M. Sigman, and S. Y. Bookheimer (2006) 'Understanding emotions in others: Mirror neuron dysfunction in children with autism spectrum disorders'. *Nature Neuroscience* 9: 28–30.

Damasio, A. (1999) *The Feeling of What Happens: Body and Emotion in the Making of Consciousness*. New York: Harcourt Brace.

—— (2003) *Looking for Spinoza: Joy, Sorrow and the Feeling Brain*. New York: Harcourt Brace.

—— ([1994] 2005) *Descartes' Error: Emotion, Reason and the Human Brain*. Harmondsworth: Penguin.

—— (2010) *Self Comes to Mind*. New York: Pantheon.

Daniels, H., M. Cole and J. V. Wertsch (eds) (2007) *The Cambridge Companion to Vygotsky*. Cambridge: Cambridge University Press.

Davidson C. N. (2011) *Now You See It: How the Brain Science of Attention Will Transform the Way We Live, Work, and Learn*. New York: Viking.

Davis, D (2010) *Gavin Bolton Essential Writings*. Stoke-on-Trent: Trentham Books.

DCMS (2006) *Culture at the Heart of Regeneration*. London: Department of Media, Culture and Sport.

Deleuze, G. ([1970] 1988) *Spinoza: Practical Philosophy*, trans. R. Hurley. San Francisco, CA: City Lights Books.

Deleuze, G. and F. Guattari ([1987] 2003) *A Thousand Plateaus*. London: Continuum.

Denzin, N. K. (2003a) *Performance Ethnography: Critical Pedagogy and the Politics of Culture*. London: Sage.

—— (2003b) 'Much Ado About Goffman', in *Goffman's Legacy*, ed. A. J. Trevino. Oxford: Roman & Littlefield: 127–42.

Derrida, J. (1998) *Archive Fever: A Freudian Impression*, trans E. Prenowitz. Chicago, IL: Chicago University Press.

Descartes, R. ([1924] 2008) *Discourse on Method and Meditations on First Philosophy*, 4th edn, trans. J. Veitch. New York: Cosimo Classics.

Diamond, E. (1989) 'Mimesis, Mimicry and the "True-Real"'. *Modern Drama* 32: 58–72.

—— (ed.) (1996) *Performance and Cultural Politics*. London and New York: Routledge.

—— (1997) *Unmaking Mimesis*. London and New York: Routledge.

Dimsdale, K. (2008) 'Schools and Experimental Theatre', http://www.stanscafe.co.uk/ helpfulthings/schoolsandexperimentaltheatre.html (accessed 25/6/2010).

Dixon, S. R. (2007) *Digital Performance: A History of New Media in Theatre, Dance, Performance Art, and Installation*. Cambridge, MA: MIT Press.

Dolan, J. (2005) *Utopia In Performance: Finding Hope at the Theatre*. Ann Arbor, MI: University of Michigan Press.

Donald, M. (1991) *Origins of the Modern Mind: Three Stages in the Evolution of Culture and Cognition*. Cambridge, MA: Harvard University Press.

Drain, R. (ed.) (1995) *Twentieth Century Theatre: A Sourcebook of Radical Thinking*. London and New York: Routledge.

Duff, C. (2010) 'On the role of affect and practice in the production of place'. *Environment and Planning D: Society and Space* 28: 881–95.

Eagleton, T. (2003) *After Theory*. New York: Basic Books.

Eco, U. ([1962] 2007) 'The Poetics of the Open Work', in C. Bishop (ed.), *Participation*: 20–40.

—— (1989) *The Open Work*. Boston, MA: Harvard University Press.

Edelman, G., and G. Tononi, (2000) *A Universe of Consciousness: How Matter Becomes Imagination*. New York: Basic Books.

Ellis, R. D., and N. Newton (2005) *Consciousness & Emotion: Agency, Conscious Choice, and Selective Perception*. Amsterdam: Benjamins.

Ellsworth, E. (2005) *Places of Learning*, London: Routledge.

Emin, T. (2010) *The Sun* (30 April), http://www.thesun.co.uk/sol/homepage/features/2953740/Tracey-Emin-rues-fate-of-Margate.html.

Etchells, T. (1999) *Certain Fragments: Contemporary Performance and Forced Entertainment*. London and New York: Routledge.

Etherton, M. (1988) 'Third World Popular Theatre', in M. Banham (ed.), *The Cambridge Guide to Theatre*. Cambridge: Cambridge University Press: 1107–8.

Ewald, W. (2005) 'Photography changes personal history'. Smithsonian Photography Initiative, http://click.si.edu/Story.aspx?story242 (accessed 1/06/2011).

—— (2006) *Towards a Promised Land*. London: Steidlville.

Fauconnier, G., and M. Turner (2003) *The Way We Think: Conceptual Blending and the Mind's Hidden Complexities*. New York: Basic Books.

Fenemore, A. (2003) 'On Being Moved by Performance'. *Performance Research* 8: 107–14.

Fenton, R., and L. Neal (2005) *The Turning World: Stories from the London International Festival of Theatre*. London: Calouste Gulbenkian Foundation.

Feral, J. (1982) 'Performance and Theatricality: the Subject Demystified', trans. T. Lyons. *Modern Drama* 25.1: 170–81.

Fischer-Lichte, E. (2008) *The Transformative Power of Performance: A New Aesthetics*, trans. J. I. Saskya Iris. London and New York: Routledge.

Foster, H. (1996) *The Return of the Real: Art and Theory at the End of the Century*. Cambridge, MA: MIT Press.

Freire, P. (1996 [1971]) *Pedagogy of the Oppressed*, trans. M. Bergman Ramos. Harmondsworth: Penguin Books.

Freshwater, H. (2009) *Theatre and Audience*. Basingstoke: Palgrave Macmillan.

Frith U. (2003) *Autism: Explaining the Enigma*. Oxford: Blackwell.

—— (2008) *Autism: A Very Short Introduction*. Oxford: Oxford University Press.

Fuchs, E. (1996) *The Death of Character: Perspectives on Theatre after Modernism*. Bloomington, IN: Indiana University Press.

Fujioka, T., B. Ross, R. Kakigi, C. Pantev, and L. J. Trainor (2006) 'One year of musical training affects development of auditory cortical-evoked fields in young children'. *Brain: A Journal of Neurology* 129: 2593–608.

Gale, M. and V. Gardner (2004) *Auto/biography and Identity: Women, Theatre and Performance*. Manchester: Manchester University Press.

Gallagher, S. (2004) 'Understanding interpersonal problems in autism: Interaction theory as an alternative to theory of mind'. *Philosophy, Psychiatry, and Psychology* 11: 199–217.

—— (2005) 'A new movement in perception: Review of Alva Noë's *Action in Perception*', *Times Literary Supplement* (17 November).

Gallese, V. (2001) 'The "shared manifold" hypothesis: From mirror neurons to empathy'. *Journal of Consciousness Studies* 8: 33–50.

—— (2008) 'What Do Mirror Neurons Mean? Intentional Attunement: The Mirror Neuron System and Its Role in Interpersonal Relations', www.interdisciplines.org/mirror/papers/1 (accessed 11/11/08).

Gallese, V., and A. Goldman (1998) 'Mirror Neurons and the Simulation Theory of Mind-Reading'. *Trends in Cognitive Sciences* 12: 493–501.

Gardner, L. (2009) 'Anxiety theatre', http://www.guardian.co.uk/stage/theatre-blog/2009/mar/02/anxiety-theatre (accessed 13/08/2011).

Garoian, C. R. (1999) *Performing Pedagogy: Toward an Art of Politics*. Albany, NY: State University of New York Press.

Gaut, B. (2006) 'Art and Cognition', in M. Kieran (ed.), *Contemporary Debates in Aesthetics and the Philosophy of Art*. Oxford: Willey-Blackwell: 115–26.

—— (2009) *Art, Emotion and Ethics*. Oxford: Oxford University Press.

Gershon, M. D. (1998) *The Second Brain: The Scientific Basis of Gut Instinct and a Groundbreaking New Understanding of Nervous Disorders of the Stomach and Intestine*. London and New York: Harper Collins.

Giannachi, G. (2004) *Virtual Theatres*. London and New York: Routledge.

—— (2007) *The Politics of the New Media Theatre*. London and New York: Routledge.

Goffman, E. (1959) *The Presentation of Self in Everyday Life*. New York: Anchor.

Goleman, D (1996) *Emotional Intelligence: Why It Can Matter More Than IQ*. London: Bloomsbury.

Govan, E., H. Nicholson and K. Normington (2007) *Making a Performance: Devising Histories and Contemporary Practices*. London: Routledge.

Gregg, M. and G. Seigworth (eds) (2010) *The Affect Theory Reader*. Durham, NC, and London: Duke University Press.

Grosz, E. (2002) 'Bodies-cities', in G. Bridge, and S. Watson (eds), *The Blackwell City Reader*. Oxford: Blackwell: 297–303.

Guss, F. (2002) 'Innovative dramaturgies in theatre for children?' *Drama Australia Journal* 26: 63–70.

—— (2005) 'Dramatic playing beyond the theory of multiple intelligences'. *Research in Drama Education* 10: 43–54.

Haddon, M. (2003) *The Curious Incident of the Dog in the Nightime*. London: Barnes & Noble.

Hagberg, G. (2010) *Art and Ethical Criticism*. Oxford: Wiley Blackwell.

Hammond, W. and D. Stuart (2008) *Verbatim, Verbatim: Techniques in Contemporary Documentary Theatre*. London: Oberon Books.

Happé, F. (1994) *Autism: An Introduction to Psychological Theory*. London: Psychology Press.

Haraway, D (1989) *Primate Visions: Gender, Race, and Nature in the World of Modern Science*. Routledge: New York and London.

Harrop, J. (1992) *Acting*. New York and London: Routledge.

Harvie, J. (2005) *Staging the UK*. Manchester: Manchester University Press.

Hauser, M. D. (2006) *Moral Minds*. London and New York: Harper Collins.

Heathcote, D. (1984). 'Role-taking', in L. Johnson and C. O'Neill (eds), *Dorothy Heathcote, Collected Writings in Education and Drama*. London: Hutchinson.

Heathfield, A. and H. Glendinning (2004) *Live: Art and Performance*. London: Tate Publishing.

Heddon, D. (2008) *Autobiography and Performance*. Basingstoke: Palgrave Macmillan.

Heidegger, M. (1971) *Poetry, Language, Thought*, trans. A. Hofstadter. New York: Harper & Row.

—— ([1977] 2003) 'The Question Concerning Technology', in R. C Scharff and V. Dusek (eds), *Philosophy of Technology: The Technological Condition*. Oxford: Blackwell: 252–64.

Herman, J. L. (2001) *Trauma and Recovery*. London: Pandora.

Higgins, C. (2009) 'Punchdrunk', http://www.guardian.co.uk/culture/charlottehigginsblog/2009/dec/07/theatre-punchdrunk (accessed 15/11/2011).

Hill, L. and H. Paris (2006) *Performance and Place*. Basingstoke: Palgrave Macmillan.

Hirsch, E. (1995) *The Anthropology of Landscape: Perspectives on Place and Space*. Oxford: Clarendon Press.

Hirsch, M. (2008) *The Generation of Post-Memory: Visual Culture After the Holocaust*. New York: Columbia University Press.

Hooper-Greenhill, E. (1994) *Museums and their Visitors*. London and New York: Routledge.

—— (2004) 'Learning from Culture: The Importance of the Museums and Galleries Education Program (Phase I) in England'. *Curator: The Museum Journal* 47: 428–49.

—— (2007) 'Museum Revolutions', in S. Knell, S. MacLeod and S. Watson (eds), *Education, Post-Modernity and the Museum*. London and New York: Routledge: 367–77.

Hornby, R. (1992) *The End of Acting: A Radical View*. New York: Applause Books.

Huizinga, J. (1971) *Homo Ludens*. Boston, MA: Beacon Press.

Hurley, S. (2005) 'The shared circuits model: How control, mirroring and simulation can enable imitation'. Strasbourg: European Science Foundation, www.interdisci-plines.org/mirror (accessed 4/02/08).

Husserl, E. (1999) *The Essential Husserl: Basic Writings in Transcendental Phenomenology*, ed. D. Welton. Bloomington, IN: Indiana University Press.

Hyde, K. et al. (2009) 'Musical Training Shapes Structural Brain Development'. *The Journal of Neuroscience* 29.10: 3019–25.

Iacoboni, M. (2005) 'Understanding Others: Imitation, Language, Empathy', in S. Hurley and N. Chater (eds), *Perspectives on Imitation: From Neuroscience to Social Science*, Vol. 1. Cambridge, MA: MIT Press: 77–101.

Iacaboni, M, I. Molnar-Szakacs, V. Gallese, G. Buccino, J. C. Maziotta and G. Rizzolatti (2005) 'Grasping the intentions of others with one's own mirror neuron system'. *Plus Biology* 3: 529–35.

Immordino-Yang, M. H. (2010), 'Toward a microdevelopmental, interdisciplinary approach to social emotion'. *Emotion Review* 2: 217–20.

Immordino-Yang, M. H. and A. Damasio (2007) 'We Feel, Therefore We Learn: The Relevance of Affective and Social Neuroscience to Education'. *Mind, Brain, and Education* 1: 3–10.

Immordino-Yang, M. H. and K. W. Fischer (2010) 'Neuroscience Bases of Learning', in E. Baker, B. McGaw and P. Peterson (eds), *International Encyclopedia of Education*. Oxford: Elsevier.

Indyk, I. (2000) 'The Critic and the Public Culture: For example, Walter Benjamin'. *Australian Humanities Review*, 18: http://www.australianhumanitiesreview.org/archive/Issue-June-2000/indyk2.html.

Irigaray, L (1992) *The Irigaray Reader*, ed. M. Whitford. Oxford: Blackwell.

Irwin K. (2002) 'What is site-specific theatre?', http://uregina.ca/weyburn_project/pages/sitespec.html.

—— (2009) *The Ambit of Performativity: How Site Makes Meaning in Performance*. Saarbruken: Lambert Academic Publishing.

Jackson, A. (2007) *Theatre, Education and the Making of Meanings: Art or Instrument?* Manchester: Manchester University Press.

Jackson A., and J. Kidd (2008) *Performance, Learning and Heritage Report*, www.plh.manchester.ac.uk (accessed 12/10/09).

Jackson, A., and J. Kidd (eds) (2010) *Performing Heritage: Research, Practice and Innovation in Museum Theatre and Live Interpretation*. Manchester: Manchester University Press.

Jackson, S. (2011) *Social Works: Performing Art, Supporting Publics*. London and New York: Routledge.

Jacob, P., and M. Jeannerod (2003) *Ways of Seeing: The Scope and Limits of Visual Cognition*. Oxford: Oxford University Press.

Jameson F. (1991) *Postmodernism, or the Cultural Logic of Late Capitalism*. Durham, NC: Duke University Press.

Jarboe, K. P. (2001) 'Inclusion in the Information Age', http://www.athenaalliance.org/pdf/AA901_Policy.pdf (accessed 20/09/2011).

Johnson, P. (2010) 'The Space of Museum Theatre', in Jackson and Kidd (eds), *Performing Heritage*: 53–66.

Kandinsky, W. ([1910] 2006) *On the Spiritual in Art*. London: Lawrence King.

Kant, I. (1999) *Critique of Pure Reason*, ed. P. Guyer and A. W. Wood. Cambridge: Cambridge University Press

Kaye, N. (2000) *Site Specific Art: Performance, Place and Documentation*. London: Routledge.

Kear, A. (1999) 'Cooking Time with Gertrude Stein'. *Performance Research* 4.1: 44–55.

Kearney, R. (2004) *On Paul Ricoeur: the Owl of Minerva*. Aldershot: Ashgate.

Keidan, L. (2004) 'This must be the place: Thoughts on place, placelessness and live art since the 1980s', in L. Hill and H. Paris (eds), *Performance and Place*. Basingstoke: Palgrave Macmillan: 8–16.

Kennedy, D. (1998) 'Shakespeare and Cultural Tourism'. *Theatre Journal* 50: 175–88.

Kershaw, B. (1998) 'Pathologies of Hope in Drama and Theatre'. *Research in Drama Education* 3: 67–8.

—— (1999) *The Radical in Performance: Between Brecht and Baudrillard*. London: Routledge.

Kershaw, B., and T. Coult (eds) (1983) *Engineers of the Imagination: The Welfare State Handbook*. London: Methuen.

Kester, G. (2004) 'Conversation Pieces: Community and Communication in Modern Art', in Z. Kucor and S. Leung (eds), *Theory in Contemporary Art Since 1985*. Oxford: Blackwell: 76–88.

Kieran, M. (ed.) (2006) *Contemporary Debates in Aesthetics and the Philosophy of Art*. Oxford: Blackwell.

Kirby, M. (1995 [1972]) 'On Acting and Not-Acting', in P. Zarilli (ed.), *Acting (Re)Considered*. London: Routledge: 43–58.

Kirshenblatt-Gimblett, B. (1998) *Destination Culture: Tourism, Museums, Heritage*. Berkeley, CA: University of California Press.

Klich, R. and E. Scheer (2011) *Multimedia Performance*. Basingstoke: Palgrave Macmillan.

Knell, S., S. MacLeod and S. Watson (2007) *Museum Revolutions: How Museums Change and are Changed*. London: Routledge.

Kourilsky, F. (1971) *Le Bread and Puppet Theatre*. Lausanne: Editions La Cité.

Kuppers, P. (2006) 'Addenda, Phenomenology, Embodiment: Cyborgs and Disability Performance', in S. Broadhurst and J. Machon (eds), *Performance and Technology*: 169–80.

—— (2007a) *Community Performance: An Introduction*. London: Routledge.

—— (2008) 'Dancing Autism: *The Curious Incident of the Dog in the Night-Time* and *Bedlam'*. *Text and Performance Quarterly* 28: 192–205.

Kuppers, P. (ed.) (2007b) *The Community Performance Reader*. London: Routledge.

Kwon, M. (2001) 'For Hamburg: Public Art and Urban Identities', http://www.art-omma.org/issue6/text/kwon.htm#1 (accessed 21/10/2010).

—— (2004) *One Place After Another: Site-Specific Art and Locational Identity*. Cambridge, MA, and London: MIT Press.

LaCapra, D. (1996) *Representing the Holocaust: History, Theory, Trauma*. New York: Cornell University Press.

Lacy, S. (ed.) (1994) *Mapping The Terrain: New Genre Public Art*. Seattle, WA: Bay Press.

Lakoff, G., and M. Johnson (1999) *Philosophy in the Flesh: The Embodied Mind and Its Challenge to Western Thought*. New York: Basic Books.

LAPD (2010) http://lapovertydept.org/state-of-incarceration/index.php.

Lave, J., and E. Wenger (1991) *Situated Learning: Legitimate Peripheral Participation*. Cambridge: University of Cambridge Press.

Lavery, C. (2007) *Walking and Autobiography: Performance Writing*. Bristol: Intellect.

Ledgard, A. (2010) '*Visiting Time* and *Boychild*: Site-specific pedagogical experiments on the boundaries of theatre and science', http://www.wellcome.ac.uk/stellent/groups/corporatesite/@msh_peda/documents/web_document/wtx050363.pdf (accessed 5/6/2011).

LeDoux, J. (2002) *Synaptic Self: How Our Brains Become Who We Are*. New York: Penguin Books.

Lefebvre, H. ([1974] 1991) *The Production of Space*, trans. Donald Nicholson-Smith. Oxford: Basil Blackwell.

Lehmann, H.-T. (2006) *Post-Dramatic Theatre*, trans. K. Jürs-Munby. London and New York: Routledge.

Levinson, J. (ed.) (2001) *Aesthetics and Ethics: Essays at the Intersection*. Cambridge: Cambridge University Press.

Lines, R. (2007) 'Why use New Media?'. *Theatre Education News*, http://www.candt.org/index.php/about/why-use-new-media (accessed 11/11/2008).

Lineskind, D. (2001) *The Space of Encounter*. London: Thames & Hudson.

Lippard, L. (1998) *The Lure of the Local: Senses of Place in a Multicentered Society*. New York: New Press.

Live Art (2009) ' What is live art', http://www.thisisliveart.co.uk/about_us/what_is_live_art.html (accessed 04/06/2011).

Los Angeles Poverty Department (2010) 'State of Incarceration', 05http://lapovertydept.org/state-of-incarceration/index.php (accessed 05/06/2011).

Low, S. M., and D. Lawrence-Zuniga (2003) *The Anthropology of Space and Place: Locating Culture*. Oxford: Blackwell.

Lutterbie, J. (2011) *Towards a General Theory of Acting: Cognitive Science and Performance*. Basingstoke and New York: Palgrave Macmillan.

Machon, J. (2009) *(Syn)aesthetics: Redefining Visceral Performance*. Basingstoke and New York: Palgrave Macmillan.

Mackey, S., and N. Whybrow (2007) 'Taking place, some reflections on site, performance and community'. *Research in Drama Education* 12.1: 1–14.

Macleod, S. (2005) *Reshaping Museum Space*. London and New York: Routledge.

Malpas, J. E. (1999) *Place and Experience: A Philosophical Topography*. Cambridge: Cambridge University Press.

Malpede-Taylor, K. (1972) *People's Theatre in America*. New York: Drama Book Specialists.

Martin, C. (2010) *Dramaturgy of the Real on the World Stage*. Basingtstoke: Palgrave Macmillan.

Martin, S. (2007) 'Critique of Relational Aesthetics'. *Third Text* 21.4, Taylor & Francis, http://www.tandfonline.com/doi/pdf/10.1080/09528820701433323.

Massey, D. (2005) *For Space*. London: Sage.

—— (2007) *World City*. Cambridge: Polity Press.

Massmoca (2011) http://www.massmoca.org/history.php (accessed 10/10/2011).

Massumi, (2002) *Parables for the Virtual: Movement, Affect, Sensation*. Durham, NC: Duke University Press.

Mayo, S. (2010) 'The LIFT Living Archive: Plunging in and bouncing off: Working with co-explorers', http://www.suemayo.co.uk/wp-content/uploads/2011/06/CILIP-LLA-paper-for-web.pdf (accessed 10/11/2010).

—— (2011) *Moving Lives* Project Report, http://www.magicme.co.uk/index.php (accessed 15/11/2010).

McAuley, G. (2006) 'Remembering and Forgetting: Place and Performance in the Memory Process', in McAuley (ed.), *Unstable Ground: Performance and the Politics of Place*. Brussels, Berlin and New York: Peter Lang: 149–76.

McAvinchey, C. (2010) 'Making an Invitation: Creative Engagement with the LIFT Living Archive', www.liftfest.com/living-archive/maling-an-invitation (accessed 01/06/2011).

McCall, M. ([2000] 2003) 'Performance Ethnography: A Brief Hisotry and Some Advice', in N. Denzin (ed.), *Strategies of Qualitative Inquiry*, London: Sage Publications.

McConachie, B. (2007) 'Falsifiable Theories for Theatre and Performance Studies'. *Theatre Journal* 59.4: 553–77.

—— (2008) *Engaging Audiences: A Cognitive Approach to Spectating in the Theatre*. Basingstoke and New York: Palgrave Macmillan.

McConachie, B., and E. F. Hart (eds) (2006) *Performance and Cognition: Theatre Studies and the Cognitive Turn*. London and New York: Routledge.

McLean, C. (2002) 'Creating the Past: Report on a Youth Project at the Royal Museum, Edinburgh', March–September 2002, Edinburgh: National Museum of Scotland.

McNeill, D (2007) *Gesture and Thought*. Chicago, IL: University of Chicago Press.

Melaney, W. D. (2006). 'Arendt's revision of praxis: On plurality and narrative experience', in A.-T. Tymieniecka (ed.), *Logos of Phenomenology and the Phenomenology of the Logos*. Book 3: *Logos of History – Logos of Life: Historicity, Time, Nature, Communication, Alterity, Culture*. Dordrecht, Netherlands: Springer.

Merleau-Ponty, M. [1962] (2002) *The Phenomenology of Perception*, trans. Colin Smith. London: Routledge.

—— (1974) 'The Primacy of Perception and its Philosophical Consequences', in J. O'Neill (ed.), *Phenomenomogy, Language and Sociology*. London: Heinemann: 280–311.

Miller, L., C. Miller, J. Taylor and M. H. Carver (2003) *Voices Made Flesh: Performing Women's Autobiography*. Madison, WI: University of Wisconsin Press.

Mills, B. (2008) 'Autism and the Imagination', in M. Osteen (ed.), *Autism and Representation*. London and New York: Routledge: 118–32.

Milling, J., and G. Ley (2001) *Modern Theories of Performance: From Stanislavski to Brecht*. Basingstoke: Palgrave Macmillan.

Molnar-Szakacs, I (2007) 'Culture Influences Brain Cells: Brain's Mirror Neurons Swayed By Ethnicity And Culture'. *Science Daily* (18 July), http://www.sciencedaily.com/releases/2007/07/070718002115.htm.

Motylewski, K. (2001) *Informal Learning: The Informal Learning Review* 53 (March–April): 3–7; www.imls.gov (accessed 27/03/2010).

Nagel, M. (2002) *Masking the Abject: A Genealogy of Play*. Lanham, MD: Lexington Books.

Nahachewsky, A. (1995) 'Participatory and presentational dance as ethnochoreological categories'. *Dance Research Journal* 27: 1–15.

National Autistic Society (2011) http://www.autism.org.uk (accessed 12/09/2011).

Neri, L., and M. Morris (eds) (2006) *Wendy Ewald: Towards a Promised Land*. Gottingen: Steidl.

Nicholson, H. (2001) 'Looking for Fruits in the Jungle: Head injury, multi-modal theatre and the politics of visibility'. *Research in Drama Education* 6.2: 161–78.

—— (2003) 'The Performance of Memory'. *The NADIE Journal Australia: New Paradigms in Drama Education* 27.2: 79–92.

—— (2005) *Applied Drama: The Gift of Theatre*. Basingstoke: Palgrave Macmillan.

—— (2006) 'Collecting Memories'. *Research in Drama Education* 11.1: 1–5.

—— (2011) *Theatre, Education and Performance*, Basingstoke: Palgrave Macmillan.

Niedenthal P. M. (2009) 'Embodiment of Emotion Concepts.' *Journal of Personality and Emotion Psychology* 6: 1120–36.

Niedenthal, P. M. et. al. (2005) 'Embodiment in the acquisition and use of emotion knowledge', in L. Feldman Barret (ed.), *Emotion and Consciousness*. New York: Guilford Press: 21–51.

—— (2009) 'Embodiment of Emotion Concepts'. *Journal of Personality and Emotion Psychology* 96.6: 1120–36.

Noë, A. (2004) *Action in Perception*. Cambridge, MA: Massachusetts Institute of Technology.

Oberman, L. M., J. Pineda and V. Ramachandran (2006) 'The human mirror neuron system: A link between action observation and social skills'. *Social, Cognitive and Affective Neuroscience* x: 1–5.

O'Toole, J. (2004) *The Process of Drama: Negotiating Art and Meaning*. London and New York: Routledge.

Oxford English Dictionary (2012), www.oup.com/uk (accessed 12/12/2011).

Paget, D. (1990) *True Stories?Documentary Drama on Radio, Screen and Stage*. Manchester: Manchester University Press.

Panskepp, J. (2005) *Affective Neuroscience: The Foundations of Human and Animal Emotions*. Oxford: Oxford University Press.

Parry, S. (2010) 'Imagining Cosmopolitan Space: Spectacle, Rice and Global Citizenship'. *Research in Drama Education* 15.3: 317–37.

Pavis, P. (2003) *Analysing Performance: Theatre, Dance and Film*, trans. D. Williams. Ann Arbor, MA: University of Michigan Press.

Pearson, M. (2010) *Site Specific Performance*. Basingstoke and New York, Palgrave Macmillan.

Phelan, P. (1993) *Unmarked: The Politics of Performance*. New York and London: Routledge.

—— (1998) 'Introduction: The Ends of Performance', in P. Phelan and J. Lane (eds), *The Ends of Performance*. New York and London: Routledge: 1–19.

—— (2004) 'Marina Abramović: Witnessing Shadows'. *Theatre Journal* 56: 569–77.

Pineda, A. J. (ed.) (2009) *Mirror Neuron Systems: The Role of Mirroring Processes in Social Cognition*. New York: Humana Press.

Pinker, S. (1998) *How the Mind Works*. Harmondsworth: Penguin.

—— (2002) *The Blank Slate: The Modern Denial of Human Nature*. London: Allen Lane.

Politis, V. (2004) *The Routledge Philosophy Guidebook to Aristotle and the Metaphysics*. London: Routledge.

Pollock, D. (1998) 'A Response to Dwight Conquergood's Essay "Beyond the Text: Towards a Performative Cultural Politics"', in S. J. Dailey (ed.), *The Future of Performance Studies: Visions and Revisions*. Washington, DC: National Communication Association: 37–46.

Poster, N. (1997) 'Cyberdemocracy: Internet and the Public Sphere', in D. Porter (ed.), *Internet Culture*. London: Routledge: 201–17.

Prendergast, M., and J. Saxton (eds) *Applied Theatre: International Case Studies and Challenges for Practice*. Bristol: Intellect.

Prensky, M. (2001a) '"Digital Natives", Digital Immigrants'. *On the Horizon 9*, http://www.marcprensky.com/writing (accessed 12/11/2008).

—— (2001b) '"Digital Natives", Digital Immigrants Part II: Do They Really Think Differently?' *On the Horizon 9*, http://www.marcprensky.com/writing (accessed 12/12/2008).

—— (2001c) *Digital Game-Based Learning*. New York: McGraw-Hill.

—— (2005) *Don't Bother Me Mom, I'm Learning*. Minnesota, MN: Paragon House.

—— (2010) *Teaching Digital Natives: Partnering for Real Learning*. London: Sage.

Prentki, T. (2003) 'Save the Children? – Change the World', *Research in Drama Education* 8.1: 39–53.

Prentki, T. and S. Preston (eds) (2008) *The Applied Theatre Reader*. London and New York: Routledge.

Preston, S. (2007) 'An argument *for* transformative theatre in development: Continuing the debate'. *Research in Drama Education* 12: 241–9.

Primary Review (2007) http://www.primaryreview.org.uk (accessed 11/11/07).

Ramachandran, V. S (2000) www.edge.org/3rd-culture/ramachandran (accessed 9/11/08).

Rancière, J. (2006) *The Politics of Aesthetics: The Distribution of the Sensible*, trans. G. Rockhill. London and New York: Continuum.

—— (2009a) *The Emancipated Spectator*, trans. G. Elliott. New York: Verso.

—— (2009b) *Aesthetics and its Discontents*, trans. S. Corcoran. Cambridge: Polity.

Reason, M. (2010) *The Young Audience: Exploring and Enhancing Children's Experience of Theatre*. Stoke on Trent: Trentham Books.

Redman, J. (2003a) (www.indymedia.org.uken/2003/09/278197.shtml.

—— (2003b) 'Guantanamo Bay prison recreated as northern art', D. Ward, *The Guardian* (11 October).

—— (2003c) http://www.inplaceofwar.net (accessed 09/05/2011.

Reinelt, J. (2001) 'Performing Europe: Identity Formation for a "New" Europe'. *Theatre Journal* 53: 365–87.

Relph, E. (1976) *Place and Placelessness*. London: Pion.

Ricoeur, P. (2004) *Memory, History, Forgetting*. Chicago, IL: University of Chicago Press.

Rizzolati, G. et. al. (1999) 'Resonance Behaviours and Mirror Neurons'. *Archives of Italian Biology* 137: 85–100.

Roach, J. (1995) 'Culture and performance in the circum-Atlantic world', in A. Parker and E. Kosofsky Sedgwick (eds), *Performativity and Performance*. London: Routledge: 45–63.

Roche, J. (2006) 'Socially Engaged Art, Critics and Discontents: An Interview with Claire Bishop'. *Community arts network*, http://www.communityarts.net/reading-room/archivefiles/2006/07/socially_engage.php (accessed 08/11/10).

Roms, H., M. Pearson and S. Daniels (eds) (2010a) 'Fieldworks'. *Performance Research* 15.4: 1–5.

—— (2010b) in H. Roms, J. McKenzie and C. W. L. Wee (eds) (2010) *Contesting Performance: Emerging Sites of Research*. Basingstoke: Palgrave Macmillan.

Roms, H., M. Pearson and S. Daniels (eds) (2010) *Fieldworks*. London: Taylor & Francis.

Rose, G. (1993) *Feminism and Geography: The Limits of Geographical Knowledge*. Minneapolis, MN: University of Minnesota Press.

Rose, G. (1995) 'Making Space for the Female Subject of Feminism: The spatial subversions of Holzer, Kruger and Sherman', in S. Pile and N. Thrift (eds), *Mapping the Subject: Geographies of Cultural Transformation.* New York and London: Routledge: 302–22.

—— (1996) 'As if the mirrors had bled: Masculine dwelling, masculinist theory and feminist masquerade', in N. Duncan (ed.), *Body Spaces: Destabilising Geographies of Gender and Sexuality.* New York: Routledge: 56–74.

Rowe, N. (2007) 'Post-Salvagism: Cultural Interventions and Cultural Evolution in a Traumatised Community: Dance in the Central West Bank'. Unpublished Doctoral thesis, University of Kent.

Saal, I. (2007) 'Vernacularising Brecht: The Political Theatre of the New Deal', in W. Demastes, W. Smith Fischer and I. Smith Fischer (eds), *Interrogating America through Theatre and Performance.* Basingstoke: Palgrave Macmillan: 100–19.

Schechner, R. (1983) *Performative Circumstances, from the Avant-Garde to Ramlila.* Calcutta: Seagull Books.

—— (1985) *Between Theatre and Anthropology.* Philadelphia, PA: University of Pennsylvania Press.

—— (2001) 'Rasaesthetics'. *TDR: The Drama Review* 45: 27–50.

—— (2003) *Performance Theory.* London and New York: Routledge.

Schechner, R. and J. Thompson (2004) 'Why "Social Theatre"?' *TDR: The Drama Review* 48.3: 11–16.

Schneider, R. (2001) 'Archives: Performance Remains'. *Performance Research* 6.2: 100–8.

—— (2011) *Performing Remains.* London and New York: Routledge.

Schwartz, S. L. (2004) *Rasa: Performing the Divine in India.* New York: Columbia University Press.

Schweitzer, P. (2006) *Reminiscence Theatre, Making Theatre from Memories.* London: Jessica Kingsley.

Shaughnessy, N. (2005) 'Truths and Lies: Towards a New Methodology of Performance Applications'. *Research in Drama Education* 10: 101–12.

—— (2007) *Gertrude Stein.* Writers and their Work. Plymouth: Northcote House.

—— (2009) 'Commentary on *The Empathising Systemising Theory of Autism*'. *Tizard Learning Disability Review* 14: 14–17.

—— (2011) 'Knowing Me Knowing You: Autism, Kinaesthetic Empathy and Applied Performance', in D. Reynolds and M. Reason (eds), *Kinaesthetic Empathy in Creative and Cultural Practices.* Bristol: Intellect: 35–50.

Shepherd, S. (2006) *Theatre, Body and Pleasure.* London and New York: Routledge.

Shepherd, S., and M. Wallis (2004) *Drama/Theatre/Performance.* London and New York: Routledge.

Siegal, L. (1984) *Fires of Love: Waters of Peace.* Honolulu: University of Hawaii Press.

Singer, T., B. Seymour, J. O'Doherty, H. Kaube, R. J. Dolan and C. D. Frith (2004) 'Empathy for pain involves the affective but not sensory components of pain'. *Science* 303: 1157–62.

Smith, S. and Watson, J. (2002) *Interfaces: Women/Autobiography/Image/Performance.* Ann Arbor, MI: University of Michigan Press.

Soja E. (1989) *Postmodern Geographies: The Reassertion of Space in Critical Social Theory.* New York: Verso.

Spinoza, B. ([1677] 1989) *The Ethics,* trans. R. H. M. Elwes. New York: Prometheus Books.

Stam, D. C. (2005) 'The informed muse: The implications of "The New Museology" for Museum Practice', in G. Gorsane (ed.), *Heritage, Museums and Galleries, an Introductory Reader.* London and New York: Routledge: 58–76.

Stan's Cafe (2003) http://www.stanscafe.co.uk/ofallthepeople/coventry1.html (accessed 22/10/2008).

—— (2005) *Of All the People in All the World: Plague Nation*, www.stanscafe.co.uk/ofall-thepeople/plaguenation (accessed 21/10/2008).

—— (2007) http://www.stanscafe.co.uk/ofallthepeople/budapest.html (accessed 21/10/2008).

—— (2010) http://www.stanscafe.co.uk/ofallthepeople/salisbury.html (accessed 07/06/2011).

Stein, G. ([1931] 1975) *How to Write*, ed. Patricia Meyerowitz. New York: Dover Publications.

—— ([1936] 1995) *The Geographical History of America; or, The Relation of Human Nature to the Human Mind*. Baltimore, MD: Johns Hopkins University Press.

Sutton, P. (2005) 'The Dramatic Property: A New Paradigm of Applied Theatre Practice for a Globalised Media Culture'. Unpublished PhD thesis, University of Kent.

—— (2009) 'Lip Sync: Performative Placebos in The Digital Age', in M. Anderson, J. Caroll and D. Cameron (eds), *Drama Education with Digital Technologies*. London and New York: Continuum: 38–51.

Sutton-Smith, B. (2001) *The Ambiguity of Play*. Cambridge, MA: Harvard University Press.

Taborsky, E. (1990) 'The Discursive Object', in S. Pearce (ed.), *Objects of Knowledge: New Research in Museum Studies 1*. London: Continuum: 50–77.

Taussig, M (1993) *Mimesis and Alterity*. New York: Routledge.

Taylor, D. (2003) *The Archive and the Repertoire: Cultural Memory and Performance in the Americas*. Durham, NC: Duke University Press.

Taylor, P. (2003) *Applied Theatre: Creating Transformative Encounters in the Community*. Portsmouth, NH: Heinemann.

Thompson, E. (2010) *Mind in Life*, Cambridge, MA: Harvard University Press.

Thompson J. (2003) *Applied Theatre: Bewilderment and Beyond*. Oxford: Peter Lang.

—— (2006) 'Performance of pain, performance of beauty'. *Research in Drama Education* 11: 45–7.

—— (2009) *Performance Affects: Applied Theatre and the End of Effect*. Basingstoke: Palgrave Macmillan.

Thrift, N. (2004) 'Intensities of feeling: Towards a spatial politics of affect'. *Geografiska Annaler* Series B, 86: 57–78, http://onlinelibrary.wiley.com/doi/10.1111/j.0435-3684.2004.00154.x/pdf

—— (2007) *Non-Representational Theory: Space, Politics, Affect*. London: Routledge.

Tilley, C. (2006) 'Introduction: Identity, place, landscape and heritage'. *Journal of Material Culture* 11: 7–32.

Trainor, L. J., A. Shahin and L. E. Roberts (2003) 'Effects of Musical Training on the Auditory Cortex in Children'. *Annals of the New York Academy of Sciences* 999: 506–13.

Trimingham, M. (2002) 'A Methodology for Practice as Research'. *Studies in Theatre and Performance* 22.1: 54–60.

—— (2010) 'Objects in transition: The puppet and the autistic child'. *Journal of Applied Arts and Health* 1.3: 251–65.

—— (2011) *The Theatre of the Bauhaus*. London and New York: Routledge.

Tuan, Y. F. (1974) *Topohilia: A Study of Environmental Perception, Attitudes and Values*. Englewood Cliffs, NJ: Prentice-Hall.

—— (1977) *Space and Place: The Perspective of Experience*. Minneapolis, MN: University of Minnesota Press.

Turner, C. and V. Turner (1986) *The Anthropology of Performance*. New York: PAJ Publications.

Tytell, J. (1997) *The Living Theatre: Art, Exile and Outrage*. London: Methuen.

Van Erven, E. (2007) 'Taking It To the Streets: Dutch Community Theatre Goes Site-Specific'. *Research in Drama Education* 12: 27–39.

Van Manen, M. (1979) 'The Phenomenology of Pedagogic Observation'. *Canadian Journal of Education* 4: 5–16.

Vergo, P. (1997) *The New Museology*. London and Chicago, IL: Reaktion.

Warschauer, M. (2003) *Technology and Social Inclusion: Rethinking the Digital Divide*. Cambridge, MA and London: MIT Press.

Weyburn Project (2002) uregina.ca/weyburn_project.

Willet, J (1964) *Brecht on Theatre*. London: Methuen.

Whatmore, S. (2006) 'Materialist returns: Practising cultural geography in and for a more-than-human world'. *Cultural Geographies* 13: 600–9.

Wicker, B., C. Keysers, J. Plailly, J. P. Royet, V. Gallese and G. Rizolatti (2003) 'Both of us disgusted in my insula: The common neural basis of seeing and feeling disgust'. *Neuron* 40: 655–64.

Wilkie, F. (2002) 'Mapping the Terrain: A Survey of Site-Specific Performance in Britain'. *New Theatre Quarterly* 18.2: 140–60.

Wilkinson, H. (2003) 'Measurable Results'. *Museums Association* 103.1: 12.

Williams, J., G. Waiter, A. Gilchrist, D. Perrett, A. Murray and A. Whiten (2006) 'Neural Mechanisms of imitation and "mirror neuron" functioning in autistic spectrum disorder'. *Neuropsychologia* 44: 610–21.

Williams, R. (1983) *Writing in Society*. London: Verso.

Wilson, E. (1998) *Neural Geographies: Feminism and the Microstructure of Cognition*. New York: Routledge.

Wilson, S. (2002) *Information Arts: Intersections of Art, Science and Technology*. Cambridge, MA: MIT Press.

Wing, L. [1996] (2003) *The Autistic Spectrum: A Guide for Parents and Professionals*. London: Robinson Publishing.

—— (2002) 'Mental Retardation and Developmental Disabilities'. *Research Reviews* 8, http://onlinelibrary.wiley.com/doi/10.1002/mrdd.10029/pdf.

Wolff, J. (2008) *The Aesthetics of Uncertainty*. New York: Colombia University Press.

Woolf, V. (1985) *Moments of Being*, ed. J. Schulkind. London: Grafton.

Yarker, J. (2005a) 'The Making Of *All the People in All the World*, Stan's Cafe', http://www.stanscafe.co.uk/helpfulthings/makingofallthepeople.html (accessed 19/12/2008).

—— (2005b) 'And So It Happened, http://www.stanscafe.co.uk/helpfulthings/ andsoithappened.html (accessed 19/12/2008).

—— (2007) 'Stan's Café and Site-Specific Performance', www.stanscafe.co.uk/ helpfulthings/sitespecificessay.html (accessed 19/12/2008).

Index

Lightning Source UK Ltd.
Milton Keynes UK
UKOW01f0134260817
307872UK00018B/283/P